T0354724

Growing Up Green

Newark Catholic Football

and the

1985 State Championship

by

William B. Evans

Order this book online at www.trafford.com
or email orders@trafford.com

Most Trafford titles are also available at major online book retailers.

Print information available on the last page.

ISBN: 978-1-5539-5822-2 (sc)

Trafford rev. 08/09/2018

 www.trafford.com

North America & international
toll-free: 1 888 232 4444 (USA & Canada)
fax: 812 355 4082

In memory of my father Robert M. Evans
Only now that he is gone do I realize how amazing he was

Intensity is shown in his eyes,
As he puts his battle armor on.

One week of his life lived in
Forty-eight minutes,

He rides the emotional roller coaster:
Joy to agony.

It's a cruel game.

The last twelve minutes are not played
By his battered body, but by his heart.

He is . . .

A football player.

—Sean Christopher Browning
Cleveland St. Joseph High School
Class of 1988

Contents

Part III: The Playoffs

Acknowledgements

Several words of thanks must be issued to those who assisted me with this project. I am humbled to have found such support:

My parents, the late Robert M. Evans and my mother M. Joan Evans for the sacrifices they made to send six children through Newark Catholic High School.

My wife Jo-Ella for supporting and tolerating me throughout this project. I love you.

My sister Nancy for her enthusiasm, support, tireless proofreading and critiques.

My brother Joe for additional critiques and suggestions.

Jill Evans for proofreading and grammar assistance.

Mr. John Cannizzaro for supplying statistical data.

Joe Bell for his input and suggestions and for the use of his home videos of our games. They proved to be invaluable resources.

Sean Browning for the use of his poetry.

Coach Bill Franks for his input and contributions.

Coach Wes Poth for his assistance and support.

Coach J.D. Graham for his assistance and input with this project, for giving us his best during his coaching years and turning us into winners. I wouldn't have wanted it any other way.

Miss Beth Hill, principal of Newark Catholic High School.

Kim Sykes for locating fonts.

Mr. John Hall of Adelphia Cable Television of Newark, Ohio.

To the many others too numerous to mention who agreed to be interrogated.

Special thanks to those who went above and beyond:

Joe Simi for the use of his game films and scrapbook, for being a "gopher" and for his priceless assistance with text and photo layout and for acting as a liaison between me and the printing industry.

Gary Van Hove for his assistance with creating photographs from videotape and for rescuing me in the midst of perplexing computer problems. Thanks Boomer!

Dan Bell for assistance with photograph preparation.

Mr. Robert Erney J. D. Attorney at Law for his legal advice and other guidance.

Mr. Tim Black, who was tracked down in New York State and graciously allowed the use of his photography.

Above all, I give thanks to God for permitting me to live in this land of blessings and freedom where pastimes such as high school football can be enjoyed. I pray that through the shed blood of Jesus Christ, God judges old football players mercifully and that there is a place in heaven even for us.

Author's Note

The story that you are about to read is absolutely true. These events are written as they are remembered by me and those interviewed. In no way do I intend to express or imply any disrespect to any of the individuals involved. This is simply an account of the 1985 football season.

In the early 1990's, an incessant thought began to fill my head that someone should write a detailed account of the J.D. Graham era at Newark Catholic. The ideal author, of course, would be J.D. Graham himself but my periodic suggestions to him to do such a work were never acted upon. (I'm still waiting, Coach!) Deciding to take a stab at it myself, I chose not to cover the entire Graham legacy, but rather, I stuck to the only portion of his legacy that I felt qualified to write about: the 1985 season.

This document literally began as a few scribbles on notebook paper in early 1995. However, due to a lack of time, motivation and a home computer, the notes were shelved until such a time when better circumstances would exist—if that time would ever come. Then on Wednesday November 21, 2001, the day before Thanksgiving, I went out for a jog and was "hit by a truck"—not a real truck, but a figurative truck in the form of *desire* and *motivation*—both of which told me that I finally had to do this. Upon returning to the house, I dusted off the notes, sat down at the computer and embarked on a journey that ended some 13 months later.

I have spent over 1000 hours on this project. It was originally intended to simply tell the story of the 1985 season the way *I* remembered it. However, the longer I worked, the more ideas I had and the larger the project became. First, I realized that writing solely from memory would never fly. Therefore, I set out to gain the facts by studying old game films, game programs, scouting reports, newspaper articles and by spending many hours staring bleary-eyed into the microfiche machines at the Newark Public Library. Secondly, in addition to relying on my own recollection, I also realized that this project would be much more enjoyable, accurate and informative if I also solicited input from teammates, coaches, friends and family. Countless phone calls and e-mail correspondence ensued, as did numerous person-to-person meetings—some of them complete with dinner and adult beverages. The end product is not only a colorful account of the 1985 Newark Catholic football season, but it is also a story of a childhood dream come true, which made room to incorporate "flashbacks" prior to 1985. Since it is still based largely on my memory, some individuals may find certain events missing or incorrect. Every effort has been made to present a truthful account of all events. No deception or misrepresentation is intended.

Profanity contained herein is not intended to offend the reader, to tarnish the reputation of those who said it, or to tarnish the reputation of Newark Catholic High School. This is intended to be an accurate account of the way it was and omission of profanity would produce a watered-down, less-humorous and less-realistic story.

Heights, weights and personnel of opposing teams were taken directly from actual scouting reports. Statistics presented herein (excluding box scores unless otherwise noted), were taken from *The Advocate* in Newark, Ohio. The accuracy of either source cannot be guaranteed. Statistics presented in box scores were supplied by John Cannizzaro, team statistician.

Numbers in parentheses following personnel names such as "(6-0, 180)" denote a player's height and weight. In the example shown, the player is six feet zero inches tall and weighs 180 pounds.

Certain statements such as, "They had never beaten us before" or "Newark Catholic's only loss to so-and-so occurred in 1976" will be encountered. These statements may be entirely incorrect today. Just remember that 1985 is the focus here and such statements were true at that time.

Procurement of photographs for this project was a struggle, to say the least. My goal was to feature one special moment from each game by using pictures from *The Advocate*. However, *The Advocate* could not grant me blanket permission to use their photographs due to copyright issues, which is understandable. As a solution, I had big plans of using images captured from videotape but the quality simply was not there, as is evident in the few such photos that I retained. I am grateful, however, for the photos I do have and my sincere thanks goes out to those who supplied them. I hope the reader will find the selections adequate.

Lastly, I would like to say that even though I despised writing in high school and college, I found this experience to be incredibly rewarding. I encourage not only other Green Wave alumni but also alumni from other fine football programs throughout Ohio to share their memories.

I hope you enjoy *Growing Up Green.* GO NC!

William B. Evans
Fall, 2002

Prologue

November 23, 1984...

"Five! Four! Three! Two! One!" A euphoric crowd clad in green and white counted the final seconds as they ticked from the giant score board. Newark Catholic's 1984 football team had just completed an incredible 13-game journey that lead to the turf of Ohio Stadium—the site where a powerful Middletown Fenwick team was defeated 14-6 in the Division V State Championship game. The victory gave the Green Wave its third state title and the second in three years.

As the November sun smiled brightly in the autumn afternoon, Head Coach J.D. Graham assembled his winning team on the eastern sideline to first hand out praises to his seniors and then to issue a challenge to his younger troops. "Juniors and sophomores," he said. "You reach down and touch that turf. Remember what it feels like and remember what it took to get here. Not every kid gets a chance to experience this. If you guys want it bad enough and work for it, you can get back here again."

I was one of those juniors. Overcome with emotion, I reached down and briskly scraped my knuckles on the abrasive surface until they were raw—the abrasions to serve as my personal trophy to remember this day. Though I was elated and stunned to be part of a state championship team—something I had long dreamed of, I also felt unfulfilled. This victory belonged to the seniors and I envied them. They had accomplished *their* dream and went out as winners. After hearing Coach Graham say, "If you work for it, you can get back here again," I really couldn't savor this moment and my thoughts turned toward next year. The 1984 team would be a tough act to follow and our class would be under immense pressure. Could we not only return to this place, but also win another one?

Introduction

On the west side of the small town of Newark, Ohio, tucked away atop the Church Street hill at "1 Green Wave Drive" rests Newark Catholic High School—home of the "Green Wave." The school appears modest and mediocre as any other small Ohio high school would. However, one step into the south lobby will expose a visitor to a collection of awards and trophies so vast and awesome that one quickly realizes this school is anything but mediocre. It is no exaggeration to say that finding space for all of the trophies is a problem. With a walk down the "Hall of Champions" and a left turn into the gymnasium, a visitor will see the upper-walls adorned with several kelly-green and white banners that proudly display the state championships achieved in several sports: Volleyball in 1979, '80, '82, '83, '84, '88 and '89; Girl's Basketball in 1984; Girls Track in 1987; Baseball in 1988, '89 and 2002; Football in 1978, '82, '84, '85, '86, '87 and '91. Newark Catholic has built such a storied past. I am awestruck when I stand in solitude in the gym and read those banners that silently scream to the world of past glories. I get lost pondering—pondering all of the average athletes with over-sized hearts, who achieved superior things under the leadership of the superior coaches who knew how to make it all happen.

Of the 19 championship banners on display, seven were secured by the football program. Each title is an amazing accomplishment and a major component of the Newark Catholic football tradition. But the one that means the most to me is the one found in the middle of them all: 1985. I was a senior on that team and I want to tell our story. My goal is to share the sad, happy and serious moments, reveal what went into preparing for a state championship, show how we dealt with adversity, rose to the challenge when it counted most and came home with a state title when many outsiders—and even ourselves at times—doubted that it could be done.

Before this journey begins, however, we must briefly discuss the evolution of the football program—events that transpired long before I ever knew what a "Green Wave" was.

Building a tradition

Newark Catholic first opened its doors in 1958 and fielded its first football team that same year under Jack Bickle. Admittedly, the program was rather abysmal for the first few years, but that is in no way a criticism of the coach or players. These were the natural growing pains, as dynasties are not born overnight.

Newark Catholic began to mix it up with some fine central Ohio teams that had been around for years and some preliminary embarrassments were to be expected. The Green Wave went 3-3-2 that first season and had established a record of 31-28-3 by the time Coach Bickle stepped down after the 1964 season.

The replacement for Coach Bickle was an intense individual named Matt Midea. Under this man, the Newark Catholic football program was molded into a force to be feared. One could also say that the best and worst happened during Coach Midea's watch. In Midea's inaugural season of 1965, which was Newark Catholic's second year in the Mid-Buckeye League, the program suffered its worst defeats in school history back to back. Week 5 resulted in a 64-7 defeat by West Jefferson, followed by a 68-0 trouncing by Columbus DeSales in week 6.

By 1967, however, coach Midea had turned things around and led the Green Wave to its first perfect season with a record of 10-0. During the '67 season, the year I was born, Newark Catholic had two running backs rush for 1,000 yards—Mike McKee for 1,495 and Denny Welsh for 1,021. The team averaged 46.5 points per game while allowing just 6 defensively. A game worth mentioning was a 50-0 blowout of Mt. Vernon St. Vincent, alma mater of a future Newark Catholic coach named J. D. Graham. This was the last time these two schools ever met.

The 1967 season was indeed awesome, but many people consider the 1968 team not only the greatest team in Newark Catholic's history, but also perhaps the greatest team ever around central Ohio. It was in 1968 that Newark Catholic won its first Associated Press State Championship. In those days, there were no playoffs or computer-points systems in place to determine who was the best. Simply going undefeated was not enough. A team had to go undefeated and steam-roll its opponents. Without question, the '68 squad delivered this and more as it *averaged* 63.7 points per game, including destructions of Lucas 89-0 and East Knox 83-0. Again, the team had two 1,000-yard rushers in Mike McKee and Gary Kutch. Defensively, the team gave up only 3.8 points per game. The 1968 season would be coach Midea's last at Newark Catholic. He left with a 29-10-0 record.

The next coach to take the helm of the now awesome Newark Catholic battleship was Lou Novak. In his first year, Coach Novak led the Green Wave to its third straight unbeaten season. Novak's second year, 1970, was his last season with the team and it was not as victorious as the first. The noteworthy game of that year would be the game against cross-town nemesis Heath in which the Newark Catholic Green Wave was the visiting team on its own home field. Newark Catholic suffered an embarrassing upset to the Bulldogs that ended a 36-game winning streak. Eyewitnesses say that in a post game meeting, Coach Novak all but destroyed a classroom and spewed out many profanities. The season ended at 8-2—a record most schools would be happy with but I dare say that after three perfect seasons, an 8-2 record must have been hard to accept. Coach Novak left Newark Catholic with a record of 18-2.

Newark Catholic's next coach had been a two-year assistant under Coach Novak named J.D. Graham. To say that the program was in good hands during his watch is the understatement of a lifetime. In his first season, 1971, J.D. Graham led the Green Wave to a 10-0 season—the notable game being a stunning victory over Portsmouth Notre Dame.

In 1973, Newark Catholic left the Mid-Buckeye League and began playing in the Licking County League (LCL). Supposedly, some members of the public claimed that it was easy for Newark Catholic to win so often because "they weren't playing anybody." Once Newark Catholic joined the LCL, it was thought, they would find out what it was like to play "real teams" and their success would be sharply curtailed. To be sure, the LCL had some outstanding football teams in Granville and Licking Valley. Once again, the "Greenies" shocked everyone by posting a perfect 10-0 record, sweeping the Licking County League and winning Newark Catholic's first LCL Championship. The fine season also qualified Newark Catholic for the 1973 state playoffs in Class A, but the Green Wave lost in the semifinal 19-8 to Montpelier. (The playoffs began in Ohio in 1972 and consisted of a three-class system: AAA, AA, and A. Only four teams in each class made the playoffs—12 from the entire state!) Newark Catholic made the playoffs again in 1974 and met up with defending state champion Middletown Fenwick in the semifinal. Fenwick won 34-6 (J.D. Graham's worst defeat) and would go on to win the championship game a week later. In 1975, Newark Catholic and Middletown Fenwick squared off again in semifinal action. This time Newark Catholic, which allowed only 18 points in 10 regular-season games, put up another tremendous defensive effort and prevailed 11-0 over Fenwick. The win secured Newark Catholic's first trip to the state final game, but they lost in overtime to Carey 15-7. Newark Catholic returned to the state final game in 1978 with a team that had not only the best defense in school history (2.08 points per game), but it also had a pair of 1,000-yard rushers in Dan McKenna and Chris Marshall. The Green Wave brought home their first state championship trophy by defeating Lorain Clearview 21-0.

In 1980, the high school playoff system in Ohio was changed to a five-division, 20-region arrangement that expanded the playoffs from twelve teams to 40 teams across the state. Newark Catholic enjoyed phenomenal success under the new playoff format and succeeded in reaching the final game regularly beginning in 1980. Make no mistake: it was no easy task to reach the final game. Many tough games were played—some of which will be mentioned later. Once the final game had been reached, victory was elusive: 1980, Newark Catholic lost to Tiffin Calvert 22-0; 1981, Newark Catholic lost again to Tiffin Calvert 3-0; 1982, Newark Catholic defeated Fostoria St. Wendelin 14-7; 1983, Newark Catholic lost to McComb 6-0; and in 1984, Newark Catholic renewed the war with Middletown Fenwick and won 14-6.

From 1971 to 1984, Coach Graham had accumulated a 141-18-1 record that included two Mid Buckeye League Championships, ten regional computer championships, four Associated Press championships, three United Press

International titles, three Division V State Championships and nine Licking County League titles.

Coach Graham had proven that he could build winners. As he stepped to the helm of the Green Wave ship once more in 1985, could he do the same with *our* class?

Source:

Newark Catholic vs. Tuscarawas Central Catholic Football Program, (Aug. 31, 1985), p. 16-19.

Your senior year is special because it's the one you remember the most.

-Coach J.D. Graham

This is what I remember…

Part I
Preparation

Laying down the Law

The school bell rang to dismiss the students on a beautiful spring afternoon just days before the summer break of 1985. Many students set out on their normal after-school activities such as going home, going to work, staying late for tutoring, reporting to detention hall, track practice, baseball practice or the weight room. Some of us, however—48 to be exact—had our normal routine altered by a mandatory team meeting in room 120 called by Coach Graham. The meeting was for those boys who intended on playing football in the coming school year. I was concerned about why this meeting was being held. Was someone in big trouble? Was Coach Graham finally confirming the nasty resignation rumor that resurfaced each time a football season ended?

I sat in my seat and watched the others listlessly shuffle into the room, giggling and unkempt with untucked shirts—good-time rock-and-rollers without a care in the world. I was briefly caught off guard when these weird freshmen began sheepishly entering the room also. *Why are they here?* I wondered. Then it sank in: They would be our new teammates in the fall, next year's sophomores who had so many titles: The Scrubs, The Clean Green, The Hamburger Defense and the Suicide Offense.

There was much laughing and carrying on in the room. It soon fell deathly silent, however, when Coach Graham finally made his authoritative entrance with a disgusted look on his face. In a highly animated fashion, he proceeded to tear us apart over the fact that many of us were doing very little to prepare for the coming football season. Only a handful of people were in the weight room after school, only a few people would go out and run, "while the rest of you aren't doing damn shit, and it ain't right!" Graham exclaimed. He accused the majority of us of being lazy, screwing off, having a good time, not caring about preparing for next year and taking for granted the storied Newark Catholic football tradition that was now being entrusted to us. He went on to warn us of the real-life consequences of laziness in adult life. "You had better change your ways!" he shouted, "unless you want to pump gas at the g-ddamn gas station the rest of your f--king lives!"

"Everybody thinks that this year will be the year the Greenies get their lunch," he said. "We have to replace 20 starters and the entire kicking game and it seems like some of you think that just because you wear that green helmet, people are going to lay down and die! If you people have any aspirations about winning a state championship, you had better wake up and get to work! Every successful team at this school has had one thing in common: They were hungry for greatness and they worked for it! There ain't no 'give-me's' in this sport! Anybody can beat you once! We are the defending state champions. Everybody will be gunning for us, baby!"

He then cited two of his core beliefs that he always mentioned at the start of each new season: "Our success will depend on how fast we mature as a team and what kind of leadership we get from our senior class." Coach Graham charged each senior with the responsibility of taking leadership of the team and then called us each by name, asking us if we even cared—rhetorically of course. We didn't dare offer an answer.

This certainly was not a good way to be heading into summer. Coach Graham was already disgusted with his future team and was sure to let us know about it on this day, one of the last chances he would have to call us together as a team until summer conditioning began. It looked to be a long year.

Summer Break

School was finally out for the summer and there was a lot on my mind. I was now a senior on the Newark Catholic football team. It did not seem possible to me. Where had the time gone? It seemed like only yesterday that I was a young punk sitting with my friends at White Field observing Newark Catholic football games and in awe of the men in the green helmets. Newark Catholic football was everything to me. If I could not be at the games, I was at home on game night glued to a radio to see if Newark Catholic could pull out yet another victory. As young boys growing up in the Catholic community, my friends and I knew all the names and numbers of these seemingly indestructible green warriors. We assigned them deity status and wanted to be just like them—Green Wave football players.

This boyhood obsession and yearning to be a Newark Catholic football player is what I refer to as *growing up green*. It is a strong and addictive force, invading a young boy's soul the first time he sees a Newark Catholic team defy the odds and do something extraordinary. At least that was the case for me. For most of the kids my age, the "infection" began when we were in the fifth grade when the awesome 1978 team completed a 12-0 season and won the Ohio High School Class A State Championship—Newark Catholic's first football playoff championship. It was the talk of the community. The players were heroes and a new standard had been set by which future teams would be judged. Ever since that time, it became our goal, our obsession, to one day wear that green helmet and win a state championship of our own.

Here I was in 1985, 7 years later after the bug first bit me. Were there young kids idolizing me? Was *I* now a hero to some schoolboy? Perhaps, but I certainly did not feel like an indestructible green warrior. In fact, I felt horribly unprepared, plagued with self-doubt and unready to assume such responsibility. I made up my mind that 1985 was going to be the best summer of preparation I had ever known.

By the time I was a senior, I had nearly forgotten two personal goals that I had set for myself during my freshman year. First was to win the Lineman of the Year award which was inspired by Joe Paul's winning of the award in Class A for his performances during Newark Catholic's 1982 State Championship season. The second goal was to be recognized as an All-Ohio athlete. In the "Hall of Champions," which leads from the school's trophy cases to the cafeteria and gym, a large board proudly displayed those past Newark Catholic athletes that had been named All-Ohio. My sister Barbara had made the list for shotput and discus in 1975. It was my goal to make that list as well one day. As I headed into the summer, however, these goals seemed like luxuries and therefore, they became secondary to the matter of survival for myself and of the team.

The term "summer break" was an oxymoron. It was a break from classes only, but not from football preparation. During the summer weeks before formal conditioning started, we were expected to workout on our own. This was specified in a letter each of us received from Coach Graham during the summer that invited us out for football in the coming school year. "The way to Ohio Stadium is through the weight room," so proclaimed the letter, and Coach Graham insisted that we lift weights. The weight room was open from 10:00 a.m. to noon and from 6:00 p.m. to 8:00 p.m. which rendered excuses about "not having enough time to lift" unacceptable. There was a handwritten workout regimen on the inside of the door. In addition to weight training, we were to "Run, Run, Run," as the note proclaimed at the bottom of the page. We were to run 20 forty-yard sprints and a couple of miles each day. Run to the store. Run to the park. Run everywhere. I don't know how many us of actually did all that Coach Graham told us to do. Not even Coach Graham could have known, as there was minimal supervision at the school. This meant that a kid could fail to do the entire workout or simply not show up at all. But those who did nothing all summer would be obvious as they were likely to show up fat, out of shape and dying on the first day of conditioning.

It should be made clear at this time that work in the weight room did not start in the summer. Newark Catholic football was not a July-to-November affair. Football was a year-round activity that began in January after the holidays were over. This was how it started for me as a freshman when the new weight room opened after the '82 season. Under the instruction of Mike Nichols and Todd Wilder, who were both NC alumni and football players, a weight-training routine was taught and was to be strictly followed. This weight routine consisted of, but was not limited to, the bench press, military press, incline press, neck machine, squats, power machine for the legs, shoulder shrugs, flies and triceps work with dumb-bells, plus shoulder work, lat work and dips on the universal machine. Coach Graham did not want us to do curls (to build biceps) at that time because he felt that the curling action "was not used in football." He later changed his stance on this when I was a junior, saying, "I want us to look good this summer."

So from freshman year onward, we were to be in the weight room three days a week to "pump the iron" as soon as school let out. It was quite intimidating to be a small, weak freshman that could barely lift the bar, having to lift along side the older kids who were bench-pressing 300 pounds. However, once that first increase in strength was realized and an "increased state of buffness" could be detected in the mirror, it instilled confidence and the intimidation factor vanished. It's just another part of growing up.

I have many fond memories of working out in the weight room in the dead of winter with classmate Mike Trotter. He was very much into weightlifting and always pushed me to go that extra mile. I can still hear the clanging of the weights as they were placed onto the bar.

The weight room could be a very crowded, busy place if several kids showed up to lift all at once and often became a swelter box. During those winter days, Coach Graham would often drop in to see who was actually working and who was there just to be seen. One day he walked in to sharply reiterate the importance of adhering to the weight program. As he spoke, the raunchy song "Whole Lotta Love" by Led Zeppelin blared from the thrashed weight-room radio in the corner, its coat-hanger antenna going in all directions. He finished talking and before leaving the weight room, looked at the radio and said, "Hey, turn that shit off. This is a catholic school." I guess Coach Graham was not into Zeppelin.

When our weight lifting had been completed for the day, we were to go out into the sophomore hallway and perform a rope-jumping routine that Coach Graham had assigned. This included 500 jumps on the left foot, 500 jumps on the right foot, 500 on both feet and then running in place for as long as we could stand it. As a freshman, I can recall seeing Rod Wilder, a junior at the time, jumping rope in the hallway for hours on end. He truly pushed himself for the coming season and this left a lasting impression on me about the work ethic expected of a Newark Catholic football player.

As a sophomore, my self-training during the summer had been half-hearted at best. My attitude was that the team belonged to the juniors and seniors and I was just a lowly sophomore. I became more disciplined as a junior, but it was not until senior year that I felt the pressure and sense of urgency to take responsibility and lead what was now *my* team. I knew I had to work like never before or those big farm boys from around the county would eat me for lunch. I hoped that my classmates were feeling the same way and were taking the appropriate actions.

What Graham had required us to do during the summer did not seem like enough to me. Therefore, motivated by fear more than anything else, I came up with some additional workouts of my own for the summer. The farm where our family lived provided several ways for me to be creative with my personal workout. A typical day for me proceeded in this fashion. Instead of running on the flat track at the school, I would run from my house down to the western end of Stewart Road and back every morning—a distance of about 1.9 miles, which took me up and down a few steep hills. Then I would go down to the barn and perform the jump rope routine in the aisle. I did this in the barn because it was the only place outdoors on the farm where the rope would not catch on the ground. The grass and the gravel driveway just did not work. Even before the summer, I had spent many cold winter nights for a few hours at a time jumping rope in the barn while listening to my cassette tapes. Periodically, the rats could be heard scurrying around in the corners, but they did not bother me—much.

I also had a homemade weight set that I used on weekends or on nights when an additional workout was desired. This consisted of a spud bar with a 16-inch concrete block hanging from each end. It wasn't the safest thing in the world to use because the blocks swung back and forth or would slide off if I leaned too far to one side. This always resulted in a large crash. With this rig, I could do curls, shoulder shrugs, military press and bench press. The "bench" was nothing more than a bale of hay.

After jumping rope, I would run my sprints but I did them in a different manner. Someone once told me that running up a hill was a great way to improve one's speed. With this in mind, I ran my 20 sprints up the steep hill in the pine grove just behind our house. It was so hard and painful—thighs burning, heart pounding, huffing and puffing, moving at what seemed like a snail's pace. Once at the top, I would jog back to the bottom figuring that maintaining a steady pace on the way down was also beneficial.

After completing my running, I would then report to school to lift weights on Monday, Wednesday and Friday. Finally, each day in the late afternoon, I would go out to the maple tree in our front yard to perform two more exercises. The first one amounted to hanging upside down with my legs hooked over a tree limb and doing three sets of as many sit-ups as I could do. The last thing I did was to move into a handstand against this same tree to do vertical pushups. The idea for this exercise was inspired by a story I saw about Hershel Walker, the great running back for the University of Georgia in 1980. The article contained a picture of him with his shirt off. The man "had no neck" because his trapezious muscles on top of the shoulder began just below his ears and extended all the way out to the ends of his shoulders. Vertical pushups were purported to have made him that way and I hoped to develop a similar physique.

Of course, as a farm kid I had plenty of physical work assigned to me, which had to be done on top of all the conditioning that I did for football. Hay had to be baled, thrown up into the hayloft and stacked. It was always brutally hot up there under the metal roof where there was no air circulating. There was a large amount of grass to be mowed around the house and barn, plus both sides of the long driveway and above the garden area. Much of it was rough terrain with steep banks. I did this all with a push mower. Lastly, as my dad burned firewood in the winter, there was plenty of wood to be split. The tool of choice for this job was the

15-pound "monster maul." Swinging that thing provided a great upper body and cardiovascular workout. (I still use it to this day and it is quite worn.)

This was how I spent my summer days of 1985 before formal conditioning began. I performed these tasks religiously. Coach Graham's chewing of us near the last day of school had prompted me to pick my training "up a notch." However, what really pushed me was that, much to my disbelief, my last year to wear the green helmet was upon me and I intended to give it all I had.

It might seem sad to some people that while I obsessed over getting prepared to play football, I deprived myself of a summer break and failed to enjoy the things that kids do at that age: screwing off, hanging out at the pool, cruising, partying, etc., etc. Oh, these things could have been pursued but it would have been at the expense of my senior year of football at Newark Catholic—something that comes along once in a lifetime. To take full advantage of the opportunity, sacrifices must be made. Coach Graham told us that each new team at Newark Catholic had a legitimate shot at winning a state championship and only a handful of other schools around Ohio could make that claim. It was not bragging or boastful. Coach Graham knew how to get the job done and it was there for the taking if the kids wanted it bad enough, had the dedication and discipline and would just listen to him. The choice was up to us. True, our summers *were* entirely consumed by the sport. But as stated earlier, the opportunity to be part of something special comes along once in a lifetime to very few kids around the state. The way I saw it, we had our entire lives ahead of us to work, chase girls and cruise in cars. I don't believe I missed a thing.

Meet the Coaches

Head Coach J.D. Graham graduated from Mt. Vernon St. Vincent High School, achieved a B.S. degree in Physical Education from St. Joseph College in Indiana and a Masters from Xavier University. Having played for the man, I can say that he was the epitome of intensity, had an intolerance for mediocrity, was a strict disciplinarian and perfectionist, ran a class act and commanded respect at all times. He had what I believed to be a God-given wisdom that enabled him to take a group of small, under-achieving kids, assemble them in just a certain way and motivate them to play above and beyond their abilities for 48 minutes on a Saturday night— often whipping superior teams.

Some are critical of Graham, saying that he ran his team like a military outfit. To that I say: *Of course, he did!* If soldiers are buddy-buddy with their commanding officer (known as "fraternization"), they have no sense of subordination or duty and will be less inclined to follow orders in the heat of battle. The same is true, I believe, of a football team. Coach Graham was our commander. Few of us may have liked him *at the time*, but we had tremendous respect for him and we carried out his orders. It's not the only way to run a team and it may not be the best way to run a team, but it was J.D. Graham's way of running a team and no one can argue with the results. He even said to us once: "I'm not your buddy, I'm your coach." Let me add that I am not mentally traumatized for having played for the man. On the contrary, I am a better man for it.

There were two sides to Coach Graham: the side the public saw and the side we, the players, saw on a daily basis. Coach Graham was a hard and demanding man to play for. He knew the correct buttons to push to get under our skin to produce the results that he wanted. This "button pushing" was achieved by powerful verbal assaults and cussing, but none of it was to be taken personally. This was the side the public did not see and it was this part of himself that Coach Graham was not proud of. In fact, Newark Catholic Linemen Coach Wes Poth said, "Coach Graham would often confide in me after a practice that he felt terrible about the way he ripped on someone and his choice of words. He knew of no other way to reach certain kids who required extra motivation."[1]

Coach Graham poured everything he had into his coaching. Often, he worked himself to the point of exhaustion by staying up until the wee hours of the morning studying game films or writing scouting reports. "He used to take a lot of Maalox," Coach Poth said, "and one time, he passed out in the parking lot after a pep rally."[2]

Offensive and Defensive Line Coach Wes "Pothy" Poth graduated from Gahanna Lincoln High School and attended Kenyon College where he played football and earned a degree in History. He began coaching at Newark Catholic in 1971. Coach Poth was (and still is) an outstanding lineman coach with a great knowledge of offensive and defensive line mechanics and techniques. Ironically, in the days when he played football, Coach Poth had been a running back but learned lineman techniques from, even more ironically, a Newark Catholic basketball coach named Jim Devine.

Coach Poth was friendly, funny and possessed a special gift of being able to teach people. Although he was laid back most of the time, he could snap and become just as intense and intimidating as Coach Graham. I can attest to this as Coach Poth was also a Social Studies teacher at Blessed Sacrament School and I had known him for eight years before I ever attended Newark Catholic. As seventh graders, we had Coach Poth ("Mr." Poth back then) for our homeroom teacher. Mr. Poth had no tolerance at all for disrespect or bad behavior from his students. Our class was so rotten and frequently in trouble, that I honestly did not think any of us would survive the school year. It was a known fact throughout the school that kids should have been on their best behaviors on Fridays during football season as Mr. Poth was likely to be stressing over the pending game that weekend. However, Mr. Poth could snap at any time if a misbehaving class deserved it—not just during football season. I remember one occasion when Mr. Poth became "unglued," picked up a metal podium, slammed it back to the floor and broke off one of the legs. Our class was not the only one to see Mr. Poth's wrath. My younger brother Mike, who had Mr. Poth for a homeroom teacher three years after me, recalls how Mr. Poth went into a rage one day, slammed his hand down onto a wooden desk and caved the top of it in. One of his patented punishments was to have a kid stand at the back of the room, arms extended out to the side and parallel to the floor while holding a large book in each hand. "Get 'em up!" he would yell when the arms sagged toward the floor. Put simply, it was suicidal to screw around in Mr. Poth's class. A good dose of catholic school discipline never hurt anyone, however, and definitely carries over into one's adult life.

As young boys at Blessed Sacrament who aspired to play for NC someday, we had a unique opportunity with Mr. Poth as our teacher. Green Wave stories always found their way into the classroom and increased in our young hearts the desire to play for Newark Catholic. I remember one time in seventh grade, Mr. Poth set up a film projector and showed to the entire class the 1975 Class A State Championship game in which NC lost to Carey. It seemed strange to show a black-and-white, silent game film to a seventh-grade class, but I loved it! If a better line coach, teacher or citizen ever existed, I sure would like to know where. Mr. Poth had a huge influence on my life both in the classroom and on the football field. I consider him the greatest teacher I ever had.

Defensive End Coach Dave Erhard graduated from Newark Catholic in 1975 and received a B.S. degree in Education from Ohio State. Like Coach Poth, Coach Erhard was also a teacher at Blessed Sacrament and therefore, we were quite familiar with him by the time we reached Newark Catholic. Coach Erhard was great to be around as he never blew up at anyone and he always brought humor to the practices. Dave was in the group known as the "Fun Bunch"—a clique of assistant coaches that would sneak candy to the players during practices without Coach Graham's knowledge.

Receiver and Defensive Back Coach Jim Campolo graduated from Newark Catholic in 1966 and received a B.S. degree from Miami of Ohio. Jim was also a teacher for the City of Newark and a member of the Fun Bunch.

Assistant Line Coach Paul Cost graduated from Newark Catholic in 1982 and was a top offensive and defensive lineman for the Green Wave. Paul had a distinct intensity about him and related to the kids well. He was also a member of the Fun Bunch.

Assistant Coach Dave Gebhart graduated from Newark Catholic in 1976 and received a B.S. degree in Education from The Ohio State University. Dave worked with the offensive and defensive backs and was a teacher at St. Francis De Sales School in Newark.

Assistant Coach Jeff "Chunky" Jones graduated from Newark High School in 1971. His main job was to scout opponents for upcoming games, plus serve as our "eyes in the sky" up in the press box on game nights.

Notes

1. Wes Poth, Conversation with author, Jan. 30, 2002.

2. Ibid.

Meet the Team

Seniors

#14 Andy Kubik (6-0, 170), Quarterback, Offensive captain, excellent quarterback skills. I first met "Captain Kubik" in eighth-grade football. He wore thick-framed glasses at the time and I thought he looked like Bob Griese of the Miami Dolphins.

#22 Joe Bell (5-11,160), Tailback, Safety, Special Teams; transferred to St Francis in seventh grade; great foot speed and a hard hitter.

#23 John Jurden (5-9, 155), Flanker, Defensive Back, Special Teams; transferred from Cincinnati to Blessed Sacrament in late seventh grade; tough hitter and a fierce competitor.

#24 Joe Simi (6-0, 165), Tight End, Defensive Back, Special Teams; a great athlete and probably the fastest man on the team.

#25 Monte Byers (6-0, 160), Split End, Outside Linebacker, Special Teams; transferred to Newark Catholic from Heath in ninth grade; caught almost every pass that was ever thrown to him. When he transferred in 1982, some of us called him "Del" as in "Del Monte," the canned fruit makers.

#28 Joe Wiley (5-9, 145), Flanker, Special Teams; solid member of special teams and practice squads; also known as "Coyote" as in "Wile E. Coyote."

#35 Jeff Ronan (6-1, 170), Fullback, Special Teams; transferred to Blessed Sacrament in third grade; a tough runner and my best friend; nicknamed "Woo Woo" by Coach Poth in seventh grade.

#42 Rob Settlemoir (5-7, 145), Middle Linebacker; new to the school and football team in 1985; lived in Columbus and commuted. Rob quit the team and Newark Catholic High School about halfway through the season. I never knew what became of him.

#51 Todd South (6-0, 180), Middle Linebacker, Special Teams, Long-snapper on punts, field goals and extra points; a transfer from the Lakewood School District to St. Francis in seventh grade; tough, quiet, hard-hitting; dubbed "Monkey Claws" or "Hook" by Coach Graham because of his stance and tackling form. Todd and I were on the YMCA Bengals together in 1978. (We were terrible).

#55 Mike Trotter (6-2, 225), Defensive tackle, Special Teams, limited action at Offensive Tackle; transferred to Newark Catholic from Newark City Schools before sophomore year; an outstanding defensive lineman with a temper; started as a junior and nicknamed "Commando" because of his enthusiasm for weapons and martial arts.

#60 Kevin "KC" Donnelly (5-9, 175), Guard, Special Teams; a transfer from the Buckeye Lake area to St. Francis in seventh grade; tough, strong, fearless, quick-footed; epitomized the Newark Catholic football player in that he was small in stature but had enormous fighting spirit; started as a junior.

#63 Tony Johns (5-10, 165), Center, Special Teams, very good and dependable at his position; a sharply dressed man with the finest clothes. I had known Tony since kindergarten.

#67 Bill Evans (5-10, 185), Guard, Defensive End, Special Teams, Defensive Captain; official "team farmer," sometimes referred to as "Sheep Man" because I raised sheep. Others called me "Billy Bob," a name Coach Poth conferred upon me at Blessed Sacrament. Dr. Trifelos, our team doctor, once told my mother that I received more crap from Coach Graham than anyone else did in 1985. Dr. Trifelos said he never knew how I tolerated it.

#76 Jim "Cal" Calvert (5-11, 225), Defensive Tackle; strong and aggressive pass-rusher; official team redneck and played with an attitude.

36

#79 Pat "Coop" Cooperrider (6-3, 250), Offensive Tackle; a valuable asset to the offensive line. I had known Pat since kindergarten and we attended grade school together at Blessed Sacrament; also called "The Refrigerator" because he was the largest and strongest Greenie in 1985; hunter, trapper, fisherman.

#86 Albert Ghiloni (6-1, 160), Tight End, Special Teams; solid member of special teams and practice squads; the team clown.

Underclassmen who started

Juniors

#15 Jeremy Montgomery (6-0, 165), Quarterback, Holder for field goals and extra points; had an extremely important job and performed it well.

#32 Billy Franks (5-11, 170), Outside Linebacker, Special Teams; alternated at Flanker with John Jurden to bring in the offensive plays; great athlete and played his positions well. Bill and I lived within a mile of each other during grade school. We road the bus home together, played ball and rode horses after school until the year his parents moved into town.

#33 Darby Riley (5-10, 150), Defensive Back, Special Teams; good foot speed.

#46 Tommy Helms (5-11, 150), Defensive Back, Special Teams; brilliant and tough kid with good foot speed.

#52 Jimmy Olson (6-1, 195), Defensive End, limited action at Offensive Tackle; played his position well.

#64 Tommy Ogilbee (5-10, 165), Guard, Special Teams; started one game in place of injured personnel.

#65 Dale Backlund (5-10, 190), Punter, Place-kicker, Offensive Tackle. He made the kicks when they mattered the most.

Sophomores

#41 Tim "Mac" McKenna (5-9, 170), Fullback, Special Teams; tough kid, hard hitter; earned a spot as a wallbreaker on the kickoff team. I took Tim to practices and back home again during three-a-days and throughout the season.

#45 Scott Saad (5-10, 165), Middle Linebacker, Special Teams, also saw much action at Fullback and Tail Back in place of injured personnel; outstanding athlete and a tough hitter.

#66 Matt Gilmore (6-1, 190), Defensive Tackle; started three games in place of injured personnel.

Remaining Players

Juniors

Jeff Poulton (5-6, 125)
Craig Cupples (5-9, 190)
Rich Walther (6-0, 170)
Kirk Lindsey (6-1, 200)
Jeff Wade (6-0, 155)
Jim Cross (6-3, 175)
Wimberly Cook (6-2, 195)
Steve Sigrist (6-1, 180)
Jeff Paul (6-0, 170)

Sophomores

Bill Sikora (6-0, 190)
Matt "Laser" Dase (5-8, 120)
Scott Rogers (5-10, 150)
Damon Schumaker (5-7, 135)
Jim Winters (5-10, 135)
Chip Elam (5-10, 135)
Bill Keaser (6-1, 170)
Hans Schell (5-9, 140)
Jerry Oder (5-10, 185)
Mike Heckmann (5-9, 185)
Craig Dye (6-1, 160)
John Price (6-2, 200)
Joe Flynn (6-2, 165)

Additional background about the author and the senior class

Boys in the catholic grade schools of Blessed Sacrament and St. Francis could officially begin their Newark Catholic football journey by joining the seventh-and-eighth-grade football team, which was coached by Mr. Jim Marquis. Our class first came together as a team in seventh-grade football with the exception of Jurden, Byers and Trotter, as noted above.

I was another one who did not join the Newark Catholic team in seventh grade. Though I was in catholic school, I chose not to join the seventh-and-eighth-grade team until the eighth grade. Now, one would think that for a kid whose life goal was to play for Newark Catholic, I would have jumped at the chance to start the process in seventh grade. The reason for not doing was based on something my father explained to me. Seventh-graders on the 1980 Newark Catholic seventh-and-eighth-grade team would be in the shadow of the fantastic eighth grade ahead of them and would see very little playing time. With that in mind, I used my last year of eligibility at the YMCA to play a second year for the Jets and what a good decision it turned out to be. After a 7-4 season in '79, the 1980 Jets dominated the YMCA league. We ripped everyone to enjoy a perfect, undefeated season.

My two years spent on the YMCA Jets had a profound impact on my process of *growing up green*. The coaching staff consisted of head coach Jim Huddy and assistant coaches Joe Tanner, Mike Tanner, Bill Giles and my brother Joe Evans. These folks were either former players of J.D. Graham, Newark Catholic alumni, or had children enrolled at Newark Catholic, in Jim Huddy's case. These men were and still are NC football junkies. It was no coincidence that the YMCA Jets were green! Under their direction, I not only received overdoses of NC football folklore, but I also learned the real ins-and-outs of football. They introduced me to NC conditioning drills and taught me that it was no crime to knock the crap out of someone and enjoy doing it—an action they described as "putting the 'bobu-later' on someone." Example: We were in the middle of a scrimmage one night against a team that had a real loudmouth on the defensive line. The kid was just a great big slob—probably outweighed me by 100 pounds and he thought he was the greatest. My coaches could put up with his mouth for only so long. While in the huddle, they instructed me to trap-block the kid as hard as I could. (See Appendix A for an explanation of a "trap block.") And just for this one play, they changed my position in the offensive line so that I could have as long a run at him as I possibly could. When the ball was snapped, I ran along the line of scrimmage and the boy never saw me coming—BOOM! He rolled around on the ground hollering and clutching an ankle—done for the day. My coaches could barely contain themselves. "Atta-baby, Billy," Coach Tanner said with smile as I returned to the huddle. The influence of those Jets coaches on me cannot be overstated.

I would be less than honest if I did not confess that I was not entirely "sold" on the sport of football right away. This is something that almost no one knows, and those who did know have probably forgotten. In 1979, my first year on the YMCA Jets, I actually quit the team. My excuse was that football was interfering with my schoolwork, which was complete hogwash. The truth was that I was finally beginning to learn how much time and hard work football really required and I was not sure that I wanted to do it for the remainder of my youth, despite my ambitions to play for Newark Catholic someday. It was a terrible internal war for me. My coaches and teammates had no clue of my intentions. I just surprised them all when I showed up on a Saturday morning—a game day—wearing street clothes and carrying my football gear. Coach Tanner asked me why I was not dressed. "I'm quitting," I said. He could not believe it and was greatly disappointed. He accompanied me to the building while I turned in my equipment but he did not permit me to go home. He made me stay and watch the entire game from the sidelines. Afterward, he had a long, poignant talk with me while my Dad waited in the truck. I remember him asking, "Now be honest. Did you miss being out there today with your friends and hitting people?"

"Yes," I answered.

"I missed you being out there too," Coach Tanner said.

That conversation put an end to my ambivalence, uncertainty and lack of commitment. I returned to the team the following Monday and the urge to quit never polluted my mind again. Had it not been for Mr. Joe Tanner, I may not be here today writing this book about my high school football days.

Eighth Grade

In eighth grade, I finally joined my classmates on the Newark Catholic seventh-and-eighth-grade team. It was the very first day of practice that I had my first experience with Mr. J.D. Graham. Mr. Graham journeyed down from the varsity team to check us out. While we performed some basic stretches, he walked between the rows of kids to assist Coach Jim Marquis in ensuring that we stretched properly. Now with all of my years spent *growing up green*, J.D. Graham was nothing short of a legend to me. Therefore, it was a big, big honor to have him working with us. It was such a big deal that it caused me to lose my concentration and bend in the wrong direction for one of the stretches. Mr. Graham spotted me right away.

"No, No, the other way son," Graham said. "What's your name," he asked as he redirected me.

"Bill Evans," I answered.

"Are you an Evans?" he replied. "Well, we're glad to have you anyway."

That was my first encounter with Coach Graham and I couldn't even tell my left from my right! It seemed that the two of us were destined to have a long, bumpy road together.

Under the fine coaching of Mr. Jim Marquis, we were introduced to the Newark Catholic football system—a prelude to what awaited those of us who chose to stick with football. Mr. Marquis worked us vigorously by making us run three or four miles after game days and by putting us through three-hour practices on Saturday mornings. We were not immune to harsh criticism at that young age either. I remember one day in which we had a lousy practice and he really got on us. "You guys stink!" he yelled. "You stink worse than that dog shit over there!" in reference to a large pile of dog feces that was found near the track that day.

I will never forget our first game that year. Since it was my first real game as a Green Wave, I was terribly nervous. My nervousness grew exponentially as we pulled in to Licking Heights High School on a gloomy, rainy afternoon. The Licking Heights team could be seen on the field warming up and they were giants! I was certain that we would be stomped into the soil of western Licking County. The day proved to be a priceless learning experience for me, however. I learned to trust in Newark Catholic coaching. I learned to trust in the Newark Catholic tradition. Most of all, I learned to trust in my teammates. We played our game that day and prevailed something in the neighborhood of 38-6.

We went 7-0 in eighth grade and trailed a team only one time all season. That took place in our very last game. Mr. Marquis put together a kickoff team with the younger boys who did not play much. Our opponent, the Northridge Vikings, ran the opening kickoff back and we were down 0-7 right away. The final score was 54-7. I believe that in eighth grade, our class demonstrated that we had the potential to be good. We were on our way into the Newark Catholic football tradition to find out.

Ninth Grade

We made the big jump into Newark Catholic High School one year later. John Stare was the head coach of the freshman football team and it was here that we were further indoctrinated into the Newark Catholic system. It did not take long to hit it off poorly with Coach Graham that year. Coach Graham taught freshman world history and this was our first official form of interaction with him. In the classroom, Coach Graham could get an idea of what kind of kids he had coming up by observing our behaviors, monitoring the types of grades we received, etc. We were all punk freshman screw-offs to be sure, but as first impressions meant everything, I tried not to be a blatant cut-up in front of Graham. On one occasion, we were in the middle of silent reading. Monte Byers, new to the school that year, broke the silence by breaking wind—quite loudly, I might add. Coach Graham looked up from his desk to find several of us suppressing laughter.

"Mr. Byers," Coach Graham said, "Is there a mouse running around in here tooting a bugle?"

"Uh, it was Evans," Monte replied.

Having been betrayed in front of the man that would rule my life for the next three years, I felt crushed, humiliated and I had several choice expletives for Byers.

That incident was provided for humor's sake. The real trespassing of our class (one of many) took place some time later. Coach Graham had finished his lecture for the day and left the room. At that moment, Joe Bell, who had been working on a supreme, extra-juicy spitball, stood up, expectorated the substance into his cupped hand and slung the mass across the room. Splat! The wad struck the clock and clung. It must have been "throw-spit-wads-at-the-clock" day because after Bell's action, dozens of others followed suit by dirtying the clock and much of the surrounding wall. Splat! Splat! Splat! It was frenzied spit-wad-throwing affair.

We returned to the room the next day. All of the spit wads had dried and became crusty formations overnight. Of course, we as freshman thought the sight was simply hilarious. Coach Graham did not share this view and was quite perturbed when he arrived. "It seems we had a little problem with spit balls being thrown in this room after I left yesterday," Coach Graham said. "This is filthy, disgusting and childish! Now I'm going to leave this room for ten minutes. I want those responsible to clean it up during that time. When I come back, all of that crap had better be off the wall! Got it, Mr. Bell?" Somehow, Coach Graham knew that the freshman football players were mostly to blame.

Then there was the time when Todd South and Kevin Donnelly skipped football practice to attend a Judas Priest concert. Coach Graham took them out into the hallway the next morning for a stern lecture. More than likely, these events and others not mentioned left a lasting negative impression with Coach Graham with regard to our freshman class—specifically the football players.

Coach Graham was sure to keep track of our activity on the football field. I remember being in world history class after our first freshman game. We had played rather poorly but defeated Big Walnut 10-0.

"What was the problem out there yesterday, fellas?" Graham asked us. He selected Todd South to answer for us, which was fine by me.

"We had a few problems on offense, but our defense was great," Todd said.

"That's not what I saw," Graham retorted. "Don't shit yourselves, fellas. You'll have to put forth a better effort than that if you want to be successful at this school."

It turned out that he was right. One week later, we choked in our game against the Wilson Tigers—a public junior high school across the street from Newark Catholic. To be fair, Wilson had an excellent team under the leadership of the venerable Bobby Klockner. They also had a superstar running back in Jackie Baltimore. (Jackie had been on the 1980 YMCA Jets team with me and was a big reason why we were undefeated.) We played poorly and were plagued with several turnovers in the game. It was a dark day for our class as it was the first time (and only time) we ever lost. Maybe we weren't so great after all. We finished freshman year 6-1.

Conditioning Begins

The first day of conditioning had arrived: July 17, 1985. The grueling journey ahead of us began here. It was a hot day, the sun beating down from the late afternoon sky. I met Tony Johns as I was headed through the gate at the edge of the parking lot.

"They've added another playoff game to the season," Tony said.

"It's going to be difficult getting psyched up for fourteen games," I replied.

We were referring to fact that the Ohio High School Athletic Association (OHSAA) had altered its playoff system that had been in place since 1980 by adding an additional regional game. This meant the possibility of having to play four post-season games as opposed to three. Therefore, beginning in 1985, any team that made it to the championship game would be playing its fourteenth game of the season.

Why did we speak of such things when we had not even been to our first practice yet? Were we over-confident and out of line? I was well aware of Newark Catholic's ability to return to the playoffs each year, but *our* class was now in charge and one must consider what we were up against. If Coach Graham didn't have enough to worry about in regard to our poor off-season work ethic, he also faced a great challenge in rebuilding this team after the school had just won its third state championship. It had been accomplished by one of the more talented group of kids ever to play at NC that had now graduated—nineteen of them, to be exact. The graduating class included Shane Montgomery, a standout quarterback, punter and place kicker who went on to have a fine career as a quarterback for the

Wolf Pack of North Carolina State. Yes, he was one of 19 reasons why in 1984, Newark Catholic went 13-0 (a new school record) and averaged 37 points per game while allowing just 4.5.

Coach Graham made public the woes caused by graduation, saying, "This is the biggest rebuilding job that we've ever had here. We have to replace 20 positions and the entire kicking game. On paper, we don't look too good right now."[1]

Hearing all of this spawned great concern on our parts and prompted many questions. Would we be able to rebuild and match last year's performance? Would we be able to emerge from the shadow of the 1984 team and be great on our own or would our team be responsible for the demise of the program—a program whose teams had made it to the state championship game five consecutive years—something that had almost come to be expected? Would 1985 indeed be the year that the Greenies finally "get their lunch?"

We were not all green with inexperience (pardon the pun). Strong-side guard Kevin Donnelly and defensive tackle Mike Trotter were our two returning starters. Additionally, there were a handful of others, including myself, that were returning lettermen thanks to several blowouts that the '84 seniors achieved that allowed us younger guys a good deal of playing time. This would make Coach Graham's job of rebuilding a little easier—but only just a little. Some of the assistant coaches referred to our class as "Jerry's Kids," the implication being that we were in dire need of assistance from the Jerry Lewis Labor Day Telethon. I don't know if we were *that* bad, but I did consider our class—me included—as an awkward bunch that had its share of clowns, partiers and internal conflicts. We had such a bad reputation that when we became seniors, no faculty member wanted to step forward to serve as our class advisor. (Someone did eventually fill this role, but with reluctance.) We seemed dense, bull-headed, hard to reach and inconsistent. Although we had good athletes, we definitely lacked the superstars, the togetherness and the panache that the '84 team had enjoyed. Coach Graham once said to our class after watching a film, "I love these people who accuse us of recruiting. Look around the room, fellas. Do you think we'd waste money on people like you?" On another occasion, when he was quite perturbed at us, he said, "If any of you people have any aspirations at all of playing college football, you're shittin' yourselves!"

Filling the shoes of the '84 team would be a daunting and stressful task. Given who we were, I thought it was insane to be talking about playing 14 games on this first day of practice. Coach Graham may have approved of the talk as healthy goal setting, but where does one draw the line between goal setting and ignorant over-confidence? Nonetheless, we would press on in pursuit of the goals which had become standard year after year at Newark Catholic: a perfect regular season, a Licking County League championship, a berth in the playoffs and a victory in the Division V State Championship game the day after Thanksgiving.

The word "conditioning" referred to the process of getting into the physical condition required to play this sport and consisted of many fun-filled activities.

The first action was an extensive stretching routine that worked every part of the body. With the team neatly ordered into rows, Coach Graham selected four seniors to stand out in front of the team and lead the exercises, a job that the quartet would have for the duration of the season. In 1985, the chosen ones were Andy Kubik, Kevin Donnelly, John Jurden and I. After a particular stretch was named, the leader yelled "Ready, exercise," and one clap initiated the stretch. After a 12-count, two claps completed the cycle. When I was *growing up green*, it impressed me tremendously on game nights to look out over White Field from high atop the home seats and watch 40 or 50 guys clapping in unison on the football field. The stretch routine is described below.

Right leg over, left leg over- consisted of first crossing the right leg over the left, bending down with the head to the knee and then repeated for the left.

Right leg, left leg, middle- standing with feet far apart and with knees locked, we bent out and touched our heads to the right knee, then the left knee, then reached back behind us between the legs for a center stretch.

Front- standing with feet apart and knees locked, we remained bent over and moved the upper body from side to side to get a good stretch in the backs of the knees.

Right leg, left leg, middle- sitting and with legs spread, the head was placed on the right knee, the left knee and then held down in the center.

Right leg up, left leg up- the legs were brought together and each was raised to touch our face to the knee while the knee was locked.

Right leg under, left leg under- involved pulling a foot back under the butt and lying on our backs for a terrific thigh stretch.

Windmill- still lying down, our right leg was crossed over our body and the foot was placed into the left hand which was flat on the ground next to our heads. This was repeated for the left leg.

Plow- involved rolling into a backward summersault and balancing on the backs of our necks with our toes touching the ground behind us with locked knees.

Cobra- moving onto our stomachs, the hips were kept to the ground while we fully extended our arms to raise our upper bodies off the ground. This was to stretch the back.

Staying physically fit is still a high priority of mine and I still go through this entire routine before jogging or any other exercise (everything but the clapping).

Coach Graham took stretching very seriously, as it was essential to preventing injuries. He would walk between the rows of players to observe techniques. If anyone failed to put forth his full effort, Coach Graham would let him know about it.

When stretching was complete, we paired up for a routine designed to strengthen the neck. A man on his hands and knees placed the side of his head against the knee of a teammate standing beside him. The idea was for the man on the ground to apply maximum force against the standing man's leg, which worked the neck muscles. After going to both the left and right, the man on the ground forced his head up while his partner pushed down, and then down while his partner provided upward resistance. The two then rotated so that the other could have his turn.

Ten jumping jacks followed the neck work. After a clap for team spirit, it was time for an exercise called Quarter Eagles. On the command "Wind it up," which meant to run in place with knees bent and butt as close to the ground as possible, we were to briefly turn to the left or right when told to do so, shout the direction that we turned and then snap back to face straight ahead. When the command "Hit it!" was issued, we were to dive on the ground and immediately bounce back up. They became less painful once we were in full pads, but they often resulted in a mouthful of soil and grass. We would typically do 25 or 30 of these, but sometimes, if the coaches were feeling particularly generous, they gave us the opportunity to do 50 or even 100. This usually occurred when some of us could not distinguish our lefts from our rights.

Quarter Eagles were followed with 25 pushups and 25 situps. Then it was time for a drill called Seat Rolls. Seat Rolls also consisted of winding it up and on the command "left" or "right," we were to drop to the respective knee, roll our butts across the ground and then come back into a running position. Again, 25 or 30 was a typical amount but any number was possible depending on a coach's mood. These were followed with another 25 pushups and 25 situps.

Another drill we did quite often was the Devine Drill. The Devine Drill consisted of winding it up, a somersault, back up on our feet and spinning to the right, a somersault, back up on our feet and spinning to the left, another somersault, spinning around on the right hand, a somersault, spinning around on the left hand, a final somersault and then sprinting for home. One was completely dizzy and momentarily disoriented after going through this and it sometimes resulted in collisions.

Another activity that I absolutely despised was the Box Drill. Cones were set up to form a box that was about 10 yards on each side. Around the entire perimeter of this box, we did such things as hopping on the left foot, hopping on the right foot, hopping on both feet, both forward and backward summersaults, and it finished up with forward and backward bear crawls. It was enough to make a guy pass out in the summer heat. I was first introduced to this drill while affiliated with the YMCA Jets. I dreaded seeing those cones come out of the shed.

After these various drills were completed, it was time to run. Twenty 40-yard sprints was the standard procedure. We were split into two groups. Backs and receivers were always in the first group and were followed by the lineman. The quarterbacks would call our cadence, "Set, thirty-eight, Go," and we fired out from a three-point stance (two feet and one hand on the ground) and hustled out to another coach standing 40 yards away. Coach Graham closely scrutinized everyone to make sure no one was loafing. We were told to not have sloppy running forms. Pumping the arms and focusing on an object in the distance would keep the head steady and focused.

After sprints, Coach Graham had another endurance-building routine for us that he called "Fences." This amounted to lining up on the right field foul line of the baseball diamond, sprinting down to the fence on the western end of the school property and sprinting back. A distance of over 100 yards each way, backs and receivers had to do these under 30 seconds and the lineman were given 40. One time, Coach Graham put me in with the backs and receivers for some reason and I was thoroughly smoked by them all. After any conditioning drill, while we gasped for air and our hearts pounded in our ears, the overwhelming tendency was to bend at the waste because standing up straight seemed difficult. The coaches would say, "Stand up! There's no air down there!"

After fences, we were permitted into the locker room for a water break before the next workout—a timed mile around the quarter-mile cinder track. Backs and receivers had to do this in less than 6 minutes and the lineman had to do it in 6:30. In the heat of the summer evenings, the cinders crunched beneath our shoes as we galloped around the track. Black dust kicked up and permeated our socks and shoes. All of this was done under the scrutiny and verbal assaults of Coach Graham. "Push it! Stretch it out!" he would yell. He always pushed us to get a better time than we had the day before. I was never a good distance runner as my best time was 5:58.

Another running exercise we did on the track was to sprint halfway around it, walk the remainder of the way around for a rest and then sprint again when we returned to the starting place. This process was repeated several times and was the final part of the workout before being dismissed to go home. It always amazed me that no matter how good of shape I thought I was in, Coach Graham's workouts always broke me and left me exhausted. How rough would it have been if I did nothing all summer?

That was a typical conditioning session at Newark Catholic during my senior year and it was conducted at 10:00 a.m. and 6:00 p.m. The evening practice was the official session that we were supposed to attend. The morning session was only open to accommodate those kids who had summer jobs or who were on baseball teams. This made missing practice inexcusable and unacceptable. Coach Graham liked to tell the story of a kid some years before us who said that he could not make it to a certain practice. Coach Graham asked him: "If this was a rock concert, could you make it here?" "Oh yea," the kid replied, after which Graham told him just to go on home and not come back because he didn't want it bad enough.

There was one of my classmates who had been missing many practices. Joe Bell, who was in line for the starting tailback position, had undergone an appendectomy in late July and was expected to miss six to eight weeks. "This was unacceptable for me,"[2] Bell said. Within a week of the surgery, not only was he at the school walking around the track, but he was also running in the pool at the house of Tom LeFevre, our team manager. "I remember walking the track," recalls Bell, "and J.D. came over to yell at me because I was walking too slowly and that I needed to stretch it out more. No rest for the ill!"[3]

The day after conditioning started, several doctors reported to the school and set up stations where our physical exams would take place. The doctor who did the heart exam told me that I had a heart murmur, something that was said to me every year after a physical. Each year, mom took me to the family doctor for further examinations and each year, the doctor found nothing and cleared me to play. This always made my mother suspect that some sort of racket was in place between family doctors and those who gave the physicals. On my trip to the family practitioner in 1985, however, the doctor did in fact detect something that he did not feel qualified to diagnose and he referred me to a heart specialist. As one might imagine, this was very upsetting, as it could have jeopardized my senior year of football. And truthfully, it was nothing to take lightly because a football player in Crooksville, Ohio had died from a heart-related problem in 1983.

My appointment was with Dr. Wee, a cardiologist. In is office, I had to do such things as pushups and stepping up and down on a stool to increase my heart rate, after which Dr. Wee listened to my heart with a stethoscope. He also hooked me up to an electrocardiogram—a heart-monitoring machine that produced a long printout of the electrical activity of the heart. After some time, Dr. Wee shook his head and smiled to announce that I did not have a heart murmur. The official report, which arrived through the mail some days later, stated that my heartbeat was so strong that it caused the whole heart to vibrate within the chest. The vibration was the noise mistakenly diagnosed as a murmur in the previous years. This was truly great news.

As conditioning proceeded for several days, another health dilemma sprang up one evening when I suddenly experienced a sharp pain in my right hip while running sprints. I tried ignoring it, but it escalated from simply slowing me down to the point where I could no longer run at all. I informed Coach Graham about my problem and without hesitation, he said that I needed to see a chiropractor. I attended the morning practice on the following day, after which Coach Graham had me follow him to Dr. Jerry Mantonya's office on the east side of Newark.

Now, my only knowledge of chiropractors had come second hand from my father. I knew that he had been to see a "back cracker" once. As told by my father, the chiropractor jumped in the middle of his back, causing my dad severe pain and it "sounded like a bunch of firecrackers going off." Never lacking disdain for physicians, Dad was not going to have that done to him twice in a lifetime and he never returned.

Based on this experience, I did not know what to expect and was quite apprehensive. One thing was certain though, and that was the fact that I was in some serious pain. If something was not done for me, I might miss my senior season.

What took place at the chiropractor's office on that first visit was a physical examination of my frame followed by a series of bizarre tests with Coach Graham observing. Individual hand strength was measured by squeezing a testing device similar to the hand brakes on a bicycle. Lung capacity was measured by blowing into another machine for as long as I could. The most bizarre test was the testing of my legs. Lying flat on my back, the doctor pulled my legs apart and told me to resist him as he tried to bring my feet together. I had almost no strength and he easily made my feet join. He then taped a small steel ball to the inside of my right wrist and we tried it again. This time, he could not move my legs! "Wow," I said. "Can I have one of those before every game?" Coach Graham seemed to appreciate my question. Another leg test with similar results was conducted. This time, the sudden increase in strength could be attributed to a Vitamin E tablet placed under my tongue.

Finally, after all the testing had been completed, Dr. Mantonya revealed to us what he had discovered. My problems were the result of a vertebra in my lower back being off center, causing misalignment of my pelvic bones and making one of my legs longer than the other. All of this manifested itself in the severe hip pain I experienced. When he put his hand on my back to show which vertebra was "out of whack," it suddenly dawned on me as to what had caused this.

Approximately eight months earlier in the state championship game against Middletown Fenwick, I was in at defensive end. Fenwick's quarterback, the tall and lanky 6-3, 180-pound John Hurlburt dropped back to pass. He was pressured to my side and decided to make a run for it. That's when I nailed him right in the legs. Unfortunately, he was so big and had enough momentum going that he just ran me over, bent me backward and I instantly felt a sharp pain in my lower back. I was scared to death at the strange, new pain in my spine. I slowly got back to my feet and was thankful that I could still stand. All of that pressure of being bent backwards had been exerted on this same area that Dr. Mantonya pointed out to me. Consequently, I stayed in the game for a few more series until I started being destroyed by the huge lineman that Fenwick had. I was yanked out and Jim Otto played the remainder of the game.

Much to Coach Graham's surprise, I revealed that the aching vertebra had plagued me for three or four months afterwards, but the pain eventually went away. He gave me flak for not having it looked at back then. Although my back and hip still give me problems periodically to this day and are "battle scars" that I must live with, they are also reminders of past glories.

49

I immediately began undergoing daily spinal adjustments. My trips out east to the chiropractor became as much a part of my daily routine as wind sprints and seat rolls. Within days, the pain was gone and I was back to normal.

As conditioning progressed, the day to begin wearing full padding steadily approached and all of the gear had to be issued. As with most other football functions, this took place in room 120 across the hall from Coach Graham's office. He would bring us into the room a few bodies at a time. A certain strong odor always accompanied the issuance of pads. I don't know if the odor was from detergents, preservatives, or simply from the pads themselves, but the odor was always present and it was the smell of football season! Every piece of equipment we had to wear was in this room, and it all had to be properly fitted. Stacked in piles were game pants, practice pants, the girdle which contained two hip pads and a butt pad, thigh pads, knee pads, shoulder pads, a shoulder harness which was additional padding worn beneath the shoulder pads, and the helmet. From the dozens of facemasks stacked on the desks, we were free to choose the style we wanted. I always thought the biggest ones with the most crossbars appeared tough and manly and those are the ones I preferred.

Finally, the remaining clothing was also issued. From stacks on the tops of the school desks, we grabbed a practice jersey, one green and one white game jersey, a gray undershirt to be worn on game day and a pair of knee-high game socks that had our "NC" logo on the side. Getting the game jerseys was exciting because the design changed slightly with each new season and there was anticipation to see what our new look would be. We were charged 30-40 dollars for the kneepads, socks, undershirt and both jerseys. We were permitted to keep them when the season ended.

This was a big day for the sophomores. From the numbers left behind by last year's seniors, the sophomores selected the number that they would wear for the next three years as a Newark Catholic football player. Even though Coach Graham allowed us to pick our numbers, we did not have total freedom. For instance, if a kid was lineman material and tried to pick a number that would normally be worn by a running back or a receiver, he was told to pick from the appropriate group— numbers 50-79. I was denied this experience as a sophomore because there were not enough numbers to go around that year. As a result, junior Tim Blasczyk had to share his #53 with me. When I finally got to select my number as a junior, I mulled over the stacks hoping to find #99, the number of Mark Gastineau, the great defensive end for the New York Jets whom I admired. When I asked Coach Graham if he had the number hiding anywhere, he laughed and said, "No, just what you see." I settled on #67 for four reasons. First, although I was a defensive end, I was also a guard and this was a guard's number. Second, Sean Farrel, weak-side guard on the '83 team was the last person to wear #67 and I always admired him for his quiet toughness. Third, the number rhymed with my last name, somewhat. Lastly, "67" is also the year I was born.

There was one last critical piece of equipment to be addressed. No—not cups—but mouthpieces. We were at liberty to use the store-bought "lizard-tongue" variety that had a strap protruding from the mouth, which fastened to the facemask. However, for the ridiculously low price of $2.00, we could go around the corner to the dentist offices of Richard Main and Jon Musser on West Church Street and have a custom mouthpiece made. All we had to do was sit in the chair, and with strawberry-flavored goop, they made a plaster mold of our upper teeth. From that, a very comfortable mouthpiece was developed. The only drawback was that they lacked the "lizard-tongue" strap and were easy to lose.

The day to begin wearing full pads was typically the first Saturday in August. It was always a shock to the body to continue doing the conditioning drills with an additional 10 or 15 pounds of dead weight suddenly added to our frames. I always had trouble with a stiff, sore neck while the neck muscles became accustomed to carrying a heavy helmet on my head.

One evening when conditioning had ended, I made my way to the locker room accompanied by Kevin Donnelly. Just as we were about to leave the track, I happened to look down and saw an old, tattered penny lying on the cinders. Being somewhat superstitious at the time, I felt that the penny was a good luck charm. I said to Kevin that if we happened to make it to the state game again, since we found it together, the two of us would come back to this part of the track and throw the penny back before we boarded the bus to Columbus. From that day forward, that penny was kept in the left rear corner of the top shelf of my locker. I checked it almost every day to be sure it had not vanished.

Notes

1. Mark Naegele, "'Biggest' rebuilding task facing Green Wave coach," *The Advocate, Football '85*, (Aug. 28, 1985), p. 6.

2. Joe Bell, Electronic mail to author, Nov. 26, 2001.

3. Ibid.

Three-a-days

Although the first Saturday in August was the first day to wear full pads, hitting was not officially permitted to begin until the following Monday. On that day, all hell broke loose. That day marked the beginning of practicing three times a day—a time known as the dreaded "three-a-days." For years, the term struck fear into the hearts of young boys, as rumors of the harshness of three-a-days filtered down into the grade schools. It was not until the first day of three-a-days as a sophomore that a kid finally discovered the rumors of barfing and passing out were mostly true. No one in his right mind would want to put himself through this, but the reality was that if we wanted to play football for J.D. Graham, for Newark Catholic and contend for a state championship, we had to go through three-a-days.

Akin to leaving home for boot camp, life as we knew it turned into the ultimate physical challenge and did not let up until school started. I have long believed that three-a-day practices were a key ingredient to Newark Catholic's success. When other teams had Newark Catholic out-manned and out-gunned, the superior conditioning, the toughness and the belligerent attitudes developed during three-a-days kept the Green Wave in the big games and enabled them to take control in the fourth quarter. Many teams may have had the edge in talent, but *no one* was in better condition than Newark Catholic.

As far as I know, three-a-days appear to be exclusive to Newark Catholic. From what I hear in the media, all other schools, even college and pro teams, only practice twice a day. That is not to say that three-a-days do not exist anywhere else in America—I am just not aware of the system anywhere else. If practicing two times a day is good enough for most other football organizations, the obvious question then becomes: Why three-a-days at all? Coach Graham answered that question and confirmed my views of three-a-days:

> Three-a-days were instituted by Matt Midea, so they were already in place when I came to Newark Catholic. We kept them going but changed the format to allow more time for developing the passing game and kicking game. Three-a-days served a threefold purpose. One, they bettered our chances of winning because of the conditioning that resulted. If we could hang with a team until the fourth quarter, which our conditioning enabled us to do, our chances of winning increased dramatically. Two, if our kids were in great shape, they were less likely to get hurt. And God forbid, if somebody did get hurt, it seemed like he recovered faster. Three, a mental toughness came from it all. We felt we deserved to win more than our opponents did because we outworked them. Winning was almost expected.[1]

While winning *may* have been expected within certain members of the team and coaching staff, for the Green Wave faithful, losing was often expected. My friend John Crowley—a father of three Newark Catholic graduates and the typical, ardent Green Wave football fan—shared his thoughts on the matter:

> I can't count the times when I would sit in the stands before a game and examine the opposing teams. They looked like monsters—like college players. I would turn to my wife Janet and say, "We're going to get our ass kicked." But by the second half, those bigger kids were tired and I would see a 175-pound lineman kicking the crap out of a 225-pound lineman. It always amazed me.[2]

The first practice of the day began bright and early at 8:30 a.m. (8:00 a.m. in 1983). Parading out into the humid, sometimes foggy mornings, we took our positions in the eastern end zone of the practice field just as the sun was breaking over the top of McGuffey School. The eerie calm and quiet of the morning would soon be shattered by the initiation of the stretching routine: "Ready, exercise!" Many groans of disgust were issued as we begrudgingly placed our butts into the dew-laden grass. The smell of the wet, freshly mowed grass on a three-a-day morning is something I have never forgotten.

After stretching, we performed all of the regular things that we had been doing in the previous weeks: Seat Rolls, Quarter Eagles, Devine Drills etc., and wearing pads made them all the more difficult.

Wearing full pads enabled us to conduct many additional exercises. We split up into two groups for the next phase of practice. Backs and receivers, sometimes referred to as the "skilled positions," would go off with Coach Graham, Coach Campolo and Coach Gebhart to delve into the complex world of pass routes and pass defenses that I, as a lineman, never understood. The linemen would head out under the supervision of Coach Poth and Coach Erhard to be put through many other conditioning drills.

The first exercise for the linemen was to do foot work in the ropes. The ropes were fastened about 12 inches above the ground in a structure made of metal tubing that was approximately 6 feet wide and 20 feet long. One rope running lengthwise through the middle across several ropes running from side to side formed many squares. We started by chopping through them down and back while facing sideways. "Come on linemen, work! Chop the feet and pump the arms!" coach Poth would shout. When that was done, we went back through facing forward. The next pass consisted of hopping in and out of each hole with both feet together and hands behind the back. Following that move came the criss-crossing of the legs over the center rope until we reached the other end. The last move was to run through the structure using as long of a stride as possible. While doing the ropes, the cleats would pound the ground and the dust would rise. These exercises were to be done with maximum effort and quickness. If Coach Poth thought we were loafing, we would do it again.

Another activity was an agility and quickness drill that consisted of chopping over and around foam dummies on the ground. First, we would chop the feet and navigate between the dummies, staying low and maintaining a good football position. The other drill was to stay as low as possible while chopping the feet and stepping sideways over the foam dummies. When we stepped over, we were to push downward and hit the dummy. This was to train for keeping blockers away from our legs.

When that drill was completed, we traveled to the old 7-man sled for some real grunt work. The first pass through was to throw a right forearm, followed by a second pass with the left forearm. I can still hear the squeaking of the sled and the dull "thud" when we struck the pads. The next time through, we performed a shoving action known as a "hand shiver." The next move was to go down the line on all fours and fire out into the foam pad with a shoulder—first the right and then the left. Rapid-fire drills followed this, which consisted of two guys firing their shoulders into the pads as hard and as fast as possible. After three hits with the right shoulder, the partners switched places by crossing over each other and finished up with the left shoulder. We were to make this change as quickly as we could, so it helped to designate ahead of time who would go under and who would go over. The final part of the sled work was the actual firing out and driving it. Seven men would approach the sled. Coach Poth, who would stand on the platform, would say, "Set …Hit!" In a symphony of grunts and squeaking iron, the sled would lurch upward. We would push it for all we were worth as Coach Poth yelled, "Drive! Drive! Drive!" Coach Poth would often stand on the platform with a cool drink in his hand, which looked so refreshing to me while working in the hot summer sun. When we had pushed it far enough, Pothy would say, "Whoa," and the next group stepped up.

Coach Poth watched the linemen closely during all of our drills. If he was not happy with our efforts, he saw to it that we received plenty of additional opportunities to get it right. On one occasion, we had finished our sled work and were moving on to the ropes, which were at the other end of the school property. Traveling between stations was to be done sharply and at a respectable jogging pace at all times. Apparently, we did not move fast enough from the sled to the ropes to suit Coach Poth and he forced us to run all the way back to the sled to try the journey again. This is just one example of how attention to detail and standards of excellence—even in something as trivial as moving from one station to the next—were to be maintained at all times.

Hitting drills were conducted as soon as possible so that the body could begin the long and painful process of becoming acclimated to the jolt of contact—the real business of football. One such hitting drill was called "Bongos." It consisted of one man who had to proceed along an entire row of eight to ten other players and smack heads with them all.

Another contact drill, known as "Root-hog or Die," pitted one man against the other. The object was to get lower than our opponent and drive him backwards. The one who got lower, scratched and clawed like a rooting hog usually won, hence the name. I often wondered if these drills were just as much entertainment for the coaches as they were for our improvement because Coach Poth would laugh and laugh at some of our performances.

I can recall my very first hit that summer, which occurred in a basic tackling drill where two men faced each other—one as the ball carrier and the other as the tackler. Usually, in an attempt to avoid injuries, the coaches tried to pair people up who were of the same size, age and ferocity. On that first day of hitting, I was paired up with Kevin Donnelly. We chopped the feet, he got the ball and we collided. Now, the first hit of the season, and all hits for that matter, are another shock to the body. If done properly, the hit should give a "buzz" to both parties involved. I definitely acquired the buzz. When I got up, I could not help but think that all of the fine work the chiropractor had been doing for me was just sent down the toilet.

Not all drills involved contact. Fundamentals and proper technique were taken seriously and addressed every week. We worked on staying low while firing out of our stances, which was done by lining up beneath a steel crossbar. If we got too high while firing out, the helmet struck the bar and could really rattle the brain.

Maintaining a wide stance while blocking was another crucial element. This was addressed by driving someone backward while straddling boards on the ground. Stances themselves were also worked on. Some guys had bad stances and needed more work than others. Those with bad stances were described as "squatting dogs looking for some place to take a shit."

Another drill without contact was known as the "Mirror Drill." This involved two men facing each other and locking together by grabbing each other's jersey. The object was to simply chop the feet faster than the other guy so that we could turn him completely around. My partner for this drill and most other drills was Kevin Donnelly. I never could turn that kid as he was stronger and had quicker feet.

One day Jeff Ulenhake, a 1984 NC grad who was a freshman on the Ohio State football team, showed up at a practice to demonstrate some of the lineman techniques he had learned at OSU. I was selected to be the "crash test dummy" for the demonstration. Kneeling on the ground and facing me, Jeff demonstrated a "swim technique" for defensive linemen to get around blockers. Jeff grabbed my right shoulder with the his left hand, pulled me toward him, brought the right arm up and over and smashed his right elbow down onto my back. What a jolt that was!

To me, these strenuous conditioning and agility drills were the worst part of football. Try to imagine performing them in the heat of the August sun—the cleats pounding the hard earth like a herd of wildebeests galloping across the African plains and sending a ton of dust into the air while heat waves shimmered in the distance. Often when there was no breeze, the dust-laden air lingered around us and entered our mouths as we groped for our next breath, which left a gritty film of soil on the teeth and mouthpiece.

Sweat invaded and burned the eyes, mingled with the dust on our arms and legs and formed a crust when it dried. Skinned knuckles and elbows were commonplace and always stung from the intrusion of dirt and sweat and re-injury. Soreness, aches, fingers bending in ways they should not and exhaustion were the norm. We were bruised, thirsty, hungry, irritable, daydreaming about a cool place to rest. Clothes were drenched with sweat and we smelled bad. Some boys puked, others occasionally had liquid bowels, also know as "the shits" in football lingo. It stretched the body to the limit. But no one forced us to be out there. This was normal. This was Newark Catholic, where expectations were high and where championship teams were born. We knew that to be a champion required the misery of the three-a-day practices. The only thing to do was to "suck it up" and support one another through the madness.

During these oppressive days, Coach Graham was generous with the water breaks. The watering device was a piece of pipe about waist-high with several holes drilled into it. When the spigot was turned on, several streams of water sprayed out in all directions and could water-down many dehydrated football players simultaneously. Desperate to extinguish our savage thirsts, we crowded around the pipe gasping, slurping, pushing and shoving each other like cattle with their big ugly heads in a feed trough trying to get the last bit of grain. If we did not stand just right, the stream of water would soak our shoes and clothes. Most of the time, we were so hot that we welcomed such a thing. Some kids filled their helmets with water just so they would get good and drenched when they put them back on. As with everything else, there was a pecking order here. If a sophomore was drinking before a senior, he was shoved off to the side and made to wait just like the runts in a feedlot.

During water breaks, the coaches always warned us not to drink too much or else we would get sick. But with us being overheated, tired and parched; when it felt as if we were on the brink of death and water was the only thing that could save us, the coaches were wasting their breath. We gulped it "like there was no tomorrow," and the "coaches be damned." Invariably, there were some that would indeed overdo it and within minutes they would go off by themselves to "ralph."

Some kids had a propensity for barfing such as Joe Bell. His recent appendectomy and resulting lag in conditioning, rather than too much water, made "ralphing" almost a daily event. On one occasion after Bell hurled, Coach Graham walked in Bell's direction saying, "Let's go see what Mr. Bell had for breakfast today."

Even during the water breaks, Coach Graham had us working. After everyone had stood in the mud hole and drunk their fill, we sat on the ground or on our helmets and worked on our offensive cadence. All quarterbacks took their turns at doing this while the coaches stood at the middle of the field talking amongst themselves. "Set, thirty-eight, go!" was our cadence and on "go," the entire team clapped one time. The counts were also mixed, some being on two and some being on three, with no particular order. If some boys clapped early, which would be akin to illegal procedure in a game, teammates berated them to "get with it." Of course, no matter how far away he stood, Coach Graham could always detect when someone screwed it up. "Get your head out of your ass and pay attention!" he would yell. It was a mental test to see if we could concentrate while we were exhausted, aching and fatigued, because that is what it would be like in a game situation.

I can recall how our cadence evolved into the form we used. Originally, "Set, go!" was all there was to it. The cadence had to change in 1984 because of a particular team we played that year. I believe the team was Crooksville and their defensive linemen would shift around after the opposing team was set to run a play. We wanted the ability to call audibles if their shifting around threatened the success of the play we had called. Once we heard "Set," we knew that the next sound out of the quarterback's mouth would be "go" and the play would begin. Therefore, if the play needed to be changed at that moment, it could not be done. So as a solution, Coach Graham added an extra element to the cadence which was "thirty-eight," a number he chose because it was easily spoken. Now, after the command "Set" was issued, if the defense switched around while we were in our stances, the quarterback could change the play. When he finally said "thirty-eight," we knew that was the point of no return and the play would go. Even though the change was instituted for that one game, the new format became permanent.

All remaining phases of the game were added once hitting began. We began running our offense: the Pro set with I backs, strong backs, slot, wing, etc. All of our plays were run from these varying formations: 13 and 14 Dives; Zero and 1 Traps; 23 and 24 Powers; 25 and 26 Isolations; Flanker Trap Zero; Counter traps; Sweeps; Quick Pitches. (See Appendix A for play diagrams.) The passes were also added. Backs and receivers had their assignments to learn. The linemen had to memorize blocking assignments and perfect blocking techniques. Coach Poth taught us so effectively that I can still hear him tirelessly drilling the rules into our heads. On pass plays: "get low, stay low and move the feet; you don't block a man, you block an area; hinge block; check (for blitz) and peel (to pick up the defensive end); call out the blitz; 'take a picture' of the quarterback with the imaginary camera in our butts." (This sounds bizarre, but it was just a rule to remember that ensured proper position for protecting the quarterback.)

For the running plays, we were told to: "check our splits (the gaps between the linemen); fire off the ball; step with the foot closest to the hole; trap-block with the proper shoulder; call an X-block when needed; anticipate the move that'll hurt you the most; don't block a man where he is—block where he's going to be; when in doubt, block down; two in, one out is our rule on traps;" and "never, ever run by one man to get to another."

As a sophomore and junior, I never had a good grasp on "line mechanics" and therefore, had difficulty learning all of the intricate blocking assignments. That changed one day during an offensive scrimmage in 1985. As if someone flipped a switch, it all finally became solidified in my brain to the point where I knew each man's responsibility for each play. I felt that I had turned the corner and made a big step toward football maturity when that occurred.

It was mentioned earlier that backs and receivers are often referred to as "skilled positions." From the first time I heard this term, I thought it asinine because it implies that it requires no skill to be a lineman and that is definitely not true. Coach Graham always said, "Blocking is the hardest part of football," and he seemed to have a slight shred of patience for the linemen. It never did last very long, however. Even though we knew what to do and constantly worked to improve our "skills," assignments were still blown from time to time—especially when pass blocking: "G-DDAMMIT BILLY EVANS! THAT'S YOUR MAN! YOU ARE NON-EXISTENT TODAY, SON! RUN IT AGAIN!"

On the subject of pass blocking, a special relationship existed between the linemen and the quarterback. As linemen, we had every confidence that Kubik would connect with his receiving corps of Monte Byers, Joe Simi, John Jurden and Billy Franks and pull us out of a tough spot. We prided ourselves in sacrificing our bodies to protect him. Kubik, in turn, while hanging back in the pocket, had to trust that the linemen would save him from the marauding horde of goons closing in to crush him. This relationship sometimes had its growing pains and an example from my sophomore year, as told by Rod Wilder, is a fine example of that growing process:

> The first-team offense was at work and Coach Graham was not in a very good mood, especially with Jim Nelson who had been having a bad practice. Coach Graham always had the ability to bring out the best in us. He could motivate like no other person in the world. During this particular practice, Coach had been riding Jim's ass all day. Jim was an easy-going guy most of the time and until this practice, I had never seen him angry before. We just ran a Zero and One Trap and I got the best of him. We helped each other up. He said "nice block," I thanked him and we went back to our huddles. Well, Coach Graham went off on Jim one more time and Jim finally had had enough. He was pissed and ready to kill. Unfortunately, the very next play I had to

block him again. I wasn't exactly a big guy. I played strong-side guard at 5-7 and 155 pounds. Jim, on the other hand, was about 5-9 and 255 pounds. When the ball was snapped, he picked me up, threw me down and just blind-sided Kirk Schell (the quarterback). Kirk got up, spiked the ball and tore into me, calling me a dumb lineman. I couldn't believe it. I thought: *Hey, I'm your friend. I protect you, and you want to talk to me this way?* I turned around and looked at Coach Poth and he just shrugged his shoulders. When I returned to the line for the next play, I turned to look at Poth and he gave me the nod. I said, "Hey Jim, you want a clean shot at him?" When the ball was snapped, I turned sideways and Nelson blindsided him again. This form of block was known as the "Look-out" block, as Pothy used to put it, because you get out of the way and yell "Look-out." I knew what was coming next and was prepared to run laps for the rest of the practice. I started to head for the track but Poth grabbed my arm and stopped me. Graham looked at us and said, "What's going on over there?" Pothy said, "Everything is okay, Coach." Coach Graham, having realized what it was all about, just nodded and said, "Huddle up!" When I returned to the huddle, Kirk apologized to me.[3]

We began running our defenses: 40; 6-2; Pinch; Goal Line. We also worked on all of the various stunts: Dogs at 2; Dogs at 4; Slant to the strength; Backer Dog Fire; Ends crash, etc. We also worked on the pass coverages: Zone cover; Man cover; Dog cover; Bandit; Red Ball; Safety Red Ball, etc. As a lineman, these pass defenses were always a mystery to me. The only thing I had to know was when the outside linebackers would run off. That is when outside containment became the defensive end's responsibility.

Coach Graham loved defense and always said, "Defense wins championships." In Kane Krizay's book, *Cheers and Tears*, Graham is quoted as saying, "Our winning tradition was based on defense...We always stressed defense first, and we excelled at that part of the game."[4]

Playing defense for Coach Graham required tremendous discipline. It was not just a matter of finding the football and making the tackle, at least not for the lineman and middle linebackers. It was all about reading keys. Everyone had them. The actions of the man across from us would indicate where the ball would go. For me as a defensive end, I had to read the tackle or tight end. If they crossed my face and blocked down, I was to look for a trap block from a pulling lineman or an isolation block from the fullback—in that order. "Trap, Iso, Pass," was the mantra drilled into the heads of Newark Catholic defensive ends. My job was not to make the tackle but to meet and destroy these blocks in the backfield. This would cause a mass of humanity where the hole should be, usually forcing the ball carrier to break outside where the outside linebacker would make the tackle. Now, in all the years of biddy football where trying to be a hero and making all the tackles was the norm, it was a real challenge for me to forget about making the tackles and concentrate on destroying the blocks. I often felt like I was not pulling my weight because I rarely made any tackles. As a senior, I remember Coach Graham saying to me, "A defensive end can have the game of his life and never make a tackle." Once I heard that, it all made perfect sense and the pressure to be a hero and make all the tackles had been removed. It was a position without glory, but I did what I was told to do and the system worked.

Another example of the need for discipline and of Coach Graham's defensive brilliance, in my opinion, was the defense of the Option. On the Option, the quarterback runs to the outside and has the option of either keeping the ball or pitching it to a running back. This could present problems for many teams if the defense did not know how to deal with it. Coach Graham's approach was simple: End has the quarterback; outside linebacker has the pitchman—plain and simple. Coach Graham taught it to me in this fashion:

> Now, defensive ends, when you see the option coming toward you, I don't want to see you dancing around out here, pussy-footin' around, waiting to see where the ball goes, trying to make the tackle so you can be a hero. We don't need heroes out here, we need smart kids. If you see that damn guy (the quarterback) head this way, you crash as hard as you can and drill his ass even if he has pitched the ball! You don't worry about the pitchman! That's the backer's responsibility! After you drill him a couple of times, he'll get gun-shy and pitch it sooner than he wants to and we'll get a turnover out of it.

It was such a simple approach but if the players did not have the discipline to stick to their assignments, it would never work.

To summarize the defensive philosophy: It was not about being some out-of-control, head-hunting, heroic lunatic. It was about being smart, under control and tending to our responsibilities—no less and no more. The opportunity to really whack someone would not present itself on every play, but when those opportunities did arise, we were to gladly oblige and make the opponent feel the wrath of Green Wave football.

Finally, there was the kicking game: Kicking game, kicking game, kicking game! The kicking game could kill or save a team and Coach Graham worked on it relentlessly. We spent many hours on punt coverage, punt returns, kickoffs, kick returns and placekicking. These were times when many devastating hits occurred. On punt returns, for example, the defensive linemen and linebackers would peel off down the field in a particular order to set up a wall of blockers known as the "return wall." This provided many opportunities to hit unwary defenders from the blind side and knock them flat. It was one of the more intimidating jobs a sophomore had to perform. On a normal day, the first-team punt return was always being scorned and forced to run the punt return over and over again. As the yelling continued, the anger of the punt return team increased and we would roam the field just looking for a body to take out. Right or wrong, we wanted to hit someone. Sophomores quickly learned to keep their heads on a swivel at all times.

When covering kickoffs and punts, there were important rules to follow as well. "Stay in your lanes" when going down the field, "break down in front of the ball carrier" so we did not over-pursue, and "keep him on your inside shoulder" to prevent a long run around the outside.

These were intense days. The "crack" of the pads, the yelling and the coach's whistle became the sounds of the season. Clouds of dust filled the air. People knocked the crap out of each other. The sophomores were officially "welcomed" to varsity football. Some of the sophomores, refusing to be outdone, answered back just as aggressively. Some boys tried to earn starting positions while last year's starters fought to keep their old jobs. Every assignment was up for grabs. It was time to put it all on the line. Those who really wanted to play would be noticed. They would refuse to take breaks. They would refuse to let someone else have a turn. They just wanted to hit someone. When a boy was really blasted, his pride, ego and competitive spirit are what picked him up off the ground to try again.

In time, certain people received more playing time at the given position where Coach Graham wanted them and that is how the team gradually took shape. By giving a kid a lot of action, this was Coach Graham's way of saying, "I think you are good enough to play for Newark Catholic and I want you here," although he never came out and said that. I was put on everything there was: offense, defense and every special team. Still, I found it hard to accept that I would see so much playing time because of the persistence of self-doubt. I expressed my concern to Coach Poth one day and his answer was this: "If Coach Graham didn't believe that you could do the job, he wouldn't have you in there." This helped tremendously.

Not everyone was eager to jump in and play. Some kids were just along for the ride and preferred to stand and watch. It was no crime to stand and watch. After all, only 22 kids could participate at any given time. However, the observers had better be paying attention and not back there "grab-assing" around. If caught, the guilty parties would be ordered to run a lap along the fence of the entire Newark Catholic property—something affectionately known as a "perimeter."

Additionally, those who stood and watched were to stand a certain way. Coach Graham wanted the hands on the hips—no arms crossed across our chests! Graham loathed this because to him, crossed arms appeared non-athletic and sissy-like. One day when he addressed this topic, he said, "You guys back there, put your damn hands on your hips! You don't look like football players with your arms crossed!" Then, assuming a pose with his own arms crossed, Coach Graham said with an effeminate voice, "Come on guys, let's just really rip their faces off." The whole team broke into laughter.

Coach Graham's temper and patience with us grew shorter as the summer grew longer. One day late in the summer, we had been heavy into an offensive scrimmage and I spied a well-dressed man with sunglasses standing across the fence in the parking lot of Egan Funeral Home. The man had been there for several minutes intently watching our practice and this bothered me as I suspected him to be some sort of spy from another team. Coach Graham, who was also aware of the unknown observer, was quite disgusted with our performance and animatedly shouted, swore and berate. While in the middle of his tirade, Coach Graham suddenly stopped yelling and approached the spectator. I fully expected the man to be asked to leave, but that was not the case at all.

"Excuse me, sir," Graham said. "Would you believe that these kids, these *idiots*, are the defending state champions?"

"No, I wouldn't," said the man. It didn't get much more humiliating than that.

On a different day shortly before school began, the pre-season football polls came out and we were ranked No. 1 in Class A. I believe that Coach Graham despised polls not only because were they meaningless, but because they also had the ability to give a team the big head and a false sense of superiority. Given that we were having another pathetic practice, Coach Graham took the opportunity to keep us in check lest we became cocky.

"Hey Wes!" Graham shouted. "Did you know the polls came out today? Where do you think we're ranked?"

"We should be ranked last, Coach, with the way we look right now," Poth said.

"NOOOOOO!" Graham shouted with a sarcastic grin. "Were number one! NUMBER ONE COACH!"

"Shit! We're cool!" Coach Graham continued as he puffed up his chest and strutted around like a cool man. "We don't have to work any more! Everybody's gonna lay down and die for us because WE'RE NUMBER ONE!" After pacing awhile in silence, he addressed every senior:

"What the hell do you guys think about that? ... Kubik? ... Bell?" (and so on). "Do you guys think you're a number one team? NUMBER ONE MY ASS! NUMBER ONE IS SOMETHING YOU HAVE TO EARN, BABY! YOU PEOPLE HAVEN'T PROVEN A THING TO ANYBODY YET! YOU COULDN'T CARRY THE JOCKSTRAPS OF SOME OF THE NUMBER ONE TEAMS I'VE HAD AROUND HERE!"

"If we're a number one team, we'll get the chance to prove it the day after Thanksgiving! Until then, if someone asks you how we'll be, tell 'em we'll be fair." That was Coach Graham's rule to us all.

Even under these stressful conditions—the constant criticism and the physical demands where one might expect people to go mad, I can recall only two occasions during my time at Newark Catholic where someone actually snapped. A senior on the 1984 team, who will remain anonymous, was in the first incident. He and coach Graham got into a disagreement about how a particular defense had been executed the previous season. Coach Graham finally told the boy to be quiet and that "no one in your family that ever played for me was worth a shit!" The kid went off: "Shut up! Quit cutting on my family, I don't cut on your f--king family!" Graham shouted right back for the kid to shut his mouth and the conflict quickly ended. After practice, Coach Graham apologized to the individual in front of the entire team and admitted that his comments were out of line.

The other incident of insubordination happened with another senior on the 1984 team. Many consider this kid somewhat of a hero because he had the guts to do what most of us only fantasized about at one time or another. This individual will also remain anonymous and will be referred to as *Jack Doe*. Coach Graham had been riding *Jack* hard about something on a particular day. Finally, the kid tore his helmet off and shouted, "I'm sick of your shit! I quit!" As *Jack* stomped off toward the locker room, he appeared ready to throw his helmet.

"Jack Doe," Coach Graham said threateningly, "don't you throw that helmet!"

"Screw you! I'm sick of your shit!" came the response and the helmet crashed to the ground. The shoulder pads appeared to be next as *Jack* disrobed as he walked.

"Jack Doe, don't you throw those shoulder pads!" Graham shouted. Too late— the shoulder pads slammed to the ground.

Coach Graham made one more futile attempt: "Jack Doe, don't you go into that locker room!"

"I'm sick of your shit!" the kid yelled once more as he completed his journey and vanished into the locker room.

The team stood in silent disbelief. Who would talk to Coach Graham like that and live to tell about it? How would Coach Graham respond? Graham stood speechless for a moment, staring toward the locker room. Finally, with an expression of incredulity on his face, he turned to us and said, "I guess he's *sick* of my shit." It sent the whole team rolling with laughter. He addressed the team after practice that day:

"Fellas, I know I've been riding you hard. If you think I'm out of line, let me know about it—not that it's going to do you any good, but you can still let me know about it. Jack did. He's *sick* of my shit."

The incident with the angry senior demonstrated another side of Coach Graham. He did not let *Jack* quit that day. He went after *Jack* and persuaded him to stay with the team. What is special is that the kid was not a starter. That made no difference to Coach Graham. Starter or not, he did not want anyone quitting because quitting could become habitual. "Once you quit something," Coach Graham told us, "it becomes easier and easier. You'll quit school, quit your job and quit your wives. Don't be quitters, fellas."

Coach Graham often said, "No one in your life will ever get on you as hard as I do. If they do, you don't deserve it. If you can handle me, you can handle anybody." Although it was always bad to receive Coach Graham's wrath, I welcomed all that he could dish out during my senior year. I enlisted into the United States Navy's Delayed Entry Program on July 9, 1985 and would ship out almost one year after that. I wanted to be pushed to the limits of physical and mental torment so that I could be fully prepared for basic training. But let me just clarify that I did not deliberately screw up so that I could received extra butt-chewings! I do not exaggerate in saying that U.S. Navy boot camp was a cakewalk in comparison to Newark Catholic football. I made Coach Graham aware of this in a letter that I sent to him in the summer of 1986. Coach Graham was absolutely right: No one in my life has ever gotten on me as he did—not even drill instructors!

When referring to three-a-days, Coach Graham often said, "No one has ever died out here." Sometimes I wondered if I would be the first. We were required to weigh ourselves before and after each practice throughout three-a-days and record the figure in the chart taped to the wall just outside of the weight room. Some weight loss was normal over the course of the summer, but major losses in a short time were not. I would drop several pounds during a single practice. This was all fluid loss and could be regained between practices if enough water was consumed. Once when I was a junior, I dropped 10 pounds during the morning practice. When I arrived home, I gulped down three large glasses of iced tea—my favorite drink at the time. My attempt to take a nap failed because of a strange ache in my gut region that I had never felt before. I stretched out on the floor for a few minutes but the pain seemed to get worse. Thinking that some fresh air might help, I hobbled out into the back yard. Suddenly, I doubled over and vomited all of the tea I had stupidly guzzled. That put an end to my tea drinking, and the end of my tea drinking put an end to my insomnia (caffeine intolerance). To this day, I am repulsed by the sight of iced tea.

On the subject of personal weights, I had put on 10 pounds per year since sophomore year and reported to summer football weighing 185 pounds in 1985. I remember Coach Graham approaching me one day asking, "Billy Evans, do you really weigh 185?" I didn't think this to be any great thing, as I would have preferred to be 6-6, 280. But as far as Newark Catholic guards were concerned, I suppose 185 pounds was considered huge in that day and age.

After the seemingly endless hours of drills and scrimmaging, we ran our sprints and the morning practice was over by 11:00 or 11:30. I would then make my daily trip to the chiropractor, go home for lunch and then lay down to " die" for a while.

The second practice of the day would begin at 2:30 in the afternoon. After picking up Tim McKenna, I usually arrived at school by 2:00 p.m. and the smell of the locker room in the middle of the day was enough to gag a rhinoceros. Once we changed into our sweat-soaked, foul-smelling practice gear, we sat outside beneath the shade trees until it was time to start. There we would lean up against trees and talk while resting our weary bodies. Sometimes we even caught a catnap but that was often risky as someone was likely to hide the helmet or contaminate the mouthpiece of the sucker napping. We always dreaded seeing Coach Graham emerge from the locker room. This signified the end to our lounging in the shade and that it was time to return to the midday sun and get back at it. The midday practice proceeded identically to the morning practice and was over by about 5:00 p.m. It was the worst practice of the three as it took place during the hottest part of the day.

There were some injuries during practice from time to time, but these were to be expected in this collision sport known as football. I don't recall any of them being particularly severe—ankle sprains, swollen elbows and the like. After Coach Graham determined a kid's injury was not that bad, he would say, "It's three feet from your heart. You're not gonna die."

One specific injury that comes to mind concerns Mike Trotter and his neck. During a scrimmage, Mike sustained what he dubbed as "ten stingers all at once" in his neck.[5] When that happened, Mike rolled around spastically in the dust, flailing his arms about and assembling a chain of profanities that rivaled anything Coach Graham ever said. "Calm Down!" Graham said as he bent down to examine the boy. "Mike Trotter, I said calm down!" Mike's injury resulted in a neck harness being installed on his shoulder pads, which would provide support for his neck and head. We had all seen neck braces before and thought they all came in one standard size. The model that Trotter received was the biggest neck brace any of us had ever seen before. We referred to it as the "toilet seat."

The third practice of the day began at 6:30 p.m. This was the most enjoyable practice of them all. It was limited to helmets and shoulder pads, which meant that no hitting took place. It was obviously much cooler since it took place in the hours when the sun was setting. Although we still performed all of the conditioning and agility drills, we spent the majority of the time working on our timing and execution of the entire offense—pass blocking, trap blocking, pass patterns—everything. The Hamburger Defense held foam practice dummies for us to hit. Running had greater emphasis during the evening practice. In addition to the twenty 40's, we would also do what was known as "The Ladder," which consisted of running two 50's, two 60's, two 70's and so on until we climbed to 100-yard sprints—of which we ran ten or twenty depending on Coach Graham's mood. After being dismissed by 9:00 or 9:30 p.m., I would go home, eat dinner, go to bed and prepare to do it all again the next day.

For those who lived close to the school, reporting to practice three times a day was no great burden. For those who lived farther out, it was a big burden especially if they could not drive themselves and had to rely on others. There were ways of coping, however. Some kids stayed in town at a teammate's house, others road their bicycles. My parents were overjoyed when I obtained my driver's license in the spring of 1984.

My dear mother would wash my practice clothes each night during three-a-days. She even went as far as soaking the pants in lemon juice to remove the grass stains. I must have been the cleanest kid out there. I remember others who were not so concerned about cleanliness. In fact, they seemed to pride themselves on achieving the maximum degree of stench. Such was the case with senior Joe Gilmore in 1983. He sought to make his practice pants as foul and rank as possible by simply neglecting to wash them for the entire season. We always believed those pants walked out of the school one night under their own power before Joe had the opportunity to burn them. Joe Gilmore refuted this rumor, however. At the 2002 Newark Catholic Stag Dinner, Joe told me that he still has the pants!

Three-a-day practices took place Monday through Friday for the remainder of the summer, except on Saturdays. On Saturdays, we had it easy: we only practiced twice but I did not know this at first. The second Saturday in August was usually the day the photographer showed up to take the team pictures. This took place in the afternoon after the morning practice. As a sophomore, I remember showing up in the afternoon for the team photo session. We all looked sharp in our game uniforms and it was a jovial time. I fully expected (and wanted) to go home after that. One could imagine my surprise when Coach Graham told us to get ready for practice after the photographer had left! That is when I learned that Newark Catholic practiced twice on Saturdays.

It was an annual tradition at Newark Catholic for the senior football players to be individually photographed in coats and ties for the senior poster. On the appointed day, we were to report to J & B Studios out in Heath between the morning and midday practices at 1:00 p.m. to have these pictures taken. Since the pictures would only show us from the shoulders up, we arrived in coats, ties and shorts! We must have appeared deranged to anyone who saw us.

Late in the summer, Coach Graham would set one Saturday aside for a recreational trip for the team. In 1983, the trip was to Canton to see the Pro Football Hall of Fame followed by a jaunt over to Massillon where we attended the North-South Ohio High School All-Star football game.

In 1984, the team excursion took us down to Oxford, Ohio to watch a Miami Redskins football game. I still have a plastic cup that came with a drink I purchased in the stadium. On the bus ride home, I thought the team acted as jerks. There was screaming, obscenities and disrespectful singing of the songs we sang at team masses. It was basically a romper-room on wheels. Coach Poth, who sat at the front of the bus, would periodically look back with a disgusted look on his face. I was certain that he would give a conduct report to Coach Graham for which we would pay dearly, but nothing ever came of it.

Strangely, in 1985, no Saturday team trip ever occurred. Perhaps Coach Graham simply did not like our team as well as the previous two. A more logical explanation, however, could be that our team was too far in the hole from a readiness standpoint and we simply could not spare the time off. After all, because of the extra regional game added in 1985, the entire season had been moved up one week.

On the night before our first scrimmage, one matter remained to be addressed: Who would be the team captains this year? No one ever dared to ask Coach Graham outright for the job. That would have seemed arrogant and ambitious. Coach Graham appointed them in his own good time. He thought about it as we headed toward the locker room and I will never forget what he said. "Oh, for team captains tomorrow, let's go with Kubik on offense and, uh...Evans on defense." I could not believe it! I had been named defensive captain of Newark Catholic! I could not have been more honored and I rushed home to inform my parents.

Notes

1. J.D. Graham, Telephone conversation with author, Mar. 3, 2002.

2. John Crowley, Conversation with author, Jun. 2, 2002.

3. Rod Wilder, Conversation with author, Dec. 19, 2001.

4. Krizay, Kane M., *Cheers and Tears: 25 Years of the Ohio High School Football Championships*, (Medina, Ohio, KMK Publishing Co., 1997), p. 147.

5. Michael Trotter, Conversation with author, Mar. 14. 2002.

The Scrimmages

During my years at Newark Catholic, the football team was given two opportunities before the season started to get some game experience against other schools. These events, known as scrimmages, not only gave the players the opportunity to demonstrate all they had learned so far, they also allowed the coaches a chance to evaluate the status of their team, find out who their gamers and hitters were, etc. The public benefited as well in that it provided them with a preview of "this year's squad."

I found scrimmages to be particularly unpleasant. They were times of great nervousness, the mistake factor was always high and Coach Graham reamed us accordingly, which was always loud enough for the entire world to hear. Spectators present for those scrimmages in 1985 must have concluded that my first name was "Dammit." In addition, both the heat and humidity often made playing conditions unbearable as one might expect on an August day in Ohio.

I can recall my first experience with scrimmages under J.D. Graham. It was in 1983. We were the defending Division V State Champions and had traveled to New Philadelphia, Ohio to scrimmage Tuscarawus Central Catholic. The weather conditions were as described above—miserably hot and humid—and the other team was thoroughly fired up to play as if it were a big game or something. Their team captains would scream, "Are you Ready!" The team would respond, "Yeah!" and they all pounded on their helmets. We found this entertaining and laughed at them. Our laughing did not last long, however. They had a big kid wearing number 54 playing nose-guard and he ate the first-team alive all day long. We had been thoroughly stuffed on both sides of the ball. Our third team seemed to handle their third team rather well, however, but it was of little consolation to Coach Graham who remained absolutely livid over the entire, pathetic performance. It just so happened that the Newark Catholic Summer Festival would take place later that day. Before boarding the bus to head back to Newark, we were addressed by Coach Graham: "When you go to that festival tonight acting all cool and people ask you how we did today, you tell them that we got our asses kicked! ... And come Monday, you're mine!"

On Monday, us younger kids on the reserve squad traveled to Bloom Carroll High School for a reserve scrimmage. We handled them easily and were feeling pretty good about ourselves. Upon returning to school, I hoped, in my sophomore naivety, that Coach Graham had already hammered the varsity while we were away and since we pounded Bloom Carroll, he might reward the reserve team by excusing us from any additional punishments that he had planned. What foolish thinking on my part! I was soon to learn one of Coach Graham's rules: "You live as a team, you die as a team."

We watched the film of the varsity scrimmage that afternoon in a hot, stuffy classroom at the end of senior hallway. The room lacked adequate seating for everyone and some of the sophomores, including Tony Johns, had to sit on the floor. Tony's floor seat was unfortunately located next to Coach Graham's chair. It remains a mystery, but somehow with all the screaming going on in that room, Tony managed to fall asleep right there beside the Coach. When Graham noticed his snoozing sophomore, he smacked him and said, "Hey sweetheart, would you like a pillow?" After we watched the film, we went out into the hot afternoon sun and Coach Graham ran us to death. Then when we were through, he said that we would *really* run the following morning.

I feared going to practice the next day. Coach Graham lined us up on the goal line of the practice field and we ran, ran, ran 100-yard sprints non-stop. Before we could even reach the far goal line, the whistle would blow and we'd have to turn around and head back the other way as if we were yo-yos—all of this while Coach Graham went on a tirade about how we were the worst team in the state of Ohio. It was just an all-around ugly week and typical of the scrimmage season at Newark Catholic.

For our first scrimmage of 1985, we made the long journey down into the hills of northeast Perry County to play the Crooksville Ceramics on Saturday, August 17th. Crooksville had a respectable program that had given NC tough games in previous meetings. Our closest game of the 1984 season was against them in week 1 when we barely escaped with an 18-13 victory. In the 1981 regional championship game, Newark Catholic prevailed over Crooksville in a 21-18 thriller.

The weather for our Crooksville scrimmage was of the typical hot and humid variety. I felt nervous and nauseated. I cannot recall many of the details about the scrimmage. We seemed to do some things well and others not so well, but I believe we won the day by a score of three touchdowns to one. I do remember them breaking a long run. I stayed with the play and made the tackle about 20 yards downfield. A film of the scrimmage was made and we watched it on Monday. Any fantasies we had that Coach Graham might have been remotely happy with our performance were just that—fantasies. He gave me some credit for making the tackle after the long run, but he wanted to know where the defensive secondary had been.

After another week of three-a-day practices, our last scrimmage took place on Saturday, August 24th. This scrimmage took place on our game field at the school and we played the Big Walnut Golden Eagles from Sunbury, Ohio. Big Walnut expected to have a promising season because, among other things, they had an "all-world" stud fullback that weighed 210 pounds. Coach Graham had warned the defensive lineman all week that if we let this "big son of a bitch" get loose into the secondary, he would physically hurt us.

What I remember of this scrimmage was that initially, we did not have a very good day at all. Big Walnut pushed us around and whooped it up. Coach Graham, completely livid that we were getting our heads handed to us, ripped us all a new place to sit until one play changed everything. We were on defense and Joe Bell, who had missed the Crooksville scrimmage because he was not cleared to play at the time, was in at safety. Big Walnut called a running play up the middle with their all-world full back. Joe came flying up from his safety position and just lit this kid up. BOOM! It was a devastating hit. "I was so pumped up to play," Bell said, "It was the greatest hit of my life and I almost knocked myself out!"[1] "I remember the hit Bell had on that kid," Tim McKenna recalls. "When Bell stood up, both of his ear pads dropped out of his helmet."[2] Big Walnut's stud was knocked out and done for the day. Coach Graham loved it. Oh, he made sure the boy was not seriously injured as he always did when a kid went down, but while back peddling from the line of scrimmage, he said something to the effect of, "That's what the game is all about, uh huh!" Then he turned to us in the huddle, looked every one of us in the eye and said, "Are you people ready to play some football now?" We were an entirely different team from that moment onward and we got the better of Big Walnut for the remainder of the day. Joe Bell's hit proved something that Coach Graham was always telling us: When our backs are to the wall and the other team is driving on us, someone has to make a play. A turnover or a big hit can swing the momentum and change the entire complexion of a game. Our scrimmage against Big Walnut was a classic example.

Notes

1. Joe Bell, Electronic mail to author, Nov. 26, 2001.

2. Tim McKenna, Telephone conversation with author, Jan. 29. 2002.

School Bells Ring

The week following the Big Walnut scrimmage was the week the 1985/86 school year began. Although I welcomed the start of classes as it meant an end to three-a-days, it also meant juggling the additional burden of schoolwork while maintaining the commitment to football. I always had a study hall on my class schedule and I used this time efficiently to keep my evening homework load to a minimum. It was common for me to become tired and groggy throughout the school day. This made it difficult to get excited about football practice, especially when inclement weather beat upon the school windows.

Being in school was what it was all about, however. Obviously, we were there for an education but that is also where the real fun began: pep rallies; dances; lunchroom antics such as sneaking a frog's eye from biology class and placing it in the tarter sauce in the cafeteria; "stacking" people's lockers so that the books would come crashing out when the door was opened; performing unauthorized and dangerous experiments with chemicals and fire in chemistry class; sending someone's purse or book bag up the flag pole; forming friendships that would last a lifetime. These were the best times of our lives and we did not even realize it.

The senior poster for which we had been photographed finally arrived during the first week of school. I can remember standing around with the other seniors and scrutinizing the poster. After so many other senior posters had come and gone over the years, it was hard to believe that our faces were finally being featured. Each new season brought with it a new team motto, which always appeared at the bottom of the senior posters. When we were seniors, that motto was *Stay Alive In '85*.

School dismissed at 2:45 and Coach Graham expected us to get to the locker room right away to prepare for practice. He could not stand guys hanging out in the hallways, leaning up against lockers, flirting with girls and acting "cool." To him, this signified a lack of total devotion to the program. He sometimes said that truly committed players cannot wait to get out onto that practice field after school so they can hit somebody.

I, personally, could not get out onto the practice field immediately because of my required daily trips to the chiropractor. I found it a burden to go out to east Newark everyday, but the chiropractic treatment kept the hip pain from reoccurring and for that I was grateful.

Practice officially began at 3:30. Special teams, however, were to be on the field by 3:00 to work on punting and placekicking. Quarterbacks and receivers also worked at perfecting their pass patterns and timing routes. When catching the ball, receivers were constantly told to "Look it in" and "If you can touch it, you can catch it."

Monday, Tuesday, and half of Wednesday were devoted to the offense. After stretching, we worked on punt coverage and extra points until the product met Coach Graham's satisfaction. Then the backs and receivers would go their way to work on passing, etc. The linemen went off with Coach Poth and Coach Erhard to hit the sled, work on techniques and fundamentals and learn new blocking assignments for any new plays that would be added. When Coach Graham blew his whistle, it was time to reconvene for a few hours of intense scrimmaging in which we ran all of our plays against every possible defense that our weekly opponent might run. This is when the younger kids—the Hamburger Defense—earned their money, so to speak. Standing behind us, Coach Graham would employ hand signals to instruct members of the Hamburger Defense to execute various stunts such as blitzes and the like. This was to see if he could catch his first-team offense sleeping. That was probably the best thing about being a sophomore: burning the first-team and getting them punished.

Thursday was defensive night. As with offensive nights, the linemen went off with Poth and Erhard to do tackling drills and to work on reading keys before any scrimmaging took place. When it was time to scrimmage, Coach Graham began by saying, "OK fellas, let's have a good night. We have 100 plays to run and we need to do 'em quick." Then he would pull out this stack of 4" x 8" file cards that contained detailed diagrams of every offensive play in the opposing team's arsenal. It must have taken hours to draw them all up. He would hold these cards up in the air, the "Suicide Squad," also called the "Gold Offense," would read the play, break the huddle and run them against the first-team. This went on for hours. Sometimes, challenges were issued to both teams such as, "If the gold team can score a touchdown, they are excused from sprints tonight." Of course, if that happened, the first-team defense was hammered and ridiculed for letting the gold team score. The whistle would blow, Graham would come walking up and start yelling, "Touchdown! ... Touchdown! ... Touchdown! Where in the hell are you Evans? You're killing us! Here you come, flying in here, wanting to be a hero. Boom! You get your ass knocked off and they go 60 yards for a score! You do that shit in a game and it's going to be a long ride back to Newark! Run it again!" And we ran it again and again until we got it right or until the effort seemed futile.

Just like in three-a-days, we scrimmaged for hours, getting after each other, hitting, hitting and more hitting. Everybody was fair game except the starting quarterback. We were expected to go full speed with maximum effort on every play. Sometimes, however, if Coach Graham felt that we were starting to beat each other up too much, he would tell us to back off to half-speed and he was serious about it. I wish to illustrate this point with a humorous incident that took place five years before our senior year.

The story comes from Gary Van Hove, senior guard and middle linebacker on the 1980 Green Wave team. Gary is from that era of Newark Catholic football players that I held in the highest regard while *growing up green*. He appeared at my place of employment in the year 2000 one day on business and I recognized his name after all those years! One could imagine the things we have talked about since that time and his story about going half-speed follows:

> We were over behind the baseball diamond on the south end of the NC property and it was getting a little dark outside. It was a Thursday practice and the first-team defense was scrimmaging against the Hamburger Offense. After a pretty rough hit by one of our first-teamers, Coach Graham suggested that we finish our practice at half-speed since it was getting difficult to see who was who. Everyone agreed! The very next play, Sherman Elliot, a sophomore at the time, took the handoff and ran right up the middle untouched. Something came over me. I don't know what it was. BOOM!
> "Dammit Van Hove! I said half speed!" screamed Coach Graham.
> "Sorry Coach," I replied, "but I just can't hit half-ass."
> Then Graham said, "Ah shit! Take it in. We're done!"
> I had nothing against Sherman. At the time, he was just hamburger to me![1]

Now that is a man after my own heart.

Coach Graham often told us that someone once calculated the total actual contact time in a high school football game to be approximately 2 minutes. Therefore, it stood to reason that after doing so much hitting throughout the week, game nights were quite often easy nights, fun nights, so long as we executed. That is why we continued to "knock the snot" out of each other even throughout the playoffs. I can say that later in the season when the nights were cooler, I often felt I could play a second game after a game had finished. Coach Graham was right: We were in the greatest shape of our lives.

Comments on being a sophomore

While the topic of scrimmaging is being addressed, it seems fitting at this time to comment further on the experience of being a sophomore. I believe that the lowest form of life at Newark Catholic was the sophomore football player. They were at the end of every line, the subjects of many jokes and the victims of many pranks such as being wrapped in athletic tape and left to rot in a corner. Whenever the freshman team needed extra bodies for scrimmaging, the sophomores were sent. Whenever someone needed a work detail around the school, sophomores were made mandatory volunteers. At the end of practices, sophomores were responsible for policing the field and gathering up the footballs, gold jerseys and tackling dummies, and even cleaning up the weight room. The common phrase was "Send a sophomore to do it."

Then there was the actual business of football. No one suffered more than the sophomores did simply because they were physically smaller, weaker and ignorant of the intensity at the varsity level, which resulted in them being hammered by the older kids.

As sophomores, we were always reminded by Coach Graham that we were competing against the number-one team in the state during scrimmages and that it was an excellent opportunity for us to improve ourselves. But more importantly, we were charged with the responsibility of putting forth our best efforts against the first-teams, because they could not improve if we did not make them work. This was known as "giving a good look," and although it was often painful, we were told to "suck it up." Because of this, a member of the scrimmage team was no less important than a starter in the whole scheme of things.

When I was a freshman, the thought of being beaten up by the older kids in the coming year was all very intimidating to me. A conversation that took place by chance helped me tremendously throughout my days on the "gold team."

It was 1982 and I was with some of my other freshmen classmates at Canton Fawcett Stadium to see Newark Catholic play Ashtabula St. John in the state semifinals. Sherman Elliot set a new Division V playoff record that night by scoring five touchdowns in one game. While roaming the stadium, we met up with Rick Booth, one of our assistant freshman football coaches who had also been an outstanding senior offensive and defensive back on the 1976 Green Wave team.

Rick proceeded to pass on some advice concerning our transition to sophomore football. Above all else, he told us not to be intimidated by the upper classmen. Being intimated would lead to playing timidly, which was not only a sure way to get hurt, but it would also lead to constant harassment. All we needed to do was to get after those older kids with everything we had and we would earn respect from them and the coaching staff.

Rick probably never knew it, but I carried this advice with me and lived by it daily as a sophomore. I knocked heads with the likes of Rod Wilder, Joe Gilmore, Jim Bayerl, Sean Farrel and Jeff Ulenhake as hard as I could go. On one occasion,

I was able to blow past Jeff Ulenhake and hit Kirk Schell. That never happened again, however, as Jeff did not appreciate being beaten by a sophomore. He made it a point to crush me on every play thereafter. Ouch!

On another occasion, I came flying in from defensive end on a pass play. Sean Farrel had checked and peeled to block me and the tops of our helmets collided with a sickening thud. It was a terrific hit, which knocked Farrel down and knocked me half senseless. As I headed back to the huddle, Coach Poth, who witnessed the whole thing, said, "I suppose you think that was good hit, don't you Evans?" I just smiled.

Was it always fun? Hardly. I hated life most of the time as a sophomore, especially when I had to go up against Chad Heffley, senior fullback in '83. I was Chad's blocking target on several 25 Isolations. Of course, the play was never right the first time and we ran it over and over and over. Junior Jim Otto and I would relieve each other every four plays at defensive end just to stay alive. In Jim's words, it was "f--king suicide." I dreaded peeling my sore body from the mattress and reporting to practice at 8:00 a.m. with *that* to look forward to. In all my years in football, no one had ever hit me as hard as Chad Heffley. I hated it, as did my peers who also had to hit him, but this was a vital step in passing on the Newark Catholic tradition to the younger kids.

Although the pounding of the younger kids was a vital and intrinsic part of the football tradition, sometimes certain seniors would get overzealous in their treatment of sophomores. When this occurred, Coach Graham would intervene but not in the manner one might think. Rather than telling his seniors to tone it down, he left the matter in the hands of the younger kids. "Sophomores," he would say, "you don't have to take any shit from these older guys! If you're being mistreated, you need to do something about it!" I loved this approach of encouraging the kids to find their own solutions to these matters. It must have been one of Coach Graham's "litmus tests" for discovering who his future "animals" would be based on how they answered the call to "do something about it." When I was a freshman, I heard secondhand from a sophomore of just such an incident where a sophomore on the 1982 team had finally been pushed too far and did something about it. Allegedly, the setting was an offensive scrimmage. Senior fullback Mike Jurden had not been merely blocking but harassing sophomore defensive end Martin Woolard on several isolation plays. As the story was told to me, one of the assistant coaches told Martin that he did not have to tolerate that kind of treatment. On the next play—BOOM! Martin crashed hard, clobbered Jurden in the backfield and had earned some respect for himself. Of course, it helped Martin's cause tremendously that he had the tools to remedy the situation as he went 6-2, 220 at the time![2]

While on the topic of encouraging the kids to solve their problems, I am reminded of a situation within the team in 1985. There was a problem with theft in the locker room and Coach Graham gave us counsel one day on how to deal with it. "Seniors," he said, "this is your team and you can decide to either let this problem go or to put a stop to it. If you guys find out who has been doing all the stealing, you have my permission to handle it in whatever way you see fit. But I don't want to know about." I never knew if the threat alone did the trick or if a little "street justice" did in fact take place, but the thievery stopped.

Despite all of the abuse we took as sophomores, there were rewards from all of this pulverization. These were the "reserve" or "junior varsity" games in which we finally received the opportunity to take out our frustrations on people of our own size and age group. Is it any wonder that the reserve teams never lost a game in those days? In the seven reserve games that were played when I was a sophomore, no team even scored on us until the very last game, which was a 38-6 win at Utica. There is one reserve game, however, that stands out in my mind as the greatest of that year.

The story begins with the 1983 varsity game against Heath. It was Homecoming weekend for Newark Catholic. We suffered a terribly humiliating 20-14 upset to the Bulldogs, who came into the game with an abysmal record of 1-2-1.[3] Coach Graham, always trying to exercise good sportsmanship, crossed the field to congratulate the Heath coach. Instead of offering a handshake, the man allegedly dropped onto his back and began kicking his legs up into the air and flailing his arms around right in Coach Graham's face. This incident was made known to the team immediately following the game. Coach Graham proclaimed, "Reserve team! You people have some unfinished business to take care of on Monday!" (A rebuttal to this story can be found at the end of this chapter.)

While losing is always a possibility, it should never be OK or acceptable. I don't care how some people try to spin it or de-emphasize it by saying that "winning isn't everything" or "you should just be out there to have fun." I agree that the game should be fun, but it's fun only if you win! Losing is a disgusting, sickening feeling that is made worse when the winners fail to conduct themselves with class and restraint. I never could handle defeat very well given the fact that there was so much hatred for us from opposing schools. Besides being hated for our success, we were also hated for being catholic which was evident in all of the endearing names hurled at us such as "Fish," "Fish Eaters," "Carp Crunchers," "Mackerel Snappers" and "Cat Lickers." We heard this stuff whether we won or lost, but being subjected to it after a loss was the highest degree of humiliation.

For the remainder of the weekend of that Heath game, I was full of rage. The next day's headline—"Heath stuns Newark Catholic"—only added fuel to the fire that burned within me. If a person has ever seen a Calvin and Hobbs comic strip where Calvin is scowling with a thunderstorm or a skull and crossbones over his head, that was me—stomping around the house, mean as a snake with an aura of death surrounding me. My parents tried to get me to lighten up, saying that it was only a game, but I did not want to hear any of that.

All through the day on Monday, I bounced off the walls and school could not end soon enough as Mike Trotter and I fed each other's anger. After school, Coach Graham called a pre-game meeting, which was very unusual for two reasons. First,

Coach Graham was not the reserve coach—Jim Campolo was. Second, I cannot remember the reserve team *ever* having a pre-game meeting, but I could be wrong. In the meeting, Coach Graham reiterated how important it was for us to do our duty and remedy this situation. Our school pride was on the line.

Game time had arrived and the Heath faithful had the welcome matt rolled out for us in a sign that read, *Welcome to the annual Fish Fry*. We had to kick off to start the game and it was at this time that a major development took place in my personal journey of *growing up green*. On all kickoff coverage teams that I had been on before, I always concentrated on running *around* people to try to tackle the ball carrier. On this day, I cared nothing about making the tackle. I just wanted to fly down the field and hurt someone. When we kicked off, I ran down the field as fast as I could, picked out the first brown-shirt-wearing Bulldog that came into view and I just kept on running—BOOM! It is hard to describe the sensation of running full-speed into another human being, but it is a terrific jolt!

I don't know if I hurt anybody that day or not, but there were plenty of opportunities to try, considering that the halftime score was 50-0. According to Coach Graham, Coach Campolo intended to run the score up to 100-0, "but I made him pull the starters out."[4] When the starters were eventually pulled, I remember being on the sideline to witness team assistant Cass Derda talking trash to Mark Collier, the Heath varsity quarterback. Collier ran the chains for the game and as he traveled up and down the sideline, Cass was right there with him to agitate. "You'll be lucky to beat us again in the next hundred years!" Cass growled. "Shut up old man! Get away from me!" snapped Collier right back. The final score was 64-0. We had dealt out a little payback and I had adopted a new approach to kickoffs. (For more information on Cass Derda, please see the chapter entitled "Other Memories.")

When Coach Graham felt that we had scrimmaged long enough, the weeknight practices finally ended by 7:00 or 7:30, but only after we ran our twenty 40-yard sprints. While sprints were run on Monday, Tuesday and Wednesday, we normally did not run on Thursday nights as this was to allow "our legs to come back" in time for game day.

I suppose most other schools would have been heading home at this point in the evening. Not Newark Catholic. It was time to watch game films of the team we were going to play. This occurred at least three nights a week, sometimes four. Graham gave us five minutes to get out of our pads and get into the film room. The lights would be off in the room and Coach Graham would sit there with the remote control in his hand to review a particular play as often as he needed to in order to show us what he saw. He might say something like, "Billy, when the backs are strong away from you, you look 'trap.' Do you see it?"

Some kids smuggled snacks into the room and tried to be discrete about eating. However, the rustling of wrappers and packaging usually caused a disturbance and gave them away. Other kids at the very back might get into a conversation and if the undertow grew too loud, Coach Graham would say, "Shut up back there!"

The man could scout a team like nobody's business. He could pick apart their offensive sets and anticipate what play they would run next with an almost psychic ability. Opposing coaches would probably be terrified to see a scouting report that Coach Graham could produce from a game film because they would discover just how thoroughly dissected their teams were. As Graham liked to say for the big games, "We're going to have this team so well-scouted that you're going to be able to tell when that guy across from you is going to fart!"

When the viewing of films was completed, there were two final housekeeping items to address. First were the eligibility reports. These came out once per week and contained the names of the students who failed to adhere to Newark Catholic's high academic and disciplinary standards. An athlete could end up academically ineligible if he or she had a course average below 70 percent—regardless of the subject. Coach Graham read the reports in front of the entire team to publicly humiliate those football players, if any, who were letting their team down. Many of us sat in fear, hoping that our names did not appear on the report. A "U" was "unsatisfactory" and an "M" was "marginal." Some starters received "marginal" ratings from time to time, which bothered Coach Graham to no end. If any "unsatisfactory" ratings appeared on the list, they usually applied to sophomores. Coach Graham would look up from the paper, find the individuals and say, "Do you realize that you can't play this week? You dumbass! How many times do I have to say it? You people hit those books. I mean it."

The other route through which students could find themselves ineligible was poor conduct. If a football player became ineligible because of poor conduct—look out! Ineligibility due to poor academic performance was one thing, but if it was due to conduct, there was no excuse for this whatsoever in Coach Graham's mind. Newark Catholic "rewarded" its students who were "disciplinarily challenged" with what was known as a "detention." A detention would cost a student one-half hour after school in detention hall where the detainees sat in silence and did nothing. Detentions, also called "pink slips," were quite easy to earn and could be issued for chewing gum, running in the hallways, violating any portion of the school's strict dress code, etc. Nine detentions in one quarter resulted in an in-school suspension. A common phrase used by some teachers to deter misbehavior was, "Think pink." I never had a serious problem with detentions. My incentive to behave was, quite simply, Coach Graham. I did not want to have to answer to him. Neither did I want to be thought of as a screwoff in his mind. I only sustained three detentions in my four years at Newark Catholic.

The last things to be taken care of were the scouting reports. Coach Graham usually had the offensive portion of the report ready for us on Monday and the defensive portion was completed by Wednesday or Thursday. Coach Graham spent hours on these reports. They were hand-written each week and were typically 8-10 pages in length, depending on the opponent. With enough copies made for everyone on the team, Coach Graham placed all the pages on the teacher's desk at the front of the classroom. When the film was over, we all went up to staple our packet together—sophomores at the end of the line of course. Sometimes, only about half of the team would take the time to pick up their scouting report. If Coach Graham stopped by the room later to find several reports left behind, he considered it an unbelievable insult and would ream us for it the next day: "I go to all that trouble to make these scouting reports for you people and most of you don't even take the damn things!" After a few times of that, we began designating a person, usually a sophomore, to go into the room and gather up the remaining pages after Coach Graham had left for the night.

After roaming through the hallways to gather up our books and homework assignments, we finally went home, often as late as 9:00 or even 9:30 at night. When I got home, before I did anything else, I went to the barn and fed the sheep. Then I would shower, eat the fine meal that Mom always had waiting for me and work on any assigned homework. It made for a very long day, but such was the time commitment for a Newark Catholic football player.

Fridays at school were the big days before the games, unless the game was on Friday itself. Evidence of the cheerleaders' and their helpers' hard work from the night before could be seen everywhere as the school would be adorned with all sorts of colorful signs and banners showing support for the team. Our lockers were also decorated with supportive notes. Sometimes, even candy was left in them. I appreciated the decorating of lockers and I still have every sign that was ever put into my locker in 1985.

Coach Graham always had us wearing ties on Friday. "If you look sharp, you feel sharp," he always said. Graham believed that a good game on Saturday depended on having a great week of school. A good week in the classroom would carry over into the practices, with the intensity increasing a little more each day until it finally peaked on game night when it was time to hit somebody.

On Fridays, all class times were equally shortened to provide time at the end of the day for a pep rally. Pep rallies were held in the gym and consisted of the cheerleaders doing cheers and dancing to a collection of pre-recorded songs performed by the OSU marching band that blared out over the P.A. system.

Sometimes the cheerleaders and other students conducted short skits about the football team. On one occasion, the cheerleaders had borrowed our helmets and jerseys to portray certain seniors. This just happened to occur the day after we had practiced in the rain, which often caused the helmet padding to absorb rainwater and to take on a foul odor. Denise Diebert, a senior cheerleader who wore my helmet, told me that when she put my helmet on, a large amount of "helmet juice" poured out from the concussion pad and ran down her face.

For the final part of all pep rallies, Coach Graham would walk out onto the floor to say a few words. He would describe our opponent, talk about the game and then proceed to whip the student body into a cheering, screaming mob. "Don't come to watch!" he would yell into the microphone. "Come to make noise! Come to win!" The music would start up when he was finished and he would signal for the team to exit the gym. We would cross the gym floor to the locker room and prepare for our Friday walkthrough practice. I was always amazed at the spirit and the energy of the student body. These rallies never failed to get me into "game mode." It was a pity that they occurred 29 hours before game time.

During the week before the first game, it was customary for a priest to visit one of the practices and have a word with the team. When the priest visited us in 1985, he spoke briefly, prayed over us for safety throughout the season and then blessed and distributed scapulars to each player. A scapular is a small, cloth medallion with an image of the Blessed Mother on one side. Some players chose to wear their scapulars around their necks, which is how a scapular is to be worn. Mine was kept inside of my helmet behind the concussion pad for the entire season. I still have it to this day.

The Friday walkthrough practice was the time to literally walk through every detail of the game. This entailed a lot of standing around and listening to Coach Graham talk for about three hours. Although walkthroughs were essential, they were often boring, monotonous and very cold during the latter weeks of the season. Some brave and stupid individuals would break the monotony by stinging people on the butt with mud balls, placing earthworms into the ear holes of helmets and throwing small rocks at helmets, which nearly deafened the recipient of the blow. Another act was to find a puffball hiding in the grass. These were strange, papery plants with a nasty, brown powder growing inside. After covering his hand with this substance, a player would smack someone on the butt or in the middle of the back. This would leave a perfect brown handprint that stuck out like a sore thumb, especially on light-colored clothing. Coach Graham caught these people in the act from time to time and they were ordered onto the track.

Late into the practice, we would go over the special teams. While lined up for the kickoff receiving team, it became a weekly superstitious ritual for me to say to Kevin Donnelly, "May we only do this once;" for kickoffs and punt return teams, "May we do this many times," and for the punt team, "May we never do this." After special teams, we briefly went over our two-minute offense.

The last item to be covered was the extra point team. After running a few of those drills, we gathered into a circle with our hands placed into the middle for a cheer. This circle always needed a center man. Whoever was chosen for this would receive pokes, head rubs and various other buffets, all in fun of course. For the cheer, if the team we were to play was called the Lions, the cheer was "Beat Lions! Beat Lions! Beat Lions Hey!"

Before dismissing us, Coach Graham would reiterate his team rules for the night. First, we were not allowed to attend the game of the team we would play the following week. This was to avoid potential fights. Second, curfew was at 11:00 p.m. Coach Graham always threatened to call a random house to see if that individual was home. If he were not home, the whole team would pay for it. Third, no drinking was allowed. "If you drink one, you might as well drink one hundred,"

Coach Graham said. "When I find out about it, I'll run your ass off, and then you're gone." Enough said.

With J.D. Graham as a deterrent, we were sure to spend our Friday nights innocently. On the nights when the Newark Wildcats had home games, a group of us would venture to White Field to see them play. Newark Catholic ball players were admitted free at the west gate. On our first excursion to a Newark High game in 1985, I can remember riding in the back of Pat Cooperrider's old Willeys jeep with Tony Johns while "A Country Boy Can Survive" by Hank Williams Jr. played over the stereo. When the Wildcat's played away games, we would eat dinner at the Burger King on 21st Street and then sit and talk while drinking free refills of pop until it was time to go home. The management never seemed to mind us being there.

Additional note: Regarding the incident of the Heath coach dropping onto his back as an alleged display of poor sportsmanship following the 1983 varsity game, it is only fair to present the other side of the story. The coach in question, who was Mr. Dave Daubenmire, explained to me that this story is only a half-truth. According to Coach Daubenmire, he located Coach Graham within the bedlam on the field and the two did shake hands. As the madness continued, Coach Daubenmire remembers someone shouting, "I feel like I'm going to faint!" Upon hearing that, Coach Daubenmire dropped to the ground to imitate a fainting motion. The "faint" was apparently witnessed by Coach Graham and others and mistaken for an offensive act, but it was not intended to be. "I was a complete gentlemen to Coach Graham and the NC faithful," Mr. Daubenmire said, "and the other version is a fabrication."[5]

Notes

1. Gary Van Hove, Electronic mail to author, Feb. 4, 2002.

2. Newark Catholic vs. Johnstown Football Program, (Sep. 18, 1982), p. 26.

3. Rick Cannizzaro, "Heath stuns Newark Catholic," *The Advocate*, (Oct. 2, 1983), p. 1C.

4. J.D. Graham, Telephone conversation with author, Mar. 3, 2002.

5. Dave Daubenmire, Electronic mail to author, Feb. 26, 2003.

Putting on the Game Face

Coach Graham gave instructions to us on how we were to spend our Saturday's before games. We were not to be out doing stupid things that could cause injuries such as riding motorcycles, playing sandlot football with the neighbors, playing basketball, climbing trees, etc. We all had a responsibility to the team and injured personnel adversely affect the team. But neither were we to lie around all day like "couch lizards," as Coach Graham put it. This caused grogginess. He preferred us to be moderately active and to steadily get into the mindset for the night's pending battle. This was known as "putting on the game face."

My Saturday morning began with the reading of the newspaper to check the scores of the Friday games. Next, I would begin the chore of polishing my cleats. Coach Graham made us polish our cleats every game day so that we would look sharp. We were permitted to wear black cleats only because as Graham said, "White shoes are for the pros and none of you are pro material." My ritual of polishing cleats was performed while listening to the "Stay Hungry" album by Twisted Sister, which contained the hit "We're Not Gonna Take It." This music was very conducive for getting into the mood to hit somebody.

After the shoes were done, I then rounded up every last article of clothing or equipment I would need and placed them on the couch. I checked and rechecked all of these items to be sure nothing was missing. I always had this fear of arriving at the stadium without my jersey. This would have been a major embarrassment!

At 3:00 p.m., Mom would fix me a high-carbohydrate dinner and I would eat while watching either the Ohio State or the Notre Dame football games on TV. I found it difficult to eat as the nervous tingles in the gut were starting to form.

The Team Mass

On each game day, a team mass was held in the Newark Catholic chapel at 4:00 or 4:30 p.m., depending on the length of the road trip we had to make. The team mass was an important part of the Newark Catholic football tradition. I do not believe that it gave us any particular advantage over anyone else. That was not the purpose of the mass. The purpose was to humble ourselves before the Lord and pray for protection against injuries.

Before mass began, nervous players would sit silently in the hallway outside of the chapel. The only sound to be heard was the shuffling of papers, as we took final glances at our scouting reports. Players who were assigned to do the readings arrived early to rehearse. Sister Maria, the school librarian, was always present to assist with the readings.

In mass, those of us at the mercy of superstitions were adamant about sitting in the same pew and next to the same person each week. I even had a special pair of blue jeans and a shirt that were for this purpose only.

The mass proceeded as any other catholic mass. There was the opening song, which was "Here We Are." The first and second readings were assigned to the senior football players. The team captains performed the readings for the first game and for all the playoff games. For the interim weeks, two new seniors got the job for each mass. A cheerleader always read the responsorial psalm. Coach Graham always encouraged us to make an effort to concentrate on these readings. His theory was that if we found ourselves able to follow the readings, then we should be able to concentrate on the football game just as easily.

After the priest's homily, it was time for the petitions. Coach Graham was the only one (other than the priest) to offer up a prayer and his was the same every week: "Dear God, we ask that our football team play to its potential tonight and that no one on either team is seriously injured." The offertory song was "Of My Hands," and for communion, we sang "Sons of God." The closing song was "They'll Know We Are Christians." These four songs never changed in the three years that I was with the team.

Before exiting the chapel, some kids stayed behind to pray awhile longer before heading to the team meeting.

The Team Meeting

Team meetings immediately followed the mass and took place in room 120. The entire chalkboard was covered with every detail about the game. This was the last chance for us to review it all. By this time, our "games faces" were to be on and our minds were to be in game mode. An "x" represented every position of the offensive and defensive sets, along with all special teams. As Coach Graham pointed to each "x," the man who had that position for the night was to say his last name. This was to assure that everyone knew where he was supposed to be and when. If a position was unclaimed or if the responses came too slowly, Coach Graham would come unglued: "WAKE UP!"

After going through personnel, the offense and defense were quickly run through one final time. Often through this, Coach Graham would direct a question at a random individual just to see if he was awake. If that person failed to come up with the answer in short order, Coach Graham would come unglued once again. I could understand that. It must have been terribly frustrating to realize just before a game that after a week of instruction, some of us still had not learned one lousy thing. It never inspired confidence when a key player did not know his assignment at this point.

Coach Graham could be nastier than usual during team meetings. I surmise that it was due to pre-game stress. I can recall a team meeting in 1984 where he really exploded. While Coach Graham was writing on the blackboard, one of our seniors ripped a big fart. At first, Coach Graham kept on writing and attempted to ignore it while the rest of us tried to contain our laughter. However, he finally threw down the chalk and screamed, "Who was that!" When the kid owned up to it, Coach Graham pointed to the door and yelled, "Get Out!"

"It was an accident," the boy pleaded.

"I SAID GET OUT!" Graham screamed again, and the kid stormed out of the room. Coach Graham then turned to the rest of us and screamed, "DO YOU PEOPLE WANT TO PLAY FOOTBALL OR DO YOU WANT TO SHIT YOUR PANTS!" Although Coach Graham was rabidly angry, it required extreme effort for many of us to suppress our laughter following that comment. As the meeting continued, the senior stood listening in the hallway and we could hear him periodically repeating his little gaseous stunt outside of the door.

The final part of the team meeting was to go over the Two Minute Offense. These were the emergency procedures we were to execute if we found ourselves behind late in the game. They were basically our bread-and-butter plays assigned to numeric codes. In rapid-fire succession, Coach Graham would speak the audible codes and the entire team would respond in unison. This drill always was an adrenaline surge for me and it proceeded in approximately this fashion:

Graham: "Two minute offense. Ball's on the left hash?"

Team: "Pro left."

Graham: "Ball's in the middle?"

Team: "Pro left."

Graham: "Ball's on the right?"

Team: "Pro right."

Graham: "All audibles are on...?"

Team: "One."

Graham: "Red, white and blue?"
Team: "Run."
Graham: "One and two?"
Team: "Dive."
Graham: "Three and four?"
Team: "Power."
Graham: "Five and six?"
Team: "Iso."
Graham: "Seven and eight?"
Team: "Sweep."
Graham: "Nine?"
Team: "There is no nine."
Graham: "Ten?"
Team: "Sprint Draw."

Graham: "What's green?"
Team: "Pass."
Graham: "One and two?"
Team: "Flood."
Graham: "Three and four?"
Team: "Flood deep."
Graham: "Five and six?"
Team: "Wisconsin."
Graham: "Seven and eight?"
Team: "Wisconsin deep."
Graham: "Nine?"
Team: "Iso out."
Graham: "Ten?"
Team: "Iso out and up."
Graham: "Eleven?"
Team: "Screen middle to the tight end."
Graham: "And that's the one pass you need to know, linemen!"

Graham: "Clock! Clock!"
Team: "Throw the ball out of bounds to the nearest receiver."
Graham: "Victory! Victory!"
Team: "14 special."
Graham: "What do we go on?"
Team: "First sound."

"Are there any questions? ... Let's be ready to go in twenty minutes."

After the team meeting, we proceeded to the locker room and changed into our game clothes. This was to be done while observing the proper pre-game rules of conduct: maintaining silence about the room, no smiling and no "grab-assing." All that was to be heard was the shuffling of clothing, flushing of toilets, the closing of locker doors and the ripping of athletic tape as the ankles were being bolstered up for the night. Sophomores were often oblivious to these unwritten rules but they usually received a quick education from angry upperclassmen if they were in violation—and woe to he that was caught by Coach Graham, himself. He could not stand inappropriate behavior before a game. I do not recall these rules ever being formally spelled out to us. It was the only sensible way to act before a game and these standards were passed down from one class to the next. Coach Graham would sometimes employ a quote from Woody Hayes concerning this topic: "I've never seen anybody make a tackle with a smile on his face."

After the dressing process had been completed, we would place our helmets and shoulder pads into Mr. Bob Franks' van and then congregate out on the basketball court until it was time to leave the school. If our game was at home, we traveled on foot to White Field. (As with the Newark Wildcats, White Field was also the home field for Newark Catholic because the game field on the Newark Catholic school grounds lacked lighting, adequate seating and adequate parking.) If the game was away, we would ride the "Blue Bomb" belonging to Blessed Sacrament School. The Blue Bomb was an old International school bus with an automatic transmission and painted dark-blue. Mr. Dick Scott, the custodian for Blessed Sacrament, usually drove the team to away games. I was always curious about what opposing teams and fans must have thought of us: a green team called the "Green Wave," whose home field was a red stadium adorned with "Wildcats," and whose transportation to road games was a blue bus with "Crusaders" painted on the side.

I remember an incident with that old bus that happened in 1984. We were en-route to the Crooksville game and were stopped near Jacksontown for speeding. This could have been a bad omen for the whole trip. We won the game 18-13. On our way out of town afterward, the bus croaked. Try as he might, Mr. Scott could not do anything to get the bus going again. A suggestion was made from one of the players that we call someone, even though we lacked a phone or a radio. "Who you gonna call?" Mr. Scott asked defiantly. "Ghostbusters!" some wisecracker in the back shouted, which was a popular movie of the day. This drew much laughter from everyone except Mr. Scott. Luckily, a Green Wave supporter on the way back to Newark spotted the bus and pulled over. After being informed of the situation, the driver headed to Newark with the mission of finding someone who could come up with another bus. In the meantime, there in the darkness sat a bus full of smelly, sweaty football players who were hungry, restless and cranky. The night was slightly chilly and the windows were heavily fogged over from all of the damp clothes and bodies. Senior Todd Weber, a man of few words who was once accused by Coach Graham of being "a communist sent to infiltrate our football team," sat in the back seat in total silence for most of the night until he finally snapped. Getting up from his seat, he screamed, "THIS F--KING SUCKS!" He sat back down and did not say another word. Finally, after a couple of hours, a caravan of cars and vans driven by the football parents arrived on the scene and took us home.

The journey to White Field from the high school was approximately eight-tenths of a mile. We always made the trip on foot. Those of us at the mercy of superstitions had a particular buddy to walk with and had to be on the same side of the sidewalk each week. Fans and supporters would wave and honk horns, while opposing fans and non-supporters had creative ways to express their sentiments. Some of us wore headphones, some ate a light snack, and some quizzed each other about what they needed to look for during the game, but all nervously contemplated the mission that awaited us. If the entire team did not make it through a crosswalk before the traffic light changed, someone yelled "Wait up!" to those leading so that the team could be kept together. Togetherness was important.

Arriving at the stadium, we would sort through the mountain of equipment that had been stacked on the locker room floor. When we had found our belongings, we then retreated to a locker and began our rituals. In addition to all of the other superstitious "requirements" to winning a game, using the same locker for each home game was certainly one of them.

As soon as it was possible, we would put our cleats on and go outside to inspect the condition of the field. The stadium would be abuzz with activity. Small groups of people mulled about in the stands. Team managers situated their equipment for the night. Cheerleading squads hung signs and banners. Lines of ticket buyers formed at the gates. Team parents purchased the football program that had the same number as their sons' football numbers. The smoke and aroma of the steak sandwiches filled the evening air. Young boys—future generations of NC football players—assembled behind the western end zone to play sandlot football where pounding each other took precedence over keeping score. Finally, Coach Graham could be seen performing his pre-game ritual of walking the entire perimeter of the field and touching the tops of every orange pylon.

For the first phase of pre-game activities, special teams, backs and receivers would go out wearing full gear except for shoulder pads. They worked on passing, punting and placekicking, just as they had done each day before practice. Some of us who remained behind would stand at the doorway to observe how our guys were catching and kicking. We would also take this time to check out the opposing team as their special teams were also warming up. I would eventually return to my locker to put on the rest of my equipment. I was always happy that I was not required to go out early with the special teams. This permitted plenty of time to think about the game without having to rush to get suited-up, as the others often had to do. While the opportunity existed, I would go down into the tunnel and sit alone to think on the game. I was often so "jacked up" and full of nervous energy that my feet would shake uncontrollably. The metal-tipped cleats tapping on the concrete produced a sound similar to that of a telegraph machine cranking out a message.

Special teams would return to the locker room and finish suiting up. Then we would all take the field to perform the remainder of our pre-game routine. As opposed to most of our opponents who employed roaring, yelling, grunting and other forms of pre-historic communication during pre-game, we calmly went about our business in a civil manner. To us it was useless, silly and an unnecessary expenditure of energy. "Let them whoop it up all they want," Coach Graham would say. "We'll do our talking during the game."

When stretching was completed, backs and receivers began running pass plays and the linemen went to the goalpost for other warm-ups. From the center of the end zone, the linemen began with a slow sprint to the sideline and then back with knees high to get loose. Running sideways while swiveling the hips, a fast sprint and a Devine Drill followed.

When the Devine Drill ended, each man took his place on the back line of the end zone in two lines facing each other to do blocking and tackling techniques. Here again, for superstitious reasons, we made it a point to always pair up with the same person for each game. I always paired up with Mike Trotter. First came right-shoulder blocks followed by left shoulder blocks. These were initiated by the command, "Set, Hit!" Coach Poth could always gauge our state of readiness by the intensity of our hitting at this time. If the pads were not cracking, he'd become angry, pace around quickly and say, "Oh we look flat tonight gentlemen! You had better wake up! You can bet that (insert opponent's name here) is fired up!"

A right-shoulder scramble block and a left-shoulder scramble block came next. A scramble block was performed by firing out low, throwing an arm up into the opponent's crotch and then scrambling around one of his legs to get between him and the ball carrier. This technique was invaluable for the smaller guys who had to block huge people.

After the scramble blocks, we briefly worked on pass blocking. We chopped in place and the command was, "Hit! Hit! Hit! Throw!" After hitting face-to-face three times, the word "throw" was the pass-blocker's cue to throw his body into the legs of the man across from him—a move known as a "cut block." Again, for small guys, this was often the only way to deal with bigger defensive linemen who charged in with a full head of steam. I don't know how many times I saved Andy Kubik by cutting people at the last moment.

One of the last things we did was a tackling drill. With one line of boys designated as the tackling dummies, they stood with arms overhead and sides exposed to the tackler. When the command was given, the tackler hit the other man in the side and carried him for a short distance. This was repeated for the left and right shoulders.

After the hitting was wrapped up, we assembled our offensive line and walked through our blocking assignments. Coach Poth welcomed any last-minute questions we may have had. At about twenty minutes before kickoff, Coach

Graham would signal that it was time to "take it in!" The team would retire to the locker room and Andy Kubik and I would go to the sideline to prepare for the coin toss.

At the coin toss, which took place at midfield, some opposing team captains held their helmets under their arms. Coach Graham did not want us to do this. We were to be always ready for business—helmets on and chinstraps snapped. I would give a firm handshake to the opposing team captains but I would not smile or appear cordial. The head official would tell us to inspect our facemasks to make sure they had no jagged edges or hardware hanging from them. It was the visiting team's place to "call it in the air" when the coin was flipped. Andy always made the call whenever we were the visiting team. The winner of the toss either chose to be on offense first or deferred their choice until the second half. When it was determined who would receive and what end of the field each team would defend, the official said, "Let's have a good, clean game tonight, gentlemen." With a final handshake, we departed to join our team in the locker room.

After the coin toss, Andy and I would return to the locker room and announce if we were on offense or defense. Being on defense usually brought the most enthusiasm from the team because it provided the opportunity to shut a team down early and set the tone of the game. We would then sit and wait for Coach Graham to appear. During this time, some kids periodically shouted supportive phrases. Others roamed around to shake a hand or to whack the shoulder pads of a teammate as an act of war preparation. Some dashed off to the toilets to take care of business one final time.

Finally, Coach Graham would enter the locker room walking briskly. The door would slam shut behind him and he would begin speaking. The first order of business was to review the major things we had to look for. If he observed the other team doing something in pre-game that we had not covered during the week, he would quickly draw it up on the chalkboard and then ask if we understood.

With a contemplative and intense look on his face, he would then pace from one end of the room to the other while staring at the floor and begin naming the starting lineup for both the offense and defense:

> Let's go with Tony at center, Kevin and Billy at the guards, Coop and Mike Trotter at the tackles. Jim Calvert stay close, Olson and Backlund stay close. Andy, Joe and Jeff at the backs, Joe at tight end, Monte split, John at flanker. Billy Franks stay close. Defensively, we'll go with Calvert and Kevin at the tackles, Billy and Mike at the ends, Todd and Scott in the middle, Billy and Monte outside, John, Joe Simi and Joe Bell back deep. Tommy Helms stay close, Darby stay close.

This was the actual starting lineup for the first game in 1985. Anyone who would be alternating or might be needed for backup in case of injury was told to "stay close." Coach Graham became instantly furious when he called for someone to go in and that individual could not be found. This was an example of someone failing to keep his "head in the game."

When all of these housekeeping items had been addressed, Coach Graham would say, "Wes," and turn the floor over to Coach Poth. Coach Poth's talks were short, motivating, to the point and were wrapped up with, "Good luck gentlemen!"

After Coach Poth finished, Coach Graham would reappear and continue to pace back and forth, sometimes looking at his watch. Occasionally, the silence of the room would be shattered by the noise of the crowd outside, as someone would open the door to announce, "Five minutes Coach." The guts tightened, the sweat rolled down the faces and heart rates increased with each passing moment as we awaited Coach Graham to deliver another one of his masterful pre-game speeches.

"Alright, let's listen up," was the start of each speech. From there, Coach Graham would proceed to deliver an inspirational message about Green Wave tradition, staying together when it got tough, swarming to the football on defense, how we should never be intimidated by anyone and if we played to our potential, no one would beat us. By the time he was finished, Coach Graham had a group of teary-eyed, frothing-at-the-mouth young men who were ready to run through a brick wall. His pep talks were simply awesome. I could never do justice to them by trying to describe them to the reader. In my years with the team, I was privileged to hear 40 of these speeches—each one of them a work of art. I wish I had them all on tape because sadly, I can only remember bits and pieces from two of them. Ironically, one is from my sophomore year and the other is from my junior year.

We faced Watkins at home in 1983—a team that had beaten Newark Catholic and had won the Licking County League championship for two consecutive years. Coach Graham told the team that his father was sick and that there was a chance his son Brian may have Leukemia. There was not a dry eye in the place. As a punk sophomore, I had seen nothing like this before in my entire life. We were all ready to tear someone apart. The unfortunate thing about getting all fired up as a sophomore in that situation was the reality that we would not get the chance to hit anyone—all pumped up and no one to hit. The Greenies prevailed that night 12-0.

The second pre-game speech that I remember occurred in 1984 at Heath. This was the revenge game for having been upset at Homecoming the previous year. While doing our stretches, Heath performed their usual classless act of jogging single file to our end of the field, encircling our team while clapping and chanting, "Kill Catholic! Kill Catholic!" Why did they do this? The only thing I could figure is that because they did it the year before and beat us, they must have felt it provided them some psychological edge. It only added fuel to the fire that we had been carrying for one year. The locker room was deathly silent and seemed to vibrate from our pent-up rage. Coach Poth said that he would give his "left nut to be in a uniform tonight!" Coach Graham was furious when he finally spoke:

> I was walking up the hill to the locker room and there's some fat ass over here with "F--k the Fish" written on his T-shirt and he's screaming at me about how they are going to kick our ass. Do you understand that your parents have to work with these people! ... Let 'em talk. We'll do our talking on the field!

It was somewhat of a long walk down the hill to Heath's field. We had to pass through a very hostile crowd—standard operating procedure at all away games. Coach Graham instructed us to walk single file, heads down, chinstraps buttoned up, "AND YOU KEEP YOUR MOUTH SHUT!"

On the way down to the field, some of us were pelted with rocks and Jim Calvert was tripped as we passed through the mob. Coach Poth recalls that Cass Derda, who just hated Heath, stood on our sideline during the game and taunted the Heath players across the way by hiking up one of his legs and shouting, "Piss on the Bulldogs! Piss on the Bulldogs!"[1] "Those kids were just livid," said Poth, "and we had to get Cass to tone it down a bit."[2] We did our talking on the field that night: Newark Catholic 41, Heath 12.

After we had all been worked into a rage to the point of near hyperventilation, the last thing to do before leaving the locker room was to say our prayer. "Alright, let's get it in here," Coach Graham would say, and we would all gather in close on one knee. We said a Hail Mary as the muffled chants of "Let's Go Green! Let's Go Green!" drifted through the walls. Coach Graham wrapped it up in this fashion:

"It'll get tough out there. Stay together! Pick each other up! Hit these people like I know we can hit! Forty-eight minutes of good, hard Newark Catholic football! … Now let's get these people.

Coach Graham: "Our Lady of victory…"
Team: "Pray for us."
Coach Graham: "Our Lady of victory…"
Team: "Pray for us!"
Coach Graham: "Our Lady of victory…"
Team: "PRAY FOR US!"

A roar followed as we leapt from our kneeling positions and began to snap on the helmets. Down the steps, up the ramp, across the track, through a corridor of cheering fans and out into the late summer evening beneath the stadium lights: The hour to begin defending our state championship had finally arrived.

Notes

1. Wes Poth, Conversation with author, Jan. 30, 2002.

2. Ibid.

Part II
The Season

Week 1

Tuscarawas Central Catholic Saints

August 31

Before getting into the first game, it is necessary to discuss the type of conduct Coach Graham demanded from his players while on the football field. No trash talking, taunting, showboating, or profanity—especially "F-bombs"—was tolerated. As Coach Graham told us, "I cuss enough for all of us and you guys don't need to be doing it." The referee was to be addressed as "sir" at all times. We were to respect our opponent, to act humbly but to fear no one. In addition, if any of us were ejected from a game for fighting, it would be better for us if we had "never been born." He wanted us to be smart on the field, be alert, have our heads in the game and be aware of the situation. The players on the sideline were expected to "get it up" and cheer constantly for those on the field. Ideally, they should be hoarse at the end of a game. We were to maintain a sharp appearance. Undershirts and belts were to be tucked in with kneepads and the knee-high game socks pulled up at all times. When a quarter ended, we were to jog, not walk, to the opposite end of the field. Helmets stayed on during water breaks. To remove them was a sign of weakness and poor conditioning.

Offensively, we were to look sharp on the field by keeping the huddle square at all times, hustling up to the line of scrimmage, snapping into our stances in unison, talking to each other, calling out the blitzes, helping the ball carrier up and jogging back to the huddle when the play ended. Defensively, when the other team broke the huddle, Coach Graham wanted all seven defensive backs shouting out the formation and the strength, reminding each other what plays to anticipate. He wanted us to be vicious, tenacious, aggressive, swarming to the ball, gang tackling and going all out until the whistle blew. If someone drilled us, we were to get right back up and pay it back on the next play. If we were behind, so long as there was time on the clock, the Green Wave always had a chance. That was the time to hustle the most. And when we had a team down and "by the balls," we were to squeeze harder, never letting up until the game ended. In the event that we lost a game, we were to maintain dignity, keep our heads up and "take our medicine" like men. If we won, it was even more essential that we maintained dignity—never gloating or rubbing the other team's nose in it. Finally, he always reminded us, "If we play our game, we'll be fine. You guys play. Let me do the worrying."

There was some cause to worry about our first game. It was a non-league game against the Tuscarawas Central Catholic Saints from the town of New Philadelphia, Ohio in Tuscarawas County. If this name seems familiar, it should. This same school embarrassed Newark Catholic in a scrimmage two years earlier. They had finished the 1984 season with a 9-1 record and had four 3-year starters aboard their 1985 squad.[1] With so much experience returning, "Tuscy" Catholic could expect continued success in 1985. They definitely had the advantage in game experience, as there were 20 of us Greenies making our first varsity start tonight. They had "nice size up front," as Coach Graham would say when describing the offensive and defensive lines of the other team. Tight end Marty Vesco (6-3, 180), quarterback Dino Nesslerode (6-0, 170), running backs Phil Stringer (5-10, 170), Matt Sciarretti (5-11, 180) and Jeff Bolden (6-0, 175) were the core group of studs on this team.

We started the game on offense heading toward the west end zone with the setting sun shining in our faces. This was before the new Route 79 was built west of the stadium, which now blocks the evening sun. The first play was to Joe Bell for a one-yard gain. Returning to the huddle, we expected the next play to be called. But instead, Andy Kubik sounded agitated as he asked us this question: "Hey guys, did somebody do something to my mouthpiece?" A few chuckles came from various individuals in the huddle. Second down was a pass that fell incomplete. Back in the huddle, Kubik asked again: "Come on guys, this isn't funny. What did you do to my mouthpiece?" More chuckles followed. I was not laughing because not only was I out of the loop on this prank, I was concerned about our focus and readiness to play. In addition, since we were huddled on the hashmark nearest to our bench, I was certain that Coach Graham could hear the laughing for which we would all surely die. Laughing in the huddle was unthinkable, especially since we had just been stuffed for two plays in a row. Third down was another incompletion—three-and-out for the first series of the year.

I later learned the mystery behind the mouthpiece incident. A common locker room prank was to spray deodorant on someone's mouthpiece. This produced a nasty, bitter taste on the recipient's palette. It turned out that Kubik had two mouthpieces—one for practices and one for games. His game mouthpiece had been "hit" sometime during the summer and the Tuscy game was the first time he actually wore it. It was an unfortunate time for a prank to have been discovered. (In addition to the mouthpiece trick, there were other creative ways to prank teammates. There was the placing of tape onto the back of a hairy person and then watching him swear in agony when he had to remove it. Black shoe polish could be smeared in someone's chinstrap. Perhaps the most advanced prank was smearing a heat-generating ointment called "Icy Hot" onto someone's jock strap. By the time practice was underway, the heat would develop and that person would be squirming in discomfort. In 1985 the pranks came to an abrupt end—by order of Coach Graham—when Monte Byers' hip pads vanished and were never found.)

Our second offensive series was another three-and-out. Our third offensive series began from the Tuscy 30-yard line thanks to a good punt return by John Jurden. We did manage to gain one first down on the drive but unfortunately, most of our yardage was cancelled out by stupid penalties that we committed. We also had some sort of weak-side tackle controversy going on because Calvert and Trotter would alternate at the position every other series.

Although our offensive effort was quite sad—people in slow motion, people not knowing whom to block, missed blocks, people delivering "love taps"—our defense was strong. Tuscy initially had a good drive going on their third possession, but three consecutive quarterback sacks shut them down. Tuscy punted on the first play of the second quarter.

Jurden took the Tuscy punt at our 25-yard line and returned it out to our 50. This too was erased by a clipping penalty and we began from our 25. We finally got some offense going on this drive. Two carries by Joe Bell netted 16 yards. These were followed by a 27-yard completion to Monte Byers. Two more running plays left us with first-and-ten at the Tuscy 23. But on the next play, Bell carried on a 30 Trap and fumbled the ball away. Tuscy Catholic recovered at their 17-yard line.

After the fumble recovery, Tuscy was fired up and they killed us with three running plays that yielded three consecutive first downs. Coach Graham called a timeout to settle us down—a common tactic of his. Following the timeout, our defense tightened up and forced the Saints to punt.

On our fifth series, we began on our 20-yard line and choked. Kubik was sacked on second down, leaving us with a third-and-twenty from our 10-yard line. To avoid any further risk, Coach Graham called for the quick kick—an emergency punt executed by the tailback. Incredibly, Marty Vesco blocked Joe Bell's punt and the Saints recovered on our 8-yard line.

A blocked punt is terribly damaging to a team because not only does it often result in a touchdown, it also causes a huge momentum swing. With our backs to the wall and Tuscy fired up, things looked very bleak. Fortunately, our defense tightened again. We were helped by an illegal procedure penalty against the Saints. Tuscy failed to get a touchdown but did manage to come away with a field goal from our miscue with 1:10 left in the first half.

On our sixth offensive series, we ran the two-minute offense only to suffer an offensive pass interference penalty that was followed by a sack of Kubik on the final play of the half. The defending state champions headed into the locker room having been embarrassed, shut out and losing at halftime. Everyone from the coaches, fans and even the players must have been thinking that it would be a very long season. I do not recall a thing about the locker room at halftime, but it is safe to assume that Coach Graham ripped us every way imaginable.

Something peculiar about this game was the fact that Tuscy Catholic kicked off to us at the start of each half. Tuscy must have elected to go on defense each time. Perhaps this was part of some bizarre strategy but to me, they made a major mistake by not taking the ball when they had the opportunity!

We looked better on this first drive of the second half. People got off the ball with more zip and seemed to hit without hesitation. We moved the ball right down the field and were set up with a first-and-goal at the 8 after a Halfback Pass from Simi to Jurden. Just when it looked like we were going to score, a delay-of-game penalty was followed by a procedure penalty. We received a gift, however, on the next play when Tuscy was called for pass interference. This set up another first-and-goal situation. Three plays later, we finally scored our first points of the season on an 8-yard pass from Kubik to Ronan. We were up 7-3 and breathed a little easier.

We ended up in another precarious situation on our next series following a Tuscy punt. On the first play, Ronan threw a crushing block on a 25 Iso that sprung Bell for a 10-yard gain. Bell fumbled again, which resulted in a Tuscy first down at our 18-yard line. The defense rose to the occasion once more. Tuscy went three-and-out and attempted a field goal that was unsuccessful.

We did not score again until early in the fourth quarter. In this series, the offensive line opened up good holes and Bell picked up nice yardage. Kubik hit Jurden for a 52-yard scoring toss that put us up 14-3 with 10:31 remaining in the fourth quarter.

On the following defensive series, I began to experience severe abdominal pains that made it difficult for me to stand up straight. Unaware of any serious hits to the abdomen, I could not figure out the cause of the pain. I simply could not move any longer and I took myself out of the game when the series ended. Junior Tom Ogilbee replaced me on offense. After I was assisted to a table behind the team, Dr. Trifelos, the team doctor, had me stretch out so he could have a look at me.

"What does the pain feel like?" he asked.

I could not tell at first, but within a few minutes, I figured it out. "It feels like...Uh...It feels like I need to take a crap."

"Well, you better get to the locker room," said the doc.

Rising from the table, I quickly dashed to the locker room hoping that no one would notice me. Fat chance. According to my brother, who was sitting with my parents in the stands, my father could tell what was happening when he saw me disappear into the tunnel. "He's OK!" my dad shouted. "He just needs to take a crap!" Allegedly, Dad repeated this several times until he was satisfied that every last person on the home side had been informed of my predicament. Upon reaching the toilets and not a moment too soon, I experienced the most painful and voluminous diarrhea attack of my entire life. To this day, it has never been surpassed in either category. No other descriptions will be provided. After a few minutes, Tom Lefevre yelled from just around the corner to see if I was OK. I snapped at him, saying, "Get the hell out of here!" I have always attributed this attack to the pre-game nerves and stress of making my first varsity start because it never occurred again. I wondered how I would ever live this down with the team and Coach Graham. Fortunately, I emerged from the locker room in time to return to the game. Although the players ribbed me about it (and still do to this day), I do not recall Coach Graham ever saying a word about the incident.

I had not been the only one in bad shape that night. Joe Bell started to wear down as the game went on and was relieved by John Jurden periodically. Bell would return to the huddle, wheezing and fighting for his next breath. After one particular play, he said, "I'd die for you guys," and then puked through his facemask. Bell had this to say about that night: "My conditioning was not where it needed to be. I nearly passed out after the game."[2]

When the game finally ended, the 20 of us that made our first varsity start had earned our first victory. "It wasn't a thing of beauty, but we're always pleased with an opening win,"[3] Coach Graham said afterward. It was an abysmal performance offensively but the defense came through when it was needed. We had a long, long way to go to become playoff material and Coach Graham's sentiments reflected as much: "We're as green as our uniforms."[4]

Many were left to wonder what kind of season it would turn out to be and were not expecting very much. My older brother Joe remembers his feelings: "As a fan and a brother, the poor performance was painful to watch because I wanted you guys to get another championship. After that first game, it didn't appear that a title was going to happen."[5]

There were no days off for the Newark Catholic football player. On Sunday mornings after the games, we reported to the school at 11:00 a.m. to review the game films. It always looked like a parade of the walking wounded when we showed up. Many of us were often sore, bruised, swollen, limping and unkempt with sleepy eyes and "bed head."

Let me clarify right now that watching game films was one of the most un-enjoyable things a Newark Catholic football player ever had to go through— especially if he played a *bad* game! Each play was dissected, each mistake was discovered and the guilty man was found out and heavily "instructed" for as long as Coach Graham felt was necessary. The film was backed up and replayed ad infinitum.

To be fair, Coach Graham was generous with the praises when they were deserved, but there would be no praises issued on this day. The Tuscarawas

Catholic films told a pathetic story. It could easily be seen that our effort was atrocious. We were in slow motion. We loafed on special teams and missed blocks as if it were the first time we ever played the game—a total lack of intensity and aggression. Coach Graham scrutinized each play as the drone of the film projector rattled in our ears as if it were an accusing enemy.

Tony Johns, while going down the field at half speed on a kickoff, could be observed pulling up his arm pads. This really set Coach Graham off. "If you got time to adjust your arm pads, you don't want to get down the field very bad!"

Jim Calvert loafed on a kickoff as well. "Calvert, you dog!" yelled Graham. Calvert was also observed delivering a block that was akin to a "love tap." "What the hell do you call that, Calvert? Tag, you're it!"

Kevin Donnelly had aggravated an old shoulder injury* during the game but did not come out, which makes my diarrhea attack seem trivial. He delivered hits gingerly and resembled a one-winged bird while he ran, holding his left arm in close to his body. "Christ sakes, Donnelly, you look ridiculous! If you're hurt that bad, get out!" Coach Graham shouted.

Joe Simi received probably the worst reprimanding of anyone. Joe had great difficulty with his blocking assignments throughout the entire game. On the one play where his most conspicuous mistake took place, Joe thought he was out of the woods when Coach Graham had not noticed. However, before he moved on to the next play, Coach Graham said, "Let's see what Simi did on that play." The film showed Joe completely missing his man, resulting in a massive hit on Bell. This made Coach Graham so angry that he forced Joe to go up to the movie screen and point himself out. "Joe Simi," Coach Graham said, "Would you mind explaining to your teammates just what the hell you're doing there!" After Joe returned to his seat, Coach Graham sent the film canisters flying across the room. When they had come to their resting place, Coach Graham said to Simi: "You had a perfect game Simi! You didn't block anybody!"

I am not mentioning these four to humiliate them. The truth is that no one was without fault. We were all equally guilty of the debacle playing out before us on the movie screen. If Coach Graham did not ream us then, he would be sure to get us tomorrow. In my three years with the team, this had to be the maddest I had ever seen Coach Graham become while watching a film—even more so than after the Tuscy Catholic scrimmage in '83. Looking back, its strange Tuscy Catholic was responsible for the two times when I recall Coach Graham being most irate.

"Films don't lie, do they Coach?" Graham said to Coach Poth, who stood in the doorway, arms crossed and with a disgusted look on his face.

After watching game films, it was time to run. The theory was that the best thing for a sore, battered body was to get right back out there and get it moving again. Although the typical Sunday workout consisted of twenty 40's, The Ladder and twenty-100's, the amount we ran was directly proportional to the degree of Coach Graham's disgust with our game effort. Rest assured that he really let us have it that day.

*In the summer of 1983, Kevin flipped over the handlebars of a bicycle and broke his left collarbone. Two operations followed—one to insert a 5-inch stainless steel screw for stabilizing the bone and another to remove the screw. The second operation occurred just two weeks before the start of our sophomore football journey.[6]

Tuscarawas Catholic	0	3	0	0	3
Newark Catholic	0	0	7	7	14

	TC	NC
First Downs	5	11
Rushing	47	115
Passing Yards	43	137
Total Yards	90	252
Att-Comp-Int	17-4-1	13-7-0
Punts / Avg	7-39	5-32
Kickoffs / Avg	3-53	2-42
Fumbles / lost	1-0	2-2
Penalties / yards	7-55	8-65

Week 1 LCL Action[7]

Big Walnut	13	Liberty Union	28
Johnstown	9	Utica	14
Philo	29	Watkins Memorial	35
Lakewood	14	Teays Valley	0
New Albany	30	Maysville	38
Northridge	6	Heath	10
Granville	21	Tri Valley	14
West Muskingum	6	Licking Valley	7

Notes

1. Newark Catholic vs. Tuscarawas Catholic game broadcast, Cable-5 Television, Newark, Ohio, (Sep. 1, 1985).

2. Joe Bell, Electronic mail to author, Nov. 26, 2001.

3. Rick Cannizzaro, "Revamped machine powers Green Wave," *The Advocate*, (Sep. 1, 1985), p. 1C.

4. Ibid.

5. Joe Evans, Electronic mail to author, Dec. 28, 2001.

6. Kevin Donnelly, Electronic mail to author, Jan. 19, 2001.

7. *The Advocate*, (Aug. 31, 1985), p. 8.

Week 2

Northridge Vikings

September 7

Week 2 of the 1985 season had us matched up against the Vikings of Northridge High School, a rural school located north of Alexandria, Ohio in northwest Licking County. Coach Graham was on the warpath during the week of practice leading up to the Northridge game. The mistakes and sorry performances of the Tuscy game were alluded to frequently and angrily with extended periods of screaming. We felt so small, so pathetic, that I wondered if we were capable of winning another game all season. I was convinced that were we not only the worst team in Ohio, we were also the worst group of seniors Coach Graham had ever coached. If that was the case, he was not going to put up with us for long. "Fellas," Coach Graham said somberly, "I've got to find some people that want to play. It's your team, seniors and you get the first shot to play, but if you aren't getting the job done, I'll start sophomores if I have to." These were very troubling words, to say the least. Only time would tell if they were enough to motivate us to get better.

For the coming game, Coach Graham had made a few personnel changes, which mainly affected special teams players who failed to perform during the Tuscy game. Another personnel change that took place was brought about by injury. Our best linemen, strong-side guard Kevin Donnelly, would sit out because of his shoulder injury. I filled in for him at strong-side guard and Tommy Ogilbee took my place on the weak side. Donnelly needed a replacement at defensive tackle as well. Mike Trotter took the tackle duties and Jim Olson filled in at defensive end for Trotter. Additionally, Joe Simi spent the week getting pounded by us linemen so that he could learn how to block!

It should be mentioned here that the terms "strong-side" and "weak-side" referred to the offensive formation (see Appendix A). It was not a classification of the physical or mental strength of the personnel in those positions. In other words, the "weak-side" guard was not a weakling himself. (At least, I *hope* that is not the reason Coach Graham put me there.)

Coach Graham began going over the personnel of Northridge. They, like most of the other Licking County schools, were populated with big farm boys. "Plows" was the term Coach Graham gave to these kids. I always wondered if Coach Graham knew that I myself was a "plow."

This year, Northridge had 9 "plows" coming back that had started in 1984.[1] Their offensive front five weighed 205, 215, 175, 190 and 200 pounds. The flanker, senior Doug Van Fossen (6-3, 180), was one of the Northridge studs and said to be "one of the better players in the league" by his coach Ron Stemen.[2] But the man considered most dangerous to us this week was their tailback, junior Jon Warga (5-11, 165). "This guy right here is their jet," Coach Graham said, pointing to Warga's position in the backfield. "If he gets loose, there's no one on this team that can catch him. Not even you, Simi, even if you have the angle." Simi was probably the fastest man on our team. If what Coach Graham said was true, things could get ugly for us on Saturday night.

With all of these things on our minds, there was an additional twist to the week that made matters even more difficult. The weather all week had been ridiculously hot and humid, which made practices unbearable. Combine this with the threat of being replaced by sophomores, plus the uncertainty about our team in general and it was nothing short of a week from hell. The weather was expected to be the same on Saturday. On Friday after our walkthroughs, Coach Graham told us: "Take it easy and drink plenty of fluids tomorrow. I don't want anyone getting dehydrated and cramping up during the game."

Throughout the day on Saturday, I had great concern about playing a football game in this extreme heat and humidity. I therefore did exactly what Coach Graham had ordered. I drank water all day long. When I thought I could not hold another drop, I forced myself to drink even more. I planned to be ready for this game. However, in my zeal to prevent dehydration, another problem arose which was the need to urinate about every 5 to 10 minutes. Realizing that I had overdone it and thoroughly waterlogged myself, I had enough sense to stop drinking late in the afternoon but it did not seem to help. It was a struggle to make it through the team mass and team meeting without having an accident.

We were all dressed and standing outside of the school waiting for the bus when the need to urinate hit me. Back into the locker room I went to take care of business. We boarded the bus when it finally arrived and as soon as I sat down, nature called again. After relieving myself yet again, I began to realize that the road trip to Northridge High School could present a real problem for me unless the bus left right away. Well, for some blasted reason, the bus did *not* leave right away. We sat for several more minutes and the longer we sat, the more the feeling of having to urinate slowly crept up on me for the "umpteenth time." I figured that it would be just my luck for the bus to leave while I attempted another trip to the restroom, so I decided not to risk it. So when the bus finally rolled out of the parking lot, I had to go—bad. All I could do was limit my movements and pray that I would make it. *This is going to be a very long trip*, I thought to myself.

I was so miserable on that bus. Every bump in the road was amplified and every mile seemed to creep by more slowly than the one before it. I remember while traveling north on Northridge Road thinking that I was not going to make it but I still tried to visualize that I would.

Upon arriving at the school, I was off that bus and into the locker room like lightning. No one was going to get to the urinal before I did. Finally, when the relieving process began, I breathed a sigh of relief. I had made it. There I stood for what seemed like five minutes and I wondered if I would ever finish.

After I was dressed, I went out as I normally did to inspect the field and I recalled what had happened the last time we played at Northridge. It was game 10 of the regular season in 1983. Northridge, which had one of their best teams in a long time, boasted a 7-2 record and was all fired up to play us. While we were heading to the locker room after completing our warm-ups, a transformer exploded on one of the power poles and half of the playing field was instantly darkened. Ted Marquis, a senior on the team that year, said that his classmate Jim Bayerl punched an electrical box as we left the field and that is what caused the power failure.[3] We went into the locker room to wait and wonder what the solution to this dilemma would be. I had an idea on a possible solution. Since it was a Saturday night, I knew that the Johnstown stadium was empty because their games were played on Friday nights. I figured the game would be moved there since it was just a short jaunt down Route 62. That never happened. I remember Mark Kane, the junior team manager, coming into the locker room, saying, "Guys, rumor has it that the game has been cancelled." The starters, who were chomping at the bit to play, nearly ripped poor Kane's head off at that moment. Coach Graham came in later to confirm the rumor and added that the game was to be played at 2:00 p.m. on Sunday.

Now this presented a dilemma. Since this was the last night of the regular season, the state high school football polls and computer rankings needed to be finalized that evening in order for round-one playoff match-ups to be determined. Coach Graham said that he had received word from the OHSAA that in light of the circumstances, they would proceed as usual and base our season on a 9-game schedule. Coach Graham added that playing a game at a strange hour would be "a blessing in disguise" in that it would prepare us for a daytime state championship game should we be fortunate enough to get there. We returned to Northridge High School on a cold, clear Sunday afternoon and put it to the Vikings 32-6. I even got to play in that game.

On game night in 1985, the weather was at the other end of the spectrum: brutally hot and humid; the worst playing conditions I ever experienced—more so than any August scrimmage. Before the game, the referees held a meeting with the team captains. They told us that because it was so hot, they were going to permit additional timeouts throughout the game just to have water brought in. "Team captains," the referee added, "You keep an eye on your players. If they look like they need a break, let me know." Well, that was good to know. I would certainly be looking out for my teammates but I did not expect that we would need any extra water breaks.

Northridge won the toss and on the opening kickoff, I somehow suffered a grass burn on my right kneecap. This was a constant annoyance all evening because the kneepad kept rubbing it raw.

On their first three plays, Northridge lost 1 yard, then 3 yards and then 18 yards on a sack by Bill Franks and me. Fourth down was an abysmal 21-yard punt.

Our first offensive series was not much better than that of Northridge. First down was a pass that was nearly intercepted. Second down was a run for no gain. Third down resulted in a Kubik sack by the backside defensive end because Tom Ogilbee failed to check and peel in time.

Northridge caught us sleeping on their second series and broke one on us. The play was a dive fake to the fullback Van Fossen and a pitch to Warga around right end. Having bit on the dive fake, the middle linebackers could not get outside to make the stop allowing the speedster to turn the corner and streak down the sideline. As I watched Warga head down the field, I remembered Coach Graham's warning about there being no one on this team fast enough to catch him and I figured it was a sure touchdown. But to everyone's surprise, Joe Simi had an angle, turned on the juice and caught the kid at the 26-yard line after a 65-yard gain.[4] What Coach Graham told him he could not do, Joe Simi had just done. How fast *was* Joe Simi?

Following the long run, the defense met the challenge and forced Northridge to turn the ball over on downs. We still were unable to do anything on our next possession and ended up punting.

After another three-and-out, Northridge got off a good punt that set us up with a first down at our 10-yard line. It was on this series of downs that the floodgates seemed to open up and Northridge could not stop us. Our line made good holes. Bell and Ronan picked up good yardage on simple dive plays. With a great block from Pat Cooperrider, Bell ran 12 yards on a 17 Quick Pitch and put us up 7-0 with 10:52 to go in the half.

I believe that the sudden inability of Northridge to contain us was a simple matter of conditioning. They were able to hang with us only so long but after that, they were zapped. Now, having said that, I must reveal that I was absolutely dying in this game from the heat and humidity. I was dragging, could not catch my breath and wondered how I would ever last four quarters. Recalling what the officials had said about special timeouts for water, I approached an official two or three different times wheezing, gasping for air and panting like an overheated dog tripping over its own tongue. "Sir," I would struggle to say, "my guys (gasp) look like (gasp) they could use (gasp) a shot of water." Of course, I was hiding behind that excuse so that *I* could get the game stopped for a little break. I suppose this was abuse of my captain authority and it was definitely conduct unbecoming of a Newark Catholic football player.

Joe Bell, who was starting to alternate out with Scott Saad, was having a rough time as well. For the second consecutive week, he puked while we were in the huddle, but it probably was not due solely to the weather. Joe Simi explained: "Bell had this huge bag of grapes on the bus up to Northridge. I told him he shouldn't be eating those things because they were full of acid and would make him sick. Sure enough, we're in the huddle and he pukes all the way down my leg."[5] Joe Bell had this to add: "I puked grapes all over Simi's shoes in the huddle against Northridge. After that incident, I changed my diet and learned to eat more carbohydrates and less acidic food before games!"[6]

Following another Northridge punt, we scored seven plays later on a 30-yard Flood pass to Saad with 6:09 left in the half.

Our fifth offensive series began with a Flood Deep to Joe Bell who was wide-open but dropped the ball. As a sort of "in-your-face" move on our part, the same play was called again on second down and it picked up 20 yards. The scouts up in the press box must have seen that this play was wide-open and could not resist trying it again. This drive was capped by another Scott Saad touchdown that came via a Sprint-Draw play that went 43 yards with 3:21 left in the second quarter.

Northridge was able to put a small drive together on their next series. With a few lucky completions and a good run, they were able to move down to our 36-yard line only to fumble the ball away shortly thereafter. Time expired on us after the fumble recovery and we went into halftime up 21-0.

Because it was so hot in the locker room, Coach Graham decided to keep us outside for halftime. We met in the grass well south of the field and away from the public. In most games, I did not care for halftime because I found it difficult to get going again after resting. That was not the case for this game. I was grateful to get the break.

We began the third quarter on offense. After running a Flood, Flood Deep and a Flanker Trap Zero, we had advanced to the Northridge 25-yard line. Ronan scored four plays later on a 28 Sweep and we went up 28-0.

Northridge had the ball briefly following the kickoff but managed to fumble again, which gave us a first down at their 27. After two plays for no gain, Kubik dropped back to pass, saw that Byers was covered and checked off to John Jurden. John hauled in a beautiful touchdown pass in the corner of the end zone at the 8:04 mark in the third period making the score 35-0.

After the ensuing kickoff, Northridge began their next series at their 27-yard line. They managed to lose yardage on each play and ended up punting from the 1-yard line. The snap from center went out of the back of the end zone and resulted in a safety, which extended our lead to 37-0.

Following the safety, John Jurden advanced the free kick to the Northridge 41 and the "Clean Green" took charge of the offense. (In any game, when the opposing team had been put away, the second and third-string kids received playing time on offense and defense. Special teams, however, were always handled by the starters regardless of the score unless otherwise specified.) They turned the ball over on downs, but Northridge was unable to do anything offensively, even against the third string. Bell returned the ensuing punt to the Northridge 25. Three plays later, Jeremy Montgomery hit Tom Helms for an 11-yard touchdown pass with 8:33 left in the game.

After holding the Vikings to another three-and-out, the Clean Green mounted an exceptional rushing attack that covered 55 yards in six plays. Tommy Parker scored a touchdown on a 13 Dive to make the final score 51-0.

Under terrible playing conditions, we had just won our second game. I thought it fortunate that we achieved a blowout because it enabled the younger kids to play and prevented the starters from having to go four quarters in the heat. Still, as a senior, I did not want the younger kids to play too much because it was the last year of my life that I would have to play this sport.

We felt that we had done better than our first game and wondered if Graham was pleased with us. Offensively, six different players scored touchdowns while defensively, we had posted our first shutout and held Northridge to minus three yards in the second half.[7] While watching the films the next day, it was evident that we looked more aggressive, sustained blocks better and hit better than we did in our first game. While Coach Graham highlighted these positives, he also pointed out many other things that we did poorly, which prevented a good game from being a great game. Because Watkins Memorial was our next opponent, he would not let us become too comfortable with this victory. "Don't shit yourselves fellas," he said. "Northridge is a terrible team. We still don't know how good we are. We'll find out this week what kind of team we are. Old Watkins is coming to town, baby, and they'll be fired up. With them it's always a war."

We exited the film room and reported to the field to do our Sunday running. After the stretching routine, the team had just started to run the first sprint when Coach Graham called out to me from the sideline.

"Billy Evans." As I approached him, he continued:

"What in *thee* hell are you doing calling timeouts for water breaks?"

Oh no, I thought. *How does he know about this?* I felt as if I was standing before God awaiting judgment. I tried the only defense I could think of, which was also my only hope of saving face.

"The ref said that if the guys looked tired that I should—"

"Bullshit!" he interrupted. "The ref told me that you personally asked for water three different times! What were you thinking?"

I had no answer. All I could do was stand there like an idiot and say, "I don't know."

"Don't ever pull a stunt like that again, you got it? Christ sakes!"

I gave an affirmative answer and joined the team to do my running. I felt completely embarrassed. I figured that this ruined Coach Graham's opinion of me, that I would probably lose my starting position and that he would name another defensive captain before the next game. I was thankful that he was considerate enough to reprimand me in private, however.

To date, Northridge has never played Newark Catholic in football after the 1985 season, as it was their last year as a member of the Licking County League. The series ended with Newark Catholic leading 13-0 by a combined score of 432-33.[8]

Newark Catholic	0	21	16	14	51
Northridge	0	0	0	0	0

	NC	N
First Downs	23	3
Rushing	293	56
Passing Yards	186	30
Total yards	479	86
Att-Comp-Int	21-11-0	9-5-0
Punts / Avg	2-38	8-33
Kickoffs / Avg	8-45	1-33
Fumbles / lost	1-1	5-3
Penalties / yards	5-45	2-20

Week 2 LCL Action[9]

Licking Valley	21		Fairfield Union	19
Heath	20		Granville	7
Watkins Memorial	42		Johnstown	35
Lakewood	6		Utica	18

Notes

1. Mark Shaw, "Northridge mentor guns for first in last," *The Advocate, Football '85*, (Aug. 28, 1985), p. 20.

2. Ibid.

3. Ted Marquis, Conversation with author, Jan. 25, 2002.

4. Sean McClelland, "NC shows no mercy in rout of Vikings," *The Advocate*, (Sep. 8, 1985), p. 1C.

5. Joseph Simi, Conversation with author, Dec. 18, 2001.

6. Joe Bell, Electronic mail to author, Nov. 26, 2001.

7. Sean McClelland, "NC shows no mercy in rout of Vikings," *The Advocate*, (Sep. 8, 1985), p. 1C.

8. Ibid.

9. *The Advocate*, (Sep. 7, 1985), p. 7.

Week 3

Watkins Memorial Warriors

September 14

Our opponent for the third week of the season was the Watkins Memorial Warriors. Located in the southwest region of Licking County near the city of Pataskala, the Warriors were probably Newark Catholic's most difficult challenge in the Licking County League year after year. The reason was simple: Watkins was a Class AAA/Division II school that was much larger than Newark Catholic and had hundreds of boys from which to build a team. Newark Catholic should not have been on the same field with some of the teams Watkins assembled—meaning that the Greenies were completely outmanned in size and talent.

The game was usually the biggest of the season in Licking County. For the previous five seasons, the contest had determined the Licking County League champion. In 1980, a shocking 13-3 Green Wave victory over a fabulous Warrior team prevented a perfect regular season for Watkins. In 1981, the eleventh meeting between the two schools, a potent Warrior team came into White Field and achieved its first-ever victory over Newark Catholic 34-21. In 1982, the year Newark Catholic won its second state championship, Watkins prevented a perfect 13-0 season by beating Newark Catholic 15-6 in week 2 and became the first LCL team to accomplish consecutive victories over the Green Wave. In 1983, the string of Warrior victories was broken by a 12-0 NC victory. The LCL title was shared between Newark Catholic and Watkins that year. The trend of this matchup being a close, classic nail-biter was broken in 1984 by the 40-0 trouncing the Greenies delivered to the Warriors. This was Watkins' worst defeat ever by the Green Wave and they would surely be seeking vengeance in '85.

The success of Watkins had been built on a fearsome running attack that usually featured three stud running backs operating from the "T" and "Power-I" formations. This season was no different as Watkins had won their first two games over Teays Valley and Lakewood by a combined score of 77-6 without completing a pass.[1] Coach Graham was correct. This week we would find out what kind of team we were.

The personnel for the 1985 Warriors team were intimidating as always. The offensive line consisted of Chris Raines (6-2, 200), Randy Foor (6-3, 215), Todd Baughman (6-0, 175), Mike Gill (6-1, 200) and Mark Cruikshank (6-0, 180). Don Van Order (6-3, 200) and Chris Wohnhas (6-1, 170) occupied the end positions. The backfield was made up of Greg Shirey (6-0, 175), Tom Murray (5-8, 160) and Dave Carman (6-1, 190). Quarterback for Watkins was Nick Lieb (5-11, 160), a tough kid who was also a state semifinalist wrestler in Class AAA.[2] The defense was made up of the same crew with the exception of Cruikshank and Baughman, who were replaced by Scott Schindler (5-11, 170) and Dwight Brown (5-11, 200). As can be seen from this lineup, Watkins had nine people playing both ways while we had only six. This would definitely be an advantage for us.

Coach Graham loved to tell us stories. Not "stories" as in "tall tales," but stories about great moments of the Newark Catholic football tradition that were intended to inspire and motivate us. These stories were regularly incorporated into practices all season long but he seemed to tell them even more frequently when a big game was on the horizon. With the Watkins game just days away, we heard these stories often but they were never boring. I enjoyed hearing them and was always ready to hit someone after he finished. With an intense expression on his face, Coach Graham paced back and forth, staring at the ground in his unmistakable fashion and proceeded in this manner:

> Classic example. I'll never forget it. We're playing Watkins in 1980. They were loaded and had been ripping people all season long. We shouldn't have even been on the field with these people. We're playing for the LCL championship and half of the county is standing five deep around the field to see the old Greenies get their asses kicked. We had a defensive tackle right here named Paul Cost. What was he Wes? Five foot nine, a hundred and eighty pounds? He was a son of a bitch! He played like a man possessed and lived in their backfield all night. They could do nothing offensively. We shut 'em down and win the game 13-3. They were stunned. There's only one thing that kept us in that game: Balls! ...Balls! That's Newark Catholic football and that's the kind of effort we're gonna need from you people Saturday night. Watkins is gonna roll in here whoopin' it up, lookin' for payback for last year. Somebody needs to step up and have the game of his life...Who's it going to be?

Then, with renewed energy, Coach Graham would say, "Let's go, here we go," and the scrimmage would resume with much harder hitting than there had been before the story was told.

It was Friday morning, the day before the big game. The school was alive with anticipation and decorated with *BEAT WARRIORS* signs in every hallway. The dress code had been slightly relaxed to permit any and all to wear green attire—events which were known as "Green Days." I had just taken my seat in the Home Economics room to await the start of my first class. Just before class began, senior cheerleader Mary Angela Reed entered the room and asked if I had looked out onto the football field lately.

"No, why?" I asked.

"There is a big sign out there and there's big birds all around it," she said.

I stepped over to the windows on the west side of the room. Looking out into the beautiful, crisp morning, I scanned the field. Sure enough, in the south end zone of the football field was a large sign facing the school building with a gang of crows congregated beneath it. The sign was too far away for me to make out what it said, but I would be sure to get out there to read it as soon as it was possible.

The school day progressed without a chance to read the sign. It was not until immediately following the pep rally that most of us were finally able to get out there and see for ourselves what the daylong mystery had been. What we saw was sickening. A large piece of cardboard affixed to two iron posts in the ground contained the following message:

> The Word is out
>
> You have no Clout
>
> We'll give You a Whacking
>
> Because We heard you're Lacking...
>
> **GUTS!!**

The word "guts" was painted in big red letters and had spots trailing away from it to appear as drops of blood. Beneath the sign, glistening in the sunlight and covered with flies, was a big, grayish-colored pile of large-caliber intestines—probably from a cow. This explained the party of crows earlier in the day. They had been sampling the wares.

Well, how is one to react to something like this? The gut reaction (pun intended) is to say, "Those rotten Bastards! Who in the hell do they think they are coming in here and defiling our school grounds like this?" This was exactly what came to my mind and I could not wait until game time. I think most of us reacted in a similar fashion but we kept our thoughts concealed until we received Coach Graham's take on the situation. One thing was certain: If it was intended to intimidate us, it failed!

The Friday walkthrough proceeded as usual with not a word said about the entrails. Before dismissing us, however, Coach Graham had us all gather around him and "take a knee" (to kneel on one knee) just a few feet away from the reeking pile of innards. He delivered another one of his perfect talks but, unfortunately, I can only recall the very end of it:

> ...There are many people who care about this team and about you as individuals and want to see you do well tomorrow night. What? Do think somebody from Watkins dumped that shit over there? Nobody from Watkins did that. Somebody who cares about this team did that. They're worried that you don't have what it's going to take tomorrow night to get the job done...Now I think we can beat these people if we play, but what I think doesn't matter. I can't do it for you, fellas. You've go to want it and you've got to get it done for the people who care about you. You people better show up tomorrow ready to play some football. Now get it in for a cheer.

As Coach Graham departed for the locker room, I pondered heavily his statement about how someone from our own community did this. Did he know this to be a fact or was he merely speculating? I didn't want to think about it. How could we properly use this for motivation if we knew one of our own was the perpetrator? I drove it from my mind. As far as I was concerned, some creep from Watkins was responsible and we would settle it in 24 hours.

The last we saw of those guts, Coach Graham scooped them into a trashcan with a snow shovel, but not before Gene Egan's dog had a taste. Mr. Egan operated the Egan funeral home just south of the school and walked his dog on the school grounds each evening.

On game day, the butterflies and tension had set in sooner and more acutely than the previous two weeks. For the seniors, it was the biggest game of our lives to date, even though we had beaten this same group of Watkins kids every year since eighth grade. This game, in all likelihood, would determine the 1985 LCL champion.

I remember being up at the school, dressed and ready to go. While standing out on the basketball court, a parade of cars full of Watkins fans drove past on Church Street with horns honking and people hanging out of windows screaming their heads off. John Jurden said, "You won't be leaving town that happy." I must confess that I was not as confident as Jurden was about the game, but his defiant attitude helped to pump me up.

We received the opening kickoff and Joe Bell had an excellent return all the way to the Watkins 35. If he could have beaten one more man, he would have gone the distance. On the first play from scrimmage, Watkins jumped offside. The game film clearly shows middle linebacker Mike Gill roughing Bell up and trash-talking after the play was blown dead. It did not take long for *that* nonsense to occur. Despite having a first-and-five, we failed to get a first down—much to the delight of the Warriors. Lining up to punt from the Watkins 30-yard line, we executed a fake to Scott Saad who dashed around the right end for 6 yards and a first down.

The fresh set of downs opened with a 25 Power Trap to my side. Ronan led up through the hole, killed the middle linebacker and sprung Joe Bell for an 11-yard gain. A 17 Quick Pitch for no gain followed on first down. Andy Kubik threw an incomplete pass on second down. Third down began with an offside penalty on Watkins, but Trotter left early on the next play to erase the small pickup. Finally, Kubik hit Joe Simi with a 13-yard touchdown pass into traffic with 9:17 left in the first quarter. The extra point (point after touchdown or PAT) was wide left. It was the first time this season that we scored on the opening drive and we did it against Watkins. Even though the drive was only 35 yards, it was a big statement by our questionable team. It must have made Watkins uncomfortable as well.

Watkins returned the kickoff out to the 35-yard line. They came out hammering my side three plays in a row that included a trap by Foor that I stuffed as I was taught to do. The defense held tough and forced the punt. Bell muffed the catch at our 30 but covered it in time at the 25-yard line.

Though we "dodged a bullet" there, we were not so lucky soon after that. Watkins prevented us from getting a first down. On the punt, the snap sailed over Bell's head. Though Bell managed to pick the ball up, he was mobbed by a gang of Warriors. Watkins was in business at our 14-yard line. The kicking game reared its ugly head again.

A fumble in the backfield caused Watkins to lose 4 yards on first down. A trap to their left side gained 6 yards on the next play. On third down, Lieb dropped back and lofted a pass. Although the ball was tipped by Jim Calvert and sailed like a wounded duck, it fell right into the hands of a wide-open Dave Carmen in the end zone. Bobbling the hold on the extra point attempt, Lieb ran to his right and threw back into the end zone. Billy Franks knocked the pass away. The game was tied at 6-6 at the 3:50 mark in the first quarter.

How ironic it was for a team that had no completions in the two previous games to have scored on a wounded duck. It was a classic example of how the kicking game can kill a team. They should not have been down there in the first place. Nevertheless, the score had been tied—something a Green Wave team had not had to deal with in the whole of the '84 season. Coach Graham said it was important to always "answer a score with a score." We had to answer now.

With a wide variety of play calls, we methodically sliced through the Watkins defense: 4 yards; 10 yards; 6 yards; 8 yards; "sha-koom, sha-koom, sha-koom," as Coach Graham liked to say when describing a good drive. The drive, which was kept alive by a Quarterback Bootleg Right on third down, went 80 yards in 14 plays and was capped by a 13-yard touchdown pass across the middle to Monte Byers.[3] The PAT was good and we led 13-6.

Unable to do anything on their next series, Watkins punted and nearly had another gift when Bell muffed the ball again. Once again, Bell covered it in time. Four plays into our next drive, a collision between Ronan and Kubik on a 23 Power caused the ball to come loose. Watkins recovered at our 39-yard line. A great defensive effort, which included a big sack by Byers and South, forced the Warriors to punt again.

Our offense had been shut down again on the next series. Watkins fielded the punt and had the ball on our 46-yard line with approximately one minute to go in the half. All that our defense had to do was sit on Watkins one last time and we could go in at halftime with the lead. On the first play, a pass-interference call on Scott Saad gave Watkins a first down on our 30. Dave Carmen caught a ten-yard pass and was hammered by Jurden. Carmen held on and gave Watkins a first down on our 20-yard line. Two plays later, Van Order was all alone and caught a 20-yard touchdown pass with just 12 seconds left in the half.[4] It was unbelievable. A team not known for its passing had scored again with a pass! The extra point was good and we went into halftime with a 13-13 deadlock. The Warriors definitely had the momentum at intermission.

At the start of the second half, our defense prevented Watkins from gaining a first down. We went on offense at our 26-yard line after the Watkins punt and moved the ball effectively with good runs and passes. A key quarterback sneak behind Coop on third down gave us a first down at the Watkins 25-yard line. Although the Watkins defense tightened at this point, we were gifted with another first down. Dave Carmen, who had been engaged in a personal war with John Jurden all evening, clobbered Jurden deep downfield and drew a pass-interference penalty. A Counter Pass Left to Byers followed and moved us down to the Watkins 13-yard line. On the next play, a poor handoff on Flanker Trap Zero caused John Jurden to fumble the ball. In a great heads-up play that kept us alive, Coop was in perfect position and pounced on the ball just before three Warriors could get on it. Two pass attempts followed that were nearly intercepted and we then faced a fourth-and-ten. Coach Graham had a decision to make and he elected to try a field goal. This decision was both gutsy and risky, given that our kicker Dale Backlund had never attempted a field goal before.[5] Dale came through, however, nailing a 30-yarder to make the score 16-13 with 2:41 left in the third quarter.

Before discussing the kickoff after our go-ahead field goal, let it be reiterated that while the speedsters occupied the outer positions on the kickoff team, the people towards the center were the somewhat psycho, bowling-ball types who had the job of breaking the opponent's return wall. Recall also that I was one of those wall breakers and I was proud of my duty. These things must be kept in mind to fully appreciate what happened next.

On the kickoff after the field goal, I had an unobstructed pathway that led straight toward Mike Gill. He was my target and I went at him as hard as I could run. BOOM! In an incredible collision, which was the greatest hit of my life, I planted my facemask squarely into Gill's, blasted right over him and continued on to assist Tommy Helms with the tackle on Chris Wohnhas. The hit seemed hard enough that one of us should have been hurt. Other than a minor hitting buzz, I was fine. Gill, on the other hand, returned slowly and gingerly to his huddle, slightly hunched over and listing to starboard. After running one more play, Gill momentarily remained face-down on the grass in a "seven-point stance," meaning he had seven points of contact with the ground: two feet, two knees, two hands and one head. After slowly rising to his feet, the 6-1, 200-pound Gill staggered to the Watkins huddle as if he were a punch-drunk boxer. He then keeled over just as an official approached him to see what the problem was. While being assisted off the field, Gill dropped to one knee and held his head before rising and completing the journey to the bench. There he would remain for the rest of the night. Mr. Gill was a key player on both the offense and defense. He had proven especially troublesome for me throughout the game from his middle linebacker position and I was glad to see him gone for the night. Blasting someone bigger than myself and putting him out of the game gave me a deep sense of satisfaction.

On the ensuing drive that began on their 45-yard line, Watkins had two fourth-and-short situations and they went for the first down on both occasions. The first one came on the last play of the third quarter. Lieb picked up the first down with a quarterback sneak. Later, on the second fourth-down situation, Lieb attempted another sneak. This time, Watkins was penalized for pushing the runner. This key penalty put Watkins into a fourth-and-five situation and forced them to punt. This pinned us back on our 8-yard line.

On our following series of downs, a Watkins defender got a hand inside Kubik's facemask and removed one of Andy's contact lenses.[6] Shortly thereafter, a pass to Byers on third down was thrown too high. Monte went up for it and made the catch for a first down. Kubik said in the post-game interview that he "really couldn't see anything for over half of the fourth quarter."[7] In my opinion, for Coach Graham to continue calling pass plays demonstrated not only courage but also the degree of confidence he had in Kubik's ability.

After our failure to get another first down, the resulting punt could have lost the game for us. Chris Wohnhas got a great return all the way down to our 25-yard line. Fortunately, it all came back because Joe Simi had been destroyed by an illegal block in the back.[8] The defensive effort that followed, which included a gang-sack of Lieb on first down, was outstanding. Watkins failed to gain a first down and had to punt one last time.

We began our last series on our 47-yard line with three minutes left to play. If we could get a few first downs, this game would be in the bag. After no gain on first down, Bell picked up 11 yards only to have the gain called back because of illegal procedure. On the next play, Kubik hit Byers on a curl route. Monte was able to cruise to the Watkins 35 and the play proved to be the backbreaker for the Warriors. After we penetrated to the 20-yard line, Kubik fell on the ball and Watkins used their final timeout. The following play, Kubik fell on the ball again. Dave Carmen came flying up over the line of scrimmage and crashed into the NC bodies protecting Kubik. Crazy stunts such as this are precisely what necessitate protection of the quarterback when he falls on the ball! After Carmen got to his feet, he head-butted Jurden in the back of the head. When Jurden turned around, Carmen head-butted him again and spit in his face, resulting in a personal foul and Carmen being ejected from the game. After the penalty was assessed, the clock restarted and time expired. We had outlasted the Warriors.

It had been a hard-hitting, physical game. For me personally, I felt it was one of the best games I ever played on either side of the ball. Coach Graham said afterward that it was "one of our biggest wins in my 17 years here."[9]

Offensively, Coach Graham said, "Kubik and Byers carried the offense for three and a half quarters."[10] The linemen could take pride in that statement. For the first time this season, Kubik played the entire game without being sacked. Defensively, we held Watkins to just 76 total yards.[11] In the locker room afterward, Coach Graham seemed pleased with us for the first time this season and told us that it was "one hell of an effort." I believe that on the night of the Watkins game, we had made a major step towards maturing as a team.

After home games, I would make the return trip to the high school with Jim Calvert and Pat Cooperrider. Jim Calvert always brought a radio with him so we could listen to WNKO's broadcast of Coach Graham's post-game comments as we walked. While walking home after the Watkins game in the block between Day and Neal Avenue, I experienced a mental "zone-out" in which I suddenly found myself back in the football game and wondering about what our next play was going to be. This bizarre phenomenon, which I estimated to be about 10 seconds in duration, was something I had not experienced before. When I had "come back to my senses," I did not know what to make of the occurrence. Maybe it did not really happen. Whatever the case, I continued the journey back to the school with my friends, discussing our victory as we traveled.

After a big victory, the locker room at the high school was always a wild place. It was noisy, filled with the shouts and laughter of wound up kids, the banging of lockers, etc. Some kids traded stories about the plays they were most proud (or ashamed) of. Bruises were compared to see who had the worst. Helmets were passed around to see which man came away with the biggest paint marks of the night. (Paint marks were badges of honor. The bigger the marks, the greater degree of "studliness" a kid had among his teammates!) Ankle wraps and tape were cut off and hurled at people. All the while, a steady stream of bodies paraded to and from the showers. The ruckus would slightly decrease when Coach Graham stepped into the room to talk to his team. He would visit with each player to see if any of us had any injuries. If we did, his instructions were to "get some ice on it and have the doc take a look at it the morning." Coach Graham knew and was impressed by the healing power of ice on an injury. "I think ice could cure cancer," he often said. Before leaving the locker room, Coach Graham was sure to remind us not to leave the place in a trashed condition because he would not tolerate it. It especially burned him up to see helmets or shoulder pads left sitting out where they could be stolen.

After the Watkins game, several of the seniors headed to a classmate's house where a post-game party had been planned. While sitting at the kitchen table talking and eating, I experienced another "zone out." I again drifted away from my location and found myself back at White Field playing the football game. It was the strangest thing. This not only happened once but twice during my stay at the party—three times total for the night. At that point, I became very uncomfortable with what was going on and just wanted to go to bed. I drove myself home. Looking back now, I probably should have had someone drive for me, but I did not know any better.

At this time of the season, my sister Nancy, a 1979 Newark Catholic graduate, was living in Atlanta and wanted to see the Watkins game. Leaving Atlanta at 9:30 a.m., she drove straight through and arrived at halftime. She permitted me to drive her car to practice on Sunday morning. With Twisted Sister cranked over the car stereo, I rolled into the parking lot in a swank, maroon-colored five-speed 1983 Thunderbird—much to my teammates' amazement. They were curious as to where this farm kid acquired such a ride. I led them on for a while by saying that my rich grandparents gave me this thing simply for beating Watkins.

While on the topic of cars and parking lots, it would be timely to incorporate Coach Graham's feelings toward our driving habits. He hated us flying out of the parking lot and burning rubber up Green Wave Drive. Of course, some of us did not need to worry about burning rubber, as some of the jalopies we drove were incapable of such a feat. Coach Graham would stay out there some nights after practice to see who was "hot-rodding" and he would chew their butts the next day. "Don't be driving like an asshole!" he would warn us. "There are young kids all over this neighborhood and I'm telling ya, one of you are going to hit one of them!"

Dr. Trifelos paid visits to the school on Sundays to examine anyone who thought they might be hurt. After I informed him of my episodes of "zoning out," he wanted to know if I had passed out, vomited, or experienced any headaches. Learning that I had none of these symptoms, Dr. Trifelos diagnosed me with a mild concussion and ordered me not to hit for three days. "Three days?" I said in shock. That seemed unnecessary to me. This mild concussion obviously occurred when I hit Mike Gill. I played the entire fourth quarter after that with no trouble at all. This I did not need. I was already on thin ice with Coach Graham with respect to my toughness and endurance. I feared that when he learned I had a concussion, Coach Graham would assume that I was on the losing end of a hit, "couldn't cut the mustard," or one of the "paper people." I don't actually know if he had any of these thoughts. It was just paranoia on my part. Even though "films don't lie," the activity of special teams that occurs upfield and away from the ball is seldom captured on film. Sadly, there is no evidence of what I did on that last kickoff. Coach Graham could not have known about the colossal blow I delivered to Mike Gill that put him out of the game. All I could do was drop the matter and sit out for the three days.

Watkins Memorial	6	7	0	0	13
Newark Catholic	6	7	3	0	16

	WM	NC
First Downs	4	18
Rushing	34	55
Passing Yards	42	163
Total yards	76	218
Att-Comp-Int	5-3-0	24-12-0
Punts / Avg	6-35	2-29
Kickoffs / Avg	3-47	4-43
Fumbles / lost	1-0	4-1
Penalties / yards	9-77	8-53

Week 3 LCL Action[12]

Licking Valley	28	Johnstown	41
Granville	0	Northridge	7
Heath	22	Amhearst	17
Utica	21	Lakewood	6

Notes

1. Mark Naegele, "NC, Watkins to battle for local bragging rights," *The Advocate*, (Sep. 13, 1985), p. 7.

2. Mark Naegele, "Warriors hoping for 'typical' year," *The Advocate, Football '85*, (Aug. 28, 1985), p. 18.

3. Rick Cannizzaro, "NC throttles Watkins for key victory," *The Advocate* (Sep. 15, 1985), p. 1C.

4. Ibid.

5. Ibid.

6. Sean McClelland, "Wave quarterback completes mission despite handicap," *The Advocate*, (Sep. 15, 1985), p. 1C.

7. Ibid.

8. Rick Cannizzaro, "NC throttles Watkins for key victory," *The Advocate*, (Sep. 15, 1985), p. 1C.

9. Ibid.

10. Sean McClelland, "Wave quarterback completes mission despite handicap," *The Advocate*, (Sep. 15, 1985), p. 1C.

11. Rick Cannizzaro, "NC throttles Watkins for key victory," *The Advocate* (Sep. 15, 1985), p. 1C.

12. *The Advocate*, (Sep. 14, 1985), p. 7.

The Licking County League disbanded after the 1990 season. In the five seasons following 1985, Watkins Memorial recorded victories over Newark Catholic in 1986, '89 and '90. The 1986 contest is clouded in great controversy, to say the least. NC trailed in the game by a point and had a first-and-goal at the 1. Four scoring attempts took place and quarterback Jeremy Montgomery allegedly broke across the goal line at least twice. The officials, however, denied the Green Wave of the touchdown. The game finished 14-13 in favor of Watkins, which ended a 31-game winning streak and prevented what would have been a state record 64-game winning streak. (It was the only loss NC suffered from the state game of 1983 until week 10 of the 1988 season.) The Newark Catholic-Watkins series ended with the Green Wave holding a 13-5 advantage in LCL play.

Week 4

Johnstown Johnnies

September 21

I do not know if the pending 1985 showdown against Johnstown was a cause for concern for anyone else in my class, but for me, the game had loomed heavy in the back of my mind for two years. Now, it may appear that I am sensationalizing just for the sake of a good story, but nothing could be further from the truth. A look back in time can explain my concern.

In 1983, because of decreased school enrollment, Johnstown had only two seniors on its football team.[1] With mostly sophomores and a few juniors filling the empty jobs, the Johnnies were basically a junior-varsity team playing a varsity schedule and their 1983 record reflected this. They had endured a humiliating 1-9 season that left them tied for last place in the LCL with Licking Heights—the only team they had beaten.[2] What all of this had to do with the 1985 season was quite obvious, in my opinion. This same group of kids that had been the doormat of the LCL in 1983 would be a tough, battle-hardened team in two years. That time had arrived.

Johnstown's 1983 season was not the norm. Under coach Tim Kidwell, the Johnnies had one of the better football programs in the county in years past and usually gave Newark Catholic a tough game. Johnstown's lone victory over Newark Catholic occurred in 1979—and what a huge victory it was. The stunning 12-7 upset of the Green Wave snapped a 25-game winning streak, denied a seventh straight LCL title and prevented a return trip to the playoffs for the defending state champions. "Coach Graham and I had a tremendous amount of respect for Coach Kidwell," Coach Poth said of the Johnstown boss. "He did a good job of preparing them. They've always been a thorn in our side and we just knew we were in for a dogfight when we played them."[3]

The 1985 Johnstown team, which had gone 5-5 in '84, had an incredible 16 starters returning from the year before—eight on either side of the ball and 18 lettermen in all.[4] The team stud was veteran running back Ed Baldwin (5-11, 185) who had been the LCL's fourth-leading rusher in 1984 with 673 yards.[5] After just 3 games into the '85 season, Baldwin was the League's leading rusher and scorer with 459 yards and 54 points,[6] including a 4-touchdown, 174-yard game against Utica[7] in week 3 and a 235-yard, 4-touchdown performance against Northridge the week before we faced him.[8]

Not only was Baldwin a big, strong, punishing runner, he was also extremely fast and Coach Graham issued his warnings to us throughout the week: "You tackles and ends better have your jocks on straight this week. If your ass gets trapped and this guy gets loose, he'll physically hurt us! And Joe Simi, you may have caught Warga, but you won't catch this guy. I don't give a shit what kind of angle you take!" We hoped that it would not be necessary for Joe to be tested.

As far as other personnel were concerned, Johnstown was not a big team. Their heaviest starter weighed 200 pounds and their offensive line averaged 180 pounds—15 pounds less than ours did. They were quick and physical, however.

Game day arrived and we made the bus trip to Johnstown High School in the northwest part of the county. There was nothing like taking an autumn road trip to a football game. Traveling through the farm country, enjoying the scenery in spite of the nervousness and proud to be with my teammates as we headed into battle.

If a contest had been held in 1985 to determine which high school in Licking County had the sorriest football field, Johnstown would have won easily. The field was hard, dry, dusty and devoid of grass cover in numerous places. Many small rocks were exposed. Playing on such a surface was sure to be a new and painful experience.

Johnstown was fired up to play from the very start. Their defense easily controlled us on the opening series and we had to punt. Johnstown took it to us offensively as well. A swing pass left to Orders on first down lost 5 yards. Six yards were gained on second down by Orders to set up third-and-nine. I was killed on a trap play and Baldwin picked up 10 yards for the first down. The same trap play hit us two plays later. I stuffed it this time, but Monte Byers had penetrated too deeply, took himself out of the play and Baldwin got 9 more yards. A tough Baldwin run picked up the first down. On the next play, Baldwin ran a dive fake, got hammered by South and Johnnies quarterback Matt Cook flipped the ball to Jay Orders around left end who gained 16 yards. The play was identical to the one Northridge's Warga got loose on and ran for 65 yards. I suspect Johnstown's coaching staff had studied the films from our Northridge game and developed that play just for us. Our defense tightened and had Johnstown stopped at our 38, but a 15-yard facemask penalty on John Jurden moved the ball down to the 23-yard line. From here, split end Steve Proffit beat John Jurden to the corner of the end zone.

He made a terrific catch good for a 23-yard touchdown with 5:30 left in the first quarter. Johnstown had gone 80 yards in 10 plays and we were shocked to be losing 7-0. Baldwin lived up to his reputation of being a tough, physical running back. He was not afraid to stick it up in there and he punished anyone who tried to tackle him.

As in the Watkins game one week earlier, we had to answer a score with a score. After a 26 Iso gained 6 yards, Kubik scrambled right to avoid a sack, threw on the run to his left across the middle and hit Franks with a 29-yard bullet. It was an awesome pass. After a juggling catch by Joe Simi and a 5-yard gain by Bell on a 1 Trap, we had progressed to the Johnstown 13-yardline. On the next play, Kubik was hit while attempting a pass and the ball came loose. It was covered by a Johnstown player but the play was ruled an incomplete pass. After that near-disaster, Donnelly knocked the defensive tackle flat on his back on a Zero Trap. This allowed Joe Bell to pick up 6 yards to the 7-yard line. The final 7 yards did not come easily as it required 4 plays to reach the end zone. The capper was a Kubik sneak on fourth down behind Cooperrider and Donnelly. The snap for the extra point was high but Jeremy Montgomery did an excellent job of pulling it down. Backlund sent the ball through the uprights to tie the game at 7-7 with 45 seconds left in the first quarter. That extra point would prove to be priceless. The amount of dust that hung in the air after each play was unbelievable and is evident on the game film. This literally was "five yards and a cloud of dust." Woody Hayes would have been proud.

On the next series, Jurden picked off a Johnstown pass on the first play of the second quarter and returned it to the Johnstown 6-yard line where he was caught by Baldwin. A Johnnie piled on and drew a personal foul. It appeared as if we were in great shape but the interception was nullified by defensive pass interference. This set Johnstown up with a first-and-twenty-five at their 36-yard line. Our defense held and forced the Johnnies to punt.

We were once again able to move the ball effectively on our third offensive series. A balanced attack of four runs and four passes covered 59 yards. The drive was wrapped up by Kevin Donnelly leading Bell on a 28 Counter Sweep that went in from 12 yards out to make the new score 14-7 with 5:59 left in the half.

Literally seconds later, we were in offensive mode again after Todd South smacked Baldwin on first down and caused a fumble. Scott Saad made the fumble recovery. A key 17-yard reception along the sideline by Joe Simi helped set up a 9-yard touchdown pass to Monte Byers on third-and-eight. The score put us up 21-7 with 3:30 left in the half. We had scored 21 unanswered points and it appeared that we would take a comfortable lead into the locker room at halftime.

Following the kickoff, The Johnnies went to work at their 38-yard line. A loss of 3 yards on first down was followed by a 5-yard run by Baldwin. On third down, Cook rolled left on an attack pass and lofted the ball to Proffit who had gotten behind Joe Simi. The Johnnie made the catch and raced 50 yards before Joe Bell finally stopped him at our 10-yard line. Now we needed a defensive stand. On first down, Johnstown ran a trap play to my side that I stuffed. Scott Saad made the stop on Baldwin after a short gain. But on second down, Cook rolled my way on a dive/option, kept the ball and cruised 9 yards untouched into the end zone 49 seconds before the half ended. Not only had we been completely spanked and faked out of our jockstraps, but it was also the first rushing touchdown inflicted against our defense in 1985. It felt terribly humiliating. Thanks to Byers, the extra point attempt was blocked, leaving the score at 21-13.

After running two offensive plays, the half expired. We withdrew to the locker room embarrassed and without momentum. The way to the locker room was up the steps of the hostile home-crowd seating, which always made us targets of sneers, stares and derisive speech. I have no recollection of what was said to us at halftime, but it is certain that Coach Graham tore into us and deservedly so. Defensively, we seemed to have been asleep in the first half whereas the offense had been in top form. This was a marked contrast from the previous three games where the defense had been our strength. Monte Byers recalls his experience during half time. "I had diarrhea and held it in the whole first half. I went straight to the shitter when we got into the locker room. While Coach Graham talked and yelled at the team, he kept yelling back to me, 'You hear me in there Byers?'"[9]

Wimberly "Boo" Cook, who performed Green Wave kickoff duties for the night, botched the second-half kickoff, which gave Johnstown great field position on their 43-yard line. During this series, the pass that had gained 50 yards just before halftime was attempted again. This time, however, Todd South clobbered Matt Cook before the pass could be thrown.

After the Johnstown punt, we began at our 30 and muscled to the Johnstown 5-yardline in 9 plays. Although we were so close to scoring, we failed to capitalize. On the tenth play of the drive, Kubik was hit while attempting a pass and lost the football. Middle linebacker Chris Nicholson scooped up the loose ball and began to move upfield. Tony Johns, who had been blocking Nicholson on the play, fell down. After regaining his feet, Tony saw the recovery, stayed with the play and made the stop at the Johnstown 33. Based on the game film, Tony probably prevented a touchdown return. Our defense held again and forced the Johnnies to punt.

Once again, the offense took it to Johnstown and moved the ball from our 42 to the Johnstown 28 in 7 plays. On the eighth play of the drive, which was the first play of the fourth quarter, a 30 Trap had been called. The backside defensive tackle, which was Tony Johns' responsibility, was unblocked and had a clean shot at Joe Bell. The hit left Joe sprawling on the ground in pain from a sprained ankle. After the officials had signaled for an injury-timeout, Coach Graham walked angrily onto the field toward his injured player. Pointing to Bell, Coach Graham looked back toward the huddle and said something to the effect of, "Atta-baby Johns, take a look at what you just did!" Bell was assisted from the field and was done for the night. The series ended when Kubik was hurried on a fourth-down pass attempt and threw an incomplete pass.

Johnstown could do nothing after they got the ball. Trotter and I combined for a big sack on third down that set the Johnnies back 13 yards and forced them to punt again.

Another Green Wave possession began at our 20-yard line with 9 minutes left in the game. Our play selection, which consisted of an 18 Quick Pitch, a 27 Sweep, three consecutive 14 Specials, a pass to Byers and a 30 Trap, moved us to the Johnstown 35-yardline. On the eighth play, Kubik threw an interception and the Johnnies were in business at their 33-yard line with 5:49 left to play.

On the ensuing Johnstown possession, Baldwin had gained 8 yards on two plays. On third down, Jim Calvert was destroyed by a trap-block that allowed Baldwin to break into the clear toward the end zone. Joe Simi, who was slightly away from the play and nearly standing still when Baldwin broke free, quickly closed on Baldwin and ran him down at our 22-yardline: Time out Newark Catholic! Once again, Simi accomplished what Coach Graham said he could not. How fast *was* Joe Simi?

After no gain on first down, Baldwin picked up 5 yards to set up third down from our 16-yardline. At this time of the drive, I was briefly rendered lame after some goon ran his cleats up the side of my left ankle. As I hobbled toward the sideline desiring a rest, Coach Graham saw me, placed his hands on his hips and just scowled at me. He didn't need to say a word. I got the message and returned to the huddle to tough it out.

So on third down from the 16-yard line, Calvert was killed again on the same trap play that came earlier in the drive and Baldwin cruised untouched into the end zone for the touchdown with 3:33 left in the game. Though it was another humiliating blow to our defense, we still had a chance to regain our pride if we could prevent the Johnnies from picking up the 2-point conversion that was needed to tie the game. Johnstown lined up and ran the dive/option that they had scored on in the second quarter. Baldwin sold the dive fake perfectly by launching himself up over the line of scrimmage. Then rolling to his left, Cook kept the ball, turned upfield and collided with Joe Simi at the goal line. When the dust cleared, an official ruled that Cook made it across. Johnstown was awarded the 2 points and the home crowd went berserk. To this day, Joe Simi maintains, "We got screwed on that play. After I tackled that kid, my facemask was right on the goal line and I'm sure I stopped him short."[10]

We found ourselves in the uncomfortable situation of being tied late in the fourth quarter. Our following offensive series was pathetic and nearly sealed our coffin. On a first-down pass-play, Scott Saad missed his block on the backside defensive end. The Johnnie crushed Kubik and the ball came loose on our 23-yardline! In a very heads-up move, Mike Trotter (God bless him), saw the loose ball and quickly pounced on it, maintaining our possession. Second down was a Flood pass to Saad for a short gain. Third down was a deep pass down the right sideline intended for Jurden. He was open but the ball was just beyond his fingertips. On fourth down and with 1:50 to play, Dale Backlund came in to punt and stood at our 10-yardline. In another near-catastrophe, the snap was high! Dale (God bless him also), had to leap skyward to get the ball. He successfully gathered the ball in and got the punt away, pushing Johnstown back to their 42-yardline.

Not surprisingly, Johnstown successfully trapped Calvert yet again. Todd South closed the hole quickly and Baldwin got minimal yardage. Now it was Johnstown's turn for a miscue. A poor exchange between the center and quarterback allowed the ball to come loose and Scott Saad recovered on the Johnnie 37-yard line. With just over a minute to play, we had one last chance to win this thing in regulation.

On the very next play, Kubik was intercepted for the second time of the night. With blockers ahead of him, the Johnstown defender returned the ball from his 10-yard line all the way to the Newark Catholic 45-yardline. Mike Trotter forced him out of bounds along our bench and the hit sent another hellacious cloud of dust into the air.

Twelve seconds remained on the clock—enough time for Johnstown to run one more play. Can the reader guess what play Johnstown called? If you guessed a trap on Jimmy Calvert, you are correct. Calvert's problem late in the game had been a matter of simply not reading his keys and thus, failing to tend to his priorities. In the plays he was burned on, all Jim saw was Baldwin coming at him. In "trying to be a hero" and make the tackle, Calvert failed to see the pulling guard closing in to "knock his ass off." This is not a cut on Jim Calvert. He was better than this. It was just that he, like the rest of us, suffered from exhaustion and the pressure of the game. When these two things set in, composure and clear thinking are usually lost and that is when bad things occur. "Fatigue makes cowards of us all," Coach Graham would say, quoting the great Vince Lombardi. It is easy to do the job when things are going well. It is *not* so easy to perform when things get tough. Calvert just happened to be the one Johnstown decided to go after the most.

On the last play of regulation, Calvert still did not look for the trap, but the pulling guard did not reach him in time, either. Calvert was able to eat Baldwin's lunch in the backfield for a 5-yard loss—a hit that caused Baldwin to get up limping. Time expired and we headed into Overtime.

High school Overtime proceeds in the following manner: After a 3-minute intermission, a coin toss is conducted to see which team will get the ball first. The team on offense first is team A. The ball is placed on the 20-yard line of team B and all game rules apply. After team A has either scored or lost the ball on downs, team B then gets the ball on the 20 (at the same end of the field) and must either outscore team A which ends the game, or match the score of team A, which mandates another overtime cycle. If team B does not match team A's score, team B loses.

In our overtime against Johnstown, we were team A. First down: Kubik threw a great strike to Byers in heavy coverage and the pass was good for 12-yards. First-and-goal from the 8: Scott Saad gained 3 tough yards on a 26 Iso. Second-and-goal from the 5: the same play was run again and Saad picked up another 3 yards.

Third-and-goal from the 2: behind Donnelly and Cooperrider, Kubik snuck into the end zone standing up and Backlund's extra point was good. We were up 28-21!

It was now Johnstown's turn. On first down, Johnstown's Cook picked up 11 yards right away on the quarterback-keep/dive/option play that had killed us all night. First-and-goal from the 9: Trotter was trapped and Baldwin smashed up the middle for 5 tough yards. On second-and-goal from the 4, Cook dropped back to attempt a pass. Kevin Donnelly, who had replaced Calvert at defensive tackle, broke through the line and slammed Cook down to the dusty earth in a big sack that cost the Johnnies 6 yards. When Cook dropped back to pass again on third-and-goal from the 10, Cook narrowly avoided another sack by Jim Olson and made it to the 5-yard line where he was belted by Scott Saad.

It was now fourth-and-goal from the 5 and the game would be decided on this next play. I can recall the stress of that moment as our backs were to the wall, the Johnstown fans roared and the Johnnies had one more shot. This was the type of situation known as "gut check" time or "nut-cuttin'" time, when "balls" were required to tough it out and to avoid the proverbial act of excreting feces down one's own leg.

Cook rolled to his right looking for a receiver. Just as he threw the ball, Cook was leveled as Scott Saad met him helmet-to-helmet. The ball sailed harmlessly out of bounds beyond the reach of Lance Hall who was guarded by Monte Byers. In looking at the game film, a fussy referee might have called Saad for roughing the passer because of the helmet contact. That, fortunately, did not occur. The game was over. We had survived.

I had never been dirtier after a football contest than after the Johnstown game. A muddy cake had formed on my gray undershirt—an obvious combination of sweat and dust. The numbers on my white jersey were illegible, the pants and socks soiled and the skin was gritty. I had dust in my eyes, ears and mouth. As we were leaving the rough field, Johnstown Coach Tim Kidwell tracked down Joe Bell to offer his condolences about the ankle injury.

A weary Newark Catholic team sat in stunned silence on the bus awaiting the trip home. Yes, we had won. However, because Coach Graham's perfectionism and standards of excellence were so infectious, there was no cause for celebration and everyone seemed to know it. All of us, not just Jim Calvert, had played sloppily, failed to read keys, made mistakes and failed to execute. After beating Watkins the week before, did we think that we were something special? Did we take Johnstown too lightly? Perhaps, but nothing should be taken away from Johnstown. They were a tough, physical group of kids who took us "out behind the woodshed" and gave us their best shot. With all the mistakes we made against a team of their quality, we were fortunate to have escaped with a "W." I wondered, and perhaps others did as well, about what kind of team we really were. Two narrow victories in as many weeks. How long could we go on like this? We certainly were not on the same plane as the '84 team who had beaten Johnstown 42-0—Johnstown's worst defeat ever by the Green Wave.

The next day at the high school when stretching was completed and we were about to run, I was "called onto the carpet" again by Coach Graham.

"Billy Evans, what in *thee* hell are you doing taking yourself out of the game in the fourth quarter when they're driving on us?"

Ah, crap. Not again, I thought to myself.

"It was my ankle," I answered.

"You were coming out because of your ankle?" he asked in disbelief.

"You said that if a kid was hurt and couldn't go, that he should get out because he could cost us the football game," I replied.

"Yeah, OK, fine," he replied sarcastically, "but who do I have to put in for you—Jimmy Cross?" (Jimmy Cross was a tall, lanky junior defensive end with little varsity game experience.)

"I don't care if your f--king foot falls off, you don't come out of that game! Not in that situation! ... Toughen up for Christ's sake!"

I was dismissed to join the team to get my running in and I was absolutely livid. We had played four games now. With each game, there was an incident that brought my toughness, durability and reliability into question. Two of those incidents moved Coach Graham to jump on me. This caused me great humiliation. I was not about to tolerate having my toughness and manhood called into question week after week. Something had to change. If he wanted toughness, I would show him toughness. I decided on that day, while running, that Coach Graham would not hear another word from me for the remainder of the season. Other than being asked a direct question, I would make no effort to speak to him. In addition, under no circumstances, other than on a stretcher or being told to do so, was I ever going to come out of a game again. Consequently, I made good on both of my resolutions.

Newark Catholic	7	14	0	0	7	28
Johnstown	7	6	0	8	0	21

	NC	J
First Downs	19	10
Rushing	128	121
Passing Yards	195	67
Total yards	332	188
Att-Comp-Int	22-14-2	5-3-0
Punts	3-37	4-41
Kickoffs / Avg	4-37	4-51
Fumbles / lost	2-1	2-2
Penalties / yards	2-25	3-25

Week 4 LCL Action[11]

Licking Valley	35	Heath	33
Lakewood	20	Northridge	15
Utica	24	Watkins Memorial	36
Granville	17	Columbus Ready	0

Notes

1. Dave Waitkus, "Young Johnnies fight inexperience," *The Advocate*, *Football '83*, (Aug. 31, 1983), p. 25.

2. Jim Wharton, "Lettermen key Johnstown secret," *The Advocate, Football '84*, (Aug. 31, 1984), p. 25.

3. Wes Poth, Conversation with author, Jan. 30, 2002.

4. Mark Naegele, "Vets help Johnnies to improve," *The Advocate, Football '85*, (Aug. 28, 1985), p. 13.

5. Ibid.

6. "Newark Catholic at Johnstown," *The Advocate*, (Sep. 19, 1985), p. 16.

7. Sean McClelland, "Baldwin leads Johnnies' attack," *The Advocate*, (Sep. 7, 1985), p. 5.

8. Dave Waitkus, "Johnstown 'traps' winless Northridge," *The Advocate*, (Sep. 14, 1985), p. 5.

9. Monte Byers, Telephone conversation with author, Jan. 1, 2002.

10. Joseph Simi, Conversation with author, Dec. 18, 2001.

11. *The Advocate*, (Sep. 21, 1985), p. 12.

In the five remaining seasons of the LCL after 1985, Newark Catholic beat Johnstown every year. The series closed with the Green Wave holding a 17-1 advantage.

Week 5

Coshocton Redskins

September 27

Early into week 5, the latest Associated Press poll had been released and we were still ranked No. 1 in Class A despite our overtime struggle with Johnstown. Apparently, it had been a bad weekend for all the No. 1 teams in Ohio. Class AAA leader Cincinnati Moeller fell 33-13 to Johnson High School of Huntsville, Alabama and Class AA leader Akron St. Vincent-St. Mary was upset 15-0 by Louisville St Thomas Aquinas.[1] We had survived the mysterious "week-four plague of the No. 1's," but after two straight hard-hitting, close games that left us slightly beaten up and unsure of ourselves, week 5 was no easier for us. We were scheduled to play our second non-league opponent, the Coshocton Redskins, and an article that appeared in *The Advocate* the night before the game summed up our predicament quite well:

This is probably the last thing Newark Catholic (4-0) needs right now. Coming off a 16-13 win over Watkins Memorial two weeks ago and last week's 28-21 overtime win against Johnstown, the Green Wave must now regroup for unbeaten Coshocton (4-0) in a non-league contest. The Redskins, who beat Ridgewood 30-7 last week, have given up just 15 points this season and are yielding about 100 total yards per game. To make matters worse, the Green Wave will be without leading rusher Joe Bell, who was injured in the Johnstown game. Newark Catholic has a 19-game winning streak on the line.

The Green Wave defense, which had been the mainstay of NC's success until Johnstown scored 21 points, will have to stop running back Matt Haines. The 5-10,

170-pound senior fullback, who rushed for 991 yards last year, has gained nearly 500 yards this season.[2]

In addition to the above information, Coshocton, a Division III school, was ranked second in Region 11 with 18.50 computer points. Interestingly enough, that was also the same point total that Newark Catholic had.[3]

Concerning their personnel, the sizes of Coshocton's offensive linemen from left to right were: 6-2, 220; 6-0, 170; 6-1, 160; 6-0, 195; and 5-11, 195. In addition to the fullback Haines, senior quarterback and defensive back Marty Arganbright (5-11, 170) was another threat we would have to deal with.

Because the Coshocton game took place on a Friday, our normal routine had to be altered. Although it was a short week, we practiced as intensely as ever. We could ill-afford another Johnstown performance and the debacles of that game were addressed relentlessly—especially the reading of keys and the stopping of trap blocks for the defensive linemen! Coach Graham continually told us that we had yet to play our best game and, "You don't know how good you can be."

Joe Bell had been making trips to Denison University all week for ankle therapy and would see limited action on defense. (Some high schools in Licking County sent injured athletes to see Dale Googins, head trainer at Denison University in Granville. Dale performed therapy on these kids and did outstanding work.) John Jurden had an ankle injury as well and was expected to play offense only. This resulted in two vacancies in our defensive secondary that were to be filled by juniors Tommy Helms and Darby Riley.

Late in the week at the end of a practice, Coach Graham called us all in around him before we retired to the locker room. He spelled out to us the scope of this game. Coshocton had their best team in several years and their community was in a euphoric state over it. Not only did Coshocton expect to make the playoffs, but they were also confident, it appeared, that they were going to smear us—so much so that they scheduled us as their Homecoming game. As most schools scheduled Homecoming games against weaker opponents so that the festivities were not likely to be ruined by a loss, Coach Graham considered this an insult and tears welled up in his eyes as he spoke to us:

> We're not some plow school! We deserve more respect than that! You people need to understand something. This will be the biggest game that community has seen in years and all the alumni will show up to see us get our asses kicked. They must think that they're the first good team we've ever played and that we're just going to lay down and die. This ain't the first big game we've ever been in! Don't get me wrong, fellas. They're a decent team, but they ain't been hit yet! You people remember who you are and what you represent and we'll show up!

Coshocton is located northeast of Newark in eastern Coshocton County and the driving distance was substantially longer than that of a Licking County League game. Because of this, the football team was released at 1:30 on Friday to begin game preparations. Most of us needed to go home first to grab clothes and something to eat. When I stepped out into the parking lot, the cold, cloudy afternoon struck me as perfect football weather—the first good game weather of the season and confirmation that autumn was finally arriving. Filled with excitement, I shouted, "YEAH, LET'S GO!" to my other teammates mingling between the parked vehicles. This moved John Jurden to chuckle and say, "Sound's like Bill is ready."

The house was quiet and empty as I got my things together. I realized that it was the first game where there was no one home to eat or to talk with. Since I was left to my own thoughts, the silence made the pre-game jitters all the more intense. Just as I was ready to walk out of the house, the phone rang. It was the Kincaid's, our neighbors over the hill to the north, calling to tell me that I had sheep running loose. *Great! This is all I need right now!* I said to myself. When I should have been en route to school getting my "game face" on, there I was on the windy, overcast afternoon, scrambling around the fields trying to get these stupid, stinking sheep back to the barn! Fortunately, of the 30 or so that we had, only five were out and I was able to corral them in relatively short order. Boy, that would have been something: To arrive late for the team mass—or worse, the team meeting—and then have to explain my tardiness to Coach Graham when confronted about it. "I was chasing sheep, Coach."

We arrived in Coshocton and as we stepped off the bus, a nearby group of Coshocton fans inspected us and one of them said, "It looks like they brought their junior high team."

Just minutes before game time, we were all crammed into a cracker box of a visitor's locker room. Coach Graham was right. This was the biggest game for Coshocton in a long, long time and the size of the crowd was indicative of that. Many of them stood outside of our locker room chanting and yelling at us in rabid fashion. I must say that I welcomed the worst treatment opposing fans could dish out. The reason was this: When it was time for the prayer and Coach Graham had us come in close together to "touch somebody," at that moment when the heads were bowed and the commotion from the vile crowd filtered in from outside, something magical happened which did more for team bonding and unity than perhaps anything else. For that reason alone, I loved away games.

Coach Graham gave us his usual instructions for leaving the locker room: single file; heads down; chinstraps snapped and "Don't say shit to anybody!" As we filed from the locker room, we were delayed from taking the field right away, which left us standing amidst the jeering, taunting mob. Off to my right, a teenage girl proclaimed, "Look, their scared to death! They can't even look at us!" Upon hearing that, I could not resist doing something. Contrary to Coach Graham's orders, I lifted my head to deliver the grimmest "death-stare" I could muster. She cowered and didn't say another word.

We started the game with the ball but did not keep it for long—only about two seconds, to be exact. On the opening kickoff, Scott Saad was drilled and lost the ball. Coshocton recovered on our 20-yard line. What a way to start a game!

After an incomplete pass and a short run, Marty Arganbright rolled left on a third-down quarterback-keep and made it all the way to the 9-yard line where Tommy Helms knocked him out of bounds. After three more running plays, Coshocton had penetrated close to the goal line to set up fourth-and-goal. The fourth-down call was a quarterback sneak. A quick read by Scott Saad kept Arganbright out of the end zone. It was an awesome defensive effort, but we then had to go on offense from this dangerous location.

Jeff Ronan got the call on first down and barely made it out of the end zone. On second down, Ronan carried again on a 23 Power and moved out to the 3 with a tough second effort. Andy Kubik rolled right on a third-down quarter-keep and picked up seven yards but was short of the first down. Standing at the goal line, Dale Backlund punted and Coshocton had a good return to our 30-yard line.

On the next three plays, Coshocton was able to pick up only 5 yards. On fourth down, an option play came to my side. I hit Arganbright just as he pitched the ball. Instead of guarding the pitchman, which was his job, Monte Byers also hit Arganbright, thus allowing the pitchman to go free and rip off 11 yards to our 14-yard line for a first down. Coshocton moved down to our 10-yard line with two more running plays. On third down, Arganbright threw a pass to the end zone. The ball went directly to Tommy Helms, who had both of his hands on the ball for an apparent interception! Helms did not intercept the ball, however. Instead, he threw it to the ground thinking that it was fourth down and that we would get the ball back. The mistake was a perfect example of someone failing to keep his head in the game and it afforded Coshocton one more play. They nailed a 27-yard field goal with 2:54 left in the first quarter. Now, Tommy Helms was a brilliant 4.0 student. Coach Graham sometimes referred to Helms as "Mr. President," joking that he would someday become President of the United States. However, it was occasional boneheaded moves such as this one that infuriated Coach Graham, often provoking him to explode with something such as: "G-DDAMMIT TOMMY HELMS! HOW CAN YOU BE THE SMARTEST KID IN THE WHOLE DAMN SCHOOL BUT THE BIGGEST DUMBASS ON THIS FOOTBALL TEAM!" (In reality, Tommy Helms did not have a monopoly on this undesirable distinction. Coach Graham would confer this title to anyone on any given day!)

Our second offensive series began at the 35-yard line. A 25 Iso on first down yielded nothing. Kubik threw an incomplete pass deep to Simi on second down. On third down, Simi picked up 11 yards on a Tight End Screen Left and we finally got a first down. The next three plays were incomplete passes and the Backlund punt rolled to the Coshocton 7-yard line.

The Redskins gained 3 yards on first down. Second down was a quarterback-keep left which lost 6 yard thanks to great containment by Billy Franks. Third down was a trap on Olson that gained only 5 yards. The Coshocton punt, which occurred on the goal line, sailed straight to Joe Bell. Bell, who was used sparingly, returned the punt to the Redskin 22-yard line.

We had a great opportunity to make something happen with a short field to work with. First down was a 23 Power that went for no gain. Then on second down, Kubik hit Simi for a 12-yard gain, which was followed by a 6-yard run from Jeff Ronan on 14 Dive. After Coshocton was penalized for encroachment, we finally scored three plays later on a sneak by Kubik behind Jim Olson and me. Backlund's extra point was good and we went up 7-3 with 8 minutes left in the second quarter.

On Coshocton's next series, a superb defensive effort took place: Trotter with a big hit on first down; Saad making the stop on second down; a Bell-Evans combo on third down. Coshocton gained only 5 yards on three running plays and the resulting punt put us back on offense at our 25-yard line.

Coshocton had somewhat of a strange stadium in that there was no visitor seating whatsoever. Instead, all fans, regardless of stripe, sat together in one big set of seats behind the home team's bench. This was a situation that just begged for trouble. Although I never heard of any skirmishes in the stands, I do remember that there was trouble between the cheerleading squads. Apparently, struggles for territory and each squad trying to out-volume the other resulted in threats and icy stares. They apparently nearly came to blows. Newark Catholic principal Ann Mullin finally intervened by placing a bench between the two squads to serve as a line of demarcation that neither squad was permitted to cross. Additional information from a fan's perspective on the seating arrangement has been provided by my brother:

> The Coshocton game was unusual in that both teams occupied one side of the field and we were seated opposite of our team. Obviously, this was strange because fans normally sat behind their team. This situation placed Coach Graham's voice coming in our direction, making it possible to hear a hell of a lot more yelling from him. I think Kubik had a rough go of it at first and J.D. was riding him hard. My friend Rick Cannizzaro was on the sideline at this game either doing stats or covering the game for *The Advocate*. He told me that J.D. hollered, "Kubik! You g-ddamn stupid quarterback!" more than once. He also told me that Poth was concerned about J.D. cussing so much during that game and allegedly was heard to say to Graham, "Coach, you better stop than g-ddamn cussin' or you'll get us thrown out!" Rick also told me that Poth said to him, "I've told him to stop that g-ddamn cussin'!"[4]

The first play of our next drive was a 17 Quick Pitch. With a great cutback, Scott Saad picked up 16 yards. Ronan then blasted for 8 yards. Our drive ended two plays later when Kubik was pressured, rolled to his right and was picked off near the sideline to set Coshocton up at their 45-yard line.

Coshocton did not keep the ball long after the interception. Bell and Simi stuffed a first-down counter-trap. Second down resulted in an incomplete pass. On third down, Arganbright had Trotter and me in his face and threw a desperate pass that was intercepted by Darby Riley and advanced to midfield.

The next Green Wave drive began with another 17 Quick Pitch that earned 6 yards. Finding no one open on second down, Kubik made a run for it and advanced to the Redskin 39-yard line. On the next play, Kubik found Byers across the middle for 11 yards. Staying on his feet, Monte went weaving and crashing between defenders to gain an additional 14 yards after the catch all the way to the Coshocton 14. Two plays later, Kubik dropped back and somehow managed to sneak the ball between three defenders to Byers at the very back of the end zone for an 11-yard touchdown pass just as the Coshocton band was assembling to take the field with 56 seconds before halftime. Time expired on the Redskins' next possession and a stunned home crowd watched the Green Wave retire to the locker room leading their "playoff-bound" team 14-3.

Poor kickoff coverage nearly let Coshocton back into the game as the second half opened. The Redskin return man fought his way to our 49-yard line where Backlund finally made the stop and perhaps saved a touchdown. Coshocton gained only 5 yards on their opening three plays of the third quarter and lined up to punt from our 44-yard line. They caught us sleeping, however, as the snap went to the up-man instead of the punter—a fake punt was underway! The up-man rolled to his left and just as Olson tagged him, he pitched the ball to the punter, resembling an option play. The punter was able to continue for 6 yards, which was enough for the first down. After two more plays with no gain, Franks and Olson were killed on a counter-trap to the left that gained 8 yards and set up another fourth-and-short situation on our 30-yard line. Rolling to his right on an apparent quarterback keep, Arganbright found himself hemmed in, backpedaled and threw an incomplete pass with a gang of Greenies in his face. It was a big defensive stand.

There was a particular play in this game while we were on defense where I was completely obliterated. I remember it vividly. Having fired off the line, I felt outside pressure and spun to my right to get out of it. Just as I had completed the spin, a Redskin, who had been split out wide, bore down on me from the outside—a block known as a "crack-back." The man hit me full-speed in the face and sent me into the air parallel to the ground. I can recall the stadium lights shining down into my face as I was momentarily suspended a few feet above the ground. Angered that someone had gotten the best of me, I placed my arms under me before hitting the ground and managed to bounce back up immediately, but was unable to assist on the play.

On our first offensive series of the second half, we were eaten alive by a rabid Coshocton team that must have been riding a wave of adrenaline from their halftime talk. First down was a 27 Counter that lost three yards. Scott Saad was crushed in the backfield for a 5-yard loss on a second-down Sprint-Draw. Third down was a pass deep down the right sideline that was badly overthrown. After Dale Backlund's punt, Coshocton had the ball at their 45-yard line. Our stingy defense forced another three-and-out with no yards gained for Coshocton.

Our next offensive series was not as bad as the preceding one. Kubik hit Simi for a 15-yard gain. Kubik then made two nice scrambles totaling 24 yards. We moved from our 25 to the Coshocton 34-yard line in 5 plays. The drive stalled, however, and the Redskins took over on downs.

Once again, Coshocton's offense could do nothing on the ground or through the air and they had to punt on the second play of the fourth quarter. After fielding the punt at our 35-yard line, Joe Simi spun away from two tacklers, got in behind the punt-return wall and motored to the Coshocton 22 where Arganbright finally stopped him.

We were now in the position to put the nail into the coffin of this close game if we could score. First down: a 27 Sweep gained 5 yards. Second down: a 23 Power was stuffed for no gain. On third down, Kubik dropped back to pass and finding no one open, took off down the middle and reached the 10-yard line. Incredibly, Kubik fumbled the football and Coshocton recovered.

Our defense, which had played infinitely better in this game than the previous week at Johnstown, gang-tackled, plugged the holes and held Coshocton to 7 yards on this latest series of downs. The Redskin punt was fair-caught at the Newark Catholic 45-yard line.

From the 45, an 11-play drive, which included an 18-yard pickup by Ronan on a Flood route and a key third-down conversion by Kubik's footwork, ended with a 25-yard field goal with 3:27 left in the game. Although it would have been nicer to get a touchdown, the drive had eaten much time off the clock and tightened the noose around Coshocton's neck.

Some problems occurred with the ensuing kickoff. Backlund's first kick went out of bounds on the left sideline and we had to re-kick after a 5-yard penalty was tacked on. The second kick had the same result. Finally, the third kick, which was short, was fielded at the Coshocton 45-yard line where the Redskins went to work for the last time.

On their last drive, Coshocton ran seven plays, six of which were passes. Although they did manage to get one first down, they moved only as far as our 41-yard line where the drive died on a fourth-down incompletion.

Behind the blocking of Scott Saad, Jeff Ronan was able to get us one more first down before Kubik fell on the ball to end the game. We had rained on Coshocton's Homecoming parade.

It had been a great defensive effort. Coshocton's total offensive output was only 112 yards.[5] Matt Haines, their top rusher, was held to 55 yards on 22 carries.[6] Coach Graham remarked after the game that "we had scouted them in all their games and their offense was unstoppable"[7] but "the defense really came through with the way the game started...We didn't think we could shut them down as effectively as we did."[8]

Coach Graham was not all praises, however. "We were sporadic on offense and struggled with the kicking game," he said, and "Our coaching staff doesn't feel we've played to our potential to date."[9] That made me wonder. What would we do to a team if we ever *did* play to our potential?

For some reason, we did not view the game film until the following Monday. I remember that we watched it after school in room 101, which was the old band room on the south end of the gymnasium. (Yes, Newark Catholic did have a marching band at one time!) I hoped that Coach Graham would not notice the play where I was sent into orbit, but the hope was wasted. When we reached the point in the game when I was destroyed, Coach Graham said, "Look out Evans." He replayed it repeatedly and muffled laughter could be heard from various locations within the darkened room. When the film was finally allowed to continue and it could be seen how quickly I was back on my feet, Coach Graham said, "I tell you what fellas. Look how fast he gets back up." After permitting *that* play to run a few times, Coach Graham said, "Billy Evans: Good job. That's a good job." I had been vindicated and was filled with pride. A compliment from J.D. Graham meant everything.

Newark Catholic	0	14	0	3	17
Coshocton	3	0	0	0	3

	NC	C
First Downs	11	5
Rushing	110	97
Passing Yards	95	15
Total yards	205	112
Att-Comp-Int	20-7-1	14-3-1
Punts / Avg	4-33	5-34
Kickoffs / Avg	4-39	2-44
Fumbles / lost	2-2	1-0
Penalties / yards	4-20	3-13

Week 5 LCL Action[10]

Johnstown	12	Licking Valley	26
Heath	7	Watkins Memorial	0
Northridge	10	Utica	32
Granville	0	Lakewood	0

Notes

1. "NC dodges loss to keep No. 1 spot," *The Advocate*, (Sep. 24. 1985), p. 11.

2. "Newark Catholic at Coshocton," *The Advocate*, (Sep. 26, 1985), p. 13.

3. *The Advocate*, (Sep. 26, 1985), p. 14.

4. Joe Evans, Electronic mail to author, Dec. 28, 2001.

5. Rick Cannizzaro, "Undefeated Green Wave frustrates Coshocton," *The Advocate*, (Sep. 28, 1985), p. 5.

6. Joe Wright, "Newark Catholic clips Coshocton," *The Times-Reporter*, (Sep. 28, 1985), p. B-5.

7. Ibid.

8. Rick Cannizzaro, "Undefeated Green Wave frustrates Coshocton," *The Advocate* (Sep. 28, 1985), p. 5.

9. Ibid.

10. *The Advocate*, (Sep. 28, 1985), p. 6.

Week 6

Heath Bulldogs

October 5

The big win over Coshocton had made us fat with computer points. We jumped from 18.5 to 32.5 points and that total topped all Division V schools.[1] We also managed to hang on to the No. 1 spot in the Associated Press poll for the third straight week.[2]

In my opinion, week 6 presented a true test of character and maturity for our team. We had just successfully completed a rough 3-week stretch of hard-hitting, emotionally draining games. Our next opponent, cross-town nemesis Heath Bulldogs, had an uncanny ability to pull upsets on Newark Catholic regardless of how poor of a team they had. As Coach Poth put it, "They always saved their best game for us."[3] (Recall that they were victorious on their last visit to White Field when Newark Catholic was the defending state champion in 1983.) Finally, our next opponent after Heath, the Licking Valley Panthers, shocked everyone by stomping Watkins Memorial 26-0 in week 5, which put them in a tie for first place in the LCL. That game would determine the LCL champion. Would we take Heath too lightly? Would we be flat? Would we be looking ahead to Licking Valley? It was a perfect formula for disaster and the reason I said that it would test our character. One of Coach Graham's favorite sayings that he always stressed was, "You win with character, not characters or charac-turds."

Coach Graham was well aware of this potential letdown and was not about to let us become lackadaisical. We heard the patented speeches about how "There ain't no give-me's in this sport!" and "Anybody can beat you once!" He made it a point to remind us that the only thing that ever mattered to Heath High School was beating Newark Catholic. The contents of their trophy case proved that. According to Coach Graham, all that Heath had on display were three dusty game balls from the three occasions they had beaten Newark Catholic:

-1970: a 22-16 victory, which was their first-ever over the Green Wave and ended a 36-game winning streak.

-1977: a 21-20 victory, Newark Catholic's first loss of a season opener since 1966, Coach Graham's one and only loss of a season opener and his first loss at White Field.

-1983: a 20-14 upset of the defending Division V State Champions, a game that ended a 15-game winning streak and forced Newark Catholic to share the LCL crown with Watkins Memorial. It was also Homecoming weekend and I watched from the sideline as a sophomore. It is interesting to note that all of these victories took place on Newark Catholic's home field.

For personnel, Heath started a "true freshman" at tailback named Jimmy Norman (5-5, 160). Despite his age, Norman was very tough, very fast, and a legitimate running threat that would test our defense of the run. The pass defense, it appeared, would also be challenged by Bulldog quarterback Rick Brown (6-1, 170). Having thrown for 1,100 yards in the '84 season, Heath coach Dave Daubenmire spoke boldly of Brown saying, "We think he is the best quarterback in the league."[4] If this was true, his numbers said otherwise as he had 594 passing yards after five games, which put him at third place in the LCL behind Andy Kubik who had 717 yards and Doug Orr of Utica who had 605 yards. [5]

Much has already been said in previous chapters about the relationship between Heath and Newark Catholic. Let me reiterate that there was no love lost between these two schools. On game night and as expected, the Bulldogs thought it necessary to encircle us again while clapping and chanting, "Kill Catholic!"

We had the ball first on our 31. A light rain fell, making for sloppy playing conditions. The first drive opened with a 24 Power and a 27 Sweep—which were both unsuccessful against a rowdy Bulldog defense. On third down, Ronan killed the middle linebacker on a 23 Power, allowing Scott Saad to slash for 8 yards and a first down at our 47. A 28 Counter was ruined by Simi's man who had penetrated too deeply, knocked me off course and caused a huge pileup in the backfield. A 30 Trap followed, which netted only 2 yards for Scott Saad. It was third down again and Coop committed the "cardinal sin of a lineman" in that while performing his trapping duties on a Flanker Trap Zero, he ran by one man to get to another. The man that Coop bypassed destroyed Billy Franks, thus ending our first drive and sending the Heath team into hysterics. After a Backlund punt, Heath began their first offensive series on their 30-yard line.

Heath must have believed they could throw the ball on us because that is what they came out doing. First down was a 9-yard completion. A quarterback sneak followed and gave the Bulldogs a first down. Heath's next three plays were an incompletion, a bad snap from center and a deep pass that fell incomplete. Heath punted and the ball rolled down to our 11-yard line.

After a 25 Iso, Saad gained 12 yards on a 30 Trap. A 23 Power and another 30 Trap followed for short gains. Facing third down, Kubik dropped back to throw but was heavily pressured and had to run. His scramble ended at our 33-yard line. Short of the first down, we had to punt again and it appeared that we could be in for another nail-biting dogfight of a game.

Heath started again from their 36 and still insisted on passing. The pass on first down fell incomplete. Here we go—second down and Jimmy Norman's first carry of the night, which was a sort of Isolation/Lead play. Franks was kicked out by the fullback and Olson was sealed. The guard led up through the hole to seal Todd South and Norman motored for 34 yards down to our 29-yard line where Darby Riley forced him out of bounds. John Jurden tried to tackle Norman at the 40 but merely bounced off the freshman's thighs. For such a young kid, Norman was very tough. Heath threw again on first down for an incompletion and then threw a deep ball that was beautifully defended by Joe Simi at the goal line. On third down, Todd South fought off blockers, strung Norman out and dropped the kid after a short gain. Heath decided to go for it on fourth-and-long. Brown rolled to his right and was crushed by Mike Trotter for a big loss: Newark Catholic's ball.

At about this point in the game, Scott Saad suffered an ankle injury and had to leave. Joe Bell, who was still not fully recovered from his Johnstown injury, came in for Saad on offense and sophomore Tim McKenna took over middle linebacker duties.

Our new series opened up with a 28 Sweep followed by a 27 Sweep. A motion penalty on third down set up a long-yardage situation. We were able to convert the third down via a pass to Jurden that took us to the Bulldog 46. A 30 Trap for no gain finished off the first quarter and we switched ends of the field as the rain continued to fall. John Jurden had another nice catch after the quarter change that took us down to the Heath 34. Flanker Trap Zero was the next call but once again, Coop ran by the man he should have trapped and Jurden was eaten alive. In addition to the botched play, a holding penalty was assessed and backed us up to our 42-yard line. An excellent sideline catch by Monte Byers moved us down to the Heath 27. That play was followed by a 30 Trap that picked up 4 yards. The next play was a 28 Counter. I pulled and got just enough of the outside linebacker to send Joe Bell on a speedy jaunt to the end zone for a 23-yard touchdown with 10:57 left in the first half. Backlund's extra point was good.

Heath resumed offensive play on their 30-yard stripe following the kick. A counter trap was shut down by South and Tim McKenna. A second-down pass fell incomplete and the Iso/Lead play that hurt us earlier was defended by Franks and yielded only 4 yards on third down. The Heath punt was fair-caught at the Newark Catholic 43-yard line.

A short run on first down was followed by a Kubik pass to Byers for a gain to the Heath 39. Following a 17 Quick Pitch, Kubik was sacked for the fifth time of the season for a 12-yard loss. Kubik, who dropped back to pass again, was soon under pressure. Just before he was whacked, he dumped the ball off to John Jurden in the right flat. John raced for 27 yards to the Heath 21.[6] What a great play for both Kubik and Jurden. The next four plays featured Joe Bell on a 30 Trap, 24 Power, 24 Power and a 30 Trap that moved us down to the Bulldog 6-yard line. After another 24 Power, Kubik found Bell wide-open on a Flood route and Joe went in to score from the 5. But wait—the play was called back for illegal motion because Coop was not in his stance—time out Newark Catholic! Coach Graham went straight to the official to find out why the penalty had been called. After his discussion with the "man in the striped shirt," Coach Graham came to the huddle. Pat Cooperrider recalls what occurred during that timeout. "The illegal procedure was my fault. Coach Graham called the timeout and said, 'Coop, get your fat f--king ass set!' The ref was standing close enough to hear him and he said, 'Hey Coach, take it easy on the kids. We don't need that kind of language.'"[7]

After being backed up 5 yards, Kubik scrambled to avoid a sack and hit Byers for a 10-yard touchdown toss. Incredibly, this score was also nullified by another illegal-motion penalty. An irate Coach Graham spent another timeout and *ran* to the official for an explanation. The problem apparently had something to do with our cadence and how the motion-man was sent in motion. (One man is permitted to go in motion parallel to the line of scrimmage before the ball is snapped). After coming onto the field, Coach Graham got down into a 3-point stance to show the ref how things ought to be. He then stormed into the huddle to berate John Jurden. Jurden's story did not jive with what the ref had seen and before it was all over with, Coach Graham had two officials standing in our huddle and he proceeded to conduct a mini-conference for them to explain the rules for sending a man in motion. My Dad always said Coach Graham knew the rules of the game better than most officials did.

Having been backed up another 5 yards, we didn't even get a play off before we were hit with another penalty for delay of game! I recall how embarrassed and frustrated I felt as this whole ordeal was a poor display of football. So now it was third-and-goal from the 20. The 15 yards of penalties did not faze our passing game in the least. Kubik threw a third touchdown pass to Joe Simi and this one finally held up. Backlund's kick was good and we led Heath 14-0 at the 3:11 mark in the second quarter.

Heath could do nothing on their next offensive series. On a second-down pitch play, I was able to get a good lick in on Norman. Heath ended up punting and we went on offense at our 41.

On first down Jurden, who had a great game, caught a deep pass from Kubik and went out of bounds at the Bulldog 37-yard line. After a pass to Byers that took us down to the 27, we went into our two-minute offensive mode. Without a huddle, a Flood Left to Bell went to the 10-yard line. The next play was a 30 Trap, which went for no gain. With the clock ticking away on us, "Clock! Clock!" was the call, which was a play intended only to stop the clock. Andy threw the ball out of bounds near Byers on the left sideline. There was enough time for one more play. The field goal team assembled for a 27-yard attempt but the kick was wide to the left. Six seconds remained and Heath fell on the ball to end the first half. The Bulldogs went to their doghouse trailing 14-0.

Heath nearly broke the second-half kickoff, which was somewhat reminiscent of the second-half kickoff in 1983 that was returned for a touchdown. This year fortunately, Tim McKenna shut it down at the Bulldog 38-yard line. They were quickly put out of business on this opening series as Norman was stuffed on first down, Calvert buried Brown in a broken play on second down and Olson made a big sack on third down. The Heath punt was fair-caught at our 30-yard line.

Our first play of the second half was a 27 Counter on which Jeff Ronan burst for a 12-yard gain. The next play was a 28 Counter to Bell that gained 6 yards. The play should have been called back because I left before the ball was snapped. I had gotten away with the mistake. Perhaps the officials chose to ignore this out of guilt for having placed three straight penalties on us in the second quarter. Then again, maybe they did not want another sermon from Coach Graham.

The following play found Joe Bell slipping and falling down on a proposed 23 Power, which left Kubik standing alone with the ball. Coach Graham had no tolerance for people slipping as Bell had just done. Sometimes during practices, when Coach Graham was on a tirade, he'd ask us, "Do you know what the number-one excuse in football is, fellas? It's 'I slipped coach,'" he'd say in a wimpy voice. "Do you know what the number-two excuse is? It's 'I didn't know. I didn't know.'" Coach Graham did not want to hear these or any other excuses coming from our mouths.

Because of Bell's slippage, Kubik had to eat the ball and take a sack. A third-down incompletion intended for Byers forced us to punt, placing Heath at their 22-yard line.

Heath's first-down call was a pass down the sideline to a wide-open man who had gotten behind Tommy Helms. Fortunately, quarterback Brown overthrew his man. Heath apparently thought they had missed an excellent opportunity and ran the same play again. This time, however, Helms picked the ball off and was able to return it 12 yards down the sideline to the Bulldog 21. Jimmy Norman made the tackle and delivered an absolutely crushing hit that upended Helms and knocked him out of bounds like a rag doll. I say again that Norman was one tough freshman. I remember this hit and thought Helms might have been hurt. But as he was also a "tough nut," Helms bounced right back up and trotted away as if it was no big deal. We were able to capitalize on the turnover two plays later as Kubik hit Simi for a 21-yard touchdown pass. Because of a penalty, the extra point had to be kicked twice but Backlund was perfect both times and we went up 21-0 with 7:04 left in the third quarter.

A penalty against Heath on the ensuing kickoff forced them to begin their next offensive series from their 9-yard line. On the second play of the series, Heath ran a reverse towards our left. Byers saw it coming and drove the kid into the end zone where Trotter helped finish him. From watching game films, this was clearly a safety and though it happened in plain view of an official, it was not awarded to us.

Instead, the ref spotted the ball as close to the goal line as possible without placing it in the end zone. A third-down run by Norman moved the ball out to the 2-yard line. On fourth down, the Heath punter had to stand at the very back of his end zone and he got off a great punt (for us) that went straight up into the lights and traveled all of 7 yards—Green Wave ball at the Bulldog 9.

Tim Mckenna, who began seeing action at tailback in the second half, muscled his way down to the 6 on a 30 Trap. A pass to Simi on second down fell incomplete. On third down, Ronan and McKenna executed counter play action, Jeff continued through the line to the left and Kubik hit him for a 6-yard touchdown pass with 4:09 left in the third quarter. The extra point was good and the score increased to 28-0. After 3 weeks of tough games, it was nice to have a comfortable lead for a change.

Heath's next offensive series was another embarrassment for them as South ate Norman's lunch on a draw play. Mike Trotter ruined a reverse, resulting in negative yardage. The Heath punt was not fielded and rolled to the Newark Catholic 30.

Our next offensive series was probably a moral victory for the 'Dogs. A first-down 30 Trap was stuffed. Kubik danced too long in the pocket and was sacked on second down. A pass to a wide-open Joe Simi was overthrown and we had to punt.

Heath again went three-and-out and we were back on offense at our 30-yard stripe just seconds into the fourth quarter. At this time, with the Clean Green starting to appear in the game, Heath was able to prevent us from getting a first down and the Bulldogs got a new set of downs at their 40.

On Heath's very next play, quarterback Brown rolled out to his left under heavy pressure from Billy Franks and launched a pass. Tommy Helms made his second interception of the game and was tackled at our 46-yard line. From here, a Jeremy Montgomery pass intended for Byers was tipped by a defender. Monte still hauled it in and made a nice run down to the Heath 24. Jeff Ronan had more shining moments on the remainder of this drive as he converted a third-and-five by breaking tackles on an 18 Quick Pitch, setting us up with first-and-goal at the Bulldog 9-yard line. The Heath defense was tough down here as they stopped us for three plays. On fourth-and-goal, Ronan made a nice cut inside on another 18 Quick Pitch and barreled in for our fifth touchdown of the evening. Wimberly "Boo" Cook received the opportunity to kick the extra point and nailed it to make the score 35-0 with 4:51 left in the game.

On the last kickoff, Curt Powell of the Bulldogs had to cover the loose football. While doing so, he was smeared into the ground by Darby Riley and Billy Franks and got up in pain. With the first-team defense still in the game, it was apparent that Coach Graham in no way wanted to risk giving up even one score to these people. Heath's next two plays were Norman-left followed by Norman-right in which Todd South belted the freshman and forced him to leave the game. As it turned out, Norman would not have much longer to play because the third-down snap sailed past Cook and Billy Franks covered the ball at the Bulldog 17.

On our last possession of the game, an offensive unit composed entirely of Clean Green began marching toward the end zone. With Jeff Poulton leading the way, Tommy Parker carried the ball 8 times, including 23 Power 5 times in a row. They could move only as far as the 3-yard line before time expired. It would have been nice to punch in another one against the Bulldogs.

The game was a solid performance for us on both sides of the ball. Offensively, we out-gained the 'Dogs 355-32 in total yardage. Defensively, Heath was held to minus 29 yards in the second half and the dangerous Jimmy Norman had been held to 43 yards in 12 carries.[8]

We had successfully avoided a letdown and a potential upset and were amazed to find ourselves 6-0. We were also fortunate to have somewhat of an easy game, which provided us the opportunity to tune-up and rest some of the guys who were bumped up. We had a bear of a game in the coming week and we needed everyone healthy.

| Heath | 0 | 0 | 0 | 0 | 0 |
| Newark Catholic | 0 | 14 | 14 | 7 | 35 |

	NC	H
First Downs	15	2
Rushing	137	18
Passing Yards	218	14
Total yards	355	32
Att-Comp-Int	18-12-0	15-3-2
Punts / Avg	5-30	7-30
Kickoffs / Avg	6-39	1-48
Fumbles / lost	0-0	2-1
Penalties / yards	5-30	4-26

Week 6 LCL Action[9]

Licking Valley	19	Northridge	34
Lexington	0	Lakewood	13
Watkins Memorial	41	Johnstown	41
Utica	3	Granville	14

Notes

1. *The Advocate*, (Oct. 3, 1985), p. 16.

2. *The Advocate*, (Oct. 1, 1985), p. 11.

3. Wes Poth, Conversation with author, Jan. 30, 2002.

4. Mark Shaw, "Heath boss expresses confidence in QB," *The Advocate, Football '85*, (Aug. 28, 1985), p. 9.

5. *The Advocate*, (Oct. 3, 1985), p. 16.

6. Sean McClelland, "Green Wave blanks Heath; Valley awaits," *The Advocate* (Oct. 6, 1985), p.1C.

7. Pat Cooperrider, Telephone conversation with author, Dec. 11, 2001.

8. Sean McClelland, "Green Wave blanks Heath; Valley awaits," *The Advocate* (Oct. 6, 1985), p. 1C.

9. *The Advocate*, (Oct. 5, 1985), p. 6.

In the five remaining seasons of the LCL after 1985, Newark Catholic beat Heath each year but 1989. In 1990, the teams met in week 9 on Heath's home field. Heath was unbeaten, while NC was 5-3 and struggling for a playoff berth. The Green Wave prevailed 24-23 in the classic battle and the victory propelled Newark Catholic into the playoffs. The series closed with the Green Wave holding a 15-3 advantage in the LCL.

Week 7

Licking Valley Panthers

October 11

Newark Catholic versus Licking Valley. For years, this contest had been an intense and bitter rivalry that could usually be counted on to produce legendary games. Consider 1973, Newark Catholic's first year in the Licking County League. It was the last game of the season and had been long anticipated. Both teams came into the contest undefeated. Valley entered the game as the defending LCL champion with a 9-0 record and had shutout 9 of their last 10 opponents. Newark Catholic came into the contest at 8-0 and had won 66 of its last 71 games.[1] The Green Wave prevailed 34-21 that night to wrap up a perfect regular season and secured the school's first LCL football crown. This after public opinion declared that once Newark Catholic entered the Licking County League, they would find out what "real football" was really like. Growing up, I had heard stories for years afterward about this game: the size of the crowd, how cars were parked from the high school all the way down Licking Valley Road to State Route 16, how cold it was and about all the money that changed hands that night. In fact, according to legend, it was a good thing Newark Catholic had won the game. Otherwise, those Green Wave faithful who had bet their houses would have had to find other places to live! By the time week 7 of the 1985 football season rolled around, this Newark Catholic-Licking Valley standoff promised to be another classic battle of epic proportions.

Recall that after defeating Watkins Memorial in week 3, it seemed that the Green Wave was in the driver's seat for the Licking County League championship. That logic and the entire LCL landscape was turned upside down as the Licking

Valley Panthers shocked Licking County by handily trouncing Watkins Memorial 26-0 in week 5 of the season. With our victory over Heath, we were 4-0 in the League and tied for first place with the Panthers—a tie that would be broken on Friday Night, October the eleventh. I do not make the claim that this game was on the same scale as the '73 contest—only that it was another "big one" with some similarities: Both contests took place after Newark Catholic had played Heath; both games were played at Licking Valley; both teams were unbeaten in the LCL and played for the League crown.

Since the Valley game was another Friday night contest, it meant another short week of practice for us. Coach Graham started going over the Panther personnel on Sunday afternoon, the day after the Heath game when our running had been completed. We would face an incredible group of Valley kids. Coach Graham said it was "...the best Licking Valley team I've ever seen."[2] Offensively, the team star was perhaps the tailback Craig Black (5-10, 165), who came into week 7 as Licking County's leading rusher with 864 yards on 131 carries—an average of 6.6 yards per attempt.[3] The key to Black's success was the offensive line he had in front of him. Panther coach Randy Baughman said it was the biggest line he had in his four years at Licking Valley.[4] From left to right, the line consisted of Tim Journey (6-2, 180), Pat Ourant (6-0, 185), Todd Gienger (6-1, 225), Charlie Cody (6-1, 190), Mark "Mooch" McNabb (6-1, 240) and tight end Brian Strausbaugh (6-1, 200). Two of these linemen had won wrestling accolades in the previous year. Cody had won the LCL title in the 175-pound class and McNabb won the district championship in the heavyweight division.[5] Other offensive players were quarterback Steve Chacey (5-10, 165), fullback Rex Redman (6-1, 190) and flanker Scott Sensibaugh (6-1, 175). Oddly enough, Chacey, Redman and Sensibaugh were also sheep farmers like me and I knew them from the 4-H club that we had been members of some years ago.

Most of these same players made up Valley's defensive unit. On the front line, Cody and McNabb were joined by tackle Shawn McClellan (5-8, 215) and Robert Armentrout (5-10, 215) at the left defensive end position. Redman and Sensibaugh made up the middle line-backing corps while Strausbaugh, Chacey and Black were joined in the defensive secondary by Corby Butler (5-11, 160) and Wes Miller (5-11, 160). My work was cut out for me, as I would be knocking heads with McNabb on both sides of the ball.

Licking Valley, a Division III school east of Newark in the town of Hanover, had made tremendous improvements since the 1984 season where they finished with a record of 5-5,[6] which included a 48-0 loss to the Green Wave. In 1985, after losing their first game to Tri Valley, Licking Valley had won five straight that included not only the big win over Watkins, but also an impressive 19-0 victory over the Lexington Minutemen on October 4. Lexington, who went into Hanover ranked 12th in the state in Division II, were out-gained 411-119 in total offense as Craig Black ran wild 35 times for 293 yards and 3 touchdowns.[7] This was solid proof that Licking Valley was no fluke and would be perhaps our toughest game of the year.

Our school week leading up to the Valley game was unusual in that there were no classes on Thursday or Friday because of parent-teacher conferences. On Thursday morning, we had an extra-long walkthrough practice in the morning hours. As usual, Coach Graham had been pumping us up with stories. He then described for us the scene at Licking Valley High School. Apparently, one person from our community had gone there to either drop off game films or to pick up some tickets and said it was a madhouse: pep rallies everyday, parades, a stuffed replica of Coach Graham with a noose around his neck hanging by the front doors of the school. Stories were alleged throughout the week that some of the Valley players had called some of our players to say that they would break our legs. Other claims were made that dead fish had been sent through the mail. "What the hell do you seniors think about all of that?" Graham said as he called us all by name. "You people need to understand that this is the biggest game of these kids' lives and you're going into that atmosphere tomorrow. Yeah, they're good fellas, but we'll show up. And knock on wood," he'd say while tapping on someone's helmet, "they've never beaten us yet." I hated when he said that.

An article appearing in the local paper the night before the game helped to fuel the hype. Valley sought to gain respect by finally beating Newark Catholic and their chances had never been better. Valley had their best team in years, had just pounded two Division II teams and all of their players were healthy. We, on the other hand, had struggled in tough games in the recent weeks and were beaten up. Coach Graham acknowledged this by saying, "We're not in good playing shape. We have two or three that are questionable."[8] Additionally, even though we were the defending state champions, Coach Baughman said most of us "were involved but from the sideline"[9] last year. Therefore, we supposedly had no advantage in big-game experience and our tradition would not be a factor. With all of this information, what else could the public conclude? The Greenies would get theirs Friday night.

On Thursday night, I went out with my regular crowd to do the usual night-before-the-game activity at Burger King on 21st Street. Now, we had a little game that we played while going through the food line and that was to see if any of us received an order number that coincided with our football number. I never had won before, but on the night before the Valley game, my order number was 67! I took that as a good omen that we were going to win this football game and that ticket resides in my scrapbook to this very day. A bacon double cheeseburger, large order of fries and a Pepsi, all for the low, low price of $3.21 was my meal that night.

On Friday morning, a team breakfast was held in the basement of Frisch's Big Boy Restaurant on Route 79 in Heath. Team breakfasts were held on the mornings of big games to further team unity and togetherness and to provide fellowship for all involved. It was our second team breakfast of the year—the first one having taken place on the morning of the Watkins Memorial game. On the way home from the meal, I stopped into Linden's Sporting Goods to follow through with a major personal decision that I had made. That decision was to say goodbye to the goliath arm pads that I had worn ever since I was a sophomore. My mom found these arm pads, which extended from the knuckles clear past the elbow, on a road trip in 1983. Since that time, they had become smelly, hard and brittle. They were also heavy to wear. For their replacement, I settled on two green hand pads that simply covered the hands and fingers. Looking back now, I wondered how I ever let myself do this. As I was somewhat superstitious, a move such as changing one's arm pads midstream through the season should have been unthinkable. Perhaps I thought I had an out with my Burger King meal ticket from the previous night!

Game day. We rolled east down Route 16 toward the showdown. The Licking Valley community had the welcome mat rolled out for us as the roadsides going up the hill to the high school were lined with signs saying *Kill Catholic* and *Flush the Wave*, etc. I was seated on the left side of the bus and when we turned into the parking lot and headed past the school building, some little twerp, who had obviously been waiting for us, had *F--k Catholic* on his shirt and he played the funeral dirge on a trumpet. I nodded and appreciated the additional motivation.

We heard more of the same crap as we walked the field upon arrival. People were already seated in the home stands and yelled all sorts of obscenities at us. I was shocked when I heard my very named called out: "Hey Evans, McNabb is going to break your legs!" We took it all in stride. Oh, it was infuriating, but as in any game, we were under strict orders from Coach Graham not to respond to any of it. "Kill 'em with kindness," Coach Graham always said. It was a good lesson in humility and restraint.

On Joe Bell's home video, Coach Graham can be seen before the game walking around with Scott Saad discussing whether Scott could go on his ankle that had been injured in the Heath game. Tim McKenna recalled the situation because it affected him in a big way. There had been no indication that Scott could not play, but "when we were in the locker room just before the game," Tim said, "Graham went through the starting line up and said, 'Mac, you're starting.' That's when I found out I was starting. It was a baptism by fire."[10] I could not imagine making my first varsity start both as a sophomore and in a game of this magnitude. I don't know how Tim did it.

It was time to for this much-hyped showdown to begin. As we stood on the field, a vast sea of people that numbered over 4,000[11] stood four and five-deep outside of the fence as Licking Valley stormed onto the field before their frenzied fans. The big games we had played in prior weeks—Watkins, Johnstown and Coshocton—all paled in comparison to the atmosphere and magnitude of this night. Win or lose, it would be a game to remember.

Receiving the opening kick at the 13, John Jurden returned it out to the 30-yard line. We were dealt a serious blow right away as Mike Trotter went down with a knee injury. Mike recalled what happened on the play:

Tom Parker bounced off the big guy that kicked for them (McNabb) and went right into my left knee. The collision tore the medial-collateral ligament. It didn't hurt, but I couldn't move my leg and I knew something was wrong. I was so angry and I missed the next three games because of it.[12]

As Mike was an anchor of our defensive line, his absence would seriously reduce our ability to stop the run. Two starters were now out on defense: Trotter and Saad. Kevin Donnelly took Trotter's place at defensive tackle.

Our first play from scrimmage was a 26 Iso for 1 yard with an unusual arrangement of Coop playing guard and Donnelly at the tackle. Second down was an incomplete pass. On third down, with Donnelly at the tackle again, the call was Flanker Trap Zero. The hole was there, but Jim Olson did not get a seal on Sensibaugh. He made the stop and engaged in some unnecessary jerking of Jurden's legs after the play. The punt was fielded at the Licking Valley 29 and returned to their 45.

Licking Valley gained 6 yards with two running plays on first and second downs. Following an incomplete pass on third down, the Panthers punted and we had the ball again at our 33.

A pass to Byers was incomplete on first down. The same call on second down gained 15 yards. Monte picked up another 16 yards on a hook pattern that got us down to the Licking Valley 37. On the next play, our line made a nice hole on Zero Trap but Jeff Ronan had the ball knocked loose by Armentrout. The first turnover of the night went to Valley at their 30.

By this time, I had hit Mark McNabb enough times to know what it would be like for me to deal with him all night. He was so strong that I was not even going to attempt going toe to toe with him while pass blocking. My approach was to get one or two bumps in on him and then throw at his legs.

On Valley's next offensive series, a key completion on third-and-eight gave the Panthers a first down at their 40-yard line. The next play was an Iso to my side in which both Monte and I fell down and Black went wide to pick up 6 yards. After a short gain on second down, Licking Valley's Chacey dropped back to pass but was pressured and decided to run. The ball popped loose when Tom Helms hit Chacey. An alert Charlie Cody fell on it at the Green Wave 46. Things appeared to be bouncing in favor of the Panthers, but we caught a break on the next play. A Panther completion to our 27 was nullified by a blocking-below-the-waste penalty that pushed Licking Valley way back to their 40 where it became "first down and a country mile." Valley then ran a wild Power/Lead play where the backside guard (Cody), the fullback (Redman) and the quarterback (Chacey) all lead Craig Black up through their left line. Franks was kicked out, Olson was sealed, South over-pursued and Black gained 8 yards before he was tackled by Darby Riley and me. After an incomplete pass on second down, third down consisted of a fake draw to Redman and a screen pass to Black in Valley's left flat. South was all over it and dropped Black for a three-yard loss. The Cody punt was fielded at the 24 where we began our third offensive set.

We finally got a good drive going on this new possession. First down, Bell ran for 7 yards on 27 Sweep. Second down, a 13-yard pass to Simi moved us out to the 44. Another Kubik pass to Simi was good for 13 yards. Then Ronan blasted for 13 yards and 5 yards on two straight Zero Traps, moving us down to the Panther 25. After an incomplete pass on second down, Bell picked up 9 tough yards on a 27 Sweep as time expired in the first quarter. On the first play of quarter two, Kubik changed the play at the line of scrimmage, dropped back to pass and finding no one open, he tucked the ball and ran to the Licking Valley 5-yard line. He was belted by Craig Black and lost the ball but John Jurden was there to cover it. On first-and-goal from the 5, every Panther had been sealed on a 26 Iso and Bell had a clear lane into the end zone had he stayed to the outside. Instead, he cut up inside the tight end and gained only 2 yards. Second and goal from the 3, a pass to Jurden in the end zone was incomplete. On third down, Bell carried on a 27 Sweep, cut up into the line and was seriously drilled by linebacker Rex Redman who put his helmet squarely into Bell's right thigh. At the spot of the tackle, Joe remained kneeling for quite some time and came up limping, much to the delight of the home crowd. He made it to the huddle just in time to hear the fourth-down play call, which was a pass intended for Byers. The pass ended up being intercepted in the end zone by Steve Chacey and the Valley fans went nuts.

It had been a humbling and humiliating end to a great drive and a devastating blow to our team. Not only had we lost a prime scoring opportunity, but we also lost Joe Bell for the night as he suffered a deep thigh bruise from the hit by Redman. "It was such a deep bruise," Bell said, "that I thought I broke my femur."[13]

We were taking a beating and losing people—Mike Trotter in the first quarter, Joe Bell in the second. With Scott Saad not playing at all, we were now short three of our starters. Who would be the next Greenie to go down? We could not afford any more personnel losses!

After the interception, Licking Valley's Black carried twice for a total of 4 yards. A third-down pass was beautifully defended as Simi knocked the ball away. The Panthers punted and the ball rolled dead to our 24-yard line where we began our fourth offensive series.

First down, a deep pass fell incomplete. Second down, I had the honors on Zero Trap. With the help of Pat Cooperrider's crushing block on Scott Sensibaugh, Jeff Ronan blasted for 12 yards.

As an interesting side note, Jeff wanted to win this game more than any other contest. The ferocity of his rushing and blocking was indicative of that. It all stemmed from the fact that he lived out in the Valley area and there was abundant motivational material for him to dwell on. "Every morning on my way to school during Valley week," recalled Ronan, "I drove past the little restaurant in Hanover and there was a sign out front that said, 'Come to the Valley victory party.' It is wrong for people to make bold claims like that. Graham taught us not to be that way. I just remember thinking, 'I hope we kick the shit out of these people.' I focused on that all week."[14]

On the new set of downs, John Jurden, who assumed tailback duties in Joe Bell's absence, caught a Flood Left on first down. The defender Chacey fell down and John picked up an additional 15 yards after the catch to the Licking Valley 47-yard line. The next play had Donnelly at strong-side tackle again for a Flanker Trap Zero. Jurden gained 6 yards on the play. (Licking Valley should have noticed the fact that Flanker Trap only occurred when Donnelly moved to tackle.) Two plays later, Ronan picked up the first down on a 14 Dive. On first down, Valley strung out a 28 Sweep that resulted in a 2-yard loss for Jurden. Second down, Kubik dropped back to pass but was immediately pressured by Charlie Cody who came through the line unblocked. Showing great athleticism, Kubik scrambled to his left, stopped, backpedaled and dumped the ball off to Byers at the Valley 41. In fighting for extra yardage, Monte got away from two Panthers but McNabb moved in and knocked the ball loose. It resulted in our third turnover of the first half!

On Valley's new possession, a 4-yard run by Black and two incomplete passes left the Panthers with fourth down at their 45-yard line. The resulting punt by Cody was not fielded and rolled dead at the Green Wave 15 with just over four minutes left in the first half.

First down, a Zero Trap with me again was stuffed by Redman who rotated to defensive tackle occasionally throughout the game. Redman attacked me, which was the proper way to defend the trap and Ronan gained only one yard. On second down, Kubik hit Byers with a short completion at the 25. With an outstanding effort, Monte twisted away from three Panthers at the 28 and raced out to the Newark Catholic 47-yard line. Another pass was called on the next play. Finding no one to throw to, Kubik had to take off again and made a nice run to the Licking Valley 35. With a fresh set of downs, we had a chance to finally score before halftime. First down, Ronan ran for 4 yards on Zero Trap. Second down, a pass to Byers was complete to the Valley 21 and we had another first down. Kubik threw an incomplete pass on the next play that was followed by a 5-yard connection to Billy Franks. A deep third-down pass was broken up and nearly intercepted by Black and we faced fourth-and-five from the Valley 16-yard line with 1:15 remaining in the half. Coach Graham elected to kick a field goal, but Backlund's 32-yard attempt was wide left. Once again, we came away empty-handed after a decent drive.

With 1:09 left in the half, Licking Valley got the ball on the 20-yard line and broke one on us. The play was a counter trap and occurred against our single-linebacker set. South bit on the dive fake, Donnelly got buried down into the center, I got my "ass knocked off" by the trap block and Black ripped us out to the 47-yard line where Jurden stopped him. A very generous official spotted the ball at the 50-yard stripe. Licking Valley did nothing else as Black had no gain on a first-down pitch and passes on second and third downs were incomplete. On fourth-and-ten from the 50 with 4 seconds left, Licking Valley punted and the ball rolled into the end zone. The first half ended in a stalemate.

The opening kickoff of the second half was a short hopper from Backlund and was returned to the Panther 40. Valley ran an Iso on first down and South absolutely rocked Craig Black for no gain. In an effort to shore up the left side of our defense that lacked two starters, Scott Saad checked into the game at his linebacker position. Saad, however, was still gimpy on the ankle and should not have been in there. Valley caught on to this and sought to exploit the weakness as they began to pound our left side. On second down, Redman gained 4 yards on a dive play. A third-down pitch to Black came my way. As Monte and I both flew out to contain, Redman kicked me out and Black picked up 10 yards to our 47. The same play happened again and added another 5 yards to Craig Black's total as he pushed to the Newark Catholic 42. On the next play, I was completely destroyed again on a trap play and Black ran for 10 more—timeout Newark Catholic!

Coach Graham's timeout did not help us. After a middle trap to Redman and an Iso to Black that had gained a total of 4 yards combined, I was destroyed again by a trap play that gave the tailback 8 more yards. *Dammit!* I thought. *I'm going to die during films tomorrow!* I can recall the frustration, the feeling of helplessness as Licking Valley blew us off the line and methodically stuffed the ball right down our throats. It was definitely a new and unpleasant experience for our defense. Mike Trotter was sorely missed and a left defensive end was needed too!

Licking Valley had a fresh set of downs at our 18-yard line. First down, Black pushed up the middle for 3 yards. On second down, an Iso came to my side. I had a chance to drop Black at the 17 but I fell down. Black made it to the 13. Third down, an Iso toward Billy Franks yielded 3 yards to the 10-yard line. This was a big stop because it set up a pivotal fourth-down play that helped to keep us in the game. On fourth-and-two from the 10, two yards was a sure thing for the Panthers based on how they pounded us during this entire drive. I doubted our chances of stopping them. We lined up and Valley attempted to draw us offside with a long count. We caught a huge break when Pat Ourant, Valley's left guard, fired out early. The illegal procedure on Valley resulted in a fourth-and-seven from the 15! Valley brought in their field goal team and Chris Chacey's 33-yard attempt was good with 6:04 left in the third quarter.[15] Licking Valley had used half of the third quarter on that drive alone!

Monte Byers fielded the Panther kickoff at the 7 and returned it to the 33-yard line. It was time to answer Valley's score. The question was, could we? John Jurden carried twice for 9 yards and Ronan picked up the first down with a 7-yard run on 14 Dive. Two incomplete passes followed. On third down, McNabb blasted past Donnelly and looked to have a sack on Andy Kubik. Kubik, who was able to shake McNabb off, directed a pass to Simi but Steve Chacey stepped in front to make a juggling interception at his 45-yard line. Chacey ran to the Newark Catholic 36 where Dale Backlund drug him down. Things did not look so good for the Greenies.

160

Author with a portion of the fine coaching staff of the YMCA Jets after the championship game, autumn 1980. Coaches from left to right are Bill Giles, Joe Evans, and Joe Tanner. Because of the many ties the coaches had to Newark Catholic, playing for the YMCA Jets was essentially the same as playing for the Green Wave.

My Newark Catholic football career officially began in 1981 when I was in the eighth grade. At 145 pounds, wasn't I simply the portrait of ferocity?

Dear *Bill,*

I hope that your summer is going well so far. The reason I am writing is to personally invite you out for the 1985 Newark Catholic varsity football team. As you all know we are the defending "State Champs" and everyone will be gunning for us.

The weight room is open from 10:00 a.m. to 12:00 noon and 6:00 p.m. to 8:00 p.m., Monday thru Friday. There is really no excuse for anyone not being able to workout......"The way to Ohio Stadium" is through the weight room.

We will start mandatory conditioning Wednesday, July 17 at 6:00 p.m. We will condition Monday thru Friday at this time. If for some reason you cannot make the evening workout you are expected to workout at 10:00 a.m. here at the high school.

At this time the physicals are set for July 18 at 5:00 p.m. for the varsity football team. You must be here on the 18th or you will have to pay for your own physical. If you have a game get here as soon as you can. There will be no make up date for the physicals.

On August 5 at 5:00 p.m., we have a salesman from Linden Sports coming to fit our helmets.....please remember that date.

Hey gang, alot of people think this is the year the Greenies are going to get their lunch. Well, we'll see won't we? Don't wait for July 17th to get ready. Run, Run and Run...okay? Get ready because if we are ready you guys know what will happen.

You people have a great opportunity to participate in one of the finest football programs in the state. With that opportunity goes the responsibility of hard work. If you want it you have to earn it. Get yourself ready now, don't wait for July 17th. One last thing, you had better be in shape by the 17th because we have alot of work to do. "You are the defending State Champs" if you want it keep it!

Yours in Sports,

J. D. Graham

J. D. Graham

P.S. If the date for the physicals changes it will be announced in The Advocate and on Cable 5.
P.S.S. If for some reason you cannot make a workout call me at home (323-   ) around 10:00 a.m.

By the way, I'm not going to Massillon next year, so you guys will have to put up with me for another year.

Bill, get yourself ready!

Coach Graham's letter inviting us out for football, which was dated June 28, 1985. His personal note to me: "Bill, Get yourself ready!"

THE 1985 NEWARK CATHOLIC GREEN WAVE

Left to Right:

Row 1: Albert Ghiloni, Mike Trotter, Joe Simi, Tony Johns, John Jurden, Andy Kubik, Monte Byers, Joe Bell, Jeff Ronan, Todd South, Bill Evans, Kevin Donnelly.

Row 2: Rob Settlemoir, Joe Wiley, Dale Backlund, Steve Sigrist, Jim Calvert, Pat Cooperrider, Jim Olson, Tom Ogilbee, Jeremy Montgomery, Tom Helms, Darby Riley.

Row 3: Craig Cupples, Bill Franks, Kirk Lindsey, Jim Cross, Wimberly Cook, Jeff Paul, Jeff Wade, Rich Walther, Jeff Poulton, Tom Parker.

Row 4: Damon Schumaker, Matt Dase, Chip Elam, Bill Sikora, Bill Keaser, Matt Gilmore, Joe Flynn, Jerry Oder, Hans Schell, Jim Winters.

Row 5: Coach J.D. Graham, Coach Wes Poth, Coach John Stare, Scott Rogers, Mike Heckman, John Price, Scott Saad, Tim McKenna, Coach Paul Cost, Coach Dave Gebhart, Manager Tom LeFever. (Photo courtesy of J & B Studio)

The 1985 Newark Catholic Homecoming Court. Pictured From left to right are: Gail Braunbeck, Monte Byers, Billie-Jean Fiore, Joe Simi, mascot (unknown occupant), Kevin Donnelly, King Jim Neumeyer, Queen Nancy Nash, Teresa Bayerl, Julie Fleming, Joe Bell, Barb Murphy, Tony Johns, Mary Angela Reed, Andy Kubik. (Photo courtesy of Joe Simi)

The interior of the offensive line on Parents Night, November 2, 1985. From left to right are Kevin Donnelly, Tony Johns, and me. Note the black armband on Tony's right wrist, which was worn in remembrance of his father.

Author standing with his proud parents on Parents Night, November 2, 1985. (Photo courtesy of J & B Studio)

Pat "Coop" Cooperrider (left) standing with author after the Lakewood game. Note the blood between Coop's eyes. This common injury occurred when the helmet rotated forward and split the skin.

During the week of our first playoff game, Channel 5 came to Newark Catholic to interview the autumn sports teams. After this program aired, Jeff Ronan (pictured) received a lot of flak—most of it in fun—for his Army T-shirt that read: *Kill 'EM ALL, LET GOD SORT 'EM OUT*, because it wasn't the type of shirt that a Catholic schoolboy should be wearing—especially for a TV program that would be seen by the public. (Adelphia Channel 5 broadcast)

The Green Wave offense preparing to run a play during the Region 19 Championship at Cooper Stadium. Garrett Trent, Paint Valley's first-team all-district linebacker, is number 52 at the far right. (Photo courtesy of Dan Bell)

An original *Thrash Mogadore* sign from 1983. After being kept in my wallet for two years, it was "resurrected" for the 1985 contest.

Joe Bell had a career-high 215 yards rushing in the state semifinal against Mogadore. Here, Bell attempts to turn the corner while Chris Yoho (44) and Richard Pierce (13) give pursuit. The formidable Jamie Popa is visible at the far left. (Photo courtesy of Dan Bell)

Joe Simi catches a pass in front of Mogadore defender Chris Yoho. Simi had a "career night" with 7 receptions for 134 yards and two touchdowns. He also threw two touchdown passes and had two interceptions on defense. (Photo courtesy of Dan Bell)

My white game jersey: last worn against Mogadore and unwashed to this very day despite my wife's threatening to sneak it into the laundry basket.

Downing an egg at the state-game pep rally as Andy Kubik
awaits his turn. (Joe Bell home video)

Coach Graham gets the crowd going during the state-game pep rally,
November 27, 1985. (Joe Bell home video)

Leaving the house for the team breakfast on the morning of the state game. The tree behind me is where I did inverted situps during the summer. Note the toilet paper in the tree and the turf shoes. The game face was already on.

Before the state game, the team paid tribute to the Newark Catholic community and then knelt for a prayer. (Photo courtesy of the Calvert family)

The greatest play of my football career: Blocking the field goal against Delphos Jefferson. The arrow points to me, and the ball is visible to the right of the holder. (Joe Bell home video)

Andy Kubik (14) hands off to Joe Bell (22) on a 25 Isolation during the second quarter of the state game. Monte Byers (25) blocks down while Scott Saad lead-blocks on a collision course with Delphos defender Joe Gorman (43). (Photo courtesy of the Calvert family)

Captain Kubik and Captain Evans at the second-half captain's meeting. "Hands on hips!" (Photo by Timothy Black)

This picture shows the size of Matt Closson and was taken as we were turning toward our respective benches. (Photo by Timothy Black)

Mike Trotter breaks through the line and looks to put a hit on Delphos tailback Jay DeWitt (34). Delphos quarterback Scot Boggs (9) stands at the far right. (Photo courtesy of the Calvert family)

Andy Kubik falls on the football and is protected by Joe Bell during the closing moments of the state game. Jeff Ronan (35) participated in these final plays and it was meaningful to have him in there. (Photo courtesy of John Ronan)

Coach Graham addresses the team after the state game. As he had done in 1984, he praised the seniors and challenged the younger kids to keep the cycle going. The scoreboard in back reads, *1985 Division V Champions Newark Catholic High School.* (Photo by Timothy Black. Used with permission)

The faithful cheerleading squad at the state game. From left to right are Deanne Crowley, Katie Shay, Kris Campolo, Denise Deibert, Mary Angela Reed, and Kelly Cummings. (Photo courtesy of Mary Angela Reed)

State Champions. Note the Green Wave logo on the giant scoreboard in the background. (Photo by Timothy Black. Used with permission)

Three friends who "grew up green," pictured at the Knights of Columbus hall after the state game. Standing with me are Jeff Ronan (left) whom I had known since the third grade, and Pat Cooperrider (center) whom I had known since kindergarten. Note my Twisted Sister T-shirt. (I still have it.)

Author listening to Coach Poth (left) and Coach Cost review the state-game statistics at the post-game celebration. Note Coach Cost's "Fun Bunch" hat.

The object of our toil: The 1985 Division V State Championship trophy.

Tim McKenna had come back in for Scott Saad at linebacker and pounded Craig Black after a 3-yard pickup. Second down, Black powered up the middle to our 24. On a third-down pitch to Black to our left, Byers penetrated and had a chance to drop Black for a 3-yard loss but fell down. Jurden also missed a tackle at the 27. Black made it down to our 20 where McKenna plastered him out of bounds with a head-snapping hit. Black, who was either exhausted or shaken-up from the lick Mac had just put on him, left the game for two plays and was replaced by Wes Miller.

On the next play for the Panthers, the call was an Iso to my side. Byers had a clean shot at Miller and dropped him 3 yards behind the line. On film, it appears that the backside guard should have pulled for a trap block but failed to do so, explaining why Monte was unblocked. On the next play, however, I was pancaked by McNabb, Byers was kicked out, Redman blocked McKenna and Miller ran for 7 yards. On third down, Valley snuck a pass in against us to Scott Sensibaugh complete at the 9-yard line to give the Panthers first-and-goal. The situation appeared bleaker for us with each passing minute. Black got the call on first-and-goal with a pitch to our left. Byers and McKenna closed quickly and dropped Black for a short loss as time expired in the third quarter.

We changed ends of the field for the final quarter. We badly needed a defensive stand or we would fall too far behind. On second-and-goal from the 10, Black bulled down to the 5-yard line on a power play. Third down was another pivotal play that would influence the outcome of this game. Using another long count, Valley tried again to pull us offside, but even with all of the pressure, we kept our heads about us and did not jump. Instead, Valley's left guard jumped a second time in a crucial situation, pushing the Panthers back to the 10-yard line. The penalty forced a pass attempt on third down into the corner of the end zone. Incredibly, the pass was nearly caught but fell incomplete to set up fourth-and-goal from the 10. Licking Valley coach Randy Baughman opted for another field goal and Chris Chacey hit from 27 yards out to put Valley ahead 6-0 with more than 10 minutes left in the game. There was still plenty of time to pull this thing out if we could just get something going.

John Jurden took the ensuing kick at the 7, ran to his left, spun out of a tackle at the 25, changed directions and then ran to his right all the way to the Panther 49. The outstanding effort gave us a short field to work with and we were finally in business to take control of this game—or so we thought. A first-down Flood Left went to Jurden who gained 5 yards with a second effort. On second down, Kubik changed the play at the line of scrimmage but took too much time in doing so. We were slapped with a 5-yard delay-of-game penalty that put us back to the Panther 49. Second and third downs resulted in incomplete passes. The resulting punt hit at the Valley 23 and took a Panther bounce up to the 29.

After that pathetic offensive series, it seemed inevitable to me that we were going to lose to these people. After all, their last two possessions had resulted in two field goals. We were simply unable to stop the running attack and were about to give the ball back to the Panthers once more. Bad thoughts filled my head. We would fail to win the LCL crown, our hopes of a perfect season would be ruined and the 19-game winning streak that had begun in 1984 would be ended. Worst of all, ours would be the first class to drop the torch and lose to Licking Valley. It was a disgusting thought.

Rex Redman began Valley's next series with a dive play and took a hard hit from Tim McKenna after a short gain. Mark McNabb was in motion on second down and the penalty pushed Valley back to their 24. On second-and-fifteen, Chacey threw a deep pass to Rod Torbert who went up, had both hands on the ball, but had it stripped from his grasp by Jurden. It was an outstanding effort by Jurden who was at a height disadvantage against the 6'3" Torbert.

Taking a play from our playbook, Licking Valley executed a Flanker Trap Zero on third down in which Scott Sensibaugh picked up 10 yards to the Valley 35. Had McNabb not been in motion on second down, the Flanker Trap would have been enough for the first down. However, it was now fourth-and-five and Valley had to punt. With less than seven minutes to play, this most likely would be our final opportunity to save ourselves.

The Cody punt traveled out of bounds and we started from our 35-yard line. It was now or never! Cody beat Pat Cooperrider on a 23 Power and tackled Jurden for a 3-yard loss. That was not exactly how we wanted this all-important drive to begin.

On this last drive, Kubik was changing plays at the line of scrimmage almost every time. That must explain the oddness of the second-down call. Some sort of trap at the zero-hole had been called because I ran a Zero Trap on the down tackle while at the same time, Cooperrider traveled down the line for a Flanker Trap Zero and smacked Joe Simi right in the back! Enough of us must have done the correct things, however, because Jeff Ronan plowed for 8 yards on the play and set up third-and-five. On the big third-down play, Kubik hit Byers on a curl route that was good for 16 yards to the Panther 44.

At this time of the drive, I was experiencing a substantial amount of pain. A full night of cut-blocking Mark McNabb and others, getting walked on, punched, tripped over and pummeled into the Hanover soil had taken a toll on my legs and ribs. I tried to conceal my discomfort but apparently did not do a very good job. I distinctly remember approaching the line of scrimmage slightly limping and somehow, a lone voice pierced through the dissonant roar of our fans and shouted, "Hang in there sixty-seven, we need you!" I have no idea who it was but it honestly helped me to suck it up.

Our new set of downs began with a deep pass along the sideline to Monte Byers and resulted in what the local paper called "a disputed interference call..." which sent "...the Valley sideline into a frenzy."[16] Controversial or not, the play gave us another first down at the Panther 29 with 5:12 left in the game.

With Kubik changing the play again to a 24 Power, he made a fine choice as Ronan crushed the middle linebacker and Jurden dashed for 12 yards to the

Licking Valley 17. I think we all sensed that something big might have been brewing but no one said a word. We simply held hands in the huddle—something we normally did not do—and we stayed focused.

On the next play, Kubik dropped to pass and hit Byers at the 3-yard line! We were in beautiful shape but the play almost did not occur as the game film reveals how dangerously close Kubik came to being sacked. I was locked up with McNabb, who had a head of steam built up. He just pushed me back, back, back and tackled Andy just after the ball was thrown. It's too scary to think about!

The jazzed-up Newark Catholic faithful anxiously waited to see if we could punch it in. First-and-goal from the 3, Tim McKenna carried on 24 Power but an untouched Scott Sensibaugh hammered Mac for a 1-yard loss. Second-and-goal from the 4, John Jurden carried on 18 Quick Pitch but ran into a wall of Panthers at the 2. It seemed that we simply could not score by running the ball. However, since Kubik had already been intercepted in the end zone once tonight, did Coach Graham dare throw it again this close to the end zone? The play came in and it was indeed a pass. Kubik set up, looked to his left and found Joe Simi alone in the end zone for the final 2 yards with 3:27 left in this gut-wrenching game. There is no one better to explain exactly what happened than Mr. Simi himself:

> The play was Tight End Delay and it was the weirdest thing. I can't remember if it was Jurden or Franks who brought the play in, but I just knew it was that play before they even got into the huddle. When I ran my route, there was absolutely no one around and I just made sure that I was in the end zone. It was almost like slow motion when Kubik threw the ball and I was watching the ball coming. It seemed like an eternity and I kept thinking: *Don't drop it!* Then I caught it and it was pure pandemonium when I got up. Everybody piled on. There was so much excitement. The best thing was that it happened right where the students and cheerleaders were.[17]

With the score now 6-6, we badly needed the all-important extra point and Coach Graham spoke to us and led us in a prayer just before the attempt. We did not want to go into overtime against this Panther team. The snap from Todd South was good and Jeremy Montgomery got the ball down. Dale Backlund's kick was perfect and put us ahead 7-6. Blessed be the field goal team!

Joe Bell offered this amazing account of the events that transpired from the time he was injured until the time we scored:

> As I sat in the locker room at halftime, I desperately wanted to return to the field of action. However, I knew I would not return to the game and the ever-increasing pain in my thigh meant a trip to the hospital for X-rays. My mom escorted me to the ambulance and she proceeded to give me her radio and headphones so I could listen to the game. Due to the overflow of the traffic and fans at this game, the ambulance driver decided to take a painfully bumpy detour out the back way to get to the hospital. Of course, the ambulance staff was comprised entirely of Licking Valley fans and they were less concerned about my discomforts. They seemed to get great joy from shoving the splint board up into my crotch and displayed great delight in rubbing in the fact that Valley

was laying a whipping on the Green Wave. They were sure to keep me abreast of the fact that Valley had just kicked their second field goal to go up 6-0 and they indicated the Greenies were finished. I never lost the faith as I listened to the final drive of the game in which the announcer indicated that Kubik hooked up with Simi in the corner of the end zone to tie the game and the extra-point put us ahead for good. I erupted into euphoria as I heard many profanity-ridden comments streaming from the front and rear of the ambulance when we entered the hospital grounds.[18]

While it was pleasing to finally be ahead, 3:27 was plenty of time for Valley to get down into field goal range. We were not in the clear yet. The first priority would be to prevent a long kick return. Backlund's kickoff was caught by Steve Chacey at the 18-yard line and incredibly, the kid found a lane! Near the 38-yard line, however, a miracle happened as Chacey simply lost the handle and the ball squirted out. Joe Wiley has fond memories of that moment:

> Steve Chacey started to bring it up the field and just before I went to hit him, he dropped the ball. It was like destiny for me. Time just stopped and I was the only one who reacted to the ball. I jumped on it and several Panthers started beating and pulling on me but I held on to it. The next thing I see is K.C. Donnelly pulling Panthers off me, tossing them aside and yelling for me to "hold it up!" My mom was in the hospital at the time and listening to the radio. Coach Graham said in the interview after the game, "That was Wiley? I just might have to kiss that boy."[19]

After Joe Wiley's fumble recovery at the Licking Valley 40-yard line, it was paramount to get at least one first down to eat up the final three minutes. Jurden carried on first down for 1 yard and Valley spent their last time out. Second down was a 27 Sweep and Scott Sensibaugh lost his cool as he tried to tear Jurden's head off by grabbing the facemask. This action drew a personal foul and moved us to the Panther 20 with 2:35 to go. That penalty sealed the victory for us by providing a first down. After the ball was set, Valley could do nothing but watch helplessly as the seconds vanished from the scoreboard. John Jurden carried the ball for the last three plays and was beaten, roughed up and abused each time as the Panthers tried to strip him of the football. Another offside penalty was assessed on Valley just before what would have been the sixth play of the drive. With 20 seconds remaining, the ball was set, the clock started and there was no need to run another play. It was over and Green Wave fans stormed the field in celebration as two exhausted and beaten-up teams formed two lines to shake hands.

I would like to think that a mutual respect develops between opposing players who, throughout the course of any game, beat each other up without either of them quitting. That is how I felt towards Mark McNabb and I could not leave the field without telling him so. I failed to locate him after a search of the entire field. Disappointed, I made my way toward the locker room and there at the edge of the field was McNabb, walking slowly and sobbing with tears streaming down his face. He probably did not want to hear from any Green Wave at that time but I just shook his hand and told him he was "one hell of a football player." McNabb was the only opponent I ever went out of my to say that to.

Offensively, we somehow out-gained Valley in total yardage 306-173.[20] The offensive line should have been proud that Kubik was never sacked and that the running backs piled up 143 yards against the Panther defense. A mark against the linemen, however, was the fact that we allowed Bell to get hurt.

Defensively, it was by far my worst performance ever. I should not have bothered suiting up as I was either buried or trapped for most of the night. With Mike Trotter and Scott Saad both missing from my side, it was no wonder that Craig Black gained most of his 126 rushing yards on 23 carries[21] through the left side of our line. I just don't know what my problem was.

What a game it had been—very exciting but too close for comfort and I wonder how many new ulcers developed that evening between both sets of fans. I believed it was the most physical game we had played to date and the grueling nature of the event would serve as a good primer for the playoffs. As Coach Graham said after this classic LCL battle: "...it's just too bad one team had to lose."[22]

The team boarded the bus for the trip home to discover a token of friendship left by the Valley faithful. The interior of the bus, from top to bottom, was littered with broken eggs. We didn't care. We were too busy celebrating the huge victory and relishing the fact that we were somehow 7-0. When I got to school, I reached into the back of my locker and kissed that lucky penny.

Our normal routine of running on the day after a game did not occur on Saturday morning because the reserve game between Newark Catholic and Licking Valley took place at our school. The running and viewing of the game film would take place on Sunday. While Saturday was a day without practice, Coach Graham still required our presence at the reserve game to support our younger teammates in their quest to also beat the Panthers. I can recall our varsity standing on one side of the field while the Valley varsity stood on the other. Although we kept our distance from them, which was required by Coach Graham to avoid potential skirmishes, the two clans stared at each other throughout the whole game.

Following the game, my Dad took me to a jewelry store on 21st Street and bought me my first wristwatch. I would turn 18 on Thursday of the coming week and a nice watch was the official gift for 18th birthdays in the Evans household.

Some months later after the football season, my friends and I continued to hang out at Burger King and it was there that we met up with Charlie Cody, Mark McNabb and Pat Ourant. Ourant was Valley's left offensive guard whose two illegal-procedure penalties help to keep us in the football game. Since I had known Ourant from YMCA football as he was on the terrible Bengals team with Todd South and me, I felt that I could razz him a bit. Offering a handshake, I told him that I wanted to thank him for helping us win that night. He smiled and took it in stride. However, after about the fourth different person followed my lead, he finally snapped and told us all where to stick it.

Joking aside, all three of them were polite and friendly men and we had a pleasant time talking to them. Somehow, we got onto the topic of belching and Charlie Cody was allegedly the unofficial belching champion at Licking Valley High School in those days. Well, my friends knew that I was rather gifted in that area as well. (Our school custodian, Bob Spear, did not call me "Belchy" for nothing!) As boys like to talk, boast and brag, the gauntlet had been thrown down and Cody and I displayed our talents right there in Burger King. In a short matter of time, Cody looked at McNabb and said, "Mooch, I think I'm beat." Chalk up another Green Wave victory!

Additional note: I had the pleasure of meeting up again with Mark McNabb at the 2002 Newark Catholic Men's Stag Dinner on April 4. We of course discussed our classic 1985 contest. McNabb revealed to me that the fence around the football field had been built during that week just for that game. McNabb also remembered five players from his team who went on to play college football: Steve Chacey to Denison; Tim Journey to West Liberty; Craig Black to Miami of Ohio; Brian Strausbaugh to Denison and also a team captain; and Mark McNabb himself, who went to Otterbein, was a team captain and earned all-Ohio Athletic Conference honors three times.

Newark Catholic	0	0	0	7	7
Licking Valley	0	0	3	3	6

	NC	LV
First Downs	19	8
Rushing	139	155
Passing Yards	154	15
Total yards	293	170
Att-Comp-Int	25-13-2	13-3-0
Punts / Avg	2-28	6-39
Kickoffs / Avg	2-33	3-50
Fumbles / lost	3-2	2-1
Penalties / yards	1-5	8-80

Week 7 LCL Action[23]

Heath	21		Johnstown	35
Granville	12		Lakewood	18
Watkins Memorial	35		Coshocton	39
Northridge	0		Utica	16

Notes

1. Rick Cannizzaro, "Irish win over Heath sets up Friday title game," *Newark (O) Advocate*, (Nov. 5, 1973), p. 18.

2. Sean McClelland, "Green Wave blanks Heath; Valley awaits," *The Advocate*, (Oct. 6, 1985), p. 1C.

3. *The Advocate*, (Oct. 10, 1985), p. 14.

4. Mark Naegele, "Valley shows power when all are healthy," *The Advocate, Football '85*, (Aug. 28, 1985), p. 19.

5. Ibid.

6. Ibid.

7. Sean McClelland, "Black, defense lead Panthers to shutout win over Lexington," *The Advocate*, (Oct. 5, 1985), p. 5.

8. Mark Naegele, "Valley hopes to gain respect with win over NC," *The Advocate*, (Oct. 10, 1985), p. 13.

9. Ibid.

10. Tim McKenna, Telephone conversation with author, Jan. 29, 2002.

11. Sean McClelland, "Green Wave trips LV; Kubik TD aerial stops Panthers," *The Advocate*, (Oct. 12, 1985), p. 12.

12. Mike Trotter, Telephone conversation with author, Jan. 3, 2002.

13. Joseph Bell, Conversation with author, Dec. 28, 2001.

14. Jeff Ronan, Telephone conversation with author, Jan. 9, 2002.

15. Sean McClelland, "Green Wave trips LV; Kubik TD aerial stops Panthers," *The Advocate*, (Oct. 12, 1985), p. 6.

16. Ibid.

17. Joe Simi, Electronic mail to author, Jan. 7, 2002.

18. Joe Bell, Electronic mail to author, Jan. 7, 2002.

19. Joe Wiley, Electronic mail to author, Nov. 25, 2001.

20. Sean, McClelland, "Green Wave trips LV; Kubik TD aerial stops Panthers," *The Advocate*, (Oct. 12, 1985), p. 6.

21. Ibid.

22. Ibid.

23. *The Advocate*, (Oct. 12, 1985), p. 7.

Newark Catholic's dominance over Licking Valley continued until 1988 when the Panthers won the contest 28-21. Licking Valley also managed to beat the Green Wave in the following two years to close out the LCL. The series ended with the Green Wave holding a 15-3 advantage.

Other Memories

Other events took place throughout the season that cannot be associated with a particular week. These will be mentioned at this time—the midpoint of the season—in no particular order. Most of them are comical in nature—at least they are to me. In order to keep the season flowing, the reader may wish to skip this section until a later time.

During the dog days of summer when three-a-days were in full swing, a large group of us lounged beneath the shade trees before the second practice one day. The discussion turned to some of the things that had occurred during track season back in the spring of the year. In front of the whole group, Tony Johns called out to a shy, polite and quiet junior teammate who will remain anonymous. "Hey (so-and-so)!" Johns said. "Remember that day during track practice when we were running and you shit your pants!" Thoroughly embarrassed, all the poor kid could do was muster a weak smile across his blushing face and say, "Oh, uh, yeah."

Continuing in the spirit of antagonizing younger kids, Kevin Donnelly offered this gem of a story:

> Three-a-days had ended but we had not yet played our first game. It was a very hot and dry day and we were in full pads running through offensive plays. On a trap play, I leveled this underclassman. He was flat on his back and I was lying on top of him. His face was completely covered in sweat and I reached down, grabbed a handful of dry, dusty dirt and dropped it through his facemask. It just covered and stuck to his face.

The next play, Coop and I got up to the line and we were laughing so hard that we could not run the next play.

Jeff Ronan had a large boil develop on his forehead that had to be lanced in order for it to disappear. Coach Graham said, "Ronan, you could probably shoot a bird out of that tree across the street with that thing!"

The boil, also known as the infamous "pimple," made it impossible for Jeff to wear a helmet, which meant that he could not practice. His replacement at fullback during this time was Scott Saad. Now, Coach Graham constantly rode Scott Saad about his lack of aggression at the fullback position. On one particular day during an offensive scrimmage, Coach Graham became disgusted with Saad and was tired of Ronan not practicing. "G-dammit Ronan!" Coach Graham screamed. "We've got Donnelly over here playing with a separated shoulder and you can't play because you have a pimple on your head!"

On the defensive day of that week, Ronan recalls that he and Andy Kubik snuck away from the practice to Graham's office, got out the film projector and watched the Mogadore game from 1983. "I sat there drinking a pop," Jeff said, "and the managers came in to say that they had been sent by Graham to find us and to get us back outside. When we appeared, Coach Graham reamed us good."

As mentioned earlier, the normal Friday-night function for us was to hang out at Burger King. We all deviated from the routine one Friday night and went to Duff's Smorgasbord on South 30th Street in Heath. There were six of us in the group, which consisted of Tony Johns, Jeff Ronan, Mike Trotter, Jim Calvert, Pat Cooperrider and me—many big boys to feed! As one might expect, we were complete gluttons, eating as if it was the last meal on earth. Adhering to restaurant policy, we grabbed a new plate each time we returned to the food line and the mountain of empty plates that we had erected by the end of the evening was unbelievable! What a shame it was that we lacked a camera.

One day during a defensive practice, the scrimmaging had stopped while Coach Graham went into teaching mode. Not a sound could be heard except for Graham's voice. Suddenly, a huge fart had been executed by one of the players. Everyone could tell that Mike Trotter was the culprit and I wondered what Coach Graham would do to him for the gaseous interruption. "Trotter, was that you?" Graham asked. Unwavering and with a straight face, Trotter simply said, "It was my shoe, Coach." Coach Graham erupted into laughter (as did the entire team) and replied, "I think you better go clean the shit out of your shoe." Much laughter followed.

During another practice, Coach Graham was so disgusted with our performance that he walked off the field and left Coach Poth in charge. Coach Poth decided that we should just do our running and go home. Now, our normal running was twenty 40-yard sprints. Coach Poth sent us down on the east goal line of the practice field and he took his place on the 40-yard line, or so we thought. The field was in such bad shape that it was impossible to tell where the 40-yard stripe was supposed to be. After a few trips down and back, a good deal of grumbling and complaining erupted from some of the boys because we were not running 40-yard sprints but 50-yard sprints. Those who complained were mainly on the south edge of the field near Egan funeral home while I was on the north edge of the field near the baseball dugout. Coach Poth stood between them and me and if I could hear them, I knew *he* could hear them. We continued to run. Each time we returned to Coach Poth, I would look at him and the sour expression on his face became more intense with each passing moment—an expression I had known since seventh grade and one indicative of someone about to explode. *Those guys had better shut up*, I thought. *He won't tolerate this crap very long and they'll get us all in trouble.* Sure enough, after we had run about 14 sprints, Coach Poth finally went off:

> Hold up, people! We got people mumblin' and complainin' because they seem to think I'm standing on the wrong line and you guys are getting screwed, running farther than you should have to. I know exactly where I'm supposed to stand! You guys sound like a bunch of babies! Whiny people like you are a disgrace to Newark Catholic football and make me want to puke! Well guess what? After we finish these 20 sprints, we're going to run 20 more! You guys who weren't complaining can thank the whiners for making you run extra! …You big bunch of babies!

…and we did indeed run 20 more!

On defensive days, the quarterbacks were to go to the far end of the football field and work on various passing drills. Coach Graham was in the middle of instructing the defensive unit and suddenly stopped when he looked to the far end of the field to see Kubik and Montgomery running in a circle throwing the ball to each other. Kubik was trying to be cute by jumping into the air and catching the ball behind his back. Coach Graham invited us all to briefly watch and then he finally yelled, "That's it Kubik! Screw around and break your fingers! …Dumbass!"

On another occasion, Kubik decided to try his hand at kicking field goals. When he finally booted one through the upright, he raised his arms to signify the score and performed a brief victory dance. While dancing, he turned to face us at the far end of the field, saw that we all were looking at him and he quickly dropped his arms hoping he had not been seen. It was too late for that. "Hey Kubik!" Graham yelled. "You can keep on dancin'—right out onto the track until I tell you to stop!"

During an offensive scrimmage, Dale Backlund was having a bad day at weak-side tackle and Coach Graham told him to "pick it up a notch." As Dale continued to screw up by falling down and missing blocks, Coach Graham finally snapped and unleashed his wrath.

"What is wrong with you Backlund?"

"I'm hurt, Coach," Dale said as an excuse.

"Hurt?" Coach Graham asked. "Hurt my ass! Backlund, you're always hurt! I bet you would say you were hurt even if you had a hangnail! In fact, that's what I'm going to call you: 'Hangnail Dale!'"

A steak-eating contest was held at the Bonanza Steak House in Heath and Coach Graham had to send three participants. He chose Jim Calvert and Pat Cooperrider right away. "Practice had not started yet," said Calvert, "and Coach Graham said to me and Coop, 'Come here, you guys hungry?' He gave us three tickets and told us to take Bernie with us." Bernie Schwartz, the junior team manager, was selected as the third member of this vaunted beef-eating trio. As Calvert recalls, the contest was between Heath and Newark Catholic, but neither he nor Pat Cooperrider can recall the purpose of the event. "After we had eaten about six steaks each," Calvert continued, "Coach Graham showed up and told us not to eat too many more. Coop and I ended up eating nineteen apiece. I went home and got sick. Coopy went home and ate the dinner his mom had waiting for him."

Pat Cooperrider recalls that "they would eat one more, then we would eat one more. Finally, it got to be about nine o'clock at night and we said to the Heath guys, 'If you just want to call it a tie, we'll leave it go at that.'"

According to both Calvert and Cooperrider, Bernie was not much help as he only ate one or two steaks. Cooperrider added, "I can't figure out why he didn't send you with us," (referring to the author). "I know we would have beaten them."

Pat says that after the contest, he went back to the school to get his homework but the place was all locked up and deserted. "I skipped half a day the next day because I had an English assignment due."

In another incident involving the big men, Coop stayed the night at Calvert's house on the eve of a game. The two wanted to go pick up a pizza but the team curfew, which was 11:00 p.m. on weeknights, had just passed. Gambling that nothing would happen, they decided to go through with their late-night snack attack. "We went to Plaza Pizza," said Calvert, "and the pizza was not quite ready. We went outside to wait and who should come driving into the parking lot but Coach Poth! Coop and I fell over each other trying to crawl into the passenger side of my red Firebird so Pothy would not see us!"

Post-game activities did not always consist of parties at someone's home. Often, Cooperrider, Calvert and I would go to Subway on 30th Street. After we had enjoyed a large sub, pop and potato chips, we would cross the street to Jolly Pirate and proceed to chow on donuts and hot chocolate for as long as we could without violating the game-night curfew of 1:00 a.m. Oh, to be young again and to eat like that without getting fat!

Believe it or not, we did have some semblance of a social life during football season and were "permitted" to attended school dances and so forth. One week after the Licking Valley game, which was the night before our game with Granville, the school held a Halloween dance. Now, I never was much of a dance attendee throughout high school, but this particular event involved wearing costumes and I could not pass up the opportunity to get weird. Other football players expressed interest in the dance and discussed their costume plans with one another. For instance, Kevin Donnelly wanted to show up dressed as a fart but was unsure about how to do it. I suggested taking several strands of cotton, painting them a sickening shade of green and have them hang from random locations on some grubby clothing.

I went to the dance as some sort of ghoulish freak akin to something out of "Night of the Living Dead." My costume consisted of baggy overalls, a steel hay-bale hook for my left hand, an arrow protruding from my chest and a dislocated eyeball, which was merely a ping-pong ball with a pupil painted on it and mounted outside of a grotesque rubber mask. A few tubes of fake blood added the finishing touches.

Admission to the dance was one dollar. As I walked into the south lobby, two girls sitting at a table to collect admission fees jumped back in their chairs when I slammed the steel hook onto the tabletop. A one-dollar bill was impaled on the steel hook and one of the girls cautiously reached for the note and pulled it free. As I headed down the hallway towards the cafeteria where the dance was held, several people followed to check out the costume and tried to guess who this freak was. "That's Evans! I can tell by the walk!" someone said, but I ignored it. I took up a position along a wall and silently observed the passersby as they gawked at the hideous sight.

At some point, I needed to hit the restroom and I almost had the arrow driven into my chest for real. While approaching the restroom door, I forgot about the arrow and it forcefully struck the door before the door opened. Luckily, the shaft broke in half and a sternum bruise was all that resulted from it. It was only after the arrow had broken that I revealed myself as I set out to find tape so that I could make repairs. Mary Angela Reed gained access to the library and snagged a roll of tape for me. I ended up winning a prize that night for the most original costume.

During another practice, there was lull in the action while Coach Graham spent some time instructing us. Suddenly, a junior teammate who will remain anonymous began sprinting toward the locker without saying a word to anyone. This caught Coach Graham's attention.

"Where are you going!" Coach Graham shouted.

"I have to take a shit!" The kid replied as he continued running.

"What did you say!" Coach Graham asked sharply in an effort to get the boy to clean up his language.

"I have to take a shit!" the kid said again.

"What did you say!" Graham asked a second time.

The kid finally got the hint and adjusted his statement: "I have to take a shit…sir!"

No book about Newark Catholic football would be complete without mentioning a gentleman by the name of Cass Derda. Cass was not a coach or a player. He was an older man who Coach Poth described as "the greatest fan Newark Catholic ever had—a 'gopher' who would do anything and everything for the football program."

Cass' main duty was to exchange game films with the team Newark Catholic would be playing in any given week. Coach Poth described for me an incident involving Cass, game films and Watkins Memorial coach Joe Ault. During one particular season, Watkins had lost to Walsh Jesuit in the opening game and Coach Ault would not let Newark Catholic borrow the game film. Coach Graham instructed Cass to make the trip to Jesuit (near Akron) and retrieve *their* copy of the game. "We won the game (against Watkins)," Coach Poth said, "and we were out on the track afterward at White Field and everybody else was gone. Cass was out there with us, holding the tapes that he drove to Cleveland to get. When he saw Coach Ault standing outside of the dressing room, Cass held the tapes in the air and shouted, 'Hey Ault! Take these tapes and stick 'em up your ass!'"

His love for Newark Catholic football knew no limits. Cass lived in the Licking Valley School District. One year, his daughter was on the Homecoming court for Licking Valley. While Newark Catholic and Valley had games the same evening, rather than see his daughter, Cass opted to see the Newark Catholic game instead. "Someone asked him about this," Poth remembers, "and his answer was, 'I can see my daughter 365 days of the year—I can only see the Green Wave ten times.'"

Cass was always one to be cracking jokes and doing the unexpected. One day during a practice, Cass came wandering in, equipped with his unmistakable ornery grin and a peculiar hat. Coach Graham was speaking at the time. As Cass drew closer, players began to chuckle—the noise growing louder by the minute. Coach Graham finally heard the ruckus and angrily asked what the disturbance was. No one said a word. We simply waited for Coach Graham to focus in on what we had seen: Cass' ball cap that said *Shithead* above a picture of Coach Graham and had a rubber dog turd on the bill. When Coach Graham saw this, he erupted into hearty laughter, which then made it OK for the rest of us to do the same. "Is that what I am, Cass?" Coach Graham asked. "A shithead, huh?" …Good old Cass: God rest his soul.

Week 8

Granville Blue Aces

October 19

For me, the euphoria from the big victory over Licking Valley would not end. I continued to dwell on the whole experience: the size of the crowd, the importance of the victory in the LCL race, the excitement and how we came from behind to win in the final minutes. I wished that every week could be so exciting and I found it difficult to let it go and to get refocused on our next opponent: the Blue Aces of Granville.

This sky-high feeling persisted all through Monday and most of Tuesday until a stunning revelation came in the newspaper that knocked us down a notch or two. To our surprise, the top spot in Class A of the Associated Press poll, the spot which we had owned for the entire season, had been taken from us and given to "the team up north." No, not that team in Ann Arbor, but another team whose name starts with the letter "M"—the Mogadore Wildcats, a team that Newark Catholic had met in playoff action twice before.

In his article that appeared in *The Advocate* a few days later, Mark Naegele explained why we dropped in the poll and he scorned the reasoning behind it: One-point victories do little to impress sportswriters who vote on which team should be No. 1 in polls, such as the Associated Press and United Press International. The fact was that while we had struggled in several of our games, the Wildcats had been busy ripping all of their opponents and week 7 was the last straw. As we squeaked by Licking Valley by one point, Mogadore stomped Ravenna Southeast 41-16, had thus appeared as the strongest Class A team to the AP and they slipped into the No. 1 ranking by just one point.[1] Though it was just an opinion poll of sportswriters, the situation irritated Coach Graham. He believed an attitude existed that northern Ohio football was somehow superior to football anywhere else in the state and that this attitude played a part in us being replaced by Mogadore.

One thing that could not be influenced by opinions and attitudes was the computer ranking system. In a comparison of computer points that each team had accumulated after the seventh game, Mogadore had 47.50, while we had 67.00[2]— nearly a 20-point lead over the Wildcats. This made it obvious that they did not play the schedule that we had to play. In addition, we had a 31-point lead on the second place team in our region which was "the largest cushion enjoyed by any of the region leaders"[3] in any division. In closing his article, Naegele said that polls were a "popularity contest" and that

> "...neither...Mogadore...nor Newark Catholic will have a legitimate claim to No. 1 until they win the state playoffs.
> So don't go out and hang any sports writer in effigy, all you Newark Catholic fans. You and your team will a get a chance to prove yourselves—if the Green Wave deserves it—Nov. 29 in the Division V state championship game."[4]

We could not allow ourselves to be distracted by the slip in the poll but in a way, it was difficult not to be. It was the '85 team's first step backward from all of the pinnacles that the '84 team had reached. I couldn't have been alone in my wondering if this was the first phase of a long slide down that so many had said was inevitable for our team. As the Naegele article said, we would get a chance to prove ourselves and it may even be against the very team that was now No. 1. We had other business to take care of in the meantime. That was to win the LCL crown, which we were in a good position to do if we could win three more games.

As mentioned earlier, our next opponent was the Granville Blue Aces. In the history of this matchup, Granville had beaten Newark Catholic in 1959 through 1961. The schools did not play each other again until the Green Wave joined the LCL in 1973.[5] Since that time, Newark Catholic never lost to Granville again.

The '85 Blue Aces were in the middle of a terrible season with a record of 1-6 with their only victory coming in week 1 against West Muskingum. Given Granville's record, it was easy for us to think that we had a sure victory coming up. However, this was exactly the type of situation Coach Graham referred to when he said, "There ain't no 'give-me's' in this sport!" and "Anybody can beat you once!" No one was to be taken lightly.

We were in a precarious situation to be sure. We had just played the biggest, most physical and emotionally draining game not only of the season but also in the entire career of our senior class. While we had everything to lose, Granville had nothing to lose and they would be looking for the upset of the year. After going over their personnel, it was obvious that they had enough good kids to be dangerous.

The Granville offensive line had good size, the largest members being Chris Fudge (6-4, 225) and Jim Wieliczko (6-2, 240). Running the ball for the Aces was senior tailback Curt Carruth (6-0, 190) and a smallish sophomore name Chad French (5-7, 145). Despite his size, French was perhaps the biggest threat on the team because he was fast, fast, fast and a great source of worry for Coach Graham. He issued all of the standard warnings to us, including the one tailor-made for our own speedster. "Joe Simi," Coach Graham said, "You may have caught Warga and you may have caught Baldwin, but you won't catch this kid. I don't give a shit what kind of angle you take!"

Game day had arrived. As the game was to be played at Granville, our student body conducted the bi-yearly tradition of walking to Granville High School for the game, which was a distance of about 5 miles. I was never sure of the exact route they took but it always seemed a great display of school spirit.

The whole scenario of this game seemed depressing and surreal to me. A dense, misty fog bank hovered about the field during pre-game. The Granville seats had a pathetically small crowd that could not have numbered more than 50. I felt tired, flat and just could not get enthused to play. Even the fans seemed spent and not into it as usual. What a stark contrast from the previous week! The setting was ripe for an upset and I just wanted to get the game behind us.

We sat in the locker room before the game and Coach Graham entered extremely irate over a few different things. First, he must have sensed that it was not just me, but the entire team was flat and almost in a daze. "YOU HAD BETTER WAKE YOUR ASSES UP!" he shouted. Secondly, the small crowd that had assembled in support of Granville bothered him. He said it was a "damn disgrace" that so few people were present to see their home team play and we, as Newark Catholic players, were fortunate to have such strong fan support. Finally, he went off on Albert Ghiloni for an incident that took place earlier that day. Albert was present at the Denison football game on Saturday morning. He wore his Newark Catholic school jacket and affixed to the collar were two offensive pins that read *Way to go Shit Head* and *Big F--king Deal*. "While I watched the game," Albert recalls, "I felt this hand reach down and grab my collar where the pins were. I looked up and it was Coach Graham. He gave me a look that could kill and he said, 'Get those f--king pins off of that coat.'"[6] This was the last issue Coach Graham raised before our Granville contest and he cleverly tied together our pre-game flatness to Albert's pins. "We ain't ready to play football, but hell, we don't care! We just want to hang out and dress cool like a bunch of hoodlums with no regard for our school's reputation! —Big f--kin' deal, huh, Ghiloni? ... Way to go, you shit head." It would be interesting to see how we responded.

We had the ball first. From the first snap, our running back corps of Ronan and Jurden cut the Granville defense apart, enjoying long carries and moving us right down the field on Traps, Power Traps, Powers and Quick Pitches. A short pass to Monte Byers set us up with first-and-goal at the 6. Three plays later, John Jurden, filling in while Joe Bell's thigh healed, scored from 2 yards out on a 17 Quick Pitch. Backlund's extra point was good and we took a 7-0 lead with 6:35 left in the first quarter. By opening the game with a 76-yard, 13-play scoring drive,[7] I think it put everyone's mind at ease.

Joe Wiley and Tommy Helms buried Curt Carruth who fielded the bouncing kickoff at the Granville 20. The Aces' first play was a run toward Jim Olson for no gain. On second down, Carruth turned the corner on a pitch around left end, ran over Tommy Helms and was on his way to the end zone but was tripped up by a shoe-string tackle from Joe Simi. The play would not have mattered as Granville was penalized for blocking below the waist. The next play was a Flanker Trap Zero but was ruined when I broke through and knocked the flanker down before he got the ball. The quarterback, having no one to hand-off to, continued to his right and attempted an unsuccessful shovel pass to Carruth. Third down was a run up the middle for a short gain. On fourth down, the Granville punter stood at his own 5-yard line and incredibly, he executed a fake punt by keeping the ball and running to his right. Byers flew up and had a chance to make the tackle inside the 5 but missed. I lost containment and the punter made it out to the 26 where he was finally knocked out of bounds short of the first down. It seemed crazy to run a fake punt from that deep in their territory, but what did Granville have to lose?

Despite the great field position, we could not score. A penalty, incomplete passes on first and second downs and a Zero Trap on third down for 5 yards was all we managed. Dale Backlund punted from near midfield and the ball rolled into the end zone for a touchback.

On first down, Carruth picked up 5 yards on a pitch to our left. On second down, Chad French was smeared for no gain. Jim Calvert, who scrapped with a Granville lineman, tried to discretely administer a gut punch but a referee directly behind him witnessed the whole thing. This gave the Blue Aces a new set of downs at their 42-yard line. Granville gained only 4 yards on the next three plays and the resulting punt rolled dead at the Green Wave 15.

Our third offensive series did not last long. It was not because of a turnover, either, which was a nice change. After Jurden ripped the defense for 12 yards on a 26 Power Trap, Kubik attempted a pass but was pressured, forced to run and was tackled at the 31. Attempting another pass on the next play, Kubik hit Simi near the left sideline. The defender fell down and Joe streaked past Granville's bench all the way to the end zone for a 69-yard touchdown—our longest play from scrimmage in 1985.[8] Backlund added the extra point and we went up 14-0 with 22 seconds left in the first quarter.

On the final play of the first quarter, Carruth was dropped for a 4-yard loss on a pitch play that was nicely strung out by Billy Franks. Two additional incomplete passes forced Granville to punt and the ball was fair-caught at our 48.

The next Green Wave offensive series was even shorter than the previous one. Kubik was back to pass, calmly stepped forward to avoid a hard-charging outside linebacker and let the ball fly. Monte Byers made a fingertip catch in full stride at the Granville 20 and cruised the rest of the way to the end zone with 11:34 left in the half. It appeared that a rout was in the works.

On Granville's next series, Coach Graham's fear was realized. I remember that I had just been relieved at defensive end by Jim Cross. On the next play, Chad French squirted around Jim's side, zipped down the sideline and looked certain to score. However, the reader should be able to guess by now what the outcome was. The speedy sophomore, who raced for 72-yards on the play, was caught from behind at the Green Wave 14 by Joe Simi. "Coach Graham called a timeout after the play," recalled Simi. "I stood at the back of the huddle grinning from ear to ear and Graham wouldn't even look at me."[9] How fast *was* Joe Simi? Looking back on this today, I am led to wonder if Coach Graham knew all along that Joe Simi had the wheels to catch all of the fast players we faced and that by telling Joe he could not catch these kids, Coach Graham was simply employing reverse psychology. If someone is told he cannot do something, pride will motivate him to succeed just to prove the entire world wrong.

Coach Graham sent all of his starters back into the game to try to prevent a Granville score. First down, a dive play gained one yard. Second down, French made it to the 7 on a pitch. Third down, the defensive game was perfect as Calvert slanted into the hole and stuffed a dive play. Granville decided to go for it on fourth down via a rollout pass to my side but the pass was incomplete.

Back on offense from the 7-yard line, Jurden slipped on a 26 Iso and lost a yard. Unbelievably, on second down, a bad exchange between Kubik and Tim McKenna resulted in a fumble that was recovered by Granville at the 10. We held them out once from here but could we do it again?

First down, French carried to the 9. Second down, Scott Saad batted a pass down. On third down, Scott Saad made another great play as he flew to the outside and dropped French for a short loss on a Quick Pitch. Again, on fourth down, Granville went for the touchdown by passing. The pass rush was incredible and the quarterback was crushed while throwing an incomplete pass. We had done it again!

We got a small drive together on the next series as we drove out to near midfield in 8 plays. The drive was plagued with penalties. On a third-down situation, Joe Simi was stopped short of the first down on a Tight End Screen Left and we punted.

Starting from their 20-yard line, Granville's first play was a quarterback sack at the 13-yard line by Byers, Franks and sophomore Matt Gilmore, who played defensive tackle in Mike Trotter's absence. Then Curt Carruth tried to go around left end but was gang-tackled by South, Saad, Franks and Helms. On third down, another pass attempt ended in a sack by Calvert, Byers and Gilmore at the Granville 8-yard line. It was time for another punt from their end zone but Granville did not fake it this time. We, however, had our punt-block game on and were "going after it." A Greenie must have gotten a piece of the ball because the punt only made it to the 26-yard line where we began our next series.

The series began with another 5-yard penalty to give us a first-and-fifteen. (I do not think that we were well-focused on the game given all the mistakes that occurred.) Granville jumped offside on the next play and we got the 5 yards right back. When we finally got a play off, it was a pass to Byers at the goal line but the play was perfectly defended by Carruth. Two more incomplete passes followed—the latter one drawing a pass interference call on Granville, giving us a first down at the 14-yard line with 45 seconds to go in the half. On the next play, the man I was to block got around me and pressured Kubik to throw too early, resulting in an interception at the 10. Granville gave the ball right back to us when Carruth dropped a pitch and Matt Gilmore, who made a great showing in his first varsity start, recovered the fumble at the 6. We lined up the offense and Kubik "threw a rope" to Billy Franks for the touchdown, extending our lead to 28 with just 5 seconds left before halftime.

Following a squib kick by Backlund, Granville did not even make a try for the end zone and simply fell on the ball to end the first half.

Granville went three-and-out on their first series of the second half. A good punt return by John Jurden was nullified by a penalty and we began at our 27 with Jeremy Montgomery in for Andy Kubik. We moved the ball well but the drive ended near midfield when Jeff Ronan fumbled. Jeff recalled this very play. "I was close to 100 yards rushing for the night and when I went to the sideline, Graham said, 'I was trying to get you 100 yards Ronan, but you had to go and fumble. Good job.'"[10]

The Clean Green began appearing in the game after the first offensive series. Our only other scoring opportunity came late in the third quarter when a Granville fumble was recovered at the Aces' 33-yard line. The Clean Green achieved a first down at the Granville 10 but could not score from there. The field goal attempt by Dale Backlund early in the fourth quarter was unsuccessful. The game ended anti-climactically. Granville was held to negative yardage in the second half.[11]

Following the game, Coach Graham said he was "...a bit concerned about our emotional status" coming in but he was "pleased with the win and happy to come out of the game injury-free."[12]

In the previous 7 weeks, we were told after every game that we had yet to play to our potential and the Granville game was no different. Coach Graham said, "We played well for about a quarter-and-a-half, then we lost some intensity."[13] While that was very true, I personally thought that the passing game finally began to gel for us as Kubik was able to connect on two "long bombs," racking up 180 yards and three touchdowns in the first half.[14] Jeff Ronan also had a good game with 87 yards on 14 carries,[15] thanks to 5 and 6 Trap which were wide-open all night.

I was just pleased that the whole thing was over and that we were not upset. For me, of all the games we played in 1985, the Granville game was the least enjoyable and least memorable.

Newark Catholic	14	14	0	0	28
Granville	0	0	0	0	0

	NC	G
First Downs	13	2
Rushing	129	76
Passing Yards	180	3
Total yards	309	79
Att-Comp-Int	18-7-1	10-1-0
Punts / Avg	4-35	7-28
Kickoffs / Avg	5-37	1-48
Fumbles / lost	5-2	3-2
Penalties / yards	8-70	7-77

Week 8 LCL Action[16]

Heath	20	Licking Valley	22
Lakewood	17	Utica	8
Watkins Memorial	7	Springsboro	38
Johnstown	3	Northridge	20

Notes

1. "Mogadore edges NC for top 'A' billing," *The Advocate* (Oct. 15, 1985), p. 11.

2. *The Advocate*, (Oct. 17, 1985), p. 16.

3. Mark Naegele, "Polls show worth again," *The Advocate*, (Oct. 18, 1985), p. 7.

4. Ibid.

5. Newark Catholic vs. Granville Football Program, (Oct. 31, 1986), p. 20-21.

6. Albert Ghiloni, Conversation with author, June 13, 2002.

7. Rick Cannizzaro, "Kubik passes Wave to victory," *The Advocate*, (Oct. 20, 1985), p. 1C.

8. John Cannizzaro, 1985 Newark Catholic Football Statistics.

9. Joseph Simi, Conversation with author, Dec. 1, 2001.

10. Jeff Ronan, Telephone conversation with author, Jan. 9, 2002.

11. Rick Cannizzaro, "Kubik passes Wave to victory," *The Advocate*, (Oct. 20, 1985), p. 1C.

12. Ibid.

13. Ibid.

14. Ibid.

15. Ibid.

16. *The Advocate*, (Oct. 5, 1985), p. 6.

Newark Catholic defeated Granville each year after the 1985 season. Granville, along with Northridge and Licking Heights (a member of the LCL until 1984), never beat Newark Catholic in LCL play.

Week 9

Utica Redskins

October 26, Homecoming

It was always a ritual of mine to study the football scores from around Ohio on Saturday and Sunday mornings to keep track of other Division V teams around the state. After they bumped us in the AP poll, Mogadore became my focal point. It was my hope that someone would knock them off so that they would not only fall from the No. 1 spot in the poll, but they might also be eliminated from the playoffs, or at least appear beatable. From what I learned about Mogadore as a sophomore, they could field a powerful team that was tough to beat. I sincerely hoped that we would not meet them in the playoffs.

There was no sign of any slipping on the part of Mogadore over the weekend of October 19th. The Wildcats had won big again 41-8 over Rootstown[1] and the new AP poll released on October 22 revealed that Mogadore had extended their lead over us by 22 points, 259-237.[2] And although we still were ahead in computer points, the gap narrowed. We had 78.50 points to Mogadore's 63.50.[3]

Our opponent for week 9 was the Utica Redskins. Located in the north-central part of the county, Utica was another school with many rural kids and that meant big farm boys on the football team. "We used to call them the 'big gray elephants,'" said Coach Poth, "because they were always so doggone big."[4]

Playing Utica also meant having to put up with a great deal of religious prejudice and Catholic bashing in the form of a barrage of dead fish jokes, literally or figuratively. According to Coach Poth, no other team in the county was more convinced than Utica that Newark Catholic recruited its football players.[5] These feelings probably stemmed from the fact that Utica could never beat Newark

Catholic legitimately. The only two "victories," which would be better termed as "incidents," the Redskins could attain were clouded in deep controversy. This only amplified the animosity between the two schools.

The first ordeal, known as the "Phantom Whistle Incident," occurred in 1974. Near the end of the game when Utica had the ball and trailed 6-0, an official blew his whistle. While the Newark Catholic kids let up on the play, the Utica kids kept going and scored a touchdown. The official denied blowing any whistle and the game ended up 8-6 in favor of Utica. It was Newark Catholic's first defeat in the Licking County League. According to Coach Poth, the official in question admitted years later that he did indeed blow the whistle before Utica had scored.[6]

The second incident took place in 1980. A Green Wave sophomore by the name of Sam Britton, a transfer from the Utica School District, caught a late touchdown pass to make the score in the already-out-of-reach game 37-0. The problem was that Sam Britton had only been a student at Newark Catholic for about six months—not enough time for him to become eligible to play sports. According to Coach Poth, no one at Newark Catholic was aware that he was ineligible. Utica, on the other hand, did know. A photographer for the Utica newspaper was present and took several pictures of Britton to document his participation in the game. The result was a Redskins' victory by way of forfeiture. Despite Coach Graham making his case at the Utica School Board meeting the following week, "They knew they had us," said Coach Poth, "and there was nothing we could do."[7] Nothing, that is, until the following season, when the Redskins came to White Field and Newark Catholic hammered them 42-0.

The Redskins did actually come close to a real victory in 1983. The contest finished 7-6 and was a horribly muddy mess of a game that took place in a cold and steady downpour. My class witnessed the game from the sideline as sophomores. Not surprisingly, Utica's worst defeat to the Green Wave was a 54-7 trouncing at the hands of the '84 team. It seemed to me that Coach Graham would run the score up on Utica whenever possible and he enjoyed every minute of it. "We enjoyed playing them." Coach Poth concluded. "You just knew something was going to happen."[8]

The 1985 Utica Redskins, who came into week 9 with a 2-6 record, had decent size on the offensive line. It consisted of Craig Rice (6-0, 185), Paul Ikehorn (6-1, 195), Bob Young (5-9, 163), Jason Lenhart (6-1, 185) and Robert Saunders (6-2, 225). Saunders was yet another person I would have to face that was bigger than me. Concerning Saunders, Utica coach Tom Russell said, he "just loves to hit people."[9] In the backfield, Doug Orr (6-0, 175) filled the quarterback spot while the dangerously speedy Dave Farley (5-8, 170), Wayne Blackburn (5-9, 175) and Daran Pratt (5-7, 165) carried the ball in Utica's "T" and "Power I" formations. Gary Selmon (5-7, 135) and Kyle Mossholder (5-11, 155) completed the offensive lineup at the end positions.

Defensively, Eric Ramseyer (6-0, 165) joined Saunders, Ikehorn and Lenhart on the front line. The middle linebackers were Rice and Todd Phelps (5-9, 155) and the outside "dogs" were Jeff Young (5-10, 155) and Rob Peters (5-9, 160). The defensive secondary consisted of Selmon, Pratt and Brad Allen (5-8, 150).

Utica week was also Homecoming week for Newark Catholic. Now, I could never be sure, but I always got the impression that Coach Graham could have done without the whole Homecoming ordeal. You see, Coach Graham was all business and Homecoming week was chocked full of things that were anything but the business of football. Instead of concentrating at practice, our minds could easily wander to such things as: who would make the Homecoming Court, float building and which class would win the contest, the bonfire, who would be crowned Homecoming king and queen, what kind of fancy cars the Court members would get to drive, who was taking whom to the dance and who was dateless for the dance, what clothes to wear to the dance, where we would go for dinner before the dance, would the band be good, etc., etc. These were all things that Coach Graham had to compete with for our attention. But he brought it into perspective for us several times during the week: "There's gonna be a whole bunch of crying eyes and broken hearts at that dance if you guys don't take care of business and win this damn football game!"

At the 2002 Newark Catholic Summer Festival, I asked Coach Graham if he did in fact dislike Homecoming:

> I never liked Homecoming. I know it's a big part of high school, but there are too many distractions. With all that goes on, it makes it difficult for people to concentrate. Obviously, I was concerned about losing the game, but the real reason was that if a kid was distracted and didn't have his head in the game, he was at a greater risk to get hurt.[10]

During the course of the week, someone got into the practice field, went out to our sled and spray-painted, with gray paint, the letters *U-T-I-C-A*—one letter on each pad of the sled. After being treated to a stinking pile of entrails during the Watkins week, we viewed this little stunt as trivial.

One night after practice, several students from our class went to a classmate's house to assist with building the senior float. It seemed a waste of time for us to build a float because ours had come in last place in the float competition ever since we were freshman. We had a devious plan for senior year, however, and that was to sabotage the floats of the other classes and prevent their arrival at the game. Therefore, with no other competition, we were sure to finally win! Joe Bell, Pat Cooperrider and I departed the float-building party and set out on a reconnaissance mission to determine the location of the other floats. We failed to locate the floats, however, and our covert operation never occurred. It was probably just as well. Had we actually succeeded, Coach Graham would have surely found out and there was no telling what disciplinary action he might have taken.

Friday night was the bonfire—an integral part of the Homecoming festivities that took place out on the track behind the school. While students began to congregate behind the school, Mr. Jim Grove, our math and religion teacher, recruited Kevin Donnelly, Pat Cooperrider and me to journey back into the school kitchen and bring out the apple cider and doughnuts that were to be served. Since Mr. Grove did not accompany us, we were given a golden opportunity that we simply could not pass up. We stayed awhile in the kitchen and quickly devoured several doughnuts before the first box ever made it out onto the track. There were plenty of leftovers at the end of the night anyway, so no harm was done. There were also a few jugs of cider left over and Mr. Grove allowed me to take one home. The stuff gave me a serious case of diarrhea in the days that followed.

Game night had arrived and a large crowd was present for the Homecoming festivities. The fancy cars from Don Maxwell Chevrolet slowly filed past the stands and around the track with our class royalty aboard. The floats also paraded around the field. Ours carried a Led Zeppelin theme, probably to Coach Graham's disgust.

Before the game, the Homecoming court had to be introduced to the community. This was one way that the festivities disrupted our game routine. As with other years, the Court was usually composed partly of football players and 1985 was no exception as football players dominated the royal clique. Joe Bell, Joe Simi, Kevin Donnelly, Monte Byers, Tony Johns and Andy Kubik made up six of the seven boys on the Court. Our routine would be disrupted when Coach Graham wanted to begin his final instructions or his pep talk. He would look at his watch with a disgusted look and say, "You guys better get out there." The rest of us would all sit and awkwardly wait for their return. It must have been impossible to keep a game face on while having to go out and be cordial in front of all the lights and cameras.

It was finally time to play some football. Utica began the game on offense after a decent kickoff return out to the 38-yard line. Joe Simi recalls that some of the Utica players had red and silver war paint on their faces and yelled at us in psychotic fashion: "We're going to kick your ass!"[11] Adding to the craziness, the Utica team looked odd because some of their helmets were painted silver while others were white.

For one whole year, Jeff Ronan had looked forward to this Utica game for the purpose of revenge. In the '84 contest, Jeff received a serious hit along the Utica sideline from a freshman named Rob Peters. Jeff was susceptible to concussions. He had suffered one each year since the eighth grade and had yet another one from the hit by the freshman. I had seen him suffer concussions before but this one seemed more severe than usual. I can vividly remember the fear that engulfed me as I stood nearby and watched the medical people tend to my motionless friend. Some of the Utica players, who crowded around from their bench to observe, were quite elated over the event and shouted, "Let's do it to more of them!" According to Jeff, a picture of Peters appeared in the newspaper at the beginning of the 1985 season. "I cut this picture out," Jeff said, "and put it inside of my helmet for the Utica game. I intended to get him back."[12]

Utica wasted no time in getting penalized. Their first trip to the line of scrimmage drew an illegal procedure call. Running-plays on first and second downs yielded short yardage. A quick pass to Blackburn and a missed tackle allowed a run to midfield for a first down. Utica was called for illegal procedure on their next two attempts to snap the ball, setting up a first-and-twenty at the Redskin 40. After two plays for no gain, Utica, notorious for the trick play, sent Mossholder in motion to the sideline. Their quarterback Orr threw a backward pass to Mossholder standing at the 28. From there, Mossholder heaved the ball nearly 50 yards in the air down to the Newark Catholic 25 where Tommy Helms broke up the pass. Utica punted and Byers returned the ball out to the 34-yard line.

Joe Bell was back with us this week and the first carry went to him on a 23 Power. After gaining 6 yards on the play, Joe took a shot on his right thigh—the one that had been bruised at Licking Valley. Joe was fine, however. Following a 24 Power for 5 yards, Kubik threw his first pass of the night complete to Joe Simi at the Utica 40. Joe fought his way to the 30 before being tackled. After a 26 Power Trap was stuffed, Kubik was under a heavy rush while searching for a deep receiver. He finally dumped the ball off to John Jurden along the sideline. John weaved his way down to the Redskin 12-yard line before being tackled. A well-executed 25 Power Trap allowed Bell to rip the defense for 11 yards down to the 1. Jeff Ronan gave the Homecoming crowd something to cheer about as he smashed across the goal line for our first points of the night with 5:03 to go in the first quarter. Backlund's PAT was good.

Utica's Paul Ikehorn picked up the "squib kick" and returned it up to the 43-yard line where Tim McKenna cut him down. On first down, Lenhart led Farley around left end and tagged Bill Franks. Olson and South were sealed and Farley dashed for 20 yards down to our 36. Coach Graham formed a "T" with his hands: Timeout Newark Catholic!

Utica went backward on each play after Coach Graham's visitation with us. They began with another procedure penalty that pushed them back to the 41 to establish first-and-fifteen. Byers dropped Pratt for a 2-yard loss on first down, leaving them with second-and-seventeen. Next, the Redskins were hit with a delay-of-game penalty to give them second-and-twenty-two from our 48. On a pitch to my side, Byers flew in to drop Farley behind the line, resulting in a third-and-twenty-four from the 50. The drive ended with a poor pass across the middle that was nearly intercepted. Another Utica penalty was declined and they punted the ball away on fourth down. After that great defensive effort, we were soon on defense again as John Jurden muffed the punt reception and the Redskins recovered at our 25-yard line. Their good fortune did not last long when on third down, Tommy Helms picked off Orr's pass at the 15 and brought it back to the 25. Jim Olson was charged with clipping during the runback, pushing us back to the 10-yard line. Olson received *two* earfuls upon his return to the sideline.

On first down, Ikehorn rotated to middle linebacker. It was unfortunate timing on his part as Jeff Ronan completely flattened Ikehorn on a 25 Power Trap. Bell enjoyed a 9-yard gain on the play. We converted a third down two plays later. Ronan barely got enough yardage on a 14 dive as the first quarter came to a close. At some point in the first quarter, I can remember approaching the line of scrimmage to see Paul Ikehorn lined up across from Tony Johns. I happened to look at the football at just the right moment and was astonished at what happened next. After Tony had placed his hands on the ball, Ikehorn blew a "hocker" (mucus wad) up through his facemask and it landed on one of Tony's hands. Though it was a vile act, I could appreciate the skill that was required to arch the mass up between the bars of the facemask with the precise amount of force to hit the target.

On the first play of the second quarter, Andy Kubik threw deep to Byers. Monte made a terrific finger-tip snag at the Redskin 43-yard line. Following a Flood Pass to Ronan that went to the 39, Kubik found Byers again on a Curl route at the 23. Monte escaped 4 defenders and cruised to the 6 where he was tripped up by Jeff Young. After the first-and-goal, we could only penetrate as far as the 3-yard line. Backlund booted a 20-yard field goal to make the score 10-0 with 9:28 left in the second quarter.

Utica's next series began at their 29-yard line. Following Blackburn's 6-yard gain on first down, our line tightened up to allow no additional yardage. The punt from Doug Orr rolled dead at the Green Wave 26 where our third offensive series began.

Coach Graham must have wanted to emphasize the passing attack against Utica. He had Kubik throw on first and second downs to start this drive. However, both passes were incomplete. Andy finally connected with Simi for 14 yards on third down to give us a first down at the 40.

After Bell gained 5 yards on a 26 Power Trap, a situation developed with one of the vehicles of the Homecoming court. The alarm system was activated and the horn began to blast repeatedly. Within a short time, the annoying disturbance was stopped and the home fans sent up a cheer of gratitude. I cannot speak for my teammates, but my level of concentration on the game was such that the car horn was unbeknownst to me. It wasn't until I got home that night and conducted my standard post-game procedure of resting on the couch with ice bags placed on various bumps and bruises that I learned about the incident from my mother.

We had been gifted 5 yards on second down when Utica jumped offside. Perhaps the car horn was to blame. Following an incomplete pass and a stuffed dive play on third down, Coach Graham decided to go for it on fourth-and-one from our 49. Bell got the ball and though he was hit solidly, his second effort made the difference and he got the first down. From the Redskin 49, Kubik dropped back to pass and was under a heavy rush from the left defensive end. I cut him down and saved Kubik—a duty that I had performed proudly since the eighth grade. The extra time allowed Kubik to find Byers all alone at the 20-yard line. Monte cruised to the end zone from there. Backlund's PAT was good and the new score was 17-0 with 4:56 left in the half.

Following another three-plays-and-out by Utica, Monte fielded the Redskin punt at our 27-yard line where our next offensive series began. On first down, Byers was interfered with on a deep pass route and we were gifted with a first down at the Newark Catholic 42. After no gain on a dive play, Kubik threw complete to Simi at the Redskin 36. Then Byers, who was simply unstoppable on this night, made a great catch near the ground for 9 more yards. On the following play, Monte was overthrown near the 15 and was hit in the back by Craig Rice. The two exchanged words as a result, which was the first evidence of tempers beginning to flare. It was third-and-short and Bell got the first down behind Donnelly and Cooperrider. The key to the play was Coop's awesome block as he got into his man, blew him 5 yards off the line and made the defender vanish into the grass. On the next play, Utica came unglued when Rice made too much contact with Joe Simi, resulting in pass interference. Rice defiantly got into the official's face, an act for which he could have been ejected. Utica head coach Tom Russell called timeout, stomped onto the field, threw his hat down and he too got into the official's face, pointing and shouting. Entertained by the event, the home fans cheered at the spectacle. This put the Utica players on the defensive. Paul Ikehorn, in particular, approached our fans and shook his fists in a defiant manner. After a 15-yard unsportsman-like conduct penalty had been assessed, the ball rested on the Utica 7-yard line. Coach Russell gathered his troops, fired them up and they appeared ready to take our heads off. As we approached the line of scrimmage, Ikehorn stood pointing at Kubik in a threatening manner. He should have known better than to ever threaten a lineman's quarterback. We can be very protective of our signal caller! As each lineman engaged in his respective battle, including Tony Johns who handled Ikehorn superbly, Kubik and Byers heaped ashes upon the enraged Redskins by teaming up for a scoring toss with 1:26 to go in the half. Utica did manage a small moral victory, however. A man broke through the line outside of Pat Cooperrider and blocked the extra point attempt.

On the ensuing kickoff, Joe Wiley made the stop on Selmon. Ramseyer blocked me in the back, which pushed Utica back to their 23-yard line. After a quick completion for 9 yards on first down, Utica converted on second down with a dive play. Following an incomplete pass on first down, Utica ran the trick play with Mossholder going in motion and receiving a throwback three times in a row. On the first attempt, which was to our bench, Mossholder caught the ball. Franks fell down and missed the tackle as Mossholder traveled along the sideline up to the 50-yard stripe with 26 seconds in the half. Paul Ikehorn blindsided Jim Calvert out of bounds just as the play ended. On the second attempt, Mossholder got the ball away and hit the wide-open Redskin quarterback downfield who ironically dropped the ball after it hit him in the hands. One of the Greenies was guilty of a personal foul on the play and Utica had a first down at the Newark Catholic 35. The third try of this trick play resulted in a poor pass from Orr, sailing past Mossholder and rolling out of bounds back at the 50-yard line. The half ended on a draw play to Dave Farley in which I had a solo tackle. The Homecoming crowd cheered as we vanished into the locker room with a 23-point lead.

The normal halftime activity in the locker room was again disrupted as the Court members had to go out for the crowning of the king and queen. With six football players out of seven boys on the Homecoming Court, it was almost certain that a teammate would be crowned as king. This was not to be, however. Jim Neumeyer, a member of the golf team, received the position of royalty. Nancy Nash was crowned as queen.

Joe Bell returned the second-half kickoff to the 30-yard line. Bell also carried on first down and was drilled in the backfield by the unblocked Craig Rice. Two Flood passes to Jeff Ronan moved the ball to the 40 for the first down. After a 26 Iso to Bell for 6 yards and a pass to Byers for 23 yards, we were in good shape at the Redskin 31. However, on the next play, Kubik was slow in getting the ball from Tony Johns. Donnelly pulled to his left and knocked the ball from Kubik's hands. Utica recovered it at the 30-yard line.

Utica began their first offensive set of the second half with an illegal procedure penalty. After a 9-yard pickup by Farley, we were called for being offside and Utica had a first down at their 42. Hindered by another procedure penalty on first down, Utica's drive stalled at their 46-yard line and they had to punt.

John Jurden returned the punt to the 30-yard line. From there, Bell ran for 18 yards on two straight 28 Sweeps. We began to get sloppy as the next three plays consisted of a holding penalty, an incomplete pass and a delay-of-game infraction. From the 27-yard line, Kubik dropped back to pass and hung in the pocket for a long time. Just as he was hit, Kubik delivered a strike to Byers good for 56 yards down to the Redskin 17. From there, Cooperrider made another pancake block and Donnelly flattened the defensive end on a 25 Power Trap. This enabled Bell to blast down to the 2-yard line. Another delay-of-game penalty prompted Coach Graham to call a timeout. He came out to chastise Andy Kubik for not getting us in and out of the huddle in an efficient manner. On first-and-goal from the 7, Bell nearly scored on another 25 Power Trap but fell down at the goal line. Bell plunged across on the following play behind the bulldozing of Donnelly and Cooperrider with 3:37 left in the third quarter. The extra point was botched when the snap from center rolled across the ground to Montgomery. Anytime a bad snap occurred on an extra point or field goal, Jeremy was to shout "Red Ball" and roll to his right. This was also the cue for the ends and wingmen to fade into the end zone and look for a pass. Jeremy was under too heavy a rush and his pass was incomplete. The score was 29-0 and it would be the final score.

Utica's next series started at their 30. They were able to gain a first down but this drive was also plagued with more penalties and died at the 35-yard line. Orr's punt rolled to the Newark Catholic 25 where several Clean Green came into the game and went to work.

The next series was a 14-play drive and was engineered by Jeremy Montgomery. It included nice runs by Darby Riley, an outstanding one-handed catch by Jurden on his back and a third-down completion to Albert Ghiloni. The drive was polluted with an offside penalty and two holding violations resulting in the drive stalling on fourth down at the Utica 28.

Against the Clean Green defense, Utica was able to effectively move the ball on the shoulders of Dave Farley. A pass interference call against Tommy Helms set the Redskins up with a first down at the Newark Catholic 30. The scoring threat was terminated with the help of another Utica procedure penalty and a sack of Orr by Jeff Wade. Utica lost the ball on downs at the Green Wave 44-yard line. After another seven offensive plays by the Clean Green, time had expired. The curtain closed on this Homecoming show.

Jeff Ronan did not get his opportunity to plaster Rob Peters. "He was injured for this game and did not play," said Ronan. "I found him afterward and he was on crutches. I told him that I was going to pay him back and he laughed." [13]

The Homecoming crowd had been treated to a fantastic aerial display. Andy Kubik had set a new Newark Catholic single-game passing record with 308 yards, breaking the previous record of 298 yards set by Doug Rodenbeck in 1968 against Watkins Memorial.[14] Monte Byers also set a new school record for receiving yards in a game with 212 on seven catches, breaking the old mark of 173 yards set by Joe Kennedy in the East Knox game in 1968.[15] We had also racked up 153 yards rushing—88 belonging to Joe Bell. Coach Graham said that the "...offensive line must have had a great night since we gained nearly 500 yards."[16]

It had not been a perfect game for us by any means. Although Utica was seriously plagued with penalties, we actually surpassed them in total penalty yardage, to which Coach Graham said "...we still have a lot of work to do on our concentration."[17]

The victory, Coach Graham's 150th in his carreer,[18] improved us to 9-0 and assured us of at least a share of the LCL title. But best of all, we had gotten the job done and there would be no "crying eyes and broken hearts" at the Homecoming dance.

Utica	0	0	0	0	0
Newark Catholic	7	16	6	0	29

	U	NC
First Downs	9	26
Rushing	68	153
Passing Yards	35	334
Total yards	103	487
Att-Comp-Int	17-4-1	26-17-0
Punts / Avg	6-34	0
Kickoffs / Avg	1-50	6-42
Fumbles / lost	0-0	3-2
Penalties / yards	14-91	11-100

Week 9 LCL Action[19]

Licking Valley	21	Watkins Memorial	34
Northridge	12	Heath	14
Johnstown	34	Lakewood	35
New Albany	14	Granville	12

Notes

1. Mark Naegele, "Mogadore, NC show similar styles," *The Advocate*, (Nov. 21, 1985), p. 13.

2. *The Advocate*, (Oct. 22, 1985), p. 12.

3. *The Advocate*, (Oct. 24, 1985), p. 26.

4. Wes Poth, Telephone conversation with author, Jan. 14, 2002.

5. Ibid.

6. Ibid.

7. Ibid.

8. Ibid.

9. Rick Cannizzaro, "Redskins' chief looks to ground attack," *The Advocate, Football '85*, (Aug. 28, 1985), p. 11.

10. J.D. Graham, Conversation with author, Aug. 3, 2002.

11. Joseph Simi, Conversation with author, Dec. 18, 2001.

12. Jeff Ronan, Conversation with author, Jan. 9, 2002.

13. Ibid.

14. Rick Cannizzaro, "NC breaks record, Redskins," *The Advocate*, (Oct. 27, 1985), p. 1C.

15. Ibid.

16. Ibid.

17. Ibid.

18.   Ibid.

19.   *The Advocate*, (Oct. 26, 1985), p. 8.

Newark Catholic beat Utica in the five remaining LCL seasons after 1985. The series closed with NC leading 16-2.

Week 10

Lakewood Lancers

November 2, Parents Night

The final week of the regular season began with a very tiring Monday. Because the Homecoming dance took place on Sunday night, most of us did not get to sleep at a decent hour and it was rough reporting to school in the morning.

The dance had been a success, although some did not view it as such. A loud, wild and heavy rock band called "Axis" provided the night's music. They inundated the school gymnasium with screaming vocals, piercing guitar solos and thunderous drumming as they covered songs from the popular "hair bands" of the day including Ratt, Van Halen, Dokken and Twisted Sister. The only opportunities for slow dancing occurred when Air Supply records were played during the band's intermissions. When we filed from the locker room to start practice on Monday afternoon, Coach Graham said, "Hey, which one of you is responsible for bringing that piece-of-shit band into this high school? Was that you, Kubik?" Although Coach Graham was quite serious in his disgust, I had to keep from laughing as he tried to pin the blame on our class vice president for the musical abomination.

In the weekly "Mogadore Watch," the Wildcats cruised past East Canton 47-7 over the weekend[1] and increased their lead over us in the Associated Press poll by 4 more points, 291-265.[2] Unless Mogadore happened to lose this coming week, we would have to accept the fact that winning the AP poll title was an impossibility.

Looking at the brighter side of things, we were on top of Region 19 with 91.00 computer points and held a 44.5-point lead over second-place Frankfort Adena.[3] This large lead assured us of a berth in the playoffs even if we happened to lose our last game of the regular season. As an interesting side note, 91 computer points after 9 games was more than the '84 Green Wave team scored in 10 games. They finished with 88.5,[4] but who's counting?

Week 10 had us matched up with the Lakewood Lancers, the last remaining LCL opponent of the 1985 season. A Class AA school in the south-central part of the county, Lakewood had lost eight straight games but entered week 10 on an up note after beating Granville 35-12 in week 9.[5] This was another week of warnings from Coach Graham not to assume victory, not to take the Lancers lightly, not to be lackadaisical, etc. Sometimes I thought that Coach Graham would rather play a 10-0 team than a team that was 0-10 simply because the kids were more easily motivated and in focus when faced with a respectable opponent. My suspicion was confirmed in a conversation with Coach Graham. "I knew the kids could stay focused for the bigger games," Graham said. "The games where the kids knew they were better than another team are what I had to worry about. Sometimes, I really had to kick ass to keep you guys focused."[6]

In the previous years of contests between the two schools, Lakewood had managed to beat Newark Catholic just one time. Pat Cooperrider recalls Coach Graham talking about it during Lakewood week. "Graham walked around talking about Lakewood," said Cooperrider, "and then he stopped and asked, 'How many trophies do you think they have in their trophy case? Coop? Evans? I'll tell ya. They've got one. It's from the year they beat us!'"[7]

The year Coach Graham referred to was 1976 in which the Lancers enjoyed a 20-6 victory over the Green Wave. When asked about that game, Coach Poth had this to say:

> They had a nice team. They had the three fastest kids in the county. I mean they could flat-out fly. They had us down 14-6 with a few seconds left to play. The Lakewood fans are all there and they're just going crazy, of course, because they're beating Newark Catholic. They had the ball and called timeout to score again. Kids like (Dan) McKenna and (Chris) Marshall—the kids who would come back and win a state championship for us eventually—they're crying, and J.D. being J.D. gives them one those speeches: "You younger kids remember this!" I'm getting fired up just talking about it. They did score on us and don't think that *that* wasn't mentioned more than once in the years we came back for Lakewood.[8]

Payback did not come the following year as the game resulted in a 7-7 stalemate—the lone tie on Coach Graham's overall record. "They were tough again that year," said Coach Poth. "We played a hell of a game. To hold that team to seven points was a good accomplishment, so it was a pretty good tie."[9]

It was not until the following season when payback finally came. The sophomores of the 1976 team who had left Lakewood High School with tears in their eyes returned in 1978 and had their vengeance to the tune of a 44-0 drubbing.

The 1985 Lancers, lead by first-year coach Chris Kubbs, had only 31 kids on the team.[10] Although the group was small, many of the players had good size. The offensive line was made of center Todd Brunton (6-0, 165); Marty Ramsey (6-2,

220) and Terry Ball (6-3, 280) at the guards; Ken Waddley (5-10, 170) and Mike Mayeux (5-11, 180) at the tackles. Defensive linemen were Ball, Brunton, Mayeux and Rick Johnson (6-0, 195). Quarterback for the Lancers was Larry Thompson (6-0, 160).[11]

As was customary, the last home game of the season was set aside to honor the parents off all the athletes involved in fall sports. In stark contrast to Homecoming, Coach Graham held Parents Night in the highest regard. We were constantly reminded that the sacrifices of our parents are what enabled us to be a part of Newark Catholic and its athletic program. We were to never take that for granted.

Parents Night required our normal game-day routine to be moved up anywhere from 30 to 60 minutes in order to accommodate the activities. Behind the west end zone of White Field, cheerleaders, golfers, volleyball players, cross country runners and football players milled about with their parents in a steady downpour as coordinators worked frantically to transform the disorganized mob into an orderly stream of bodies. The line snaked its way to a gate beneath the west goal post. This was the last stop where we waited for our names to be announced. After a family was introduced, the athlete and parents walked out to the 50-yard line, turned left toward the home seating and then stopped to have a picture taken. Coach Graham issued instructions to his football players on what he expected of us. Our helmets were to be off and carried under the right arm. We were to lead our mothers by the arm and smile for the picture. After we had reached the sideline, he wanted us to kiss our mother, shake our father's hand and tell them that we loved them. It was a special time to be able to take our parents out onto the very battlefield where a war would rage in less than an hour. It was also an emotional time for those of us who were seniors as it would be our last Parents Night at White Field. Depending on the playoff pairings, this could also be our last time to play at White Field—a point Coach Graham drove home in the locker room for additional motivation.

Before the game, it was Coach Graham's custom to invite all of the football fathers into the locker room. This made for a very crowded locker room, but no one seemed to mind. It was all about togetherness. Standing behind their sons with hands on the shoulder pads, the fathers got a taste of the pre-game atmosphere, speeches, nervousness and intensity that we as players thrived on week after week. There's no doubt in my mind that this was a rewarding experience for my father who had gone through the same thing in this very locker room as a Newark Wildcat 40 years earlier. Coach Graham was quite close to his own father. He always became emotional and teary-eyed on us during the pep talk while speaking about fathers, causing most of us to follow suit.

This night had to be rough for two of our seniors: Albert Ghiloni and Tony Johns. Albert's father Eugene had passed away some years ago and Tony's father Robert passed away unexpectedly during our junior year. When asked about how he handled it, Tony simply described what he did to remember his father throughout the season.

I mentioned in the pre-season of our senior year that I intended to wear a black wristband so I could do something to remind me that my father was there with me. But the first game of the season came before I had time to stop by the sports store and pick up my wristband. John Jurden came up to me in the locker room before the first game and put out his hand. In it was a black wristband. All he said was, "You mentioned this in the summer." Then he just walked away. I wore that wristband for every game and it seemed to bring me pretty good luck.[12]

When the last prayer had been said and it was time to head outside into the fray, we carried out Coach Graham's last instruction: "Turn around and shake your father's hand." Some went so far as to hug their dads, which was even better.

In a steady downpour and on a slick, soggy field, Lakewood took the opening kickoff at the 20 and returned it 8 yards. Our defense was wired from the very start as the first two plays netted –1 yard, thanks to Calvert slanting into the running back and crushing him on second down. After fumbling a pitch on third down, Lakewood punted. Monte Byers flew in on a punt block and roughed the kicker, giving Lakewood a new set of downs at their 40. Lakewood's good fortune ended there when Simi intercepted a pass on the next play at the Newark Catholic 49.

After Kubik threw a dud on first down, Joe Bell sliced for 26 yards on a 26 Iso to the Lancer 25—not bad for the first carry of the night. Yardage came slowly on the next three plays and we faced fourth-and-three from the 17. Coach Graham elected to go for it. Joe Bell, lead by Dale Backlund, gained the required yardage to the 11-yard line on a 17 Quick Pitch. Bell penetrated to the 4-yard line on a 26 Power Trap—a play in which Donnelly's man ended up on the ground as usual. Another standoff on the play—a battle that would occur all night—was Coop against the large 6-3, 280-pound Terry Ball at defensive tackle. Coop successfully bulldozed the larger man. Terry Ball was handled again on the ensuing play as Bell found a lane to the end zone inside of Cooperrider on a 24 Power with 6:27 left in the first quarter. Backlund's PAT was good.

After fielding the kickoff at the 10, Lakewood's return man slipped and his knee touched, leaving 90 yards between the Lancers and pay dirt. It was an abysmal series for Lakewood as first down went for no gain. Byers blitzed and drilled the quarterback on a second-down option, causing a fumble that we nearly recovered. On third down, an option play went to Billy Franks' side. The ball sailed behind the running back and into the end zone. Todd South, "The Claw," recovered for our second touchdown on Parents Night. Backlund converted the extra point and we lead 14-0 with 4:48 left in quarter one.

Lakewood again generated no offense on their next series thanks to a swarming defense that was aided by Monte's quarterback sack for a 4-yard loss. The Lancer punt rolled dead at the Green Wave 36.

After Bell carried for 5 yards on 26 Power Trap, he then fumbled the ball on a 25 Power Trap. Luckily, I happened to be in position to cover the loose pigskin. The following play featured Scott Saad on a 17 Quick Pitch for 18 yards, but a holding penalty brought it all back. A pass interference call gave us a first down on the next play. Then a 2-yard run by Bell was followed with a pass to Monte Byers at the Lakewood 34-yard line good for another first down. Lakewood then had defensive success as Saad was held to 4 yards on first down. Ronan was wiped out on second down and then slipped on a third-down Flood pass. On fourth-and-five from the Lancer 28, Saad was leveled after a short gain and Lakewood returned to offense just moments into the second quarter.

Lakewood failed to gain any positive yardage on their next possession. We had a new series of downs at the Newark Catholic 45 following the Lancer punt. Jeff Ronan gained one yard on a Flood Left. Scott Saad jetted for 17 yards on 26 Iso to the Lancer 37. Ronan found another 15 yards on a 27 Counter Sweep. That play was called back for blocking below the waist and left us with first-and-eighteen at the Lancer 45-yard line. This was no problem as Kubik hit Simi for 15-yards and the remaining distance was earned by Ronan on a 6 Trap. On the following play, Joe Bell caught a Flood pass from Kubik at the Lancer 16 and made it to the 7 before he was stopped. Jeff Ronan finished off the drive with 5:58 to go in the half with a 6 Trap and a 14 Dive. Backlund's PAT was perfect: Newark Catholic 21, Lakewood 0.

On the ensuing kickoff, the return man lost the ball at the 20-yard line after Tim McKenna hit him. Another Lancer managed to cover it in time. The Lancers were dominated by our defense once more and gained only minimal yardage in three plays. Joe Simi fielded the punt at the 30 and returned it out to the 38-yard line before slipping in the wet grass.

Our offense operated as a well-oiled machine on the next possession. On first down, I lead Jeff Ronan on a 6 Trap. The senior fullback broke two tackles and rumbled for 12 yards. On the next play, I trapped again for Scott Saad on 5 Trap, which was good for 6 yards. The third play of the drive was somewhat unusual. It was a 23 Power to the weak side and Joe Bell blocked for Jeff Ronan. Jeff blasted through the line, ran over the first man that tried to tackle him and gained 10 yards down to the Lancer 30. Joe Bell stole the show on the final three plays of the drive as he gained 4 yards via 28 Counter Sweep, cruised to the Lancer 3 on a Flood Left pass and completed the scoring journey with a 13 Dive behind Donnelly and Cooperrider. Dale Backlund's extra point attempt sailed awkwardly into the air and just cleared the crossbar to set the score at 28-0 with 2:04 left in the half.

The Lancers had great field position after the kickoff was returned out to the 40-yard line. The drive went 20 yards the wrong way for Lakewood, however, thanks to an aggressive defense and a blocking-below-the-waist penalty. Time expired in the second quarter after Lakewood's third play and we withdrew to the locker room with the game well under control as the rain continued to fall.

At half time, Coach Graham was pleased we were up 28-0. An entirely new lineup composed of substitutes was assembled for both the offense and defense for the second half. Except for special teams, the first-teamers were finished for the night. This served two purposes: First, it rested the starters and eliminated the risk of further injuries before the playoffs. Second, it gave all of the younger kids their final game action of the season as the playoff games were likely to be low-scoring, ulcer-producing dog fights where the Clean Green were unlikely to participate.

On the opening kickoff of the second quarter, sophomore Damon Shumaker was one of the deep men and the ball went right to him. Damon had great difficulty getting a handle on the loose, wet ball at the 12-yard line. When he finally picked it up, Schumaker raced 57 yards along our sideline to the Lancer 30. Nothing came of this drive due to a penalty. A punt by Jim Winters set Lakewood up at the 15.

On Lakewood's first snap, Jimmy Cross nailed the quarterback on an option play, causing the ball to come loose. After a mad scramble for the ball, Lakewood retained possession at their 3-yard line. Lakewood ended up punting from inside the 5. The punt, fielded by Darby Riley at the Lancer 40, was returned to the 22.

The short field was made even shorter by a late hit out of bounds, moving the ball to the Lancer 11. Despite the great field position, 20 yards in penalties and a sack of Jeremy Montgomery forced us to punt from the 35. Lakewood went to work again from inside the 5-yard line. From there, the Lancers had limited success running the ball and moved out to the 20-yard line before they finally punted.

After the punt was downed at the Lakewood 47, the Clean Green mounted a ground assault on the backs of Riley and Tommy Parker. The 10-play drive included a 21-yard jaunt by Riley and a pass interference penalty against Lakewood that set up first-and-goal at the 3. Tommy Parker capped the series with a 3-yard touchdown run with 11:10 left in the final period. Matt Dase, also known as "Laser," kicked the extra point and the new tally was 35-0.

Lakewood was able to move the ball again on their next series. The drive did not last long. On the fifth play, a quick pass over the middle advanced the ball to the Newark Catholic 35, but the ball came loose and the Greenies recovered. Both in jubilation and to indicate a first down, junior Jeff Wade spun around while quickly extending his arm and tagged an approaching referee right in the head. This was a source of much laughter during films the following day as Coach Graham repeated the scene several times.

The younger Wave players made good use of this next offensive opportunity. Tommy Parker ran left on a 17 Quick Pitch, made a nice cutback to the right and scampered 65 yards for a touchdown—the longest rushing play for a score up to this point in the season. Matt Dase nailed his second PAT of the night to make the score 42-0 with 8:15 left in the game.

Following the touchdown, Lakewood moved the ball out near midfield on a pass completion, but a sack by Jeff Wade and Craig Dye brought about the end of the drive and Lakewood punted for the last time. The clock was then kept in motion by the rushing of Riley and Parker. After 12 more plays, time expired and the 1985 regular season came to a close.

The newspaper article that covered the game contained some interesting facts that our team did not know. We had the state's longest regular season winning streak at 25 games. We had amassed 23 consecutive victories and the defeat of

Lakewood tied a Licking County League record of consecutive league victories at 21—a record set by Johnstown in 1966.[13] Coach Graham said that he was "...very pleased with this team. They've come a long way since the start of the year."[14]

It had been an outstanding defensive effort as we posted our third consecutive shutout and fifth of the season, limiting Lakewood to just 34 total yards and –10 yards rushing.[15] The best part about the entire game, aside from winning for our parents, was that three out of four goals of the season had been realized that night: We wrapped up a perfect regular season, we achieved an LCL championship and we secured a trip to the playoffs. We were ready to set sail!

The night of the Lakewood game was the night the clocks were rolled back for daylight savings time in 1985. While our curfew was 1:00 a.m. on game nights, some of us thought that we could roll our watches back to midnight when the bell tolled one to give us an extra hour out on the town. Technically, we were not violating curfew. I know this was probably stretching things just a bit. If we had gone home at the normal time, the following incident would have been avoided.

I was in the school parking lot late after the game with Pat Cooperrider and some others, just talking and having a good time. Jimmy Cross decided that it was time to go and he headed home. A few minutes later, Cross returned to inform us that he had just struck an opossum out on Church Street and asked us if we would help him catch it. I do not know why Jimmy Cross wanted to go opossum chasing after midnight on a Saturday night, but we agreed to assist him and piled into his car.

Jim drove us to the telephone building situated on the south side of Church Street between Neal and Day Avenue. On the way, Jim explained that he had nicked one of the opossum's feet with the front tire and it scurried off under a bush. We searched the area when we arrived at the site and sure enough, we found the beady-eyed, prehensile-tailed beast staring back at us from beneath a bush next to a building. None of us had the guts to reach in and grab the thing because it would assume a defensive posture when it saw us. Thinking that he could smoke the beast out from its secure location, Jim backed his car up tightly against the bush with the tailpipe pointed toward the critter and began to rev the engine. Now keep in mind that this occurred late into the evening and the revving of the car engine plus our laughing and yelling must have been a great disturbance to the surrounding homes.

When it was apparent that smoking the animal out would not work, Cross decided that we should just attempt to stun the thing by throwing rocks at it. There were not many rocks to be found in the area but the few we did find were tossed at the animal. It was difficult to get a clear shot because the bush provided plenty of cover. When the rocks had all been used up, I got the bright idea of pulling chunks of broken pavement up from the alley surface. Just as I bent down to extract a piece of asphalt, I was caught dead in the headlight beams of a sheriff's car that pulled into the alley from Church Street. Because the car approached from the east, which was the blind side of the building, I suspect that a neighborhood resident reported us because the officer knew exactly where to pull in.

When the headlights hit me, I instantly dropped the asphalt and retreated up the alley to join the others. I never had a run-in with the law before and was scared to death.

"We're dead, guys," I said to my accomplices.

"No we're not. Just let me handle this," Cross said as he confidently awaited the interrogation process to begin.

"What's going on here gentleman?" asked the sheriff as he looked us over. It was my bad luck to be wearing my school jacket, which had my full name stitched across the front. I stood sideways to the officer so he could not read my name. As I contemplated the possible fallout from this incident, terrible thoughts filled my mind. I could envision the headline in tomorrow's paper: *Newark Catholic team captain arrested for cruelty to animal; killed by coach.*

Jimmy Cross began to answer the sheriff and his approach was masterful.

"Well sir, we were driving down Church Street and accidentally hit a possum. It was hurt and wandered up under this bush. We thought that if we let it go, it might get all crazy and angry and try to bite some little kid, so we we're going to kill it before that happened."

"Where is the possum now?" asked the sheriff.

"Under there," Jim said, pointing to the bush.

After peering under the bush, the sheriff turned to us and said, "I think the possum has had enough for one night and I don't think you need to worry about it. Why don't you boys just go on home now."

Anything you say, sir! I thought. Words could not describe the relief I felt after that. Thanks to Jim's creativity and the generosity of a sheriff, Coach Graham would not have to kill any of us!

Lakewood	0	0	0	0	0
Newark Catholic	14	14	0	14	42

	L	NC
First Downs	5	19
Rushing	-10	281
Passing Yards	44	83
Total yards	34	364
Att-Comp-Int	10-3-1	9-7-0
Punts	6-32	2-27
Kickoffs / Avg	1-48	7-43
Fumbles / lost	6-2	1-0
Penalties / yards	5-49	7-75

Week 10 LCL Action[16]

Licking Valley	44		Watkins Memorial	47
Johnstown	14		Granville	8
Clear Fork	26		Utica	40
Heath	2		Northridge	30

Notes

1. Mark Naegele, "Mogadore, NC show similar styles," *The Advocate*, (Nov. 21, 1985), p. 13.

2. *The Advocate*, (Oct. 29, 1985), p. 11.

3. *The Advocate*, (Oct. 31, 1985), p. 15.

4. *The Advocate, Football '85*, (Aug. 28, 1985), p. 8.

5. *The Advocate*, (Oct. 26, 1985), p. 8.

6. J.D. Graham, Telephone conversation with author, Mar. 3, 2002.

7. Pat Cooperrider, Conversation with author, Dec. 11, 2001.

8. Wes Poth, Conversation with author, Jan. 30, 2002.

9. Ibid.

10. Mark Shaw, "New Lancer boss begins to search for game players," *The Advocate, Football '85*, (Aug. 28, 1985), p. 12.

11. Ibid.

12. Anthony Johns, Electronic mail to author, Jan. 21, 2002.

13. Rick Cannizzaro, "Newark Catholic crushes Lancers; playoffs await," *The Advocate*, (Nov. 3, 1985), p. 1C.

14. Ibid.

15. Ibid.

16. *The Advocate*, (Nov. 2, 1985), p. 7.

After the 1985 season, Lakewood would get one more victory in on Newark Catholic before the LCL broke up. That victory occurred in 1989—Coach Graham's worst season in which the Green Wave finished 5-4 and failed to make the playoffs for the first time since 1979. The series ended with NC holding a 15-2-1 advantage.

1985 Licking County League Statistics[1]

Final Records

	Overall					LCL			
	W	**L**	**PF**	**PA**		**W**	**L**	**PF**	**PA**
Newark Catholic	10	0	267	46	Newark Catholic	8	0	236	40
Licking Valley	8	2	229	95	Licking Valley	7	1	203	81
Watkins	8	2	290	75	Watkins	6	2	219	75
Johnstown	6	4	242	170	Johnstown	5	3	202	143
Heath	4	6	155	231	Heath	4	4	137	167
Utica	3	7	179	260	Utica	3	5	149	195
Northridge	2	8	134	302	Northridge	2	6	108	253
Lakewood	1	9	129	308	Lakewood	1	6	115	269
Granville	1	9	87	292	Granville	0	8	59	237

Rushing

	Att.	**Yds.**
Baldwin, Johns.	210	1,357
Black, LV	191	1,216
Norman, Heath	164	1,051
Farley, Utica	195	929
Carruth, Gran.	159	776
Miller, LV	108	675
Warga, NR	153	593
French, Gran.	103	576
Shirey, WM	123	566
Bell, NC	119	563
Jones, LK	95	480
Murray, WM	72	390

Passing

	Att.	**Comp.**	**Yds.**
Kubik, NC	180	99	1,624
Rice, NR	163	78	1,112
Brown, Heath	159	71	957
Orr, Utica	155	69	906
Thompson, LK	126	46	670
Chacey, LV	94	38	538
Cook, Johns.	91	43	523
Lieb, WM	61	29	486
Engle, Gran.	73	29	325

	Receiving	
	No.	**Yds.**
Byers, NC	40	728
Simi, NC	26	410
Powell, Heath	25	396
Newkirk, NR	23	329
Warga, NR	22	341
Farley, Utica	18	174
Jurden, NC	16	301
Strausbaugh, LV	15	180
Selmon, Utica	14	255
French, Gran.	14	216

	Scoring				
	TD	**PAT**	**2PT**	**FG**	**Pts**
Baldwin, Johns.	17	0	1	0	104
Black, LV	16	0	0	0	96
Farley, Utica	11	0	5	0	94
Warga, NR	9	0	2	0	56
Shirey, WM	9	0	0	0	54
Norman, Heath	8	0	1	0	48
Backlund, NC	0	29	0	3	38
Byers, NC	6	0	0	0	36
Ronan, NC	5	0	0	0	30
Simi, NC	5	0	0	0	30

Notes

1. *The Advocate*, (Nov. 7, 1985), p. 14.

Part III
The Playoffs

Mr. Graham

We're so sorry Mr. Graham,
But we do the best we can,
While you stomp around and cuss,
Saying no one's worse than us.
Seems like all you do is yell;
Make our lives a living hell.

In the summer sun we fry,
And we scrimmage 'til we die.
You say, "No one's died here yet,"
As we drown in stinking sweat.
And quite common during sprints,
Are the puking incidents.
We watch films 'til 9 p.m.,
Then we watch them all again.

But we know it's for the best,
Even though we get no rest.
For when game day comes around,
We're prepared for the battleground.
And then someday, who knows when,
We might make that trip again,
And hope to win the prize for you,
On the turf at O.S.U.

—William B. Evans
September 1985

Week 11

Richmond Dale Southeastern Panthers

November 9, Regional Semifinals

The post season had an incredible atmosphere all its own that is difficult to put into words. Everything seemed new, fresh and more exciting than in previous weeks. School spirit and pride were everywhere and swelled in the hearts of those within the NC community. Radio, TV and newspaper personalities snooped around the school almost daily to interview Coach Graham and key players. These people would often bring the TV cameras right out onto the practice field. Coach Graham faced the challenge of not only keeping these distractions to a minimum but of also keeping us from getting big heads from all of the media attention.

With respect to the practices, there was extra excitement among the players. We got after each other more intensely and were more attentive to the coaches. The November weather was usually cold, wet and overcast. We often had to practice in muddy areas. In my opinion, this was perfect football weather. I preferred these conditions to a 90-degree August day anytime! I personally could not wait for practices to begin when school let out. The regular season games seemed like eons ago once the playoffs began. They also seemed small and boring in comparison to a playoff game and I often wondered how we ever got fired up for them.

Each playoff game became increasingly bigger and brought more pressure than the one before it. This stemmed from the fact that not only did the quality of opponents constantly increase, but also a harsh reality existed that it was now a one-game season. If we slipped up, our dream of reaching that final destination—the hallowed turf of Ohio Stadium—would be ruined. Coach Graham had a way of using that fact in a positive manner. He always managed to fill us with immense confidence no matter how formidable our opponent seemed.

Painting the Playoff Picture

In 1985, high schools were separated into five divisions "based upon the male enrollment in grades 10-12."[1] The smallest schools in the State—those with male enrollments between 30-142—were assigned to Division V and there were 144 schools of this size in Ohio in 1985.[2] Twenty computer regions existed in Ohio in 1985—four regions for each of the five Divisions in the State. Division V teams were assigned to the last four regions: 17-20. As mentioned earlier, the OHSAA expanded the playoff system in 1985 by allowing the top four teams in each region into the post season as opposed to the top two, which had been the case since 1980. We were one of 16 Division V schools in Ohio to make it to the post season. This number would be cut in half each week until one team was left standing. Below are the 16 Division V schools that made the playoffs in 1985 along with their final computer rankings:

> **Region 17**: Mogadore (88.7222), Sycamore Mohawk (65.50), New Washington Buckeye Central (63.00), New Philadelphia Tuscarawas Catholic (53.5).
> **Region 18:** McComb, (62.5), Attica Seneca East (61.5), Fremont St. Joseph (60.00), Delphos Jefferson (57.277).
> **Region 19:** Newark Catholic (103.50), Frankfort Adena (50.50), Richmond Dale Southeastern (45.00), Bainbridge Paint Valley (44.00).
> **Region 20:** Middletown Fenwick (78.50), S. Charleston Southeastern (74.50), Covington (71.50), Cincinnati Summit Country Day (70.3888).[3]

Special note should be taken of the computer point total that Newark Catholic had amassed. The 53-point advantage over second-place Frankfort Adena was "...the largest winning margin of any region champion..." in 1985.[4] With that point total, our team could have qualified for the playoffs in every region in Divisions III and IV. Only 7 teams between both divisions had more points than Newark Catholic did.[5] More impressive was the fact that we were the first Division V team in the State of Ohio to score more than 100 computer points in a season.[6]

The point total was a testament to the strength of schedule that we endured in the regular season. It should be noted in the above list that the fourth-place team in Region 17 was Tuscarawas Catholic, our opponent in week 1. They finished the year with a 9-1 record, their only loss being to us of course.[7] Our other non-league opponent, the Coshocton Redskins, had a fine season as well and also finished 9-1. They did not qualify for the playoffs, however.[8] These non-league games not only provided abundant computer points but they also brought struggles and tests of character that served as primers for the playoffs.

As can also be seen from the list of playoff qualifiers, our friends to the north, the Mogadore Wildcats finished on top of their region as well. We all watched the paper with interest to see which school would be awarded the AP poll championship. Mogadore had made an impressive showing in week 10 by ripping Crestwood 54-12.[9] When the voting was finished, Mogadore did in fact win the poll title. Several of the voters, however, must have thought that the old Green Wave had gotten things back on track with our 42-0 defeat of Lakewood because Mogadore's margin of victory was just three points![10] It was almost sickening to think that we lost by such a small margin, but we did manage to edge out Mogadore for the top spot in the UPI poll[11] and we could take consolation in that fact.

As mentioned earlier, it was typical for media hounds to flock to the school throughout the playoffs and they began to hit us on Monday of the first playoff week. One or two new articles would appear in the paper each night that concentrated on certain players, qualities of our team or our opponent for the week. One afternoon, Mark Shaw from *The Advocate* wanted to do a story about our defense and the "new kids" that comprised it. Coach Graham selected Todd South and me to be interviewed and it took place in room 120 before practice. The article, which was entitled, "New kids uphold Catholic tradition with stingy defense," even included a picture of Todd and me. It was our moment in the spotlight. Pat Cooperrider and Joe Simi were chosen to share their thoughts with the *Columbus Dispatch* about what the season had meant to them.

On still another night of the week, the local cable TV station (Channel 5) brought a camera to the school and set up in room 101 to interview all of the fall sports teams. Before practice started, Coach Graham sent the senior players to be interviewed. We were clad in our football pants and other mangy clothing. Ed Jobes, a Cable 5 sports commentator, conducted the interviews. He called each of us up one at a time, asked questions and stuck a microphone in our faces, causing some awkward moments for us all. Jeff Ronan, ever the warrior, wore an Army shirt which read *Kill 'em all, Let God Sort 'em Out.*

The program aired on Thursday of that week for the "LCL Show." On the day after the interview, many of us received unbelievable amounts of ribbing and teasing from the coaching staff, younger teammates and each other. Coach Graham jumped on Joe Simi and John Jurden, saying that they needed haircuts. (Simi and Jurden were fearful of cutting their hair for superstitious reasons.) Coach Poth had critiques of everyone's performances and seemed to enjoy giving us a hard time. He said that our catholic school, a place that supposedly taught God's love, was painted in a bad light by Ronan's shirt but that it was also funny in a sick sort of way. He also jumped on me about my answer to Ed Jobes' question, "What does it mean to be a team captain." I said that one of my jobs was to keep people in line.

"What kind of answer was that, Evans?" Poth jeered. "Keep people in line? Gee-ma-nee frost!"

227

Coach Poth thought I literally meant keeping people in straight lines on the football field during pre-game, but that's not what I meant at all. What I meant was keeping people in line with respect to their behavior during the game. Coach Poth was entirely justified in ripping on me, however. I did not want to do that interview and my stuttering and stammering was indicative of that. I came off sounding dumber than a box of rocks. It pains me still to watch it.

The biggest news of the week that set the school abuzz was the Associated Press all-district football awards. Andy Kubik had been named Class A Central District Back of the Year,[12] following in the footsteps of Newark Catholic quarterback Shane Montgomery who won the award in 1984.

The awards did not end there. Kevin Donnelly, all 5-9, 175 pounds of him, was selected as the Class A Central District Offensive Lineman of the Year.[13] The reader may recall that way back at the beginning of the season, I mentioned that winning this very award was a goal of mine. Obviously, I had failed in this quest but I was in no way jealous of Kevin. He was strong, tough as nails and played most of the year with a separated shoulder. He clearly deserved this award several times over. Kevin joined three other Green Wave linemen who won this award in previous years: Paul Cost in 1981, Joe Paul in 1982 and Jeff Ulenhake in 1983.[14]

The amazing aspect of all of this was that for the first time in Newark Catholic's history, two players on the same team won these awards.[15] Coach Graham remarked that the school had "...been fortunate to have the Lineman of the Year or Back of the Year, but never both in the same year. It's a great honor for our young people and I'm sure their teammates share in the recognition."[16]

The awards still did not end there. In addition to Andy and Kevin being named to the first-team all-district, Pat Cooperrider, Monte Byers and Joe Simi were selected to the first-team for their offensive efforts.[17]

A sixth player from our team received first-team all-district recognition on the defensive side of the ball: me! Now, I considered myself a much better guard than defensive end and for the life of me, I don't know how I was selected for this award. Obviously, those that were involved in the selection process must have overlooked my performance in the Licking Valley game! It was definitely an honor nonetheless.

Somewhere in the middle of all of this commotion, there was a football game to prepare for. Our opponent for the regional semi-final was Region 19's third-place team, the Richmond Dale Southeastern Panthers. Richmond Dale is located in the southeast corner of Ross County, approximately 13 miles southeast of Chillicothe on U.S. Route 35. Richmond Dale, whose football program had been in existence for only 11 years by 1985, finished second in the Scioto Valley Conference with a 7-3 record and were making their first-ever playoff appearance.[18] Their three losses came by a combined total of just 5 points in a league that was represented in the playoffs not only by themselves but also by Bainbridge Paint Valley and Frankfort Adena.[19]

Richmond Dale brought with them a balanced running and passing attack commanded by quarterback Jeff Fairchild (5-11, 165), a senior who had been named as the Scioto Valley Conference Back of the Year with 926 yards passing and 238 on the ground.[20] Fairchild's receivers were Dean Cartee (6-4, 205) and Todd Alley (5-11, 150). The running back corps was made up of Craig McGarvey (5-10, 160) and Chris Higley (5-9, 150).[21]

As far as the linemen were concerned, they were not a huge team on either side of the ball. Only two men weighed over 200 pounds. These were offensive and defensive tackle Bill Kimbler (6-0 and 240) and the aforementioned Dean Cartee at defensive end.[22] Both of these guys would be across from me on offense and defense.

Panther Record[23] 7-3		
14	Racine Southern	7
13	Southwestern	14
14	North Gallia	7
13	Adena	17
29	Huntington	6
27	Piketon	6
9	Paint Valley	7
35	Zane Trace	6
23	Unioto	0
12	Westfall	13

We went about our business of preparing for the Panthers during a week that brought rain, wind and cold weather every day. We became saturated and smeared with mud from head to toe as we pounded one another. Some days, when the weather was bad enough, Coach Graham moved us into the gymnasium and we walked through everything. Although we were indoors, we still had to wear helmets but the shoulder pads were allowed to come off.

We were somewhat handicapped when preparing for Richmond Dale. The playoff picture was still unclear in week 10, so our scouts had gone to see the four or five different teams that had the best chance of being our first-round opponent. While Richmond Dale occupied third place in Region 19, they were expected to lose to Westfall and fall out of contention. For this reason, Richmond Dale was never scouted.[24] Even though Southeastern did lose to Westfall, the team behind them, Patriot Southwestern, "failed to pick up any secondary points in the complicated computer system and dropped to fifth."[25] "I don't know if we've ever gone into a playoff game without scouting a team," Coach Graham told the local paper. "It's very hard to evaluate a team when you haven't seen them live."[26] What we lacked by not scouting this team would be compensated for with Coach Graham's uncanny ability to dissect the game films.

Recall that daylight savings time had gone into effect during the previous weekend. Coach Graham had no use for this as it shortened the time available for practicing. I remember Coach Graham saying that week, "Whoever came up with this daylight-savings nonsense sure didn't take high school football into consideration."

While *growing up green*, I remember hearing stories about how Coach Graham attempted to cope with this dilemma. Allegedly, all of the football players with cars were instructed to park them nose-in to the fence and to turn the lights on. The practices then continued within the headlight beams! Although we were not asked to do this in 1985, we practiced well into the darkness until we could no longer see.

Then we ran our sprints. It certainly was an experience running wind sprints after dark. It was nearly impossible to see the ground and we proceeded cautiously, hoping that we would not encounter any holes and "jack-up" an ankle or a knee. Some of the more daring individuals on the team would take advantage of the darkness to get out of running sprints. While Coach Graham stood at the east edge of the game field to watch us, they would simply drop out of the sprints and lay down on the ground at the back of the end zone until the team finished! I never considered doing this because the penalty surely would have been worse than the twenty 40's.

Friday walkthrough practices were extremely cold this time of year. Multiple pairs of socks, sweatpants and several sweatshirts were donned in vain attempts to stay warm. Keeping the head warm was probably the biggest challenge as the helmet was a very poor insulator. To do this, as much padding as possible was removed from the helmet so that it would fit down over the hood of a sweatshirt. Others put tape over the ear holes in an effort to block the wind.

Unshelled sunflower seeds were a popular snack at this time, probably because they took so much effort to eat, which diverted our attention from the cold. With a mouth full off seeds akin to a chaw of tobacco, we would separate the shells from the fruit and spit the shells onto the ground. It required some skill to spit the shells in such a way that they would miss all of the bars in the facemask. Some guys didn't care and would have a mass of spit-laden shells attached to their facemasks by the time practice ended.

During the playoffs, the Friday walkthroughs always ended with a solemn ritual. Since it was indeed a one-game season, a loss ensured that the seniors would never return to this practice field. With the juniors and sophomores gathered in the south end zone of the game field, Coach Graham sent the seniors on a leisurely jog down to the far goal line for possibly the "last sprint." "Don't let it be the last one," he would say upon our return.

Obviously, there was much to contemplate on the journey to the stadium on game day. On the very sidewalk where autumn leaves crunched beneath the feet of previous Green Wave warriors making their last walk to White Field, our senior class also made its final trek. This had always been a special part of town for me. On the north side of Church Street was the YMCA—the site where most of us had played our first football game. To the south was White Field where all of us would play our last game in Newark, Ohio (and if we lost, our last game period). Both Coach Poth and Coach Graham addressed this point during their pre-game speeches. "Seniors, tonight is the last time you'll wear that green uniform on this football field," Coach Poth said. "I'd sure hate to have it end with a loss. Make it count, gentlemen!" Once again, the tears flowed as we exited the locker room. We had tradition on our side. Newark Catholic had never lost a playoff game on this field. We were not about to let that happen.

Playing conditions were not the best. Rain throughout the week had left the field saturated and muddy. Light rain showers—remnants of storms earlier in the evening—also fell at game time and it was somewhat chilly. Low temperatures became a concern for me in the playoffs. As my Mom was always a stickler for dressing warmly, I debated before each cold game whether to put on a sweatshirt. I did not want to become sick, but neither did I want to be too warm. It usually turned out that once we got moving, a sweatshirt was not needed.

Southeastern began on offense from the 32-yard line and came out throwing. After two quick completions, Southeastern had a first down just shy of midfield. On the next play, I nearly had a sack on quarterback Fairchild at the 37 but he broke free and made it back to the 45 before going out of bounds. The kid was quick, strong, agile and as good as he was said to be. An incomplete pass on third down forced Richmond Dale to punt and we went on offense at our 20.

We ran two 24 Powers back to back. Ronan's crushing blocks on the linebacker allowed Bell to get 16 yards. Ronan then blasted for 16 yards on a 6 Trap and moved us out to midfield. Three plays later on third-and-long, Kubik hit Simi with a nice pass down to the Panther 27. Six Trap, Flood Right and Zero Trap comprised the next sequence of plays and netted only 4 yards. On fourth-and-seven from the 23, Coach Graham called a Counter Pass Left. I pulled, got a seal on the defensive end and Kubik made a nice run down to the 5-yard line. He was roughed up out of bounds but no foul was called. A great collision of humanity occurred on the 24 Power that followed. Bell kept his legs churning through it all and punched over for our first points of the postseason at the 5:49 mark in the first quarter. Backlund's PAT was good.

Richmond Dale's second series began at their 33-yard line. Mike Trotter, who had missed the last three games because of the knee injury sustained at Licking Valley, announced his return by dropping the running back for a three-yard loss. The series amounted to three-and-out for Richmond Dale. Joe Simi caught the Panther punt but couldn't quite make it to the wall and was knocked out of bounds at the Newark Catholic 46.

Our second series opened with a 12-yard completion to Byers followed by an 11-yard scamper by Joe Bell. Shortly afterward, we faced another fourth-and-long situation at the Southeastern 29. Coach Graham decided to go for it again. Kubik dropped back and zipped the ball to Simi at the 16. Joe penetrated to the 2-yard line before he was stopped. Behind Pat Cooperrider, Scott Saad went into the end zone standing up on a 14 Dive. Backlund nailed the extra point and we led 14-0 with 1:26 left in the first quarter.

Things got a bit scary on the ensuing kickoff. Billy Franks lost outside containment on the coverage. The return man turned the corner and made it out to the 46-yard line where Albert Ghiloni and I ran him out of bounds. The game film shows Albert crashing over me. I can remember taking a serious blow to my left kidney region during the collision. Man, did *that* hurt. Recall the resolution I had made for myself the day after the Johnstown game: The only way I would come out of a game, other than being told to, was on a stretcher. This was the only time after the Johnstown game that my resolve was tested but I toughed it out and the pain departed. Besides, this was a playoff game—the big time—and I did not want to miss one single play.

The scoring threat that Southeastern posed with the good field position quickly vanished. On first down, a quick pass to the wide receiver was complete to our 44 but the man fumbled and Tommy Helms came up with the recovery.

Coach Graham "went for the jugular" by calling a deep pass to Monte on first down but the pass was incomplete. The series was a short-lived three-and-out for us. Backlund's punt rolled briefly, was scooped up off the ground and then advanced by a Panther. A host of Greenies standing guard quickly dropped the man at the Southeastern 30. The first quarter had just ended.

After switching ends of the field, Southeastern shot themselves in the foot again. Fairchild had the ball knocked from his hands while running a play-action fake and Monte Byers came up with the big recovery at the Panther 21-yard line.

To start our new series, Kubik attempted a pass but had to throw the ball away to avoid a sack. This drew an intentional-grounding penalty. From the 31-yard line, Bell got the call on a 17 Quick Pitch and "took it to the house" for a touchdown! But it all came back because Dale Backlund blocked someone in the back—what a shame, too, because Coop threw a crushing block as he pulled outside and Bell made a terrific cut. Two plays later, Jurden executed an out-and-up pattern and was heavily guarded by a man that was not even looking for the ball. The ball was thrown a little short. Jurden slowed, hauled it in and reached the end zone for a 36-yard touchdown pass at the 11:07 mark in the second quarter.[27] The extra point was no good and the new score was 20-0.

Richmond Dale's next drive started from their 31 and Fairchild got his passing arm going. Following a short run and an incomplete pass, Fairchild completed a deep pass down to our 31-yard line. On the next play, another pass was completed to the 19-yard line. Then, looking to his right, Fairchild rolled out to avoid Trotter and me and eased the ball just over Monte Byers and into the hands of his receiver at the 10. Just as the receiver turned toward the end zone, John Jurden was there to deliver a devastating hit that jarred the ball loose. Monte, who had fallen down, was in perfect position as the ball rolled to him and he notched his second fumble recovery of the game. The boy that Jurden smacked was shaken up and remained on the turf for a short time. The big hit thwarted a potential scoring drive.

From the 10-yard line, Joe Bell got the call on 24 Power. By twisting, fighting and breaking three tackles, Joe gained 11 yards to the 21. With a 6 Trap and a 27 Counter Sweep, Scott Saad picked up 11 yards to the 32. Following an incomplete pass, Coach Graham called Screen Middle on second down. On Screen Middle, the linemen block the defensive linemen for about two seconds and then let them go. While this is occurring, the tight end runs to the middle behind the defenders who have taken off on the pass rush and he awaits a short pass from the quarterback. Upon catching the ball, the tight end yells, "Go!" and the linemen head downfield to block. We executed this play perfectly. Five defensive linemen fell for the trick and went after Kubik. Simi fell in behind to catch the pass. With five blockers out

in front, Joe found open field down the left sideline, turned on the afterburners and
went 68 yards for the touchdown with John Jurden escorting. Backlund's kick was
good and we lead 27-0 with 7:10 left in the half. When asked about that particular
play, Coach Graham said, "We've had that tight end screen play for years. We
haven't run it often but we found a good time for it tonight."[28] Given the speed of
Joe Simi, it is interesting to note that Fairchild actually closed on Joe and tripped
him up at the goal line. How fast was Fairchild?

Southeastern's next series ended with a punt to Joe Simi after three plays. On
the punt return, Joe took the ball at our 45 and was freed for a 14-yard runback
thanks to a crushing blind-side block by Mike Trotter. A block of that nature is
easily visible (and audible) to the seated fans and moves them all to shout, "Ooo!"
in unison. That is how we practiced it on the sophomores!

John Jurden carried on a Flanker Trap Zero and gained 17 yards. Scott Saad
carried next on Zero Trap but gained very little. On 28 Counter Sweep, Joe Bell
turned the corner, stuck his head right into a tackler and raised the kid off the
ground. Joe made it to the 12-yard line with the effort. Kubik and Simi then
connected for a 12-yard touchdown pass via Tight End Delay—the play that saved
us at Licking Valley. With Dale Backlund's extra point, we had assembled a 34-
point lead with 3:39 left in the half.

Richmond Dale opened their next series with a Flanker Trap of their own, but
Jim Calvert shut it down. On second down, Fairchild was pressured to my side and
tackled by a gang of us after a short pickup. On third down, I had another
opportunity to get a sack on the quarterback but he managed to escape me a second
time. Trotter finished him off at the Panther 30. The punt was taken at the Newark
Catholic 41 and we went to work again.

A first-down pass deep to Byers was right on the money but Fairchild made a
great defensive play on the ball and knocked it away. On second down, Bell, who
was running better than he had all season, blasted for 16 yards on a 26 Iso. Bell got
the call again on a Flood Left pass and went out of bounds at the 26. The play set
up a 43-yard field goal attempt by Dale Backlund on the last play of the half. The
kick never came close. We went to the locker room with our first playoff game
well under control.

If a game was going well, the halftime locker room scene was always one of
noisy celebrations and jubilation until Coach Graham entered. "Everybody sit
down and shut up!" he would yell and the jubilation would quickly die. He was not
angry about the show of emotion—just that there were things that needed to be
addressed and he needed silence. Once he had our attention, he would proceed
with that gleam in his eye—the gleam that proclaimed: *We've got this team by the
balls and we're not letting go!* The attitude was infectious. Whatever successes we
had realized, we were not to be content. Rather, we were encouraged to try to
surpass them and constantly strive for excellence. He drilled that into us and it was
a lesson he wanted us to carry into our adult lives long after high school football.
Any kid who played for J.D. Graham cannot, in good conscience, be a quitter or do

things half-heartedly in his adult life. It goes against everything Coach Graham hammered home to us year after year. I know that when I become tired and feel like cutting corners, a voice in my head asks: *What would Coach Graham think if he saw you like this?* He is still "coaching" me today! While some may view this long-term influence as "haunting" rather than "coaching," I do not see it as such.

How well had the first half gone for us? In addition to the lopsided score, we racked up 347 total yards and 16 first downs to Southeastern's 68 yards and 3 first downs.[29] Without question, it had been the best first-half of football we had played to date.

Southeastern opened the second half with a little trickery as they employed an on-side kick. An on-side kick occurs when the team kicking attempts to gain possession of the ball by kicking it a short distance rather than all the way down the field. The ball is eligible for recovery by either team once it has traveled 10 yards. The Southeastern kick was botched as it traveled only 7 yards, resulting in excellent field position for us at the Panther 43. We came out in a double tight end formation and ran a pro left 23 Power. Everyone nailed his blocks beautifully and Joe Bell cruised for 33 yards to the Panther 10—not a bad way to start after a halftime break! Bell crashed into the line for the next three plays and scored on a dive play behind Coop and Donnelly. With Backlund's PAT, we lead 41-0 with 10:35 left in the third quarter and the rout was on.

Despite being down in such a deep hole, Southeastern did not lie down and die. From the Panther 33-yard line, Fairchild went to work scrambling, throwing quick strikes and running the ball when nothing was open. On the tenth play of the drive, a key completion was made on the sideline as Fairchild was under heavy pressure near our bench. That play set up a 20-yard touchdown pass in which Tom Helms was so far out of position that he left the receiver wide-open in the end zone. Southeastern's two-point attempt was unsuccessful and the score was 41-6 with 5:03 left in the third quarter—so much for posting a shutout.

For our next offensive series, Bell and Kubik were relieved for the night by Darby Riley and Jeremy Montgomery, respectively. Darby Riley made nice runs on three straight power plays, including a 13-yard gain where Donnelly drove his man 10 yards backwards before finally burying him. Joe Simi received a Montgomery pass at the Panther 30 and turned downfield for more yardage. Reminiscent of the great Houston Oiler running back Earl Campbell, Simi lowered his head into a would-be tackler at the 20, put the kid on the ground and made it to the 16. Two plays later, Montgomery hit Simi with a 14-yard scoring toss with 1:37 left in the third quarter. Backlund's extra point made the score 48-6 and it was safe to assume at that point that we would live to play another day.

Following the Simi touchdown, Fairchild was picked off near midfield by Monte Byers three plays into the fourth quarter. A second-team offensive unit came into the game for the Green Wave but the drive resulted in a punt.

From their 20-yard line, Southeastern had driven out to midfield again. On the fourth play of the drive, a quick pass from Fairchild was complete but then fumbled at the Newark Catholic 44. Tom Parker made the fumble recovery for the Greenies.

The Clean Green returned to offense and managed to get one first down before we had to punt again. On the punt, Backlund stood at our 44 and the snap sailed over his head. Dale ran back to fall on the ball and the Panthers took possession on our 26. On the next play, Fairchild stepped back and lofted a pass to the end zone that was good for another touchdown with 3:26 left in the game. An attack pass went to the right for the two-point conversion attempt. The pass was complete at the back of the end zone but an official ruled that the receiver's feet were out of bounds. The score was now 48-12 and our dominating lead began to disappear.

Southeastern executed another on-side kick for the ensuing kickoff. Billy Franks had a chance to cover the ball near our sideline but couldn't quite get there. Southeastern had the ball again at our 40.

This Fairchild kid was tough. It was easy to see why he had been selected as the Scioto Valley Conference Back of the Year. On Southeastern's final possession, Fairchild was all over the field scrambling, taking hits, breaking tackles, escaping when it appeared he was sure to be sacked and scrapping for all he could get. After racking up 22 rushing yards on the drive, Fairchild scrambled to his right under heavy pressure, threw on the run and nailed his third touchdown pass of the game with just 54 seconds remaining. I remember standing on the sideline in utter disbelief as the third touchdown occurred and the Southeastern kids celebrated. They did not seem to care that they were losing. All they knew was that they had scored three touchdowns in a playoff game against Newark Catholic.

Southeastern attempted another on-side kick toward Donnelly and me but Donnelly fell on the ball. With time enough for one more play, the offensive unit took the field and ran the clock out. Round one of the playoffs was in the history books.

After all ten games of the regular season, we were told, "We've still not played to our potential" or "We've yet to play our best game." Following the Southeastern game, I could not help but think that things had finally come together for us and for once, we *did* play to our potential. Almost everything went right for us. Joe Simi had what Coach Graham would term as a "career night" with six receptions for 169 yards and three touchdowns—the touchdown tally equaling a school record.[30] Coach Graham said that Simi "...did everything well tonight" and probably had "...his best game ever."[31] On the ground, Joe Bell was in top form as he enjoyed a career-high 131 yards rushing.[32] Additionally, the 48 points scored was a new Division V playoff record.[33]

After studying this game, I realized that after our first offensive series, Jeff Ronan was not seen again. When asked about this, Jeff said that on the opening kickoff, he tried to make an arm tackle on the return man and nearly had his left arm ripped off. "That hurt like hell," Jeff said. "I played the first offensive series in a lot of pain. I could not lift my arm and had to use my right one to go into a three-point stance. I just couldn't return after the first series."[34]

Southeastern	0	0	6	12	18
Newark Catholic	14	20	14	0	48

	SE	NC
First Downs	13	22
Rushing	42	199
Passing Yards	204	254
Total yards	246	453
Att-Comp-Int	28-17-1	22-11-0
Punts	4-30	2-32
Kickoffs / Avg	4-14	4-42
Fumbles / lost	5-4	0-0
Penalties / yards	0-0	4-43

Regional Semi-Final Results[35]

Region 17

Mogadore	36
New Phil. Tuscy Catholic	7
Sycamore Mohawk	21
New Wash. Buckeye Central	7

Region 18

Delphos Jefferson	40
McComb	0
Fremont St. Joseph	22
Attica Seneca East	15

Region 19

Newark Catholic	48
Richmond Dale S.E.	18
Bainbridge Paint Valley	3
Frankfort Adena	0

Region 20

Middletown Fenwick	16
Cinn. Summit Country Day	10
Covington	35
Southcharleston S.E.	0

Notes

1. 1985 Regional Football Tournament Program, Division I, II, III, IV, V, (Nov. 1985), p. 1.

2. Ibid.

3. *The Advocate*, (Nov. 4, 1985), p. 14.

4. "NC, Sheridan in playoffs; unbeatens left out," *The Advocate*, (Nov. 4, 1985), p. 13.

5. *The Advocate*, (Nov. 4, 1985), p. 14.

6. Mark Naegele, "Wave offsets rush shortage with defense," *The Advocate*, (Nov. 8, 1985), p. 11.

7. Derek Monroe, "Wave's crowns piling up," *The Columbus Dispatch*, (Nov. 30, 1985), p. 3B.

8. Ibid.

9. Mark Naegele, "Mogadore, NC show similar styles," *The Advocate*, (Nov. 21, 1985), p. 13.

10. "Poll champs named; real titles undecided," *The Advocate*, (Nov. 5, 1985), p. 11.

11. Mark Naegele, "Mogadore, NC show similar styles," *The Advocate*, (Nov. 21, 1985), p. 13.

12. "NC, area gridders grab top honors on all-district team," *The Advocate*, (Nov. 6, 1985), p. 15.

13. Ibid.

14. Ibid.

15. Ibid.

16. Ibid.

17. Ibid.

18. Mark Shaw, "Football takes huge strides at Southeastern," *The Advocate*, (Nov. 6, 1985), p. 15.

19. Ibid.

20. Ibid.

21. Ibid.

22. Ibid.

23. 1985 Regional Football Tournament Program, Division I, II, III, IV, V, (Nov. 1985), p. 2.

24. Mark Naegele, "NC prepares to tackle 'unseen' Southeastern," *The Advocate*, (Nov. 7, 1985), p. 13.

25. Ibid.

26. Ibid.

27. Mark Shaw, "Wave thrashes Southeastern in round one," *The Advocate*, (Nov. 10, 1985), p. 1C.

28. Sean McClelland, "Simi stars with three TD receptions," *The Advocate*, (Nov. 10, 1985), p. 1C.

29. Mark Shaw, "Wave thrashes Southeastern in round one," *The Advocate*, (Nov. 10, 1985), p. 1C.

30. Sean McClelland, "Simi stars with three TD receptions," *The Advocate*, (Nov. 10, 1985), p. 1C.

31. Mark Shaw, "Wave thrashes Southeastern in round one," *The Advocate*, (Nov. 10, 1985), p. 1C.

32. Ibid.

33. Ibid.

34. Jeff Ronan, Conversation with author, Feb. 11, 2002.

35. Kane M. Krizay, *Cheers and Tears: 25 Years of the Ohio High School Football Championships*, (Medina, Ohio, KMK Publishing Co., 1997), p. 256.

Week 12

Bainbridge Paint Valley Bearcats

November 16, Region 19 Championship

One exciting aspect about all the playoff games after round one was that with each new game came an opportunity to travel around the state and play in a different stadium. The thought of taking our show on the road and suiting up in fancy facilities was an endless source of excitement for me. I always waited with great anticipation to find out where that next site would be.

Site selection was performed by the commissioner of the OHSAA and was based on the following criteria:[1]

- Seating capacity of home and visitor sides to handle the projected crowd.
- Seating capacity of the press box.
- Condition of the playing surface.
- Availability of adequate parking.
- Capacity of dressing rooms.
- Availability of field phones for coaching.
- Presence of a fence to keep spectators separated from the playing surface.
- Proximity of stadium to the teams playing.
- Size and proximity of the officials' dressing room.

News of the playoff site and opponent was released on Sunday afternoons and announced over the local radio stations but for whatever reasons, I always managed to miss this information. I usually never found out until Monday morning at school. It was from Jeff Ronan that I learned our next game would be in Cooper Stadium in Columbus. Home field to the minor league baseball team Columbus Clippers and able to seat ten thousand people, Cooper Stadium was equipped with artificial turf—a new experience and/or obstacle in the 1985 season.

Eight teams in Division V had been eliminated over the weekend and eight teams remained—two in each region. The winners in each region would now battle each other for the regional championship. Those match-ups were: [2]

Region 17: Mogadore (11-0) vs. Sycamore Mohawk (9-2).
Region 18: Delphos Jefferson (11-0) vs. Fremont St. Joseph (8-3).
Region 19: Newark Catholic (11-0) vs. Bainbridge Paint Valley (7-4).
Region 20: Covington (10-1) vs. Middletown Fenwick (8-3).

It was always interesting to observe the results of playoff game action. We were debriefed by our scouts Doug Heffley and Jeff "Chunky" Jones on what they had gleaned on their missions to the distant corners of the state. Mogadore had won easily over Tuscarawas Catholic—the team we struggled against in week 1. The word on Mogadore was that they were "loaded" and every bit as good as they were said to be. Another team that caught our attention was Delphos Jefferson. They enjoyed the largest margin of victory over the weekend: a 40-0 defeat of the 1983 Division V State Champion McComb Panthers. No one had ever heard of Delphos before and this was a red flag. My older brother has a theory that newcomers to the playoff scene are a cause for concern because they usually have a once-in-a-lifetime compliment of studs that no one can beat.

Paint Valley Record[3] 7-4		
23	Albany Alexander	0
3	Waverly	20
20	East Clinton	6
10	Piketon	0
0	Westfall	14
13	Zane Trace	0
7	Southeastern	9
9	Adena	0
7	Huntington	14
20	Unioto	0
3	Adena	0

As in any other situation, we could not afford to look ahead to any of our potential opponents. We had to take care of the next task that awaited us: the Region 19 Championship game against the Paint Valley Bearcats. The Bearcats belonged to the Scioto Valley Conference and were from the town of Bainbridge in western Ross County, approximately 20 miles southwest of Chillicothe on U.S. Route 50. The good news for our team was that Paint Valley had a rather weak offense that averaged only 10.5 points per game.[4] They had decent size on the offensive line with tackles Larry Tennant (6-0, 210) and Joe Cowman (6-2, 225). The guards were Cliff Kinnison (5-11, 170) and Eldon Smalley (6-0, 195). Garrett Trent (6-1, 195) was the center for the Bearcats. They ran a wishbone offense (three running backs) with Joey McFadden (5-10, 180), Brad Hager (5-10, 185) and Joey Like (5-6, 150). Signal caller for the Bearcats was Todd Chaney (6-0, 170).

How could a team make the playoffs with such little offensive output? The answer (and the bad news for us) was in their stingy and tenacious defense that had recorded six shutouts and given up only 63 points in 11 games.[5] Paint Valley's defensive set was the 5-2 (five linemen and two middle linebackers) and consisted of Brad Hager at middle guard; Cowman and Tennant at the tackles; Mike Lough (6-0, 180) and Dave Page (6-1, 175) occupying the defensive end positions. The middle-linebacker positions were filled by McFadden and Trent. The secondary was composed of the quarterback Chaney, Benji Ligett (5-8, 155), Glenn Barker (5-11, 160) and Jim Thompson (5-10, 160). The standout members of the defense were Trent and Hager. Both had been selected as first-team all-district players. Trent had 159 tackles while Hager had 93 tackles and 10 quarterback sacks to his credit.[6]

As Monday rolled around and we began preparing for this defense, I can recall a sophomore at the middle linebacker position who I had been "swapping paint" with throughout the scrimmage. After one particular play, I remember the kid looking at me with a smart-aleck expression and saying, "You ain't much." I was instantly infuriated! Maybe I wasn't much, but it certainly was not a punk sophomore's place to say. I could not imagine a sophomore deliberately provoking the wrath of a senior. Deciding to exact a little payback for his unwise choice of words, I went out of my way to rock that kid as often as possible for the reminder of the practice. It cranked the intensity of the scrimmage up to a nice, respectable level.

As mentioned earlier, this pending game would be played on artificial turf. Coach Graham saw to it that we had the opportunity for at least one practice on the synthetic surface in order to get the feel of it. On Tuesday of that week, we boarded the "Blue Bomb" Crusader bus and headed for Cooper Stadium. Because it was just a practice and not a game, no one was stressed or in game mode and it was quite a rowdy trip complete with food, obnoxious jokes, laughing, hurling of tape balls, etc. I had my Walkman with me and intended to listen to some music on the trip. Jim Calvert sat down beside me with his own musical device but lamented the fact that his batteries were dead. "Not to worry," I told him. My unit happened to have not one, but two, headphone jacks. I let Jim tap into my machine so long as I chose the music. I introduced Jim Calvert to "You Can't Stop Rock and Roll" by Twisted Sister that day. Although it was not Hank Williams, Jr., Jim still seemed to enjoy himself.

The fact that we would play on turf required special shoes other than the grass cleats we normally wore. Several boxes of turf shoes—some black and some white—arrived at our school and we picked through them until we found a pair that fit. Sophomores were low priority and if they had grabbed a pair while a starter was still shoeless, they were forced to give them up and find another set. Everyone could be fitted from what we had to pick from—everyone except Pat Cooperrider. His feet were just too large and he needed a special size that did not come with the lot. Fortunately, we had a "man on the inside" at The Ohio State

University who helped remedy the problem. Pat Cooperrider explained, "Jeff Ulenhake personally brought me some high-top Nikes when we practiced at Cooper Stadium. They said 'Bucs' on the heel. I told him I would see that he got them back but he said, 'Just keep 'em.' That was a very nice gesture and I think I still have them."[7]

A TV station joined us at Cooper Stadium and did a lengthy story about the Newark Catholic tradition. Not only did they talk to Coach Graham, but they also talked with our two District players of the Year: Andy Kubik and Kevin Donnelly.

The practice at Cooper Stadium brought terrible misfortune to one of our starters. The backs and receivers had been conducting a tackling drill that involved hitting a man in the side, wrapping the arms and spinning him to the ground. Billy Franks was paired up with Jeff Ronan and he executed the move on the senior fullback. When Jeff went down, the back of his head struck the artificial turf with such force that it resulted in a concussion—his fifth one in as many years. It was a blow to the entire team. It was bad enough to be without Jeff's crushing blocks and the warrior mentality with which he played. But the hardest thing was sharing in Jeff's grief that came with the ruling from Doctor Trifelos. It restricted Jeff from hitting for such a time that he would miss the remainder of the season— his senior season—his last chance to be a Green Wave. Sophomore Scott Saad would be called upon to step up and fill the void. Jeff was someone that I began _growing up green_ with in the third grade and we dreamed of winning a state championship _together_. I could not imagine how difficult that must have been. Jeff says that to this day, Billy Franks apologizes for the incident whenever the two see each other. "It wasn't his fault," says Ronan. "It could have been anyone."[8]

On game day, Coach Graham instructed us to dress nicely for the trip to the game—coats and ties, sweaters, etc. This was his dress code while traveling to playoff games. "We're going on the road to take care of business," he said, "and we're going to dress like businessmen." This also had a practical purpose, as it was nice to have dry, comfortable clothing to change into after the game.

We arrived at Cooper Stadium far ahead of the 7:00 p.m. kickoff time. There was not another soul in the place and we took advantage of the quiet time by leisurely walking the field and imbibing the pre-game atmosphere. The towering light poles, the vast seating, the expansive press boxes and the artificial turf—all proclaimed that this was the big time. What an exciting place this was for a young kid to play a football game! It was also a bizarre place for a football game. Given that the facility was designed for baseball, it seemed a struggle to comfortably fit a 100-yard football field into the place. In addition, the seating was situated on one side only. This meant that opposing fans would be required to sit together as they had done at Coshocton—another situation for skirmishes to occur.

We began to retreat to the locker room when we saw the Paint Valley kids arrive. Several of us stood near our locker room door and watched in disbelief as they ran around on the field, yelling and throwing a Frisbee. Others went up into the seats and ran through the aisles like children in a toy store. I believe this was a classic example of the advantage of one team having playoff experience over another. Though we were in awe of the surroundings just as Paint Valley was, we knew we had a job to do and we could not let ourselves become distracted. In contrast, the Paint Valley kids seemed overwhelmed by the whole experience. Their pre-game antics were not those of a team ready to play a football game, in my opinion. "Most kids are just happy to be here," Coach Graham would say of other teams. "Act like you've been here before."

It was a chilly night as we took the field for pre-game warm-ups. Several days of rain rendered the turf totally saturated. By the time we finished rolling around on the ground for stretching, we were completely soaked to the bone. Combine that with the cold air and a slight breeze and we were freezing before the game ever started. It got nearly unbearable for a short time when a helicopter from one of the Columbus TV stations touched down behind the end zone where we did our warm-ups. It was quite a rush to be so close to that whirly bird, but the great blast of air that it generated cut through our wet clothes like razor blades. That was COLD!

Our kickoff team assembled on the field. The waterlogged turf had a dull glare beneath the glow of the stadium lighting. With the kick from Dale Backlund, this regional championship game was underway. Paint Valley broke a run off our left side for four yards on first down. Jurden wrapped the kid up and slammed him to the turf, forcing water to splash out and fly in all directions. Calvert dropped the quarterback for a loss on second down and Saad broke up a pass on the third play from scrimmage. Jurden fielded the Bearcat punt at our 40-yardline.

Our first play was a 6 Trap with Saad and Donnelly that gained 2 yards. After an incomplete pass, Kubik threaded the needle between two defenders to Joe Simi for a 15-yard gain. This drive stalled, however, after two incomplete passes on second and third downs. Dale's punt rolled into the end zone for a touchback.

On Paint Valley's next play, I jumped offside but was fortunate that the tackle across from me moved simultaneously. It backed the Bearcats up 5 yards. With first-and-fifteen, quarterback Chaney faked the handoff and rolled my way on an option. After getting hung up in traffic, Chaney was belted by Todd South and lost the football. Billy Franks recovered it at the 15.

The yardage came slowly but surely for us after the fumble recovery. Saad gained 5 yards on a dive play. On 24 Power, Garret Trent, Paint Valley's standout linebacker, filled the hole and met Scott Saad's block in the backfield. Bell still was able to skirt around the collision and find four yards. Another dive by Saad took us to the 4-yard line. On the next play, Kubik changed the play to a 30 Trap. I sent a lineman rolling with a solid trap block but Trent had the middle shut down. The play failed. Finally, on the next play, Bell followed on a 24 Power and punched across the goal line with 4:40 remaining in the first quarter. Backlund's extra point was good.

On the ensuing kickoff, the Paint Valley return man brought the ball back 13 yards until—BOOM! —he was instantly halted and knocked onto his backside by Scott Saad. That was a "hit for the highlight reels," as the saying goes. Paint

Valley's first two plays resulted in no gain. Matt Gilmore checked into the game on third down to relieve Trotter and shared a quarterback sack with Calvert and Franks. On the resulting punt, Byers and Simi drew close together beneath the ball as neither could decide who should make the catch. They both caught it. Then they both dropped it. An incoming Bearcat nearly pounced on the ball but Simi covered it in time. I guarantee Byers and Simi received an earful from Coach Graham because of that miscommunication and near-disaster.

Starting from our 42, we gained nothing on a 14 Dive. On second down, Andy Kubik threw a wobbly pass down the field to Byers. When Monte made his cut to the outside, he fell to the turf as the ball was tipped up into the air by a defender. What happened next was unreal. As Monte was *on his side* and sliding across the turf, he maintained his concentration, extended an arm while the ball passed over him and made an incredible one-handed catch at the Bearcat 26. Those of us who witnessed this feat consider it the greatest catch we have ever seen on any level of football. Outstanding efforts such as that are what win playoff games. A 28 Counter Sweep to Scott Saad failed to develop as the nose guard Hager penetrated and dropped Saad for a loss.

I had a "wake up call" on the following play. On pass plays against the 5-2 defense, it was my job to first check for a blitzing linebacker and if he did not attack, I then peeled to pick up the defensive end. Well, I remember on this play that the stud linebacker Garret Trent was over me and did not blitz. Nor did I find a charging defensive end after looking to my left. After letting my guard down and turning back to center, the 195-pound Trent flew in on a delayed blitz, caught me standing up too high and just blasted me. I did not go down even though he had me stood up and back on my heels, helpless to do anything about it. I did not like the feeling of being burned in that fashion and I was sure not to be lulled to sleep again. For those younger kids out there who want to play football someday, believe what your coaches tell you: *The man that gets the lowest wins the battle!*

Kubik's pass fell incomplete on the play where Trent nailed me but a nice connection was made to Byers on the following down, moving us to the 10. Then, after Bell picked up 3 yards on a power, he blocked for Scott Saad on a 28 Sweep. There was little running room around the right end but Saad stuck it up in there and actually made it to the 1-yard line on the last play of the quarter. On the next play, Bell muscled across the white chalk for his second touchdown of the game. Dale missed the extra point, which bothered Coach Graham to no end. Extra points were so critical, especially in the playoffs when the games were likely to be close.

Todd South and Joe Wiley combined to make the stop on the kickoff at the Paint Valley 26. On first down, I slanted inside of Cowman—the big offensive tackle—right into the ball carrier and dropped him for a 1-yard loss. A gang-tackle on second down and an incomplete pass on third down forced Paint Valley to punt again. No one could get under the high, short punt that hit at the 47 and rolled to the 27. Coach Graham always told our punt returners not to let the ball bounce on artificial turf because it would roll for miles. Sometimes, however, it was just impossible to catch them.

Our next offensive series was rather pathetic. Kubik did not get a handle on the first-down snap from Johns. He fell on the ball and we lost a yard. Second down was an incomplete pass. On third down, a Sprint-Draw to Bell picked up 7 yards but was well short of the first down marker. Backlund stood near our 20 to punt. The snap, slightly high, glanced up off Backlund's hands and sailed over his head. Dale scrambled to pick up the football as two Bearcats rapidly closed in for the kill. While running to his right, Dale escaped what looked like a sure tackle and somehow punted the ball out of there just before he was knocked to the turf! It was an outstanding effort and resulted in the Bearcats starting from our 46 instead of our 20-yard line. I think Dale properly made amends for the missed extra point.

Our defense did not permit Paint Valley to capitalize on the good field position. First down was a pass complete for 5 yards and a third-down pass fell incomplete. On second down of the drive, I flew into the backfield untouched and saw Chaney pitch the ball out to the halfback Joey Like. The ball traveled just beyond my grasp and I have always thought that had I been just a bit quicker, I could have intercepted this pitch and "taken it to the house" for a touchdown. Byers and Jurden teamed up to stop the kid for no gain. Another high, short punt hit at the 15 and took a Green Wave bounce out to the 21.

Our next series was off to a good start as Bell cut the defense for 7 yards on three straight plays. On the fourth play of the drive, Saad led Joe Bell to the right on a 26 Iso for an 8-yard gain. Flying over to make the tackle, Garret Trent slammed Bell to the turf well out of bounds. When Joe finally came to a stop, he found himself literally lying underneath Paint Valley's bench. The action should have been a late hit out of bounds but nothing was called. The following three plays were incomplete passes and we had to punt.

Paint Valley went back to work on offense at their 29. It was another terrible series for them. Between penalties and our aggressive defense that swarmed and gang-tackled, the Bearcats ended up with a fourth-and-twenty-one from the 8-yard line. A horrible punt ensued that traveled all of 7 yards, hitting at the 15 but rolling out to the 32-yard line.

On first down, Kubik hit Joe Simi for an 11-yard completion. On second down, Kubik was nearly intercepted and we were hit with a holding penalty. This pushed us back to the 31. A funny thing occurred after breaking the huddle for the next play. We were always instructed to look sharp and hustle up to the line. Before the third play, Tony Johns was a little too aggressive in his approach to the line. When he planted his feet on the wet turf, his feet kept going and he ended up on his butt. This drew a collective chuckle from the onlookers. The drive was plagued with penalties and incomplete passes. Kubik made an unsuccessful shot for the end zone on fourth down.

The Bearcats took over at their 24-yard line. A first-down dive play gained nothing. A completion was made for 20 yards to the 44 with time left for one more play. Chaney scrambled, eluded a would-be sack from Jim Olson and threw a pass downfield that was broken up by John Jurden. The first half had ended and we withdrew to the locker room leading 13-0.

The second-half kick was taken by Bell at the 20 and returned to the 40. It had been decided at halftime that we were going to come out and "run the hell out of the Power and Counter Sweep" in the second half and we went to work. First down was a 23 Power. Saad made a great hit on Trent, enabling Bell to pick up 6 yards. We came back with the same play again. This time, however, Trent angrily filled the hole and destroyed both Saad and Bell, sending them backwards as if they were "paper people." After a 28 Sweep and a 23 Power had moved us to the Bearcat 46, Coach Graham called 28 Counter Sweep. I enjoyed the Counter Sweep because it gave me a chance to lead-block. Bell gained 12 yards on the play. Tim McKenna checked into the game and picked up 1 yard on a Dive play. The next call was 27 Counter Sweep. I went outside and was in a position to seal the defender, which would have allowed Bell substantial running room to the outside. Instead, Bell cut inside of me but he still gained 13 yards to the Bearcat 20. After another 23 Power, the old Flanker Trap Zero was thrown in. Jurden gained about 4 yards on the play but it came back because of a clipping penalty. The penalty would be too much to overcome. On third-and-sixteen, we ran Screen Middle to Joe Simi but the play only netted 10 yards. A dive play to Joe Bell on fourth-and-six gained only 2 yards and Paint Valley took over on downs at their 14. Even though we failed to score, we still managed to consume nearly half of the third quarter on the drive.

Paint Valley could do nothing offensively. A short-lived drive, ensured by Mike Trotter's quarterback sack at the 10-yard line on second down, forced the Bearcats to punt from deep within their territory. The punt was not caught and rolled out to the 44.

The first play of our next series was a 27 Counter Sweep. Once again, rather than reading my seal block and going outside, Joe Bell decided to cut it inside of me. Although Bell got 14 yards on the play, he would hear about this from Coach Graham the next day during the films: "Joe Bell, what are you doing going inside like that? If you stay to the outside, you walk in!"

Following a dive play to Saad and a pass to John Jurden to the 19, the call was 27 Counter once again. This time, I knocked the defender to the outside and Bell made a nice move to the inside for a 10-yard gain. Joe Bell seemed to get better the farther we advanced into the playoffs. He was finally healthy, running with confidence, power and authority. On this particular 27 Counter play, Brad Hager, the standout Bearcat middle guard, had flown outside to make the stop on Bell. At the moment of contact, Bell put his head down and punished Hager. Hager began to slowly rise from the turf. After ascending into a kneeling position, he quickly reached for his right collarbone and made no attempt to stop himself as he fell back to the turf as if he had just been shot. He assumed the infamous "seven-point stance" just for an instant and then finally rose to his feet, continuing to hold his right arm. Hager cannot be seen in the game film after that play.

The 27 Counter set up first-and-goal from the 9. Following a 3-yard gain to the 6, Bell dashed around left end for a 6-yard touchdown run. Bell also punched across the goal line for a 2-point conversion to improve our lead to 21-0 with 1:52 left in the third quarter.[9]

Paint Valley began the next series from their 26 and opened up with a 10-yard pass completion. Chaney stepped back and threw again on the next play. Just after the ball left his hands, the quarterback was drilled in the side and sent to the turf by Mike Trotter. Chaney remained flat on his back as the official signaled for a timeout. On his return to the huddle, Trotter could not contain himself: "Did you see what I did to that kid! Did you see it! Did you see it!" Mike was nearly yelling in his excitement. I remember fearing that his exuberance would draw a penalty and I told him to tone it down a bit. It was indeed an awesome hit and Chaney missed the remainder of the game. After a short dive play, Byers blitzed and stuffed the third-down pass attempt of substitute quarterback Jim Thompson (5-9, 150). The resulting punt died at the Newark Catholic 29.

On first down, Kubik delivered a perfect pass to Monte Byers near the 50-yard line along the Paint Valley sideline. Turning downfield, Monte fought his way to the Bearcat 27-yard line—a play that closed out the third quarter. Darby Riley, who relieved Joe Bell, picked up 18 yards on a 28 Counter Sweep. Unfortunately, the gain was killed by a penalty. After a first-down pass fell incomplete, Coach Graham called for the Flanker Trap Zero. Despite all of the shifting around by the Paint Valley defensive linemen, we blocked the Flanker Trap perfectly and Jurden picked up 17 yards to the Bearcat 19. After Jurden's run, Darby carried on a 23 Power and dashed through the traffic down to the 10. Darby lost 2 yards on the next play and nearly had his head removed as he was "clotheslined" (tackled around the neck) by an untouched Larry Tennant (6-0, 205). This drive ended on the ensuing play when Coach Graham employed some trickery known as the 48 Counter Pass. This play consisted of Joe Simi lining up at left end, running to his right behind the line of scrimmage and taking the ball from Kubik. Similar to a counter sweep, I pulled on this play as well and the scheme was intended to trick the defense into thinking that Simi would run with the ball. Instead of running, Simi would set up to throw a pass and it was my job to provide the protection. On second down from the 12-yard line, Simi set up and found Monte Byers dragging through end zone for a 12-yard scoring toss with 9:52 left in the game. Not only was Joe Simi fast, but he could also throw the football very well. The extra point was blocked by an outside man from the left and the score was 27-0.

Paint Valley had not been able to move the ball on us the entire game. That changed briefly after our fourth touchdown. Perhaps Paint Valley cranked it up a notch because they saw their season slipping away or perhaps we lost some intensity. From their 34-yard line, the Bearcats ripped us for runs of 13 yards, 9 yards and 11 yards. Coach Graham called a timeout to deliver an attitude adjustment to his defense. The timeout was effective. When play resumed, Joey Like went around left end and appeared to be off to the races but fumbled the ball out of bounds at the 30 when Tommy Helms hit him. On second down, I was assisted by Tim McKenna with a tackle of McFadden for no gain. A third-down pitch to our right was squelched by South, Franks and Helms. On fourth down, Jim Calvert got his arms up into the face of substitute quarterback Thompson and ruined a pass attempt.

A Clean Green offensive unit took the field at the Newark Catholic 30. After executing eight running plays, the offense faced a long-yardage situation at the Paint Valley 44. While dropping back to pass, Jeremy Montgomery was sacked and lost the football. Paint Valley recovered the ball well into our territory. Aided by an offensive pass interference penalty, the Clean Green defense was able to contain the Bearcats thereafter and forced one more punt. Two more plays were all it took to consume the time left on the game clock.

With the victory, we became the Region 19 Champions. It was the sixth time Newark Catholic had won this award—something that was accomplished for as long as Region 19 had been in existence. This distinction brought with it the Region 19 trophy that was presented to the team immediately following the game.

It had been a very solid performance for us. Defensively, we held the Bearcats to 71 total yards and 4 first downs.[10] Offensively, Kubik did not have his greatest night passing the ball. He completed only 38 percent of his passes for 142 yards.[11] That was not really an issue. What the passing game had lacked, the running game compensated for to the tune of 213 yards—126 of those belonging to Joe Bell.[12] It did not matter to any of us how we won. We were 12-0 and advancing to the state semifinals. As we headed back to Newark, many of us wondered who our next opponent would be.

Paint Valley	0	0	0	0	0
Newark Catholic	7	6	8	6	27

	PV	NC
First Downs	4	17
Rushing	34	213
Passing Yards	37	153
Total yards	71	366
Att-Comp-Int	11-3-0	22-9-0
Punts / Avg	8-32	3-28
Kickoffs / Avg	1-39	5-40
Fumbles / lost	3-1	2-1
Penalties / yards	3-30	3-25

Regional Championship Results[13]

Region 17	
Mogadore	25
Sycamore Mohawk	6

Region 18	
Delphos Jefferson	22
Fremont St. Joseph	0

Region 19	
Newark Catholic	27
Bainbridge Paint Valley	0

Region 20	
Covington	3
Middletown Fenwick	0

Notes

1. 1985 Regional Football Tournament Program, Division I, II, III, IV, V, (Nov. 1985), p. 1.

2. Krizay, p. 256

3. Mark Naegele, "Weak offense, strong defense propel Bearcats," *The Advocate*, (Nov. 15, 1985), p. 7.

4. Ibid.

5. Ibid.

6. Ibid.

7. Pat Cooperrider, Conversation with author, Dec 11, 2001.

8. Jeff Ronan, Conversation with author, Feb. 11, 2002.

9. Rick Cannizzaro, "Catholic defense gives PV dose of own medicine," *The Advocate*, (Nov. 17, 1985), p. 1C.

10. Ibid.

11. Ibid.

12. Ibid.

13. Krizay, p. 256.

Week 13

Mogadore Wildcats

November 23, State Semifinals

Four teams were left standing in Division V after the completion of the regional final games: Newark Catholic, Delphos Jefferson, Covington and Mogadore. Of these four teams, three were playoff veterans who had played each other at some point in the past. Newark Catholic and Covington locked horns in the 1980 semifinals—a game the Green Wave won 14-10.[1] One year before that, with the old three-division playoff system still in place, Mogadore and Covington battled each other for the Class A State Championship. Mogadore prevailed 23-17 in double-overtime.[2] Mogadore and Newark Catholic crossed paths twice before in state semifinal action in 1981 and 1983.

The newcomer to this "final foursome" was Delphos Jefferson. They had never even made it to the playoffs before, let alone to the semifinals. Although they had finished 10-0 in 1984 and second in the AP poll,[3] Delphos lacked sufficient computer points to qualify for the playoffs that year. They were one of many teams throughout the state that benefited from the expansion of the playoffs in 1985. Recall that in 1985, the playoffs expanded to take the top four teams from each region rather than the top two. Delphos had occupied fourth-place in region 18 and edged Archbold from tournament action by just .27 of one computer point.[4] Delphos was no fluke, however. They won their first two playoff games by a combined score of 62-0 and boasted a 23-game winning streak—second only to our streak of 25 games.[5]

This group of semi-finalists had a combined record of 47-1 and Coach Graham remarked that it was "...probably the strongest four teams ever that I can remember in Division V."[6] It was up in the air as to what team we would draw for the semifinal contest. Based on previous years, many people speculated that it would be Mogadore, but no one could be certain.

I do not remember exactly when or where we heard the announcement, but when the news came down, it was as suspected: Our next opponent was Mogadore. Our hearts sank. Just the mere mention of the name struck a collective nerve within the Newark Catholic camp and unleashed a potpourri of thoughts and emotions: excitement, respect, fear and disbelief that we would play them again. What was so earth-shattering about Mogadore? Were they not just another team similar to the others we had beaten? The answer was *No!* A look back in time is essential to understanding this situation.

As mentioned earlier, Newark Catholic and Mogadore played each other twice before. The first meeting took place in the 1981 Division V semifinals at Canton Fawcett Stadium. The result was a hard-fought 7-0 victory in the snow for the Green Wave. "We had a pretty good football team," Coach Poth said, "and to be held to seven points sort of got our attention with respect to their program."[7] Coach Poth also remembered senior defensive tackle Paul Cost having a hand injury that required an enormous amount of tape and this became a source of controversy before the game. "For the previous five weeks," Poth said, "Cost taped his hand up for our games. We go up to Canton to play and here come the officials telling Cost, 'You can't play with that hand taped like that.' I forget how we got around it, but there was some confrontation before the game and J.D. just about went crazy."[8]

If the rivalry was not officially established in 1981, it certainly was in 1983. Once again, the scenario was the Division V state semifinals at Canton Fawcett Stadium—home of the National Football League's annual Hall of Fame game. It had been Newark Catholic's third straight semi-final game in this stadium. I was just blown away by the size and majestic nature of the place. I remember that when we first arrived at the stadium, juniors Tim Musselman, Todd Weber and others walked over to the fence behind the scoreboard. There, at the base of a fencepost, they unearthed a coin that they had planted one year earlier as sophomores on the 1982 team. They were confident that they could return to this place and retrieve it!

Mogadore came into the 1983 game with an incredible team that had an 11-0 record. They had it all: a 205-pound fullback, great linemen and a terrific quarterback named Steve Poth—no relation to our beloved lineman coach.

The game was a seesaw of emotion. They would score, we would tie. They would score, we would tie it again. Steve Poth just picked us apart with his incredibly accurate passing. Green Wave quarterback Kirk Schell was on target as well and both teams went into halftime locked in a 14-14 tie. Late in the third quarter, Mogadore marched 80 yards and took a 7-point lead. With 5:11 left in the game and trailing 21-14, the Green Wave took over at their 45-yard line after a timely 20-yard punt return by junior Tom Hickman. Yardage came steadily as us younger players on the sideline screamed for all we were worth. On the sixth play of the drive, Rod Wilder made a huge fumble recovery at the Wildcat 26 that kept the ball in Newark Catholic's possession. Then, John Stephens caught a screen pass on the seventh play of the drive and barely got a first down at the Wildcat 18. Mogadore contained the Green Wave on the next three plays and our season came down to a critical fourth-and-eight situation from the Mogadore 16. Jim Parker kept us alive when he made a diving 9-yard reception for the first down at the Wildcat 5. Two plays later, Mike Helfer made an outstanding catch at the back of the end zone with 1:17 left in the game. Shane Montgomery's kick secured a trip into overtime.

Mogadore won the toss and chose to go on defense first. On the first play, Kirk Schell hit Todd Weber for a 14-yard completion to the Wildcat 6. Chad Heffley then gained 4 yards on a Zero Trap. On the third play, Heffley followed Jeff Ulenhake around right end for a 2-yard touchdown run. Montgomery's kick was perfect and the Green Wave took the lead 28-21.

When it was Mogadore's turn, Steve Poth was sacked by Scott Sanders on first down. Poth threw complete on second down to set up a third-and-three from the 13. Two successive penalties against the Wildcats and a tipped pass on third down ultimately set up the final play of the game. On fourth-and-thirteen from the 23-yard line, Mogadore attempted what looked like an old "Hook and Trailer" pass, but the ball fell incomplete. Newark Catholic faithful stormed onto the field to celebrate the Green Wave securing their first trip to Ohio Stadium and their fourth consecutive appearance in the state finals.

The game was a classic contest between two teams that simply refused to give up. They battered one another, tore up the field and were plastered with dark soil by game's end. Mogadore quarterback Steve Poth finished the game with 21 completions in 30 attempts for 239 yards. The two teams combined for 578 yards of total offense and 38 first downs.[9] The announcer at the game said that he had "...been around high school football for 40 years and that was the finest game..." he ever witnessed in Fawcett Stadium.[10] I totally exhausted myself and lost my voice just from screaming and running from one end of the bench to the other. I even "hyperventilated" myself in the process.

In the week following the 1983 contest, all that anyone could talk about was "the Mogadore game." Coach Graham said "...some of our players and many of our fans were still talking about that game when we were lining up for the kickoff of the state championship game" the following week against McComb.[11] I personally wanted some memento to remember the fantastic occasion. On one of the school walls, I had found a small sign made by a cheerleader that read *Thrash Mogadore*. I folded it up and kept it inside of my wallet. (The *Thrash Mogadore* sign stayed in my wallet for two years and was "resurrected" for the 1985 contest. I gave it to cheerleader Denise Diebert, explained that it was "charmed," and expressed my wishes of having it copied and placed all over the school just as it had been in 1983. This was done and I still have it today.)

We (the 1983 team) had paid a price for the stellar victory over Mogadore, however. Chad Heffley suffered a bruised kidney on the go-ahead touchdown in overtime and spent most of the following week in therapy. Additionally, the coaches, players and probably even the fans were physically and emotionally drained, making it impossible to be at our collective best. McComb nipped us the following week 6-0. I called the phenomenon the "Mogadore Jinx." Twice our school had beaten Mogadore in the semifinals only to go on and experience heartbreaking losses in the championship game one week later.

It should now be clear why the prospect of playing Mogadore was such a daunting task. They had a fine, tradition-rich football program under the direction of head coach Norm Lingle. We would need to have our best game against them if we had any hopes of winning.

The city of Mogadore is located in southeastern Summit County about eight miles as a crow flies southeast of Akron. Mogadore may be better termed as a "town" as it had a population of only 2,656 in 1985.[12] With such a small number of people, it was quite a feat, in my opinion, to continually find great athletes and assemble such powerful football teams year after year. Visit the OHSAA website sometime to see how many Mogadore players hold individual performance records in football—some records dating as far back as the 50's.

I do not remember Coach Graham's exact words but during Mogadore week, he explained how a certain mystique, deserved or not, seemed to accompany any football team from northern Ohio. Some sort of pervasive attitude held that northern Ohio football was somehow superior to other brands of football from the rest of the state. With Mogadore being the AP poll champion-media-darling and scoring an average of 37 points per game while allowing 7.6, it amplified the theory (Coach Graham alleged) and influenced people to conclude that we did not stand a chance against the top-rated Wildcats. This angered Coach Graham but he used it for motivation. I remember him mocking this mindset one day during a practice: "Northern Ohio football: 'Our shit don't stink!' Well, we'll find out, won't we fellas?"

It was said by the media that the 1985 Mogadore and Newark Catholic teams were mirror images of each other in that each had a strong passing attack, a strong running game and a tough defense. Mark Naegele, *Advocate* sports editor, wrote that the two teams "...are so close to each other in talent that neither the Associated Press nor the United Press International could decide who was better."[13] Even the team colors—green and white—were similar, although Mogadore's green was just a bit darker.

The offensive line for Mogadore consisted of Larry Murphy (6-3, 270) at center, Dan Sentelik (6-0, 190) and Tom Hardesty (5-10, 170) at the guards and Dave Bramlett (6-2, 205) and Kevin Kinnan (6-3, 225) at the tackles. The ends were occupied by Ron Pierce (6-2, 180) and Eric Barker (5-11, 180). Quarterback for the Wildcats was Richard Pierce, brother to Ron, who had completed 109 passes in 302 attempts for 1,510 yards and 20 touchdowns.[14] For his efforts, Pierce had been named as the Northeastern Inland Class A Back of the Year.[15] Mogadore operated from the "T" and Power I formations quite often, which utilized three running backs. Two of those backs were Mike Murphy (6-1, 170) and Doug Sharpless (5-10, 155). Murphy was a key multi-purpose player in the offense with 478 yards receiving and 708 yards on the ground.[16]

The last offensive position to be discussed is the third running back. Mogadore could always be counted on to have at least one big, physical running back on the roster. In 1985, that individual, dubbed as "the most outstanding athlete on the team,"[17] was 5-11, 210-pound Jamie Popa. Popa's numbers included 153 carries for 862 yards and 20 touchdowns, nine pass receptions for 138 yards, over a 30-yard average per kickoff return, over a 41-yard average per punt and he was one of Mogadore's leading tacklers.[18] Coach Graham came up with a little play on Popa's name when talking about this kid. He combined the two phrases *Does a bear shit in the woods* and *Is the pope catholic*. Graham's name for the kid was "Jamie does-the-popa-shit-in-the-woods Popa." The team would break into laughter whenever he said this and I believe that to laugh was the whole idea. It was not intended to be disrespectful toward Popa. Instead, it was a way to incorporate moments of levity into a terribly stressful weak in order to keep us all from going crazy. We *had* to laugh just to keep from crying!

Mogadore Record[19] 12-0		
28	Rittman	0
33	Atwater Waterloo	0
47	Peninsula Woodridge	3
38	Garretsville Garfield	8
28	Streetsboro	7
27	Windham	17
41	Ravenna Southeast	16
41	Rootstown	8
47	East Canton	7
54	Mantua Crestwood	12
36	Tuscy Catholic	7
25	Sycamore Mohawk	6

The Wildcat defensive corps had Hardesty and Larry Murphy at the tackles and Sentelik and Charles Martin (5-9, 160) at the ends. Mr. Popa was accompanied at middle linebacker by either Mike Morris (5-8, 160) or Chris Yoho (5-11, 180). Sharpless and Bill Brake (5-10, 165) filled the outside linebacker jobs while Mike Murphy, Barker and Aaron Carlton (6-0, 175) were in the defensive secondary.

Having to face a team with these kinds of numbers, one would think that it would be enough to cause a coach to develop ulcers. Coach Graham, however, never lacked confidence. If he thought we were going to get our butts kicked, he kept it well-hidden. It would have been devastating for us to have sensed uncertainty in him and he knew that. All great coaches know that. If the leader is scared, the troops will follow suit. With that said, I have always been curious as to how the coaching staff approached a team such as Mogadore and maintained this positive attitude. Although they put up a good front for the team, did they run off to the coach's office after practice and ingest copious amounts of Maalox? What was *really* said when the team was not around? Coach Poth had this to say:

> Well, it all stemmed from J.D. You know he always preached, "Anybody can beat you once." The same was true in reverse: We could beat anybody *one time*. J.D. would say, "Pothy, if we play these people ten times, they'll beat us nine. We don't have to

play 'em ten times—just once—and I think we can get 'em." He would form a plan and then just get us to believe that somehow, there was a way to win.[20]

Coach Graham also shared his thoughts on this topic: "I felt going in that we would have to play a perfect game in order to beat them. I knew there was no way we would be able to shut them down offensively and that we would have to simply outscore them."[21]

The week of practice was mind-boggling in pursuing that objective—so much to go over and so little time. New plays had been added regularly throughout the season and the Mogadore week was no exception. Joe Bell remembered that the Option play was added. "Coach Graham was excited about putting the option in," Joe said. "He told us, 'We're going to score on this play!'"[22] Coach Graham also tried to tweak and improve everything else offensively. If he felt that he was getting too fancy or refining things too much, he would consult Coaches Poth and Campolo. After taking their counsel and going through careful considerations, Coach Graham would say, "No, I'm not gonna change anything. We're gonna go with what got us here."

Defensive preparation for the Wildcats was a massive undertaking in itself. Of the 10-page scouting report Coach Graham developed, seven pages were devoted to defense. He had actually put in a 50 defense with three middle linebackers. Joe Simi was to move up as the third middle linebacker and stay on Mike Murphy like "flies on shit." Scott Saad was assigned to do the same with Popa—quite a task with which to charge any sophomore. We went over every offensive set that Coach Graham felt Mogadore might try. The goofiest was a "spread" formation that consisted of a center and two guards in the middle of the field, the quarterback and one running back behind them and two linemen split out wide to each side of the field with a receiver standing behind them. "They haven't shown this at all this year fellas," Coach Graham said, "but this formation was in my notes from two years ago and there's no telling what these people might try on us." According to the scouting report, if they lined up in the spread while we were in the 50, I was to rush the quarterback. However, if we were in a 40 and they showed the spread, Jimmy Olson was to take my end position and I had to split out with the receiver to provide pass coverage. Me on pass defense—now that was a terrifying thought!

After the Thursday practice, we rushed to get cleaned up and find a meal because a pep rally, open to the public, was held in the school gymnasium at 7:00 p.m. This was a very rowdy occasion just as a pep rally should be with the noise level, the intensity and the excitement far surpassing the previous ones.

Several different things took place during this pep rally. I remember the fathers of all the seniors, each wearing his son's green jersey, marched onto the floor and performed the "Script NC." This was done to the same music used by the Ohio State marching band to perform "Script Ohio." The fathers wrapped up their act with the "Give me an I-R-I-S-H" cheer, which was led by Mr. Byers.

Also present was Steve Minich, a sports reporter from Channel 6 in Columbus. He was there to award us the "Team-of-the-Week" trophy for having won the

Region 19 championship. He finished by saying, "I'll make you a promise right now: Beat Mogadore and I'll be back next week with another team-of-the-week trophy!" This sent the student body into a screaming frenzy. A camera operator, present to film the event for the 11 o'clock news, turned the camera on the student body. The volume instantly doubled to a level that was nearly deafening within the confines of the gym. It was *that* loud. What incredible school spirit!

The Friday walkthrough practice was intense. Recall that a walkthrough was just as it sounds—walking through every play, doing everything correctly right down to the very last detail. When Coach Graham would call an offensive play, for example, he might say, "Pro left, 24 Power, block it." We stepped with the proper foot, hit with proper shoulder and positioned ourselves on the correct side of the defender. Joe Simi recalls that during this practice, we had just gone over a play and a new one had been called. Joe says that he failed to realize the play had been changed. When Coach Graham said, "Block it," Joe blocked for the previous play, which was completely incompatible with the current call. "Coach Graham caught this," said Simi, "and just tore into me like never before. I honestly did not know the play had changed."[23]

When the walkthrough practice had ended, we did not leave school as we normally did. Coach Graham told us all to report to the film room for something special. After all, this was not a typical game and, therefore, atypical procedures were in order. For additional inspiration, motivation and a classic example of guts, balls and underdogs rising to the challenge to literally shock the world, Coach Graham played for us a movie about the 1980 U.S. Olympic Hockey Team. American boys pulled off "the biggest upset in Olympic history"[24] and won the gold medal by defeating the highly favored Soviets and Finns. The room was deathly silent as we sat with lumps in our throats, entranced by the "Miracle on Ice." Coach Graham was visibly choked up as his voice wavered when he called for the lights to be turned on. He had tears in his eyes, as did many of us. Not a word was spoken when we were dismissed. Graham later told a reporter: "...you could hear a pin drop when those kids walked out of that room."[25]

Bang! Bang! Bang! Bang! The sound of a metallic collision resonated from within the locker room immediately following the hockey film. Players filed in to determine the cause of the disturbance. There stood Jeff Ronan, tears in his eyes as he drove his fist repeatedly into the door of his football locker. No one needed to ask why. It was understood.

On Friday night, the cheerleaders made their usual rounds to the players' homes for toilet-papering. Not only did they do the outside of the home, but for Mogadore, they went a step further and "T-P'ed" our bedrooms. When they came to my house, I waited downstairs while they went aloft to decorate. I was somewhat concerned about the event because my room was full of fragile plastic model ships and airplanes that I had built over the years. I listened closely to the ruckus upstairs and sure enough, something crashed to the floor. I went to view my room when the ladies had departed. They certainly did a nice job as there was so much toilet paper draped from wall to wall that it was impossible to walk through. After a careful entry, I found my model of the aircraft carrier *USS Yorktown* in several pieces on the dresser. I still have this model and it is still broken.

Our contest with Mogadore was to be played at Crater Stadium in Dover, Ohio. We were no strangers to this field. We played there just 12 months earlier in the 1984 semifinal game against the Smithville Smithies and won 41-6. The trip, which involved an easterly jaunt on State Route 16 and then north on Interstate 77, was around 2 hours long and meant that our game-day routine had to be moved up accordingly.

Our Saturday began with another team breakfast at Frisch's Big Boy. The day flew by and before we knew it, it was time for the team mass and the team meeting. Joe Simi recalls something unique about the team meeting. "Graham came in and said, 'Before I do anything else, where is Joe Simi? Joe, I've been up all night and have just felt terrible about the way I exploded on you yesterday. Dammit, I'm sorry.'"[26]

When it was time to hit the road, we went to the parking lot to the ride that awaited us. Instead of the "Blue Bomb," we had a fancy charter bus to take us to Dover, complete with comfortable reclining chairs, overhead storage and even a restroom. We rolled out between 3:00 and 3:30. There was something very special about traveling to a big game in style.

The trip itself was great. It was a nice, clear autumn day—perfect traveling weather. Some kids reclined and slept. Others engaged in subdued conversations that were barely audible over the incessant growl of the big diesel engine in the aft of the rig. Paper would rattle as other kids raided the care packages that parents had prepared for the trip. Though I was so nervous, as I am sure we all were, the trip was comforting to me as a faithful old friend. I felt right at home and it stemmed from the fact that for the third straight year, we were making a November road trip to a semifinal game on a charter bus and on the very same roads. Most of all, we had never returned from this trip disappointed. Another similarity with all three trips was that Ohio State was always playing Michigan on this day. Those of us with walkmans were either listening to music or the big game. My older brother recalls the '85 game vividly. "We listened to the OSU-Michigan game on the way up to Dover. That was unusual in that the OSU game started at 2:30 that day and not the usual 12-noon kickoff. The Buckeyes lost and I wondered if it was a bad omen for the evening's tilt."[27]

Our locker room at Crater Stadium was the same one we had been assigned to the previous year. It was an expansive facility, fully stocked with the latest weight-lifting equipment. It was strange to me, however, that for all the money that had obviously been spent on the place, one important provision had been overlooked: privacy walls around the toilet. As the team went about its silent business of game preparations, one of our assistant coaches was the first to use the "toilet from hell." He appeared humbled and humiliated and I was thankful that it was not me sitting there. Minutes later, however, after being fully dressed, I also had an intestinal attack and was forced to endure the humiliation. Afterward, I approached Joe Bell, who had been getting his ankles taped on a nearby table. "Joe," I said, "I may have looked like an idiot, but now I'm ready to kick some ass." That was very true. All joking aside, I had never felt more ready to play a football game than that night in Dover.

After we completed our warm-ups, we returned to the locker room for the final 20 minutes before kickoff. At that time, each player received a supportive note addressed to him from a grade school boy in either St. Francis or Blessed Sacrament. It was very touching and a stunning realization hit me: We were now the heroes to a new generation that was *growing up green.*

I was always one to notice obscure details and to make them superstitiously significant. Three similarities existed between the '83 and '85 Newark Catholic-Mogadore contests that I felt were in our favor: We were playing Mogadore in a stadium where we had been victorious the previous year against a different team; Mogadore was #1 in the AP poll; we wore white jerseys. These things probably meant nothing, but history does have a strange way of repeating itself.

The stage was set: Mogadore and Newark Catholic; AP Champion against UPI Champion; 12-0 against 12-0; No. 1 against No. 2. It was time to settle it.

We kicked off. The ball was caught at the 12 and returned to the 31-yard line. When Mogadore broke the huddle for the first time, I was stunned at the size of their offensive line. With their dark-green uniforms, it was as if five huge pine trees were walking toward us. The first play was a pitch my way to Popa. He and I collided head-on and Calvert and Trotter assisted in holding the man to no gain. On second down, we lined up in the 50-defense. Olson was trapped and Popa gained 5 yards. A quick pass down the center of the field to Ron Pierce was broken up on third down. The man across from me, Dave Bramlett, roughed me up after the play and gave me a dirty look. *Great,* I thought. *Me and this hothead are going to have a long night together.* The Wildcat punt was fair-caught at our 39.

Our first offensive play was a disaster. It was a 23 Power with Joe Bell blocking for Scott Saad. Saad failed to properly take the handoff and fumbled the ball. The Wildcats recovered it at our 40. That is *not* the preferred way to start out against the top team in the state!

Quarterback Richard Pierce, who had a quick release and threw "bullets," fired to Barker at the 20 but Jurden broke it up. Popa carried up the middle on second and third downs for 9 hard-earned yards to set up fourth-and-one at the 31. Pierce carried on a quarterback sneak and was so close to the first down that the chains were called out. Monte Byers began to celebrate as the measurement appeared short to him. The officials saw it differently and Mogadore had the first down by ever so little.

It was pure smash-mouth football on the next three plays. Sharpless, escorted by Popa, gained 6 yards and punished Riley and Simi—just put them on their butts. Running back Aaron Carlton (6-0, 174) was cut down by Saad and Byers for no gain. On third down with our goal-line defense in (all of our biggest boys), a trap to my side gained 2 yards and set up another fourth-down situation. With our goal-line D still in, we were prepared to stop the run. Mogadore, however, ran a swing pass left to Murphy. The all-star raced down the field and was finally forced out of bounds by Saad at the 6-yard line. Now it was gut-check time. First-and-goal: Murphy takes a pitch and penetrates to the 3. Second-and-goal: Popa carries up the middle and is stacked up for no gain. Third-and-goal: a pass into the end zone sails over a Wildcat's head. On fourth and goal, Pierce rolled out to his right. Setting up to pass, he had Monte Byers in his face and the pass was knocked away. The play by Byers was huge because Popa, whom Pierce was throwing to, was wide-open. That was a big-time defensive stand!

We took over from our 3-yard line. Saad crushed the defensive end on a 25 Iso and Bell moved us out to the 7. The same play was run again and an unblocked Popa filled the hole to punish Bell after a 1-yard advance. Coach Graham wisely called for the Quick Kick on third down. Bell got a nice punt away that rolled dead to the Wildcat 49. The play went much better than it had in the Tuscy Catholic game!

Mogadore came at us again. Olson was trapped on first down. Popa rumbled for 5 yards and pounded Tommy Helms at the end of the run. Popa carried again on a trap-lead for 4 yards. This time Simi made the stop and felt the wrath of the big running back. On third down, Carlton launched himself up into the pile and got enough to move the chains. Someone finally laid a good lick on Popa on the next play. It was another trap to Olson's side. Todd South fired into the hole. BOOM! Popa was merely stood-up by the solid hit and did not go down. Franks, Byers and Simi quickly swarmed to the scene to put the "hoss" to the ground. Pierce dropped to pass on second down and threw the ball into the ground when he was hit from behind by Byers. Attempting another pass on third down, Pierce threw a rope to Barker crossing the field at the 25. The kid had the ball in his hands but could not hold on as Jurden blasted him in the legs. Mogadore had to punt.

Our next series began from our 24. At this point, we had a total of 5 yards in the first quarter and desperately needed to get something going. Bell gained 1 yard on 18 Quick Pitch. Kubik connected with Byers for 12 yards on second down. Following another 18 Quick Pitch to Bell for 3 yards, time expired in the scoreless first quarter.

To start the second quarter, Kubik dropped back to pass. He had to elude a fast-closing defensive end coming from his right and while doing so, he threw complete to Monte Byers at our 48. Monte earned 9 yards after the catch and set us up with a first down at the Mogadore 43. A 17 Quick Pitch to Bell was good for 7 yards. On second down, Joe Simi lined up in the backfield, took a pitch from Kubik and threw a Halfback Pass to Byers. Although the pass was complete to the 10-yard line, a penalty nullified the gain. Our "eyes in the sky"—coaches Campolo, Cost and Gebhart up in the press box, can be heard on the home video voicing their disgust when the play came back. Screen Left to the tight end was executed on the next play. Simi only got 5 yards out of it but Mogadore was penalized for illegal use of hands and we had new life at the 30. Kubik connected with Joe Simi at the sideline for 11 yards. Bell picked up 4 yards on a 24 Power. The next call was 28 Counter Sweep. I did not get a very good block for Joe but he somehow slashed his way to the Wildcat 4-yard line before being knocked out of bonds. We were in a great position to score and that is exactly what happened on the following play. Behind Saad, Donnelly and Cooperrider, Bell slashed into the end zone for our first touchdown of the night with 9:43 left in the first half. Dale Backlund nailed the extra point.

Mogadore was back in business at their 30 following the kickoff. They seemed desperate to even the score because they came out throwing. Pierce threw for 11 yards on first down. Pierce connected again with Popa on a dump-off pass. The big running back roamed downfield after the catch and was nailed by Scott Saad. The ball came loose on the hit but rolled out of bounds. Mogadore retained possession and the play was good for 18 yards—timeout Newark Catholic! After Coach Graham had reiterated our responsibilities, Popa ran to our left on a flood route and Saad was there to drop him for a 1-yard loss. On second-and-eleven from our 43, a quick trap to Sharpless netted 2 yards. Pierce attempted a deep pass along the sideline on third down. Joe Simi was in position and made an easy interception at our 19.

Bell made a nice gain on a 25 Iso to begin our new series, but an illegal-motion penalty left us with first-and-fifteen from the 14-yard line. We ran a 27 Counter next. The defensive end penetrated, tripped me up and prevented me from getting outside. Bell had no one to block for him and was gang-tackled after a 3-yard pickup. Kubik then found John Jurden on a curl route at the 27, leaving us with a third-and-two. With our crowd chanting *Go-Go-Go,* Kubik changed the cadence and drew the Wildcat defense offside. We had a first down at the 32. Following an incomplete pass, Kubik set up and threw a beautiful pass complete to Joe Simi crossing the field at our 49. Joe stayed on his feet and his momentum carried him to the 39. A 28 Counter was the next call. I was nearly tripped again by Sharpless, who had penetrated after running over John Jurden. This time, however, I was able to step over the man, get outside and get a block for Bell. The play was good for 7 yards. Facing a second-and-three, Kubik connected with Joe Simi at the Wildcat 24. Once again, Simi was able to get more yardage after the catch and his journey ended just inside the 10-yard line, leaving us with first-and-goal. Mogadore burned a timeout and our fans loved it. Coach Graham came out to see us and called for the 48 Counter Pass. When play resumed, Simi set up, snuck the ball over the head of Mike Murphy and into the hands of Monte Byers—touchdown! Backlund nailed the extra point and with 3:50 remaining in the first half, the Greenies had a 14-point lead on mighty Mogadore. The home video of the game, complete with audio, reveals just how incredibly loud and animated our fans were. Equipped with bells, air-horns and indefatigable voices, Newark Catholic fans were second to no one!

Dale Backlund's kickoff rolled out of bounds. We tried it again after a 5-yard penalty was assessed. Jamie Popa picked the ball up at his 23 and was stopped at the 34. Trailing 14-0, the Wildcats needed to make something happen. First down was a middle trap and Popa ripped us for 11 yards to the 45. On the next play, Monte Byers gave too much cushion to Barker. This allowed Pierce to shoot a pass to the receiver good for a 15-yard pickup. On the next play, I blew it big-time. We were lined up in the 40-defense and I was exponentially destroyed on a trap play. Sharpless, the ball carrier, enjoyed an 11-yard gain to our 29. I knew what was coming next: Timeout Newark Catholic! Coach Graham angrily paced onto the field and came right for me. After finishing with me, he then turned to Jimmy Olson and whacked him on the side of the helmet. I did not understand that move. Of the 11 guys standing in the huddle, I was the one most recently burned. I should have been the one to get whacked. A slap on the helmet was one of Coach Graham's techniques for getting a kid's attention. It was not employed nearly as often as a simple grab of the facemask combined with an intense lecture.

Mogadore attempted a pass on the next play but Todd South broke it up. On second down, a short pass was completed to Barker and the kid was slammed out of bounds at the 17 by Monte Byers. Pierce set up to pass again and sent the ball near the left corner of the end zone. Tommy Helms was there in position to defend it but his legs became tangled up and he fell down. Mike Murphy was all alone and reeled the ball in to put Mogadore on the scoreboard. Popa's extra point attempt was good and our lead had been cut it half. It was very impressive for Mogadore to drive down and score after being down 14-0. They were right back in it.

The left-footed Popa kicked off for Mogadore and sent the ball deep to John Jurden at the 7. He did not try anything fancy. Running straight up the field to take what he could get, Jurden got us out to the 30-yard line and plowed a few Wildcats over in the process. We went to work with 2:23 remaining in the half. The first-down call was 27 Counter. I got a good kick-out on Barker. Bell turned inside, ran right over Carlton and gained 10 yards. Andy Kubik, who was on target all night, threw a 20-yard completion to Joe Simi, leaving us with a first down at the Wildcat 40. The next play was awesome. It was Screen Left to the tight end, which works the same way as Screen Middle, with the exception that everyone goes to the left of the field rather than staying in the middle. Kubik, backpedaling from the four defenders in his face, dumped the ball to Simi crossing the field at the 44. At the same time, Backlund, Johns, Byers and I had to run to the left to find someone to block. Aaron Carlton came up and was in position to make a tackle. I got into him, kept my feet moving and put the kid on his back. When that happened, I remember seeing a white streak in the corner of my right eye. It was Simi, cutting inside my block and motoring down the field. Tony Johns and Dale Backlund also had key blocks on the play, providing the seam for Joe to travel unmolested to the end zone. I vividly remember this entire play and could not believe we had scored another one on the Wildcats in only three plays and so close to halftime.

Backlund's extra point attempt was wide right and the score stood at 20-7 with 1:06 left in the half.

Murphy took the kickoff at the 16 and was tackled at the 33 by Albert Ghiloni and Darby Riley. Mogadore's first play was a quick pass to Barker for 7 yards. The Wildcats spent a timeout with 43 seconds remaining. Junior team manager Bernie Schwartz brought water to us during the timeout. It was his season-long trademark to get the crowd fired up by twirling his towel around in the air while leaving the field. In the Mogadore game, that towel worked overtime!

After the timeout, Mogadore attempted what looked like a double pass. This consisted of the quarterback throwing laterally to a man split to the outside and the man who caught the ball would then look downfield for a deep receiver. The play never developed for the Wildcats. Popa was the split man who received the first pass. Joe Bell, reading the play immediately, attacked Popa and dropped the man for an 8-yard loss at the Mogadore 32. On third down, Pierce dropped back to pass and was nailed by Mike Trotter. The ball came loose, but an alert Mogadore lineman fell on the ball. The first half had ended. The Wildcats must have been concerned going into halftime trailing by 13 points. We were concerned as well. There was no way that 20 points would be enough to beat these people.

The start of our halftime session is still fresh in my memory. We all found places to sit and quietly awaited Coach Graham's entry into the locker room. When he came in, I was the very first one he came looking for. "WHERE'S BILLY EVANS!" he roared. This surprised me, but a thought came to mind: *Oh, he must want to give me an "atta-boy" for that great block I had that sprung Simi to the end zone.* That wasn't quite the case. When he located me, he pointed in my face, shouting, "THEY SCORED BECAUSE OF *YOU*! YOU GOT YOUR ASS KNOCKED OFF ON THAT TRAP PLAY AND IT'S *YOUR* FAULT THAT THEY SCORED!" That was all the longer it lasted. He quickly moved on to someone else.

Mogadore kicked to us to start the second half. Popa's kick hit and died at the 20. Jurden picked the ball up and in a superb display of athleticism, he twisted, dodged, spun and made six Wildcats miss during the 15-yard runback. A 25 Iso was the first call and Bell ran for 3 yards. On second down, Kubik threw the ball away just before he was clobbered. There was no receiver near the ball, but "intentional grounding" was not called. Third down went better as Kubik zipped the ball between two Wildcats and into the hands of Monte Byers. The pass was good for 15 yards to the Mogadore 47. Bell got the next call on a 28 Counter Sweep. As he turned up into the line, he was hit low by Richard Piece and fumbled the ball. Mogadore came up with it on their 45 and their fans came to life.

Jamie Popa carried on first down and was buried by Olson and Calvert for a 2-yard loss. Second down was a trap on me. I was ready for it this time and upended the blocker. Murphy bounced it to the outside but Byers had briefly gone downfield on pass coverage and was not outside to contain. Murphy had room to run and was knocked out of bounds by Jurden and Byers after a 17-yard gain. On first down from the Newark Catholic 40, Popa ran for three yards. A late flag was thrown for a personal foul against Mogadore. The 15-yard penalty moved the Wildcats back into their territory. They quickly recovered this yardage on the next play when Pierce threw complete for 14 yards. Then, on the ensuing play, Pierce saw Murphy all alone at the Green Wave 25 and connected. From there, it was a footrace to the end zone between Murphy and Jurden. Murphy scored on the play and the Mogadore fans just went crazy. Popa nailed the extra point to make the new score 20-14. With 8:57 left in the third quarter, Mogadore had not only gotten themselves right back into the game, but they had also taken the momentum. They were fired up, their fans were going nuts and we were concerned.

We went back on offense at our 30 following a 20-yard kick return by Joe Bell. Joe carried on first down for 4 yards. Kubik threw to Byers on second down. The pass was quite low but Monte made a nice grab at our 46-yard line. On the new set of downs, an incomplete pass, a Sprint-Draw to Bell and a flood pass to Bell left us with a fourth-and-two at the Mogadore 46. Coach Graham sent a play in that he called "Take the Penalty." It was not really a play at all. The offensive unit simply lined up and the quarterback yelled, "Go" several times in an attempt to pull the defense offside. It usually did not work and resulted in a delay-of-game penalty— hence the name. Mogadore was too disciplined of a team to fall for this trick and it was a big moral victory for them. We punted to Mogadore after the penalty was assessed, wondering if we could shut them down and get some of that momentum back.

Mogadore began at their 22-yard line following the punt. On first down, Sharpless carried into the middle for 2 yards and then came to sudden stop as if he had run into a brick wall. He ran into Mike Trotter. That was one good stop. *Let's see if we can do it again.* On second down, Pierce was hurried and threw a pass into the ground: another good play. *One more like that and we can get the ball back.* On third down, Pierce tried to pass again but found Kevin Donnelly in his face immediately. Pierce dumped the ball off to Popa 2 yards behind the line of scrimmage. Scott Saad was all over the play and dropped Popa for a 2-yard loss— three plays and out and zero yards for Mogadore at a time when they seemed to be taking control of the game. The significance of that series cannot be overstated, but was very nearly all-for-not. On the punt, Joe Simi tried to make an over-the-shoulder catch and dropped the ball! The ball was up for grabs on our 34-yard line, but Joe covered it just before a gang of Wildcats piled on top of him.

We had new life at the 34-yard line and it was extremely critical that we took control of the game. What happened next was not only timely, but also incredible and the memory has never left my mind. Pat Cooperrider was the first part of the puzzle. While Pat was out of the game as our defense was on the field, he had been in-conference with Coach Poth. "Poth kept asking me what play I thought would work," Pat said. "I told him that we should go with the Power. Pothy approached Coach Graham and said, 'J.D., Coop says to run the Power.'"[28]

As we were huddled, Kubik came in with the call: Pro Right, 23 Power. Scott Saad would lead-block for Joe Bell. Now, I wish to make one thing very clear with regard to Scott Saad and the play we were about to run. Saad was a terrific athlete at 5-10, 165 pounds and had talent to spare. With his size and all of the responsibilities that were placed upon him, it was often easy to forget that he was still just a sophomore with sophomore tendencies. Throughout the 1985 season, Saad constantly received verbal annihilations from Coach Graham for a lack of aggression and hitting people too timidly while blocking from his fullback position. That all changed on the night of the Mogadore game. When Kubik called the play, Saad stood up and said, "I'm going to open one up for you, Joe." When the ball was snapped, I blocked down to cut the man over me and I heard the most hellacious hit—WHUMP! The roar of a crowd immediately followed but I was caught beneath the man I had just blocked and could see nothing. Neither could I tell whose fans were cheering. My initial fear was that Bell had been hammered (WHUMP) and fumbled the football, resulting in a Mogadore recovery. When I had finally been able to sit up and look around, I couldn't believe what I saw: Joe Bell tearing down the field and throwing grass from his cleats on his way to a 66-yard touchdown run! The game film reveals just how perfectly we all executed our blocking assignments and opened a huge hole for Bell. The devastating hit that I heard was Scott Saad putting the hurts on Jamie Popa. When asked about his approach to this game, how he dealt with the pressure of being assigned to Popa and if he remembered this particular play, Saad said, "I do remember this play. I was so keyed up when he (Coach Graham) called a power. I felt there was no way that I would let Graham or the team down. I didn't focus on the pressure. My only focus was how I was going to destroy the middle backer."[29]

After Bell had been praised in the end zone by several teammates, he made his way to the sideline. Bell explains what happened next:

> I came off the field because I was not part of the extra-point team. When I reached the sideline, my brother Dan, who was in the Marines at the time and home on leave from Japan, was there to give me a big hug. As we hugged, I felt someone tugging on the back of my jersey. I thought, "Alright, someone else wants to get in on this celebration." I turned around to find Coach Graham and he began to yell. "What the hell are you doing!" he said. "Get your ass back in there! We're going for two!" Because of the time spent with my brother, it took awhile for Coach Graham to locate me. As a result, we could not get organized in time and we were forced to burn a timeout. Coach Graham was not happy.[30]

With the score 26-14 and Mogadore being so dangerous, it was very important for us to get those two extra points. Bell remembers that the play call was the Option Right—the play added during Mogadore week about which Coach Graham said we would score on. When the play went off, I remember Bell turning the corner as two Wildcats—one being Popa—stood between him and the goal line. I did not think he would make it. Joe lowered his head and gave it everything he had. BOOM! A crushing hit could be heard from the great collision. Although it was two against one, Bell was not to be denied. He smashed across the goal line and we got our two points.

Popa took the kickoff at the 15 and was stripped of the ball by Todd South near the 33. Mogadore managed to cover the ball and their offense went to work. On first down, Trotter shed his blocker instantly and sacked Pierce 6 yards in the backfield. We had the momentum back! Popa carried on second down and got 5 yards back. Pierce attempted another pass on third down. Fleeing from Trotter and about to be hit by me, the quarterback got rid of the ball. Joe Simi stepped in front of Sharpless, making a huge interception and going out of bounds at the Mogadore 30-yard line.

The 48 Counter Pass was called upon one more time. Byers was wide-open and notched a 30-yard touchdown reception with 2:26 left in the third quarter. Backlund's PAT made the score 35-14. Things certainly looked rosy for us. It was incredible to think that we had a three-touchdown lead on this Mogadore team. However, as much as our most recent touchdown should have been the proverbial "back-breaker" or "nail in the coffin," the turning point of this game still had not been reached. As coach Poth said in our visit together: "What are most teams going to do being down 35-14? They're going to pack it in. It just made *them* mad. They just came right back at us."[31]

Mogadore returned to offense at their 28. Calvert jumped offside on first down and gave the Wildcats 5 easy yards. Next, a sweep to Murphy followed on first-and-five. Saad flew outside and made a terrific tackle, stopping Murphy for no gain. That was all the longer we could contain the Wildcats. On the next play, Popa went straight down the field and caught a right-on-the-money pass from Pierce, good for 28 yards to our 40—timeout Newark Catholic! Coach Graham's attempt to break Mogadore's momentum and shore up the defense failed. After a completion for 5 yards, Mogadore came back with a screen-middle to Popa good for 14 yards. The big man then broke through the line on a trap play and rumbled for 18 yards to our 3-yard line, punishing the tackler John Jurden. Coach Graham sent Calvert and Cooperrider into the game for our goal-line defense. They were no sooner set when Pierce took the handoff and gave it to Popa. Calvert and Saad nailed him after a 1-yard pickup on the last play of the third quarter. Twelve minutes remained.

After switching ends of the field, we lined up for second-and-goal from the 2. Popa took the handoff around left end and was stopped just shy of the goal line by South, Simi and Saad. Mogadore came right back to the line without a huddle for third-and-goal. Pierce ran a quarterback sneak but was denied. Despite our valiant effort on three plays, we could not do it a fourth time. Popa took the ball on fourth-and-goal, launched himself into the air and somersaulted over the mass of bodies for the touchdown. Popa's extra point was good, making the new score 35-21 with 11:10 left in the game.

Joe Bell took the ensuing kickoff at the 2 and returned it 30 yards. Bell carried into the line on first down and was hammered after a gain of 2 yards. On second down, Kubik attempted a pass to Simi into heavy traffic. Ron Pierce stepped in front, making the interception and running down to our 32-yard line. Needless to say, the Mogadore team and fans were ecstatic over this development.

After an incomplete pass on first down, a Pierce-to-Pierce connection was good for 14 yards. From the 18-yard line, Pierce was under a heavy rush and threw incomplete. Before the ball was snapped, however, Calvert had been sent into the game late to relieve Donnelly. Donnelly hustled to get off the field before the snap but could not. We were penalized for having too many men on the field and Mogadore moved 5 yards closer to the end zone. After the penalty, Richard Pierce connected again with his brother Ron at the 2-yard line. Jurden made the kid pay for it, though, as he stuck the Wildcat right in the back after the catch, leaving him sprawled on the ground in agony. From two yards out, it was obvious that Popa would be called upon as he had been on the last Mogadore drive. He went skyward on first down but was kept out of the end zone by a host of Greenies. Popa carried again and although he was smacked squarely in the face by Saad and South, he had just enough push to break the plane of the goal line. The Mogadore faithful exploded into a celebratory roar that became even more intense when Popa kicked the extra point and cut our lead to 7 points.

As I headed toward midfield to prepare for the kickoff, I can recall my feelings of concern while surveying the scoreboard. Although we were still ahead by a touchdown, it was quite clear that Mogadore was in control of this game. They were so jacked up from having chipped away at our lead that I doubted our chances of thwarting their comeback in the 8:42 remaining on the clock. The time appeared as an eternity to me.

The ensuing kickoff nearly spelled our demise. Joe Bell ran up to field the ball at the 12-yard line. The ball passed through his hands, bounced off his gut and was kicked away from him by his knee! Bell frantically chased the ball and covered it on our 25 just in time as three Wildcats closed in and smashed him. The heart palpitations that must have shot through our crowd at that moment were incalculable. Kubik threw complete to John Jurden in the right flat for 6 yards on first down. The second-down call was the 23 Power again. Saad flew into the middle linebacker Chris Yoho (5-11, 180) with unbridled fury and wiped him out. Jamie Popa, however, was unblocked and laid a big-time hit on Joe Bell. BOOM! The Mogadore crowd let loose with a chorus of roars, sirens and air horns to express their satisfaction. Bell gained 2 yards but most importantly, he held on to the ball and got up from the hit.

Popa putting the hurts on Joe Bell was a recurring theme throughout the entire game. It could have been a separate news story in and of itself with a fitting title of "Popa rings Bell." "Without question," Bell said, "Jamie Popa was the greatest linebacker we faced all season. There were numerous crunches delivered by him, which left me in a frail and painful condition the next day. Playing on adrenaline always seemed to kill the pain though."[32]

With third-and-two from our 23, Coach Graham called a 14 Dive to Scott Saad. Scott crashed into the stack of bodies and appeared to have the first down—but he was short. Facing fourth-and-inches from our 35, conventional wisdom says to punt the ball away. Coach Graham did not waver in the least. He was going to go for it on fourth down. Mogadore must have expected us to punt because when they saw us break the huddle intending to run a play, they called a timeout. That was good. *Maybe we should re-think this, Coach.* Coach Graham came into the huddle and I will never forget this. "We're going for it, guys. You up to it?" he said. Incredibly, the only one who answered him was Scott Saad—the sophomore! I can still see Scott pulling up his arm pad, looking past us linemen and into the Mogadore huddle and saying, "Hell yes. Let's go!" In his eyes was a distinct confidence and ferocity that had not been there before this game. With the way he had played the entire evening—big plays on defense and obliterating middle linebackers on offense—it was clear to me that the timid boy who could never please Coach Graham had died. As far as football was concerned, Scott Saad became a man on the night of November the 23rd, 1985.

When we as seniors saw this sophomore so fired-up and confident, how could we not follow suit? I know that it lifted me. It is one of the most awesome and special memories I have as a Green Wave. The reason I say that is I truly believe it had everything to do with what occurred after the timeout.

"What play do you guys want to run?" Coach Graham asked us.

"Give me the damn ball!" Joe Bell demanded.

Coach Graham wanted none of us to use foul language, but in this instance, he overlooked Bell's transgression. After surveying the Mogadore huddle in the distance, Coach Graham made his decision. "OK," he said, "Let's go Pro Right…17 Quick Pitch. All we need is a yard." We approached the line of scrimmage with breath steaming through our facemasks and into the cold night air. All fans were on their feet pouring out support for their respective teams—the Green Wave community chanting *Go-Go-Go!* This was the play of the game. If we made it, we could keep the ball awhile longer. If we failed, it would be a huge momentum swing in Mogadore's favor—not to mention that they would have terrific field position. Kubik approached center. "Set! …Thirty-eight! …Go!" Bodies collided. Joe Simi got a good seal-block on the defensive end. Billy Franks kicked the outside linebacker out. Kevin Donnelly ruined the pursuit angle of *two* men inside including Popa. Pat Cooperrider pulled and buried the middle linebacker who had flown into the hole. Keep in mind that these blocks only lasted for a fraction of a second. That was all it took for Joe Bell to squeak through a tiny opening and tear down the field for a 58-yard run! Bell appeared to have an easy touchdown but Mike Murphy was in close pursuit. The Wildcat dove and got just a piece of Joe's right foot, bringing Joe down at the Mogadore 6-yard line. The ball popped loose and rolled into the end zone when Joe was tackled. Joe quickly bounced up and covered the ball just in case it was still live.

The play was an incredibly courageous but risky move. Fortunately, it paid huge dividends and I asked Coach Graham what prompted him to take such a gamble. "We knew going in to this game that we would have to take some risks and do things we did not normally do, such as going for it on fourth down, end-around passes, that sort of thing. On the fourth-down play, I looked at Poth and said, 'We have got to keep the ball because we just can't stop them.'"[33]

Jurden relieved Bell and gained 1 yard on first down. On the next play, Simi bounced off Richard Pierce, cut out to the right and reeled in a 5-yard touchdown pass from Andy Kubik with 5:30 left in the game. Backlund's PAT made the score 42-28.

Tony Johns had been battling all night with Larry Murphy—the big 6-4, 270-pound defensive tackle for Mogadore. On the touchdown pass to Simi, the two "tangoed" in such a way that it resulted in them both being ejected from the game. Tony explains:

> Kevin Donnelly and I had been double-teaming the big tackle they had. The guy threw me aside and made it through Kevin also. I saw that Andy had thrown the ball and the tackle made a beeline toward him. I did a seat roll and took out his legs. He rolled up on me and began punching me in the face. I did a good job stopping the punches with my helmet! The referees threw us both out for fighting. When I went to the sideline, my cousin Bill Sikora was informed that he was going in to replace me. I stopped him because his eyes were as big as basketballs and I told him to remember one thing: "Just get the ball to Andy and the rest will take care of itself." I was worried about what Graham would say, however. Poth came over to me to say that I did the right thing and not to sweat it. Graham never did say anything to me.[34]

The ensuing kickoff was taken at the 10 and returned to the 20. Todd South was guilty of a 15-yard facemask penalty, moving Mogadore out to the 35-yard line. Just over five minutes remained and Mogadore was desperate to keep their state championship hopes alive. I was not convinced that we were out of the woods yet, either. They lined up and ran the old "Hook and Trailer" pass—a bit of trickery in which the receiver turns to catch a short pass and then pitches the ball to a man trailing to the outside. The play gained 13 yards. Mogadore's chances of winning this game were greatly reduced, however, on the following play. Pierce threw straight down the field to Mike Murphy. Todd South, who had perfect coverage on Murphy, made a huge interception at the Newark Catholic 31 with 5:01 left on the clock.

Mogadore still did not quit after the interception. Yardage was very hard to come by and Bell continued to be rocked by Popa. Bell remembers at this point in the game that Popa tried to gouge his eyes out after a run. "I slapped his hand away," Joe recalls, "and said, 'What the hell are you doing!' Popa says, 'Ah man, I'm sorry, I thought you were number twenty-three.' After another play, he helped me up and said, 'Really man, I didn't mean anything by it. I thought you were twenty-three.'"[35] Apparently, John Jurden, who was number 23, had done something to anger Jamie Popa and became a marked man.

Two 23 Powers and a 17 Quick pitch left us facing a fourth-and-short from our 41. Coach Graham decided to go for it again and called a simple dive play with Bell. Bell was nailed at the line but his second effort was just enough for the first down. With 3:30 remaining, the situation looked bleak for Mogadore and their fans can be seen on the game film making a mass exodus from the stadium. Although we could not move the ball after the first down, Mogadore was helpless to stop the clock. The time remaining moved inside of two minutes as we faced third-and-eleven. We failed to get the first down and Mogadore got the ball back one last time following Dale Backlund's punt.

Running a no-huddle offense, Mogadore came out throwing and got a first down at our 49-yard line. Three straight incomplete passes, however, left the Wildcats with fourth-and-ten with 54 seconds left. Our fans erupted when Mogadore failed to get the first down. All that was left to do was for Andy Kubik to fall on the ball until time expired. We were headed to state!

The game was another classic in the storied Mogadore-Newark Catholic series. The two teams combined for 802 yards of total offense.[36] Mogadore quarterback Richard Pierce was 18 of 34 for 244 yards and two touchdowns.[37]

For the Green Wave, Coach Graham remarked, "We had a couple of kids tonight play totally to their potential."[38] He was speaking of Joe Simi and Joe Bell. Simi caught seven passes for 134 yards and two touchdowns, threw two touchdown passes to Monte Byers and had two interceptions.[39] Joe Bell tallied an incredible 215 yards rushing and two touchdowns on 26 carries.[40] "I consider this to be my single greatest moment in sports," Bell said. "I remember Graham saying that we wouldn't run on Mogadore based on the film reviews. He was right until the second half, which is when our offensive line took control of the game. I was simply the beneficiary."[41]

Andy Kubik hit 13 passes in 18 attempts for 213 yards and two touchdowns.[42] Kubik was never sacked. This was a deep source of pride and satisfaction for me and the entire offensive line. In fact, with the end of the Mogadore game, Kubik had not been sacked for seven consecutive games and had only been sacked six times all season. That spoke volumes not only of our line but also of the job Coach Poth had done with us.

The scene in the locker room, of course, was filled with jubilation—whoops and hollers typical of a team that was headed to the state championship game for the sixth straight time. The celebration was restrained, however. We had one more game left to play and were all too conscious of the fact that now we had beaten Mogadore, we were subject to the Mogadore Jinx (discussed earlier). "Enjoy this one tonight, fellas!" Coach Graham said loudly. "We have 48 minutes of great football left to play and we'll start tomorrow."

We showered and changed into our "businessman clothes." A throng of fans was present outside of the locker room to congratulate us as we boarded the bus for home. We were provided with a sack-lunch for the journey, as it had been several hours since we had last eaten.

On the trip home, a busload of happy young men laughed and shared war stories of our incredible victory over an incredible team. At some point, nature called for Monte Byers and he withdrew to the rear of the bus to use the restroom. When he later emerged, a vile stench immediately overtook the bus like a wildfire, causing us to grimace and cover our noses. "Damn Byers!" someone yelled. "You stink!" Monte simply laughed and smiled as he triumphantly waded back to his seat amid a showering of pats on the back, high-fives and "atta-boys" for the scene he had just wrought. In time, the commotion died down. As the bus rolled on through the darkness, many of us drifted off into a fitful sleep, dreaming of the turf of Ohio Stadium that awaited us.

We arrived at school the next day sore and beaten to a pulp. None were as thrashed and unsightly as Joe Bell was, however. He came around the corner of the building, hobbling and resembling a side of beef that had escaped the butcher shop and wandered into the school property. "It was the sorest I had ever been in my life," Joe said. "My dad could barely get me out of bed on Sunday morning. When Coach Graham arrived and unlocked the door to let us in, he looked me up and down and said with a smirk on his face, 'Those guys didn't hit that hard, did they?'"[43]

Although we were hurting, it was easy to overlook our pains with the exhilaration of the victory still pulsing through us. We sat in the film room and it was perhaps the only time all season that we actually looked forward to watching a game film. Coach Graham was sure to be in a great mood and issue praises by the dozens, so I expected. Wasting no time in taking measures to break the Mogadore Jinx, however, he threw us all for a loop when he entered the room and said, "Hell of a game fellas...and it's over. We're not going to dwell on it. We're not going to talk about it. We're not even going to watch the film. We've got a state game to get ready for. Let's go run." And just like that, the last word concerning Mogadore had been spoken.

I never did get to see this game until about 10 years later when I purchased the 1985 season on videotape. Joe Simi and two others, however, did something incredibly brave and stupid after we ran that day. "Bell, Jurden and I waited around for Coach Graham to leave," Simi said. "We set the projector up, figured out how to thread the tape through it and watched the game ourselves!"[44]

Additional note: The Newark Catholic-Mogadore contest has become a recurring battle of small-school football powers. As of autumn 2002, the two programs have met in postseason action 7 times: 1981, '83, '85, '87, '88, 2000 and 2002. All games have been semifinal contest except 1987, which was a state final. Newark Catholic leads the series 4-3. As another bizarre observation on my part, NC has won whenever the game occurred in an odd-numbered year. Mogadore's first victory over Newark Catholic—1988—ended the "Drive for Five,"—Newark

Catholic's attempt to win a fifth straight state championship. As my brother said after the game: "Even though we lost, losing to a program like Mogadore is nothing to be ashamed of. It's almost like 'keeping it in the family.'"

Newark Catholic	0	20	15	7	42
Mogadore	0	7	7	14	28

	NC	M
First Downs	17	19
Rushing	207	94
Passing Yards	253	242
Total yards	460	336
Att-Comp-Int	20-16-1	34-18-3
Punts / Avg	3-32	3-28
Kickoffs / Avg	7-43	5-48
Fumbles / lost	2-2	2-0
Penalties / yards	8-40	3-25

Notes

1. Krizay, p. 253.

2. Ibid., p. 252.

3. *The Advocate*, Football '85, (Aug. 28, 1985), p. 10.

4. *The Advocate*, (Nov. 4, 1985), p. 14.

5. *The Advocate*, (Nov. 17, 1985), p. 1C.

6. Mark Naegele, "Newark Catholic to renew battle with Mogadore," *The Advocate*, (Nov. 18, 1985), p. 13.

7. Wes Poth, Conversation with author, Jan. 30, 2002.

8. Ibid.

9. Rick Cannizzaro, "Catholic makes title game with playoff win," *The Advocate*, (Nov. 20, 1983), p. 1C.

10. Mark Naegele, "Mogadore game stirs emotions in Catholic camp," *The Advocate*, (Nov. 22, 1985), p. 7.

11. Ibid.

12. World-wide web, http://www3.uakron.edu/src/Demographics/Mogadore-Demographics-CPS.htm (Jan. 2002).

13. Mark Naegele, "Mogadore, NC show similar styles," *The Advocate*, (Nov. 21, 1985), p. 13.

14. Mark Naegele, "Newark Catholic faces season's toughest test," *The Advocate*, (Nov. 20, 1985), p. 7.

15. Ibid.

16. Ibid.

17. Ibid.

18. Ibid.

19. Mark Naegele, "Mogadore, NC show similar styles," *The Advocate*, (Nov. 21, 1985), p. 13.

20. Wes Poth, Conversation with author, Jan. 30, 2002.

21. J.D. Graham, Telephone conversation with author, Mar. 3, 2002.

22. Joseph Bell, Conversation with author, Jan. 25, 2002.

23. Joseph Simi, Conversation with author, Dec. 1, 2001.

24. World-wide web, http://memoryInsports.com/usahkremarkable.html (Jan. 2002).

25. Derek Monroe, "Wave's crowns piling up," *The Columbus Dispatch*, (Nov. 30, 1985), p. 3B.

26. Joseph Simi, Conversation with author, Dec. 1, 2001.

27. Joe Evans, Electronic mail to author, Dec. 28, 2001.

28. Pat Cooperrider, Conversation with author, Dec. 11, 2001.

29. Scott Saad, Electronic mail to author, Feb. 16, 2002.

30. Joseph Bell, Conversation with author, Jan. 25, 2002.

31. Wes Poth, Conversation with author, Jan. 30, 2002.

32. Joe Bell, Electronic mail to author, Feb. 28, 2002.

33. J.D. Graham, Telephone conversation with author, Mar. 3, 2002.

34. Anthony Johns, Electronic mail to author, Jan. 7, 2002.

35. Joe Bell, Electronic mail to author, Feb. 28, 2002.

36. *The Advocate*, (Nov. 24, 1985), p. 2C.

37. David Waitkus, "'Attitude adjustment' pays dividends for NC," *The Advocate*, (Nov. 24, 1985), p. 1C.

38. Ibid.

39. Ibid.

40. John Cannizzaro, Game statistics report, Newark Catholic vs. Mogadore, 1985 Division V State Semifinals.

41. Joe Bell, Electronic mail to author, Feb. 28, 2002.

42. David Waitkus, "'Attitude adjustment' pays dividends for NC," *The Advocate*, (Nov. 24, 1985), p. 1C.

43. Joe Bell, Electronic mail to author, Feb. 28, 2002.

44. Joseph Simi, Conversation with author, Dec. 1, 2001.

Week 14

Delphos Jefferson Fighting Wildcats

November 29, Division V State Finals

For the sixth straight year, state week was upon Newark Catholic High School. Although the event had become as intrinsic to the school year as semester exams and Christmas breaks, state week never lost its appeal or excitement. It provided each new team the opportunity to achieve greatness, make a name for itself and add to the collection of state crowns that first began in 1978.

State week was always a short and hectic week. There was a holiday to work around as the game always took place on the day after Thanksgiving. The media came around more frequently and inquisitively than ever.

I think many of us on the 1985 team were still in a state of shock that we had gotten past Mogadore and secured another trip to the state championship. We had overcome so much and had come so far to get to this point: replacing 20 starters and the entire kicking game, dealing with the questions that arose from our poor season debut against Tuscarawas Catholic, surviving the stretch of three tough games that included the big win against Watkins Memorial, the overtime win at Johnstown and the defeat of Coshocton's best team in several years. Moreover, who could forget the narrow victory at Licking Valley that was accomplished without three of our starters? We certainly came a long way. Coach Graham said that he and the other coaches "...were very proud to take this team to the Stadium. Maybe more so than any other team before."[1] Did we possess the fortitude to pull off one more miraculous win?

Our opponent for the championship game would be the newcomer to the playoff scene, the Delphos Jefferson Fighting Wildcats. A town of 7,000 people,[2]

Delphos is located in northwest Allen County on the Allen County-Van Wert County borders about halfway between the towns of Lima and Van Wert, Ohio. Their "stomping ground," —the flat, open farm country of northwest Ohio—was and is to this day, a hotbed of high school football where so many powerful teams have originated. This did not bode well for our team. Delphos was the next in a long line of teams from that area of the state that Newark Catholic seemed destined to meet and lose to in the state finals. The phenomenon was uncanny: Carey in 1975; Tiffin Calvert in 1980 and '81; McComb in 1983. The only victory Newark Catholic managed over a team from that area came against Fostoria St. Wendelin in 1982, making our school's championship game record 1-4 against northwest-Ohio teams.

Not only was history against us, but I feared it had a good chance of being repeated. We faced an unbelievable Delphos team. To me, they were even more intimidating, more formidable than Mogadore, if that were even possible. They had the second-longest winning streak in the state at 24 games,[3] had outscored their opponents 570-41 in 13 games for an average score of 43.8-3.2 per game and achieved some insane scores of 62-7, 80-0 and 84-0![4] Although this was their first year in the playoffs, Delphos proved themselves to be legitimate contenders as they smashed their first three opponents by a combined score of 94-14—the latest victory coming against Covington 32-14 in the other Division V semifinal game.[5] "This is supposedly the greatest Division V team of all time," Coach Poth said when asked about Delphos. "They were just steam-rolling people and nobody could stop them."[7]

Delphos Record[6] 13-0		
48	Haviland Wayne Trace	0
40	New Bremen	0
54	Columbus Grove	0
22	Bluffton	8
84	McGuffey Up. Scioto Val.	0
62	Ada	7
14	Perry	0
22	Lafayette Allen East	6
50	Paulding	6
80	Spencerville	0
40	McComb	0
22	Fremont St. Joseph	0
32	Covington	14

What exactly did Delphos Jefferson have going for them that enabled them to coast to the state finals in their first year of playoff action? There was the offense—primarily ground-oriented and one that accrued over 3,500 yards rushing.[8] The front line for this running attack was made of Bob Fish (6-0, 190) at center, Sam Miller (5-8, 180) and Dave Maxwell (5-8, 165) at the guards and Mark Downey (6-2, 185) and Keith Dickman (6-4, 275) at the tackles. The end positions were occupied by Toby Kimmett (5-10, 160) and Alan Syphrit (6-3, 180). Flanker duties were handled by Steve Buzard (5-8, 145). Quarterback for the Fighting Wildcats was Scot Boggs (6-0, 165). Throwing for over 1,000 yards and 18 touchdowns with just four interceptions, Boggs' main target was Syphrit who had 41 receptions, 570 yards and 11 scores.[9]

At center stage for a team with such a vaunted running attack was, of course, the running backs. At tailback was Jay DeWitt (5-10, 170). He was the team's leading rusher with 162 carries for 1,138 yards and 27 touchdowns. [10] DeWitt was also a track star with a 100-meter dash time of 11 seconds.[11] Delphos Jefferson's fullback was a beast named Matt Closson who had rushed for 816 yards and 13 touchdowns on 126 carries.[12] His 6-2, 220-pound frame was not the only thing that was staggering. The man could bench-press 420 pounds, squat 600 pounds and run the 40-yard dash in 4.6 seconds. He had colleges such as Penn State, Ohio State and Michigan drooling over him.[13]

Delphos Jefferson also had a fine defensive unit to complement their offensive power. They ran a 5-2 Monster with Randy Bonifas (6-0, 170) at middle guard, Downey and Eric Arthur (6-0, 200) at the tackles and Closson and Joe Gorman (5-10, 165) at the ends. The middle linebacker duties were performed by Bob Ladd (6-0, 190) and sophomore Tony Closson, younger brother to Matt, who went 6-0, 230 pounds. Tony started every game since he was a freshman and the Wildcats were undefeated with him in the lineup.[14] During state week, a rumor circulated within our camp about Tony Closson. Supposedly, as a child, Tony Closson was such a mean and devastating hitter that he was banned from biddy-league football because he injured too many kids!

The third middle linebacker for Delphos, known as the "monster," was Tim Brock (5-9, 150). DeWitt, Boggs and Kimmett were the defensive backs for Delphos.

So that was what we were up against—big, strong farm boys who rolled up some big numbers. As with the Mogadore game, I was curious about how Delphos was viewed by our coaching staff. "They were big," Coach Erhard remembered, "but we felt we could prevail with our quickness. The plan was to shut down the run and make them throw."[15]

Coach Graham had this to say:

> I felt more comfortable facing Delphos than I did Mogadore. Mogadore was just so versatile. They ran well and had an outstanding quarterback. Delphos was more of a one-dimensional team in that they primarily ran the ball. I didn't expect to shut them out but I felt that we could score on them. If we could keep the score close into the fourth quarter, we had a chance. They would panic because they had never been pushed.[16]

When asked if those scores of 80-0 and 84-0 were a cause for concern, he had this to say: "They were a good team but we questioned their level of competition. You just don't beat good teams fifty-to-nothing. And let's face it: Had we left our starters in until the ends of some of our games, we too could have had scores like that."[17]

Monday

Coach Graham always said that the foundations of a great football game began on Monday morning with a great week of school—concentration, intensity and discipline serving as the cornerstones. Our state week in 1985, the biggest week of them all, got off to a very poor start on Monday morning. A few of us were sitting at the end of senior hallway just outside of the chapel, which was our normal morning ritual before school began. A huge disturbance arose upstairs in the junior hallway and we went aloft to check it out. Upon entering the hallway, I saw only a few souls present, as it was early in the morning yet. These people were giggling and appeared to be fleeing from something. After walking a short distance, it was easy to determine what they had been running from. I was nearly knocked to the floor by a powerful, very foul, eye-watering, flatulent odor. *I know this smell from somewhere before*, I thought. Jimmy Cross stood nearby with an ornery look on his face. "What is that smell!" I asked him. He was reluctant to divulge any information at first, but finally did so after much persistence from me. Pointing to a broken glass vile on the floor, he informed me that the smell had come from a stink bomb—also known as a fart bomb. The stench was identical to that experienced on the bus coming home from the Mogadore game when Monte Byers exited the restroom. Suddenly, it became clear to me: The odor on the bus, which had been attributed to Monte's intestinal prowess, turned out to be nothing more than a perfectly timed stink bomb.

The smell eventually crept its way down the staircase and took up residence in senior hallway. This made the morning very unpleasant for everyone. The principal's office was at this end of the building as well. I wondered what would happen when she found out. Before school began, a second huge ruckus could be heard upstairs—Cross had struck again.

The first bell rang and we all settled into our first class of the day. Not long afterward, an announcement came over the school's public address system: "Will the entire varsity football team please report to the principal's office immediately." *Holy cow! This sounds serious!* I had an inkling of what this was regarding. Still, I could not be sure. There was always the chance that the odor had vanished before Mrs. Mullin arrived at school.

Mrs. Mullin stood in the doorway of her office, arms crossed with a disgusted expression on her face as she waited for every last football player to crowd into the congested hallway.

"Do any of you care to take a guess why I've called you all here?" she said sharply.

Forty-eight boys had never been so silent.

"There was an incident this morning of stink-oil being let loose in this school and I've been told that members of the football team are responsible! Now I want to know who is responsible for setting off these stink bombs, or stink-oil bombs, or whatever you call them. I want to know where they are coming from and I want to know right now!"

From the back of the crowd, someone spoke up and stepped forward. It was Jimmy Cross. "Mrs. Mullin," he said. "I don't know who set them off but I'm the one that's been supplying them."

Astonishment befell many of us when Cross spoke. We could not believe he actually admitted guilt.

"Thank you for coming forward Jim," Mrs. Mullin said. "I'll deal with you later. Now this setting-off of stink bombs or stink-oil is going to stop! Is that understood? ...You may return to class."

Throughout the entire ordeal, I surveyed the far end of the hallway expecting to see Coach Graham round the corner any minute so that he too could give us "what-for." He never appeared, however. *Good*, I thought. *Maybe this whole thing will blow over and he will never find out.*

That afternoon, the last week of practice began as we went to work preparing for Delphos Jefferson. It was a cold and miserable day, overcast, drizzling and windy. I remember that we had set up for the offensive scrimmage near the track, just beyond the doors at the end of sophomore hallway. This was just about the only place remaining that had not become a quagmire throughout the fall months.

Practice progressed well for awhile and was uneventful. It was inevitable, however, that someone would screw-up (probably me) and Coach Graham went off on a tirade. And while he had our attention, he made a smooth transition into another topic and ripped on us all the more.

"Hey Wes! Have you heard the latest!" he said while pacing around in an irate fashion. "It seems we've had a little problem in school today." *Here it comes.* "Somebody tried to be cute by playing with stinky-ass bombs! What do you think of that, Coach?"

"I don't know, Coach," Poth said shaking his head.

Coach Graham was not trying to be funny. He was quite irate! With respect to his verbal assaults on us, we had developed rather thick skins by week 14 of our senior year. And as was the case with most of his other past explosions, his terminology was so comical that it required great restraint not to burst into laughter. Even the assistant coaches—those in the "Fun Bunch"—had to turn away for fear of being caught laughing.

"I just can't figure you people out," Coach Graham continued. "Biggest g-ddam week of you peoples' f--kin' lives and you want to screw around and let off stinky-ass bombs! I guarantee Delphos ain't doin' that shit! Wes, do you think Delphos is lettin' off stinky-ass bombs?"

"I don't see how they could have time for it, Coach," Poth answered. "They have a state game to get ready for."

After continuing to pace, Coach Graham said it once more: "Stinky-ass bombs! Shit!" He spat out of disgust and we resumed the scrimmage.

Tuesday

The site for the championship game, Ohio Stadium, was equipped with artificial turf. Similar to Paint Valley week, Coach Graham had us dismissed from school early on Tuesday so that we could journey to Columbus for another practice on artificial turf. The site was not Cooper Stadium, however, but the actual practice facility used by the Ohio State Buckeyes. The complex is located on the Ohio State campus, north of Lane Avenue and west of Olentangy River Road. It was our third straight year that we had the privilege of practicing in this place and it was always an incredible thrill. Two fields existed in the area—one natural grass and one artificial turf. The artificial field where we practiced was situated parallel to Olentangy River Road and was surrounded by a chain-link fence. On the fence hung a green curtain that shielded the activities inside the fence from any prying eyes on the outside—such as spies for opposing teams. It was here that we did our preparations for Delphos while the incessant roar of traffic on Olentangy River Road could be heard in the distance.

We were permitted to go inside the building for such things as getting ankles taped, changing clothes, using the restroom, etc. The place was just so impressive. It had "the mother of all weight rooms" in both size and complements of equipment. A huge training room contained dozens of tables for taping the athletes, endless supplies of athletic tape and long rows of football shoes for both grass and artificial turf. The corridors of the place were adorned with amazing photographs of past Buckeye teams, coaches and many of the past superstars such as Archie Griffin, *et al.* The place was even equipped with privacy walls around the toilets!

In our years with Newark Catholic football, our class made three trips to Ohio State's football facility to prepare for championship games. While every trip was special for obvious reasons, none could compare to the very first time, which took place in 1983 when we were sophomores. The year 1983 was special in itself because that is when Ohio Stadium became the official site for all of the state championship games.

I vividly remember that practice day in 1983. It had been my first trip ever to the Ohio State University. The practice itself, thrilling in its own right, was not the highlight of the day. It had been a very cold day and we practiced until darkness fell. As we made our way toward the building, I expected to go in, gather up our belongings and go back to Newark. However, Coach Graham made an announcement, saying, "Guys, we're not going home just yet. We've got one more thing to do."

We went into the locker room area and shed our pads. On the way, I remember seeing Tim Spencer, the great Buckeye running back, in a distant room talking to someone. Coach Graham directed us into a classroom and told us to find a seat and wait. I assumed that this "one more thing to do" would be the viewing of one last game film of McComb. No projector was set up, however, and the longer we waited the more restless and noisy we became. Finally, Coach Graham appeared, walked to the head of the room and said, "Fellas, there's more to football than just blocking, tackling and hard work. We've got a special treat lined up for you." And when he finished, who should come walking into the room but the one, the only, Mr. Woody Hayes! I nearly fell out of my seat. I do not know how Coach Graham was able to pull this off, but what an honor it was to have Woody speak to our team! I sat captivated, soaking in every word that he spoke. The one thing I can remember Mr. Hayes saying had to do with us listening to our coaches. "Pay attention to your coaches," he said. "They have the knowledge to turn you into winners."

Wednesday

As state week progressed, the school was abuzz with activity. People streamed in and out of the school throughout each day to purchase their game tickets. The TV stations from Columbus came around for one last time to interview players and to film portions of our practices. The cheerleaders worked overtime to decorate the school like never before.

The local paper had a new article each night concerning the big game. Joe Bell was featured in his very own article entitled, "Newark Catholic tailback has message for Jefferson." In the piece, Joe said, "We can still play better on offense and defense."[18] Additionally, the *growing-up-green* phenomenon, a subject near and dear to my heart, was touched upon:

> In the Newark Catholic scheme, where tradition permeates even the grade school and junior high levels, the desire to excel is implanted at an early age. "I can remember being back in the seventh grade waiting for this to happen. We've all come up and matured together," Bell said.[19]

The pep rally for the state game took place on Wednesday night and was captured on home video by the Bell family. A rowdy, full-house crowd was present that included representatives from the mayor's office, Newark Chamber of Commerce and the sheriff's department. As promised, Steve Minich from Channel 6 in Columbus returned to award us a second Team-of-the-Week trophy.

From the two previous football seasons, I had learned that one particular event was standard operating procedure during a state-final pep rally. That event was the drinking of an egg by the team captains. This was done in the spirit of Rocky Balboa from the movie "Rocky," who drank eggs in the morning before his workout. I knew that if we made it to the finals, Andy Kubik and I would have to do this. It was somewhat of a concern for me because I was not an egg-drinker—who is? If it were to make me sick, I could not think of anything more embarrassing than to upchuck on the gymnasium floor in front of a few hundred Green Wave fans. I intended to be fully prepared for the event. After we beat Mogadore, I drank one egg each day after I returned home from football practices. I was apprehensive at first and stood close to the sink in the event that I had an accident. There was really nothing to it—just open up and let it slide on down!

When it was time to do it for real, Coach Graham explained it to the fans. "We've had a tradition around here before the big game that we've had a lot of fun with," Coach Graham said. "Kubik and Billy Evans, come on out here." Kubik and I walked out to the center of the gym floor. Jeff Ulenhake and Shane Montgomery, who were home from their respective colleges for the Thanksgiving holiday, assisted Coach Graham in administering the eggs to us. "Now, if you guys really want this game," Coach Graham said while the eggs were cracked, "you're going to take one of those eggs and just chow that baby down right now!" As Kubik and I stood with glasses at the ready, Coach Graham looked at us and asked, "Who wants to be first?" "Right here," I said, eagerly stepping forward. I turned the glass bottom-up and bam—the egg was history. I issued a thumbs-up and the crowd cheered. The attention then turned to Kubik. Andy did not have the same zeal and confidence as I did for this event, which was apparent in the way he stared down into the glass with uncertainty on his face. "Andy, what do you think?" Graham asked him. "Rocky did it!" Kubik finally got up the nerve and pounded the egg. Although it appeared that he might lose it, he kept it down and the crowd erupted into more cheering and applause.

Another event of the pep rally was a bit of comic relief. Someone dressed as a turkey had a bunch of gag gifts for the seniors. The gifts were from our parents and probably did not have any significance to the general public. The turkey called each senior out individually and we unwrapped our gifts in front of everyone. Jeff Ronan, after peering into his gift-bag, simply waived his hand and refused to reveal the bag's contents—must have been embarrassing. The most interesting gift was presented to Calvert and Cooperrider simultaneously. It was a 5-foot, gift-wrapped hoagie sandwich.

After the gift distribution, the cheerleaders received green-and-white flowers from their parents that were to be worn for the state game. Later, Coach Graham presented each senior cheerleader with a bundle of red roses.

While Coach Graham had the floor, he talked briefly about our team and the senior class. "We've gone through all kinds of adversity," Coach Graham said. "People didn't think we'd get this far, especially going into last week and now we're here and this is what counts. I don't know another group of kids that has come so far as this football team."

I can remember Coach Graham singling out the seniors and offering praises. He talked about Donnelly and me at the same time, saying, "Kevin Donnelly and Billy Evans are probably the best pair of guards I ever had here." I was stunned at that remark and have never forgotten it.

The last event was a special tribute to Coach Graham and was snuck into the night's lineup without his knowledge. Coach Graham's amazing list of accomplishments while at Newark Catholic (up to that point in his career) was displayed on huge sheets of paper and read to the crowd by Sheriff Gerry Billy. The list was as follows:

- 155 wins, 17 losses and one tie—a winning percentage of .901
- Three state playoff championships
- Four Associated Press poll championships
- Four United Press International championships

- 10 Licking County League championships
- Two Mid-Buckeye League championships
- Seven teams with undefeated regular seasons
- 83 players with All-Ohio recognition including 16 first-team
- Named as Class A Coach of the Year six times
- Leader of all Ohio coaches in playoff competition with 26 games including 18 wins, seven losses and eight appearances in the title game

Coach Graham, who appeared humbled from the event, received a standing ovation as he took the floor one last time to address the crowd:

> I really didn't expect anything like this. We saw all these things on paper. I really believe in my heart we should have won six state championships instead of three. I love to death that we got the three. But right now my big concern: I just pray that this football team can really show what they can do and bring back a state championship. Because I'll just tell you right now: If it happens, it's the biggest one of my career and our coaching staff's career. So I just pray that we can get it for you and bring it back to Newark Catholic and Newark and Licking County. Thank you.

Thursday

As the week rolled on by, an unpleasant reality began to slowly sink in. I was haunted by a voice in my head that nagged me like an annoying little dog nipping at the heels of my soul. It was the undeniable truth that this was the last week of my life as a Green Wave football player. The time comes to us all eventually. I am sure my classmates were tormented by this "ghost" as well and that we all had varying ways to deal with it. My approach was to totally engross myself in the preparation process and to focus as hard as I could on the game itself, not thinking about anything beyond that day. This became increasingly difficult with each new day, however, especially on Thursday—Thanksgiving Day.

Thanksgiving Day was the eve of the big game, as it had always been. School was out, of course, and we met in the morning hours for the most thorough, attention-demanding walkthrough we had ever known. Moreover, this was our very last football practice at Newark Catholic. How fitting for it to have taken place on the very field where we all played our first games in the green helmet as either seventh or eighth-graders. As mentioned in the Richmond Dale chapter, walkthroughs during the playoffs ended with the solemn ritual of the seniors running possibly our "last sprint"—last only if we were to lose. On the day before our state game, there was no "if" about it. This definitely was our last sprint. Coach Graham gathered the team in the south end zone and sent the seniors down the field one final time. As we returned to the end zone, Coach Graham began to applaud. The juniors and sophomores joined him. It was a very special moment. When I was a sophomore and junior, I remember watching the other senior classes make their last sprint. While they were out of earshot, Coach Graham issued a mixture of compliments and good-natured humor about them all. I often wondered what he said about us.

Another newspaper story that appeared on Thursday caused a big stir in our camp. It was the story by Mark Naegele that listed all of the astronomical numbers Delphos had accumulated throughout the season. The juicy bit of information that sparked the most interest in our camp concerned Matt Closson, the supreme stud of the Fighting Wildcats. According to the paper, Closson strained some knee ligaments during Delphos' semifinal game against Covington and it was uncertain if he would be able to play in the state game.[20] I guess we had mixed emotions about that. Closson missing the game would definitely be favorable for us. At the same time, however, we did not want to play a team in a weakened condition. In the event that we won, the victory might seem illegitimate and we might never hear the end of it.

Thanksgiving nights were special times in the Newark Catholic community. Since 1980, it was a tradition to have a state championship game to attend on the following day. Newark Catholic in the state finals was as much a part of the Thanksgiving holiday as gravy and pumpkin pie and it was always the center of discussion. As a senior, I was humbled to be blessed with the opportunity to continue and participate in that tradition.

Our Thanksgiving meal in 1985 was a very stressful time. After we said grace, my brother Joe followed up by adding, "And may we have a victory at the state title game tomorrow." Much discussion followed pertaining to the previously mentioned article by Mark Naegele, revealing Delphos to be a football juggernaut. The story caused concern and aroused questions in our home, as it must have also done at other Newark Catholic dinner tables that evening. Is this team for real? What does Graham think? What is our plan? Do we have a chance? I was not much for discussing these matters. As one could imagine, I was a complete bundle of nerves, wrapped tighter than an eight-day clock. My mother recalls that my eyes were glazed over, I was in a fog and although I was at the table physically, my mind was elsewhere.[21]

While the Thanksgiving meal always presents the opportunity to gorge upon the spread of food and become bloated, this would have been an imprudent act the night before the big game. Eating in that fashion, however, —even eating at all— was next to impossible because of the tension. My sister-in-law Cara remembers me pushing the chair away from the table and hardly eating a thing. "This was very rare," she said. "You were eating a lot at that time in your life."[22] Later in the evening, the family wished me well as I headed off to bed at a decent hour, hoping for a good night of sleep.

Through the week, I wondered which game jersey we would wear for the state game. Coach Graham usually never told us until the night before a game. While it never was a major issue, it happened to be so for me during state week. The reason was that our white jerseys were last worn against Mogadore. The game was such a huge victory that as a perpetual symbol of that night, it was my intention to never wash the jersey. This would have been impossible if we had to wear white for the state game. So it was very good news to me when I heard that we would be wearing green for the state finals. To this day, my white game jersey remains soiled and grass-stained, as it did the night I walked off the field in Dover, Ohio.

Game Day

The morning of the state finals began very early. In 1983 and '84, game time was 11:30 in the morning. To conduct a team mass, team meeting and travel to Columbus, we had to report to school as early as 6:00 a.m. In 1985 however, our game time was set for 2:30 in the afternoon, giving us three more hours to prepare. One last team breakfast had been planned for us on the day of the state game, however, so we still had to leave our homes under cover of darkness.

I walked out of the house into the very cold morning. Mom was there to see me off for this momentous occasion. She hugged and kissed me and wished me luck. I threw my bag onto the seat of the truck and rolled out of the driveway nearly sick to my stomach.

The first thing Coach Graham did when we arrived at school was to send us out for a morning walk so that we could "wake up." Coach Graham instructed us to relax, take our time, stay together and come back with a clear head. The route took us south on Green Wave Drive, east though the alley by McGuffey School, north on 21st Street and west on Church Street back to the school. I always wondered if any local homeowners were struck with fear at the site of 48 boys walking through the alley in the early morning.

Upon our return from the walk, we gathered into the cold chapel for the last team mass, then on to room 120 for one more team meeting. Finally, we were released to the locker room to make final preparations and then wait until it was time to depart.

The time to board the bus had arrived. Little by little, the locker room grew more vacant and silent as teammates walked out. I purposely was one of the last ones to leave and caught Kevin Donnelly on his way to the door. "KC," I said, "there is one more thing you and I need to do." Reaching into the shelf of my locker, I pulled out that tattered penny that Kevin and I found on the track way back in July. "Do you remember this penny?" I asked. "We found it together and I said that if we made it to state, we would return it to the track together for the next team to find." We walked out to the track side by side to the very spot where we found the coin. After a short moment of silence, I tossed the coin to the cinders and Kevin and I boarded the bus.

The scene at Ohio Stadium upon our arrival was much different from the previous two years. We had been the first game of the day and found the stadium quiet and empty in 1983 and '84. In 1985, we arrived with the Division III title game between Orrville and Columbus DeSales still in progress. The moment I stepped off the bus, the shrieks and roars of a cheering crowd within the towering structure seemed to vibrate the very ground. What an adrenaline surge that caused within me!

We were dropped off at the southwest corner of the stadium where our locker room was. A sheet of notebook paper, which read *Newark, Upper*, was taped to a doorway at the bottom of a staircase, indicating to us that our dressing room was on the second deck. Once inside, we found our equipment, withdrew to an area of our choice and settled in.

Having arrived with plenty of time to spare, we were permitted to go out and sit as a team to watch the remainder of the Orrville-DeSales game. (DeSales won 21-13.) There were plenty of places to sit in the southwest corner just outside of our dressing room and this is where we congregated. The weather was very cold and damp with heavy cloud cover and some wind. There would be no sunshine today. I remember sitting there and pulling my sport coat tightly around me in an attempt to stay warm.

After several minutes of watching the football game, a great deal of movement below the gigantic scoreboard in the southeast corner of the stadium caught our attention. Our challenger, the Delphos Jefferson Fighting Wildcats, had arrived. We were finally seeing in-person this wrecking machine from northwest Ohio—and they were huge! Clad in blue jeans and white game jerseys that hung down to their knees, they were a tough-looking bunch—not the type of people I would want to meet up with in a street-fight unless they were on my side. With us in our "businessman clothes," we must have appeared as soft, preppy pretty-boys to them. I forgot about the cold when our two teams began to stare at one another, similar to two boxers in the ring competing for a psychological edge before a fight. Someone in our group suggested that it was probably a good time to go inside and we withdrew to our quarters.

As we went about our pre-game rituals, the pressure was unreal. Not only were we about to play the biggest game of our lives, but those of us who had been together since the eighth grade were also donning the green jersey for the last time. The voice that haunted me all week spoke louder than ever. By the look on some of the other seniors' faces, I could tell that the voice hounded them as well.

The low temperature outside resulted in me going through a personal superstitious dilemma. To wear a sweatshirt or not to wear a sweatshirt: That was the question. I had not worn a sweatshirt all season and surely did not want to start now! It was cold enough to justify one, however, and I opted to wear it. If we were to lose, I would never forgive myself.

After completing our pre-game rituals, Andy Kubik and I ventured out to midfield for the coin toss. Team captains for Delphos were Jay DeWitt and Matt Closson. Both Andy and I were overwhelmed by the construction of Closson.

It is with shame that I admit my inability to recall anything about the last pre-game speech Coach Graham gave to our class. If I may be afforded some artistic license, however, I would guess that the speech contained classic J.D. Graham-isms that drove us all to tears. Such items were possibly, "We are 4 quarters of great football away from being state champions. You guys have put up with me and have gone through hell for four months. Stay together, pick each other up when it gets ugly out there—and it will get ugly. Believe in yourself and believe in miracles. Seniors, this is the last time you'll wear that helmet. This is what we've worked for all season long. Let's go out and have fun today. Now let's get it in here for a prayer."

Upon our exit from the locker room, Coach Graham had us repeat a tradition that was instituted at the start of the 1984 state final game one year earlier. We slowly walked single file and spread out before our fans. Cheering, applause and chants of *Let's Go Green* came forth as we walked. We then looked up into the sea of green and white, held hands and raised them skyward in tribute to the Newark Catholic community. It was special to me that my position in the line was next to Pat Cooperrider—my friend and classmate since kindergarten. On Graham's signal, we dropped to one knee, said a prayer, made the sign of the cross and finally took our positions on the field.

Delphos made a grand entrance as well. Their starting offensive unit ran in formation to the north end of the field with the remainder of the team following. After the team gathered in the end zone, they exploded from their location and broke through a paper banner as scores of red and white balloons were set free.

A season's worth of weightlifting, rope jumping, seat rolls, wind sprints, scrimmaging past dark, viewing of game films, heartaches, hassles, peaks and valleys, came down to this one day. Literally, for years, my teammates and I dreamt of this opportunity. We were 48 minutes away from fulfilling that dream.

We kicked off toward the closed end of the stadium. Fielding the ball at the 11, Jay DeWitt made it to the 33 where Albert Ghiloni and Tommy Parker punched him out of bounds. When Delphos broke the huddle for the first time, we saw that Matt Closson was not in the game. His brother Tony took the fullback duties for the day. On first down, the humongous Keith Dickman drove me down the line almost into the center. Saad stuffed the power block of Closson. DeWitt was tackled by Byers after a 1-yard gain. On second down...well...let me just say that second down was unbelievable and rendered the entire Green Wave community shell-shocked. The play came to my side. Closson put an Iso block on me. Monte Byers was trapped by the backside guard and Jay DeWitt turned the corner with plenty of green space in front. John Jurden flew to the scene and got a piece of DeWitt at our 45. DeWitt shrugged Jurden off and continued down the sideline. Monte Byers, although in pursuit, was obliterated out of bounds at the 25. DeWitt kept going and appeared to have an easy score. A touchdown was prevented, however, by a wonderful effort from Tommy Helms. From the far side of the field, Helms turned on the jets, had a good pursuit angle, stayed with the play and made a solid hit on DeWitt at our 5-yard line.

We were grateful for Helm's tackle, but also in disbelief that Delphos ripped us for 61 yards on the second play of the game. The Delphos fans must have been thinking that it was business as usual—another 80-0 blowout in the works. Our fans must have been thinking something similar to what Coach Erhard said to Joe Bell after the long run: "Joey, no matter what happens today, I just want you to know that you guys are all winners in *my* book." Bell answered back, saying, "Hey! We are *not* going out of here losers today!"[23]

The whole scenario was hauntingly familiar to the 1983 State Championship game against McComb. Although it only took Delphos two plays to reach our 5-yard line as opposed to McComb's seven, other things were similar. Delphos opened the game on offense as McComb had done. Delphos gained big yardage by running to their right side just as McComb had done. Delphos was in white jerseys as McComb had been. Delphos was heading toward the south end zone of Ohio Stadium just as McComb had been. And at the risk of sounding like a broken record, let me reiterate that the Delphos game was being played after a terrific triumph over Mogadore—just as the McComb game had been! Would this day turn out to be McComb all over again? Would the Mogadore Jinx rare its ugly head a third time? Would our dream of being state champions go up in smoke?

With the game just 49 seconds old, Coach Graham called a timeout. I remember watching him approach the huddle, expecting any and all of us to receive the verbal assault of a lifetime. Incredibly, Coach Graham was quite calm when he reached the huddle. There was even a hint of a smile on his face when he said, "OK, they broke one on us fellas and now we've got us a game." I could not believe how calm he was—calmer than I had *ever* seen him. Instead of chewing on us, he first exhorted us to pull together and get into the game. Then he had us all huddle close together and say a Hail Mary right there on the 5-yard line. I asked Coach Graham just what kept him so calm in that situation. "The bigger the game," Coach Graham said, "the calmer and more focused I tried to be. I just tried to keep you guys from panicking there in the Delphos game."[24]

Kane Krizay, author of *Cheers and Tears*, wrote that Coach Graham's strategy of calling defensive timeouts early in a game "was considered unorthodox by many observers."[25] Krizay himself, however, gave this particular timeout a place of honor as an all-time championship game highlight, saying, "Graham's timeout maneuver was the turning point of the game."[25] Here's why:

First-and-goal from the 5: Tony Closson plowed forward to the 3-yard line. Olson, South and Simi combined for the tackle.

Second-and-goal from the 3: Trotter slanted to his left directly into the path of DeWitt. BOOM! Dewitt lost 3 yards.

Third-and-goal from the 6: Dickman pulled left for a Flanker Trap Zero. He and the guard Dave Maxwell double-teamed Jim Calvert and buried him 5 yards deep in the end zone. Their effort had been in vain. Monte Byers flew in on a Backer-Dog Fire and caught the flanker Buzard from behind for a 2-yard loss at the 8.

On fourth down, *it* happened—my one moment of fame, stardom and heroism. Delphos sent out their field goal team for a 25-yard attempt. My job at defensive end in this situation was to shoot the gap between the end and the wingman. This was intended to draw the wingman in to block me, thus providing a shorter distance for Byers to travel on a block attempt. After stepping into the gap, I was then supposed to get outside and look for a fake coming around the end. When Delphos attempted this field goal, the end blocked down and the wingman blocked out on Byers. When I stepped into the gap, I found myself unblocked! Instinct just took over when I saw a clear path between the holder and me. Instead of getting to the outside, as was my duty, I accelerated, dove and felt the football impact on my left hand. I had blocked the kick! It was the biggest play of my football career in the biggest game of my life and it could not have come at a better moment. Although my timing and position were perfect, it was not as if I knew what I was doing. It was just an instinctual reaction, graced with a bit of divine guidance and I probably could not have done it again if I tried.

The block was a fitting end to an awesome defensive effort that sent the Delphos offensive machine away with nothing. For a team averaging 44 points per game, that had to be one of the few times, perhaps the only time, that they were turned away after being inside the 5-yard line. I wonder if the Delphos faithful took it as a bad omen.

After the kick was blocked, a scramble ensued for the pigskin and Jim Olson fell on it at our 17-yard line. When we went to work on offense, I was so "jacked up" during the next couple of plays. I knew I had to come back down to earth because there was a great deal of football left to be played. Bell carried on first down on a 25 Iso for 4 yards. On second down, Kubik threw a beautiful, deep pass to Byers for 45 yards to the Wildcat 34. What a rapid change of field position!

On the new set of downs, Delphos jumped offside and left us with first-and-five at the 28. After Bell gained 3 yards on a 23 Power, he was able to push to the 20-yard line via 27 Counter Sweep. This play was called back because of an illegal-procedure penalty. Delphos jumped offside again and gave us the 5 yards back. Bell carried on a 27 Counter again and gained only 2 yards. On the next play, Kubik dropped to pass. Much to the disgust of the offensive lineman, Delphos safety Scot Boggs came in on a safety blitz and sacked Kubik—the first sack on Andy since the Heath game. Kubik attempted another pass on second down and was again under heavy pressure from the safety blitz. He was able to dump the ball off to Bell who made a nice run to the Delphos 21-yard line. On third down, John Jurden penetrated to the 16 on the Flanker Trap Zero, setting up a 26-yard field goal attempt by Dale Backlund. The kick sailed wide left.

Jefferson's second series began with a first-and-five after our entire defensive line encroached into the neutral zone. Boggs attempted a pass under heavy pressure from Byers. Simi was in position for the interception but was denied by Syphrit acting as a defender. On second down, DeWitt lost 3 yards on a carry around left end after being buried by South, Calvert, Saad and Franks. Third down resulted in another gang-tackle of DeWitt and Delphos had to punt for the first time of the day. The low punt from Boggs hit the turf at the 50 and did not stop until it reached the Newark Catholic 23-yard line.

We came out with a 28 Counter on first down. The play was a disaster as the unblocked defensive tackle penetrated and wrapped Bell up for no gain. Counter-Pass Left was the second-down call and resulted in a 10-yard pickup by Monte Byers. Monte had his leg bent beneath him on the tackle and came up limping. He was able to "walk it off." Time expired in the first quarter after we ran a Flanker Trap Zero for no gain. Only 7 yards rushing for the Green Wave showed on the scoreboard.

On the first play of the second quarter, Kubik attempted a pass but fled from the pocket under a tremendous rush. He threw the ball into the ground to avoid a sack and the refs nailed us with intentional grounding. The officials failed to notice that Kubik had been face-masked on the play. The penalty moved us back to our 21. From there, a deep pass to Byers on third down fell incomplete.

Backlund's punt was taken at the 50 by DeWitt. The speedster, attempting to reach the return wall, lost 7 yards on the runback. Additionally, Delphos was called for clipping and was pushed back to their 23-yard line. Tony Closson plowed into the middle on first down. South and Saad combined to hold the big back to no gain. On second down, Boggs wanted to throw but had Monte Byers in his face immediately. The ball was released in desperation, floated in the air and gathered in by John Jurden, resulting in the game's first turnover.

At about this time in the second quarter, I remember detecting a stinging sensation on my right hand. I discovered this to be caused by a divot of meat that had been removed from the base of my right thumb. This eventually scarred and is now a daily reminder of the state game against Delphos.

We went back to work at the Delphos 43-yard line. On first down, Kubik connected with Monte Byers for a 12-yard completion. Kubik threw to Byers again on the next play. This time, Monte went up for the ball, took a shot in the gut and landed flat on his back onto the hard surface. Amazingly, he was not hurt. In addition, Delphos was called for roughing the passer, resulting in a first down at the Wildcat 16. Bell carried on first down and, not surprisingly, gained nothing. That is not a cut on Bell but a credit to the tenacious Delphos defense. They pursued to the ball well and we just could not run against them. Luckily, we had the passing game to carry us.

After throwing an incomplete pass to Franks, Kubik zipped the ball between three Delphos defenders to Joe Simi, resulting in a first-and-goal at the 4-yard line! Bell carried on a 26 Iso and penetrated the Wildcat wall to the 3. Bell carried again on a 27 Counter. The play was totally disrupted by a blitzing Tony Closson, resulting in a 1-yard loss. On third down, Coach Graham called upon the tried and tested Tight End Delay one more time. Joe Simi faded to the left. Although Simi was well-covered by the defender, Kubik put the ball where only Simi could get it. Simi made a great sideline catch in the end zone with 7:53 to go in the second quarter. The extra point, however, was no good.

Taking the kickoff at the 12-yard line, Jay DeWitt tried the left side of the field and found no room. Turning back to the center, the Wildcat was smeared at the 24-

yard line by Albert Ghiloni and Tim McKenna. DeWitt remained on the turf for quite some time in proximity to our defensive huddle. I can remember him rolling around and moaning loudly. After he finally got up, he walked off the field in a manner indicative of someone who had taken a shot to the testicles.

Tony Closson plowed into the line on first down, picking up 5 yards. On second down, Andy Mox (6-0, 165), who was in for DeWitt, was drilled by Scott Saad for no gain. Boggs and DeWitt rolled left on third down for an option play. Although Billy Franks closed quickly and drilled Boggs, the ball had been pitched just in time. DeWitt ripped us for 19 yards to the Delphos Jefferson 46. On the next play, Boggs rolled to his right and completed a 9-yard pass to Steve Buzard at our 45-yard line—timeout NC! Following an incomplete pass and an illegal-procedure penalty, Delphos faced a third-and-six at midfield. Buzard carried on a Flanker Trap for 4 yards, setting up a fourth-and-two from our 46. Trying to employ some trickery, Delphos attempted a fake punt by snapping the ball to DeWitt. The ball glanced off DeWitt's hands, however, and rolled to the punter at the Wildcat 45. Billy Franks closed quickly and dropped the punter, leaving us with a great opportunity at the Delphos 42-yard line.

Realizing the ineffectiveness of our running game, Coach Graham tried to "air it out." On first down, Andy Kubik zipped the ball perfectly to Byers at the Delphos 5. It appeared to be a sure touchdown but Toby Kimmett made a nice play on the ball and knocked it away. Kubik found himself under another intense rush on second down and had to throw the ball away. On third down, Byers went up for a pass and had his paws on the ball until his legs were violently cut out from under him. Monte landed on the rock-hard turf on his back again. We failed to capitalize on the short field and had to punt.

The Wildcats went back to work on offense from their 20. DeWitt carried around the right end for 5 yards and was forced out of bounds. After a 3-yard gain by Closson, DeWitt picked up a first down with a run out to the 34-yard line. John Jurden knocked a pass away on first down. DeWitt ran for 5 yards on second down to set up third-and-five from the 39. Boggs stepped back as if to pass, then took off down the field on a quarterback draw play, gaining 32 yards to the Newark Catholic 29. The scoring threat was quickly snuffed out on the next play when Boggs threw a wounded-duck pass straight down the field. Joe Simi was in position for an easy interception at the 12 and ran it out to the 23-yard line. However, a clipping penalty occurring on the runback pushed us back to the 12-yard line.

Joe Bell carried on first down for a 3-yard gain. Another 3 tough yards came on second down as Bell plowed ahead on a dive play. On third down, Kubik came dangerously close to being intercepted when he threw to Byers at the 27. The pass was complete for a first down. In addition to the pass yardage, Delphos was penalized for roughing the passer, moving us out to the 33. After a deep pass toward Byers fell incomplete, Bell found 9 yards on a draw play as time expired in the first half.

At halftime, the scene in the locker room was very downhearted. We were flat, subdued and appeared exhausted. I remember Joe Bell sitting on the floor with a look of great concern etched across his face. His expression was no different from that of anyone else on the team. To my continued amazement, Coach Graham maintained his calm demeanor and was gentle as a dove when he spoke. "What's the matter with you guys? Look at you. You act like you're losing."

I suppose that we should have been ecstatic over the fact that we had shut Delphos out of the first half and were winning 6-0. There were many things to be concerned about, however. According to the scoreboard, Delphos had the advantage in total yardage 134-107. All but 9 of their yards were earned on the ground. How long could we expect to keep their high-powered running attack out of the end zone? And that defense—it was unlike anything we had faced all season. We managed only 8 yards rushing in the first half. We were also in a precarious situation having missed that extra point. These were just a few of the thoughts going through my head.

After Coach Graham addressed all of our dilemmas, he led us in a Hail Mary and gave his final thoughts:

"Are we better than this team, fellas?" Graham asked.

"Yes," the team said weakly.

"Can we beat this team?"

"Yes!" we said a little louder.

"Seniors, this is your last half of football in that green helmet! Don't go out there all scared and worried that you're going to lose! Go out there with your tradition and play to win!"

Almost as if he had done something wrong, Coach Graham caught himself after he had raised his voice.

"Listen to me, still giving you guys hell even now. Hey, I love you guys. Remember that. Now let's go out and have fun this second half."

"Our Lady of victory..."

"Pray for us!"

"Our Lady of victory..."

"Pray for us!"

"Our Lady of victory..."

"Pray for us!"

We emerged from the dressing room to find that the day had grown considerably darker while we had been inside. (It was about 4:00 p.m. by this time.) This necessitated the stadium lights being turned on. Although the lighting was not much, I considered it a rare privilege to see this. All Ohio State games I had ever watched on TV were played during the day and the lights were never used.

Kubik and I went out to the middle of the field to perform our captain duties one last time. My mother was able to talk a photographer (Tim Black) into going out there with us and capturing the moment on film. These photos are a prized-possession of mine.

We had the ball to start the second half. A nice 17-yard kick return by John Jurden took us out to the 42-yard line. On first down, Bell carried on a 13 Dive for 5 yards. Then on second down, just seconds into the third quarter, a major step toward winning this game took place. The play was a Counter Pass Left. I pulled out to keep the defensive end away from Kubik. He set up and sent the ball deep for Billy Franks. Jay DeWitt had the coverage on Franks and both men went up for the ball at the 15-yard line. The ball was tipped once but Franks maintained his concentration and made an outstanding catch. He was able to fight for additional yardage and was finally pulled down by Tim Brock (5-9, 150) inside the Delphos 1-yard line. Bill Franks recalled this momentous catch. "I was the third option on the play. Dewitt was in position to make the interception. Coach Graham always taught us to go into defensive mode if we could not make the catch. I tipped the ball up to keep it away from DeWitt and was just able to pull it in."[27]

It was interesting that Delphos ripped us on play two of the first quarter and that conversely, we ripped them on play two of the third quarter. The play was not a complete bed of roses for us, however. Joe Simi, while executing his pass pattern by dragging across the middle, suffered a vicious hit that left him unconscious for a brief period. "It was a cheap shot," Simi recalls. "I was looking up at the ball as it left Kubik's hand and just got plowed from the blind side."[28] The game film revealed the perpetrator to be Scot Boggs. Boggs led with his helmet and tagged Joe on the right side of his face. Several people came onto the field to tend to Simi including Dr. Trifelos, Newark Catholic teacher and basketball coach Gary Wheeler, Coach Graham and Dale Googins with one of his assistants from Denison University. Although Joe eventually got to his feet and left the field under his own power, his day, his Green Wave career, was over two quarters before the rest of ours.

After the great catch by Franks, Kubik went behind Donnelly on a sneak and punched across the goal line. Coach Graham decided to go for two points. A pass to Byers fell incomplete and the score stood at 12-0 with 10:42 left in the third quarter. Scoring that quickly and establishing dominance so soon after halftime did wonders for our confidence.

Dale Backlund's first kickoff after the score rolled out of bounds. On the re-kick, DeWitt took the ball at the 16 and brought it out to the 41 where Tim McKenna put a crunch on him. Now it was time to see how Delphos would react being down by two scores. Amazingly, they did not attempt to throw the ball. Closson carried once for 3 yards and DeWitt carried twice for a total of 4 yards. Our defense contained them!

We went back on offense at our 15-yard line after a 5-yard Byers punt return. Rushing yardage continued to come with great difficulty. After 3 yards apiece for Bell and Saad, Kubik threw to Byers for a first down at our 30-yard line. First down again and Saad ran into a wall at the line of scrimmage for no gain. On second down, Kubik looked to pass but the bothersome safety blitz put him on the run just as it had in the first half. Fleeing from Boggs and being driven back to the 20, Kubik finally turned upfield and made a nice run out to the 41-yard line, good for 11 yards and a first down. On the next three plays, Bell carried on a 17 Quick Pitch, 26 Iso and 18 Quick Pitch, earning 6, 3 and 10 yards, respectively. Just when it appeared that our running game was finally starting to assert itself, linebacker Bob Ladd blitzed on a 26 Iso and dropped Bell for a 3-yard loss. On the next play, a Kubik pass was tipped off the hand of Byers and intercepted by Scot Boggs. The Delphos fans erupted as their team had new life at the Wildcat 44-yard line.

A procedure penalty on first down pushed Delphos back to their 39, leaving them with first-and-fifteen. DeWitt carried first and was buried by Calvert and Olson after a 1-yard gain. On second down, DeWitt rolled out to our left for a swing pass. After catching the ball, DeWitt appeared to have an opportunity for a substantial gain. Scott Saad closed quickly, however, and made a big-time solo tackle in the open field, dropping DeWitt for a 5-yard loss and sending our fans into an uproar. Third down gave our fans more reason to celebrate. Running to his right again, DeWitt took a pitch from Boggs and tried to set up for a halfback pass. Trotter and Calvert provided immediate pressure, forcing DeWitt back across the middle of the field in search of more favorable conditions to the left. Todd South suddenly appeared and had DeWitt on the run. South eventually caught up and slammed DeWitt to the turf back at the Wildcat 18-yard line—a loss of 17 yards on the play.

After humiliating Delphos in that fashion when they had an opportunity to get back into the game, I think we began to realize that we could handle this team. It was still too early to declare victory, though, and no one brought it up. We merely pressed on with our assignments. This type of mentality—not declaring victory until a game is over—is one of the biggest standards of good, smart sportsmanship that I learned from playing for J.D. Graham. We were warned to never be so arrogant or do something so ludicrous as guaranteeing a victory or assuming we would easily stomp another team. Sooner or later, these words will always come back to haunt those who speak them, as well they should. It galls me to no end when I see present-day football players, whether they are high school, college or pro, shooting off their mouths in this fashion. This usually drives me to shout at the TV: "You idiot! You never would have played football for J.D. Graham!"

Following the Delphos punt, we had the ball again at our 27-yard line. The series turned out to be a zero-yardage affair for us. Scott Saad gained nothing on a first-down dive play. Andy Kubik threw incomplete passes on second and third downs. Scot Boggs took Dale Backlund's punt at the Wildcat 35 and returned it to the 49 where I made the stop. That was the last play of the third quarter. Twelve minutes were all that remained in the game, the season and my Green Wave career. If we could just hold on…

In the meantime, Joe Simi had been sitting on the bench wrapped in a blanket while recovering from the hit in the head. He offers an account of what took place after he had gotten his senses back:

> When our offense was in the game, Trotter would come up to me just madder than a hornet, asking, "Who was it Joe! Who did this to you!" I would say the first number that came to mind and Trotter would go stomping away, growling and seething. He would come back later and say, "I got him for you, Joe! I really nailed him!" Then I would say, "Actually, I think it was number so-and-so instead." Mike would go away angry again and then come back saying that he had nailed someone else. I don't know how many times we repeated this.[29]

Joe Simi essentially had his very own hit man in Mike Trotter!

To start the fourth quarter, Delphos ran the trap play with DeWitt that ripped us in the first quarter. Although a huge hole was there again, Trotter shed his block and ran DeWitt down, preventing any gain. On second down, Delphos tried the other play that brought them earlier success—the quarterback draw. When Boggs took off this time, he gained only 3 yards before I nailed him. Delphos tried a rollout pass to my side on third down. The pass from Boggs, intended for a wide-open DeWitt, was another ailing duck that hung in the air. The extra flight time of the ball was just enough to allow Joe Bell to cross the field, step in front of DeWitt and make the interception at our 34-yard line.

Scott Saad carried on first down. Once again, there were no yards to be found. The passing game, which had carried us all day, was called upon again. Kubik sent the ball deep. With a defender all over him, Monte Byers made a great catch at the Delphos 25-yard line. Delphos was guilty of pass interference but the penalty was declined. The next play was Flanker Trap Zero from the Pro-Right formation. To this day, I can remember being at the line of scrimmage and Dale Backlund asking me what his blocking assignment was. I told him to block out on the defensive end. He did so. I blocked down on the middle linebacker and Coop trapped the nose tackle. No one blocked the tackle on my side but it did not matter. The kid took himself so far out of the play that John Jurden easily cut inside of him. The play was good for 10 yards.

First-and-ten from the 15, Bell carried around left end on a 17 Quick Pitch and was hammered—no gain on the play. As was the case all day, Kubik connected with Byers again for a first down inside the Delphos 5. Wildcat defensive back Tim Brock was penalized for spearing on the tackle. The personal foul left us with first-and-goal at the 2. Bell carried to within a half-yard of the goal line on first down. On second down, Kubik scored on a quarterback sneak but the play did not stand. Donnelly had been in motion and we were pushed back to the 5-yard line. Joe Bell carried two more times, finally scoring from 2 yards out on 17 Quick Pitch. Backlund's extra point was good, making the score 19-0 with 7:05 left in the game.

DeWitt took the kickoff at the 7 and returned it to the 19 where Albert Ghiloni threw him out of bounds. Some rough hits occurred at the end of the run and a flag was thrown. Seeing the flag on the ground, Delphos defensive end Joe Gorman believed the flag was against Newark Catholic and he brazenly applauded in the faces of our coaches standing nearby. Too bad the flag was against Delphos—a clipping penalty that pushed them back to their 12-yard line.

Delphos could do nothing as our defense was all over them once again. Boggs rolled my way on first down. I could have sacked him had he not thrown the ball. Monte Byers nearly made an interception. On second down, another Boggs pass was broken up and nearly intercepted by Joe Bell. Mike Trotter limited DeWitt to 6 yards on third down and Delphos punted one more time.

We began from our 31-yard line with 5:47 left in the game. From this point, it was just a matter of getting a few first downs to grind out the clock and our dream of being state champions would be realized. Scott Saad carried first for no gain. Joe Bell carried on second down and gained 9 yards with a tough, twisting run. On third-and-one, Bell blasted for 5 yards and a first down to our 45-yard line.

Joe Bell began our next set of downs with a dive play that gained nothing. On the play, I remember being pushed over backwards and landing on an object that seemed to give beneath my weight. It had been the upright-pointed left foot of Tony Johns. Tony was assisted from the field and Bill Sikora entered the game. Scott Saad picked up 9 more yards after carrying on second and third downs, leaving us with a fourth-and-one at the Delphos 46. Saad charged ahead for 2 yards and our fans began to celebrate.

After the first down was achieved, the reality began to sink in that we were going to win this game. At the same time, I was also acutely aware, as I am sure my fellow seniors were, that the curtain was slowly closing on our careers in a sport that we loved so much. I knew I would never play the game again and I did my best to hit the Delphos linemen as hard as I could while the opportunity remained.

After two more rushing plays had moved us down to the 42-yard line, Coach Graham signaled for a timeout with 38 seconds remaining. On his way to our huddle, he brought with him Mike Trotter, Joe Wiley, Albert Ghiloni and Jeff Ronan. Coach Graham sent all underclassmen to the sideline in order for there to be an offensive unit composed entirely of seniors for the game's final moments. Even Tony Johns, injured though he was, hobbled out to join us so as not to miss this special time.

Kubik was instructed to fall on the ball on the next play. After Andy had done so, Coach Graham unorthodoxly signaled for another timeout with 26 seconds left. This time, he brought with him every remaining senior from the sideline. At Coach Graham's direction, all 15 of us joined hands and spread out in a line facing our fans, similar to before the game. It was the ultimate "senior moment" and was selected as the cover photo for this book. "I didn't want to be a hotdog or show anybody up," Coach Graham said of the act. "I just wanted to give the senior class a last hurrah. They deserved it."[30] This scene still chokes me up when I see it on film.

After a brief huddle for one more prayer, we lined up in the formation in which the quarterback downs the ball to run out the clock. Joe Wiley was back deep. After Kubik fell on the ball at midfield, some of the Delphos players, understandably crushed by the day's events, unloaded on some of us. Joe Gorman drove Byers 8 yards off the line of scrimmage and slammed him to the turf at the 45-yard line. Ironically, the flag that had been thrown was against us for illegal procedure. The clock stopped with 23 seconds left while the 5-yard penalty was assessed.

Kubik fell on the ball a third time. Again, we were guilty of illegal procedure and the clock stopped with 18 seconds left. The penalty seemed so typical for a team that experienced so many problems and frustrations throughout the season. We could not even execute a kill-the-clock play without screwing it up!

Because it had been fourth down, the ball changed hands and the Delphos offense had time enough for a few more plays. One play was all they would get, however. Delphos backup-quarterback Rob Poling, trying to make something happen, threw deep and was intercepted by John Jurden. Our bench cleared as the rest of the team stormed the field to begin the celebration.

No combination of mere words can properly describe the thoughts, the emotions and the euphoria that followed. The scene was almost surreal—my head spinning in a whirlwind that spanned the entire emotional spectrum. There was the ultimate joy and disbelief of having achieved a goal that was set back in the fifth grade. There was also a feeling of great sadness and finality from the fact that my days of being a Green Wave football player were over forever. The tears flowed, but I knew not if they were from sadness or joy. Tears are funny that way.

We mingled about the field, hugging and screaming. "I'm so proud of you guys!" Coach Poth shouted when he saw me. Mike Trotter and Jim Calvert hoisted Coach Graham upon their shoulders and carried him across the field. They carried him until he asked to be put down so that he could address the team. With his team huddled close around, Coach Graham launched into a post-game speech quite similar to the one spoken just 365 days earlier. Our class, the first to successfully defend a state title, had come full-circle.

When Coach Graham dismissed us, we made our way over to celebrate with the many fans that were still present including classmate Jim Neumeyer, who was shirtless. "I made a deal with Kubik," Jim said, "that if you guys made it to the state game, I would go without a shirt and have 'NC' painted on my chest. It was thirty-four degrees that day and I was sicker than a dog for days after that."[31]

When we returned to the dressing room, I finally met up with Kevin Donnelly and asked him to join me over in one of the corners. With our battle gear still on, the two of us stood weeping and staring at ourselves in a large mirror. "There we are," I said, quoting that which Coach Graham had said just days ago. "The best pair of guards J.D. ever had."

Sometime later an official from the Ohio High School Athletic Association appeared to present us with the glamorous 1985 Division V State Championship trophy. Coach Graham designated Jeff Ronan to accept the award on behalf of the team. It was an awesome moment.

As it had been following the Mogadore game, a sizable crowd greeted us as we emerged from the locker room. On my way out, I noticed the sheet of notebook paper that had directed us to our dressing room upon our arrival still hanging in place. I removed it and took it with me—and yes, I still have it. I saved everything.

With many of the players catching rides back to Newark with their parents, those of us who rode the bus home found it spacious and desolate. Despite the reduced number of kids, the trip was no less rowdy or boisterous than if the entire team had been on-board. I remember saying to Kevin Donnelly that I could not think of a better example of simpletons and no-namers putting their differences aside and coming together for a common purpose.

"How did we do this?" I asked him.

"Coach Graham believed in us," Kevin said, "and he got *us* to believe in us."

Jefferson	0	0	0	0	0
Newark Catholic	0	6	6	7	19

	Jef	NC
First Downs	4	16
By Rush	4	6
By Pass	0	8
By Penalty	0	2
Rushing	26-123	41-88
Passing Yards	5	209
Total yards	128	297
Passes	2-11-4	10-19-1
Punts	4-51	3-32
Fumbles / lost	0-0	0-0
Penalties / yards	8-66	9-51
Time of Possession	17:31	30:29

Box score from *The Advocate*, (Nov. 30, 1985), p. 11.

Notes

1. Mark Naegele, "Berth in championship tilt 'special' for NC squad," *The Advocate*, (Nov. 25, 1985), p. 11.

2. World-wide web, http://www.noacsc.org/allen/dl/high/highschool.htm, Jan. 2002.

3. Mark Naegele, "Delphos gridders take advantage of initial chance," *The Advocate*, (Nov. 26, 1985), p. 11.

4. Mark Naegele, "Jefferson rushes into title contest with big numbers," *The Advocate*, (Nov. 28, 1985), p. 1C.

5. Ibid.

6. 1985 OHSAA Football Championship Game Program, Division I, II, III, IV, V, (Nov. 1985), p. 17.

7. Wes Poth, Conversation with author, Jan. 30, 2002.

8. Mark Naegele, "Jefferson rushes into title contest with big numbers," *The Advocate*, (Nov. 28, 1985), p. 1C.

9. Ibid.

10. Ibid.

11. Ibid.

12. Ibid.

13. Ibid.

14. Ibid.

15. Dave Erhard, Telephone conversation with author, Mar. 3, 2002.

16. J.D. Graham, Telephone conversation with author, Mar. 3, 2002.

17. Ibid.

18. Sean McClelland, "Newark Catholic tailback has message for Jefferson," *The Advocate*, (Nov. 27, 1985), p. 9.

19. Ibid.

20. Mark Naegele, "Jefferson rushes into title contest with big numbers," *The Advocate*, (Nov. 28, 1985), p. 1C.

21.   Marilyn J. Evans, Conversation with author, Mar. 10, 2002.

22.   Cara Evans, Telephone conversation with author, Mar. 10, 2002.

23.   Joseph Bell, Conversation with author, Feb. 28, 2002.

24.   J.D. Graham, Telephone conversation with author, Mar. 3, 2002.

25.   Krizay, p. 147.

26.   Ibid., p. 235.

27.   Bill Franks, Telephone conversation with author, Feb. 14, 2002.

28.   Joseph Simi, Conversation with author, Dec. 1, 2001.

29.   Ibid.

30.   Mark Naegele, "'Biggest win' for NC coach," *The Advocate*, (Nov. 30, 1985), p. 10.

31.   James Neumeyer, Telephone conversation with author, Mar. 14, 2002.

Accolades

The house was dark and empty when I finally arrived home after the state game. Not one family member was present. That was OK. I guessed that they were already celebrating at the reception that had been planned, win or lose, at 7:30 p.m. at the Knights of Columbus hall on Everett Avenue in east Newark. I was excited to get there as well and I hurriedly showered and got dressed. Before leaving the house, however, I realized that it was several hours since I had last eaten and I raided the refrigerator and finally got something to eat! (Thanksgiving leftovers, of course.)

On my way to the reception, I cruised down Hudson Avenue, just I as had done all summer, to pick up my sophomore buddy Tim McKenna one last time. We arrived at the reception to a scene of great jubilation. Many members of the proud Newark Catholic community were present to offer hugs, handshakes and praises. A TV was set up to play the videotape of the game. Naturally, we all crowded around to see ourselves playing in the biggest game of our lives. This video had been recorded by a hired professional. For the low, low price of thirty dollars, anyone could obtain a copy. In a corner of the hall, the result of all our hard work stood proudly upon a table: the Division V State Championship trophy. We all took our turns at paying homage to this latest addition to Newark Catholic's trophy cases.

Strangely enough, there was nothing for us to do after the reception. My circle of friends and I were unaware of any other parties being held. Driving around town in search of an activity worthy of celebrating a state championship proved fruitless also. It was as if we were directionless now that the season was over. So, what did we finally end up doing? We stopped at the convenient store at the corner of 11th and Church Streets, just outside of our home stadium. There we purchased a mess of cigars and we went up to the high school and smoked for the rest of the night. There is nothing like a good Swisher Sweet to help celebrate a state championship!

When Saturday morning arrived, I could not wait to get the newspaper to read all the game statistics and to see all the things Coach Graham had to say. Our outstanding defensive performance was the hot topic in most of the news stories. Except for two or three broken plays, our defense had never played better all season. We held Delphos to 128 total yards—minus six yards and no first downs in the second half![1] Scot Boggs, who had thrown for over 1,200 yards with only four interceptions all season, was picked off three times and completed only two of 10 passes for 9 yards.[2] The speedster Jay DeWitt was limited to 83 yards in 15 carries.[3] (And remember, 61 of those yards came on one play!) Coach Graham said that it "was probably one of the greatest defensive efforts of all time."[4]

The terrific defensive stand and blocked field goal early in the first quarter was alluded to often. My suspicion of Delphos never experiencing rejection so close to the end zone was confirmed by a quote from Delphos coach Kevin Fell: "That is the first time this year that we have had the ball inside the ten and failed to score."[5] *Advocate* Sports Editor Mark Naegele printed a quote from me regarding the defensive effort. I said that in our minds, "it planted the seed that we were able to shut them down in critical situations."[6] Coach Poth razzed me about this comment a few days later, saying, "Only you Evans, the farmer that you are, could find a way to sneak in a comment about 'planting seeds' while discussing a football game!"

Offensively, our running game was not nearly as effective as it had been in the preceding playoff games. We managed only 80 total yards on the ground—74 belonging to Joe Bell in 25 carries.[7] Had it not been for our top-notch passing attack to pick up the slack, we would have had a long bus ride back to Newark. Andy Kubik completed 10 of 19 passes for 209 yards and one touchdown.[8] Monte Byers had an excellent day as he grabbed six passes for 129 yards.[9] The biggest play, of course, was the 52-yard tipped pass reception by Billy Franks that took us to the Delphos 1-yard line. Coach Graham expected the passing game to be the difference in the contest: "If we had to throw 50 times today, we would have. Passing is what got us here and we knew we needed to throw the football to win."[10]

Was our victory any less legitimate because Matt Closson did not play? The answer depends on to whom the question is posed. Delphos fans think so. Jeff Ronan has a brother who lives out in that part of the state. According to him, Delphos believes to this day that if the elder Closson had played, the outcome would have been entirely different. Coach Graham disagrees: "I know that the Closson kid being out was a factor. But honestly, I don't think it would have made any difference—not the way our defense played."[11]

I don't remember which day it was—either Saturday or Sunday morning following the state game, but Coach Graham called us to the school for one final team meeting. The purpose of this meeting was for us, the players, to vote for our teammates who were most deserving of the following awards: Most Valuable Offensive Lineman, Most Valuable Defensive Lineman, Most Valuable Offensive Back, Most Valuable Defensive Back and Most Valuable Player. The results of the voting would be announced at the annual Fall Sports Banquet to be held on Saturday, December 7, 1985.

For days after the state game, several people asked me if I could tell a difference between playing on grass and playing on artificial turf. Playing on artificial turf seemed like an issue to me before the game as the surface was so hard and capable of producing carpet burns. Once the game was underway, however, the "turf factor" was forgotten and the game was just like any other—until the following day. On Saturday night, just 24 hours after our championship victory, some friends and I went to see Rocky IV at the Newark Cinema Four movie theater, also known as the "cheap seats" because of the low admission fee. I can remember sitting in that theater with the highest degree of post-game pain and soreness that I had ever experienced. It is no exaggeration when I say that my entire body ached. It literally hurt to breath with the expansion of the ribcage as my lungs filled with air. I believed this to be a consequence of playing on the hard turf. Of course, I suppose that part of the soreness must also be attributed to those big boys of the Delphos team. They definitely knew how to hit people and the game was a bruising, physical struggle every step of the way. I often wondered if they ended up as sore as we were.

One night during the following week, our team was to be honored by the City of Newark at City Hall. We were treated to a ride on a large fire truck as our transportation from the high school to City Hall. It was a challenge for the entire team to find a safe place to ride aboard the truck, but we managed. The ride took place after dark and was somewhat cold and miserable. Once we reached City Hall and crammed into the chambers, the Newark City Council read a proclamation to officially recognize and congratulate our football team for the wonderful season.

Another celebration that took place was sponsored by the Newark Elks Lodge #391. They have a long-standing policy of honoring any state championship team from Licking County with a steak dinner.

On Friday, December 6, a gathering of the entire student body had been planned to further celebrate the state championship. This was not to be a big affair, but just a brief get-together at the end of the school day for people to express their thoughts about the season. Now, the nasty rumor circulating throughout the school that day was that Coach Graham planned to call on the team captains to get up and speak. The prospect was terrifying to me. I wanted no part of giving a speech in front of the entire school. I dismissed these claims as idle chatter intended to agitate me.

The time for the meeting had arrived. We gathered into the gymnasium, which was already filled with tables and chairs to accommodate the fall sports banquet on the following evening. Coach Graham gave a splendid speech about our team and the fantastic season. "Now," Coach Graham said in conclusion, "I'd like to get a few seniors to come down here and say a few words." I froze in fear. *Don't call on me!* Coach Graham scanned the crowd and he confirmed the rumor. Kubik and I were chosen. Andy took the microphone first. This was good for me as it provided time to think of something to say for my public speaking debut. Kubik improvised well and his speech was well-received. Taking the microphone from Kubik, I was still unprepared and stood staring at the floor for a moment. I finally began and talked about how most of us had limited varsity game experience and were unsure of what kind of season we would have. I touched on the fact that nearly every team was bigger than we were and that I usually had a man across from me that was 30 or 40, even 90 pounds heavier. My closing comments were concerning the thrill of winning the state championship: "In Psychology class, we were told that a person requires seven hugs per day to maintain good mental health. I received enough hugs that day to last me the rest of my life. It's been a great year."

The Fall Sports Banquet

The Fall Sports Banquet was a large affair designed to recognize all athletes involved in fall sports in grades 9-12. The units recognized were: freshman, reserve and varsity cheerleading squads; girls and boys cross country teams; the golf team; freshman, reserve and varsity volleyball teams; the freshman football team and varsity football team. According to the printed program from this night, 164 students were involved in the fall sports program in 1985! This was a large percentage of the total school enrollment and was indicative of the pride and commitment to Newark Catholic athletics.

The varsity football team was the last group to be honored. There were several awards for Coach Graham to bestow upon his championship team. Four of our players received Licking County League recognition. Andy Kubik, Monte Byers and Kevin Donnelly were selected as first-team All-LCL offensive players. Todd South was named as a first-team All-LCL defensive player.

For Class A Region XI, to which Newark Catholic belonged, Monte Byers, Pat Cooperrider, Kevin Donnelly and Andy Kubik were first-team offensive players. Todd South and I were named to the first-team defense. Second-team recognition went to Joe Simi, Tony Johns, Mike Trotter and Jim Calvert. John Jurden, Billy Franks, Jim Olson and Scott Saad received honorable mention.

On a statewide scale, Andy Kubik was named as Class A Back of the Year by the United Press International. Kubik's final numbers on the season were 138 completions in 255 attempts for 2,379 yards and 23 touchdowns—all were new Newark Catholic records except for the touchdown total.[12] Monte Byers was selected as a first-team All-Ohio athlete for having 56 receptions for 1,050 yards and nine touchdowns. Monte's reception and yardage total were also new school records.[13]

Still on a statewide scale, a number of our players received recognition by the Associated Press. Andy Kubik again was named the Class A Back of the Year. Monte Byers and Kevin Donnelly were both selected as first-team All-Ohio offensive players. One player was selected as a first-team All-Ohio defensive player under the AP banner: Me! I could not believe that I received this award. Several chapters earlier, I mentioned that two of my pre-season goals were to win the Lineman of the Year award and to be selected as an All-Ohio athlete. While I did not win the former, my goal of having my name placed upon the All-Ohio board in the "Hall of Champions" was realized. It was an incredible honor. Other teammates receiving AP honors were Joe Simi and Pat Cooperrider, who were named to the third team. Todd South received honorable mention.

There was an elite category of awards exclusive to Newark Catholic football in which the coaches selected the winners. These awards were ways of remembering certain individuals who were instrumental in the Newark Catholic community over the years:

-**The Connolly Award**, in honor of Mr. Bill Connolly, who had two sons play football for Newark Catholic. The members of the Connolly family financed Newark Catholic's first weight room, known as the Bill Connolly "Press" Room. The 1985 Connolly Award, which went to the player who reflected the spirit and attitude of Newark Catholic and achieved greatness on the football field, went to Joe Simi.

-**The Duffy Award**, in honor of Mr. Bill Duffy, who had a daughter married to a Licking Valley graduate. It was very important to Mr. Duffy that Newark Catholic beat Licking Valley. Thus, the Duffy Award went to the one player whose effort was a deciding factor in the Newark Catholic-Licking Valley game. The 1985 Duffy Award recipient was John Jurden. Recall that John was pressed into tailback duties for the night when Joe Bell went out with a thigh injury. John performed valiantly as he received tremendous abuse from the Licking Valley defense.

-**The Ghiloni Award**, to honor the memory the late Eugene "Ding" Ghiloni, was awarded to the player who best exemplified the Newark Catholic spirit. Ding Ghiloni was a huge supporter of Newark Catholic and sent all seven of his children there. Mrs. Nancy Ghiloni, Ding's widow, had the honor of bestowing this award to the recipient. In 1985, she had the special privilege of awarding it to her very own son Albert. With tears in his eyes, Albert stepped forward and hugged his mother while the team united in a standing ovation. "Winning this award," Albert said, "was one of the highlights of my time at Newark Catholic."[14]

-**The Loewendick Award** was in honor of Art Loewendick, a 1975 Newark Catholic graduate who died shortly after high school in an industrial accident. Art started two seasons at center and although he played the game with several physical disabilities, he played with courage and was an inspiration to many. (And don't think that his name was not mentioned many times over the years to serve as an example of Green Wave determination that all players were to emulate.) This

305

award went to the player who was most dedicated, hardworking, with not the most ability but the most drive—the "over-achiever" award, if you will. This award usually went to a lineman. The 1985 Loewendick Award recipient was Kevin Donnelly, who persisted in his efforts in spite of a separated shoulder and achieved Lineman-of-the-Year honors in the process. Incredible.

-**The Coach's Award** went to those players who had outstanding work ethics and played above their abilities. The 1985 Coach's Award recipients were Jeff Ronan and Joe Wiley.

The last group of awards was the "players' choice" awards that we voted on after the state game. The results were:

Most Valuable Player: Andy Kubik
Most Improved Player: Jim Calvert
Most Valuable Offensive Back: Monte Byers
Most Valuable Defensive Back: Todd South
Most Valuable Offensive Lineman: Pat Cooperrider
Most Valuable Defensive Lineman: Bill Evans

Once again, I was in shock for having won an award that I did not expect. My mother said that of all the awards I received, this one was the most special because it came from my friends.

There was one player, in my opinion, that was totally overlooked and should have received recognition with the rest of us in one form or another: Joe Bell. Despite struggling much of the season with injuries (appendix, sprained ankle, thigh bruise), which resulted in him missing the equivalent of four games, Joe still managed to get his 1,000 yards rushing for the season—1,108 to be exact and 14 touchdowns on 208 carries.[15]

In January of 1986, a salesman for Jostens (manufacturer of class rings) came to the school to offer the football players a chance to purchase a commemorative state championship ring. I was never one to wear or even own jewelry, but this football ring was something that I definitely wanted. The cost was over one hundred dollars. Not having the finances myself, I asked my father if he could spare the money for this ring. Now, Dad had no use for jewelry and was not keen on spending his hard-earned money on a luxury. He also explained that he did not have the money to spare. Still, he reluctantly wrote me a check for the full amount. When I went to school on the day the payment was due, I did not feel right about the whole situation. I tore up the check and never ordered the ring.

Fast-forward eight years to 1994. I told the above story to my future wife Jo-Ella. With the help of Sue Schilling (an employee in the Newark Catholic school office at the time), Jo-Ella learned the name of the ring company and even the name of the salesman that she needed to speak with. The ring was still available! She bought the ring and surprised me with it on my 27th birthday. It has everything: my name, my position, my number, *1985 Green Wave* on the sides and *Newark*

Catholic Division V State Champions bordering a handsome green stone. There is even a small wave on one side. I wear this gem proudly and it was the best gift I ever received!

Notes

1. Sean McClelland, "Catholic claims second straight title," *The Advocate*, (Nov. 30, 1985), p. 9.

2. Mark Naegele, "Long Wildcat run spurs defense," *The Advocate*, (Nov. 30, 1985), p. 9.

3. John Cannizzaro, Game statistics report, 1985 Division V State Finals.

4. Mark Naegele, "Long Wildcat run spurs defense," *The Advocate*, (Nov. 30, 1985), p. 9.

5. Mark Shaw, "High-tech NC puts byte on Jefferson," *The Advocate*, (Nov. 30. 1985), p. 9.

6. Mark Naegele, "Long Wildcat run spurs defense," *The Advocate*, (Nov. 30, 1985), p. 9.

7. John Cannizzaro, Game statistics report, 1985 Division V State Finals.

8. Sean McClelland, "Catholic claims second straight title," *The Advocate*, (Nov. 30, 1985), p. 9.

9. Mark Shaw, "High-tech NC puts byte on Jefferson," *The Advocate*, (Nov. 30. 1985), p. 9.

10. Sean McClelland, "Catholic's unlikely hero emerges from shadow," *The Advocate*, (Nov. 30, 1985), p. 10.

11. J.D. Graham, Telephone conversation with author, Mar. 3, 2002.

12. John Cannizzaro, 1985 Newark Catholic Football Statistics report.

13. Ibid.

14. Albert Ghiloni, Electronic mail to author, March 26, 2002.

15. John Cannizzaro, 1985 Newark Catholic Football Statistics report.

Growing Old Green

While working on this project, it dawned on me that I did not merely play football for Newark Catholic—it was my entire life during my high school days. I guess that is why I am able to remember so much and have the desire to write about it. Putting it all into words was the only thing missing from the experience of playing for one the finest football programs in Ohio.

Although Coach Graham was very hard on me, I harbor no ill feelings toward him. I understand now that he was driven by a tremendous desire to win, which is *not* a bad thing. I also realize the tremendous pressure he was under to produce winning teams for an expectant Newark Catholic community year after year. He did what he had to do to achieve this end and while some of his tactics may have been harsh on occasion, I am convinced that he always had the players' best interests in mind, such as outstanding physical readiness to prevent injuries and to have fun by winning as often as possible, just to name two. I also believe that Coach Graham had a bigger purpose in mind and that was to mold us into decent young men. If this were not true, he would never have spent so much time talking to us about manners, respect for elders, good sportsmanship, responsibility, honor and integrity.

Although I am no longer *growing up green*, I am still growing. And just as Coach Graham had predicted and planned, the lessons learned in football went with me into adult life and continue to shape who I am today. I learned that it is possible to be confident without being arrogant. I learned that if a person is willing to work hard enough and make the necessary sacrifices, almost any goal is attainable. I learned that when you think you have nothing left to give, that is the time to reach deep inside—there may be a little fight left after all. I learned that the people who are always on your case just might be the ones who care about you the most. Most importantly, I learned that a person should intend to be a winner in any undertaking. If total victory is not the goal, don't bother showing up. The rule applies to sports, to careers and to life in general. The world is full of whiners and people all too ready to make excuses. Playing for J.D. Graham taught me that it is best to just shut up and do the job.

The longer I watch football, whether it be high school, college or professional, the more I realize that it is often a game of chance. A dropped pass here, a fumble or an untimely penalty there can mean the difference between victory and defeat. Given the unpredictability of this often-infuriating game, what Coach Graham achieved at Newark Catholic is nothing short of incredible. He was one great coach and I, for one, consider it an honor to have played for him. He has been one of the greatest influences on my life, second only to my father.

As I write this in the fall of 2002, it has been 17 years since I last wore the green helmet. My journey of *growing up green* could not have ended any better than winning a state championship. I am so proud of what our class, our team was able to accomplish. I suppose that had our season been anything less than perfect, I would not have bothered telling our story. But our season *was* perfect, and those of us who experienced it together share a common, life-long bond. We continue to relive it, no matter how many years have passed between our meetings. We can be proud, knowing that we kept the program together under our watch. I shall never forget that cold day in November when we earned a title that can never be taken away from us.

We are brothers.

We are...*State Champions*.

Appendix A

Formations and Plays

Offense

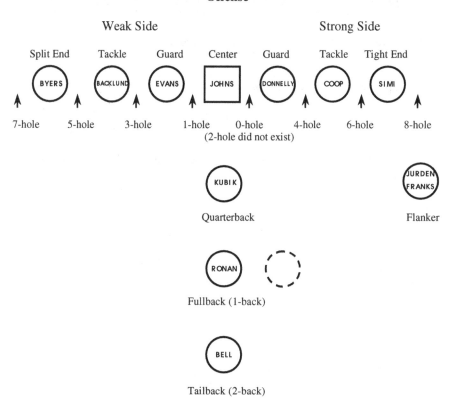

- ♣ Spaces between linemen are called "holes" or "gaps."
- ♣ Holes left-of-center were assigned odd numbers. Holes right of center were even.
- ♣ The Pro-Left formation is shown here. When changing to Pro-Right, everyone left of center moved to the right and vice-versa.
- ♣ "I"-backs are pictured. Backs could be strong to either side as dashed circle implies.

Naming conventions of plays

For the most part, all running plays had a first number and a last number. (Example: 24 Power.) The first number designated which back would carry the ball. The second number denoted which hole the play would go through. For a 24 Power, the 2-back (Bell) would carry through the 4-hole. For plays such as 0-1 and 5-6 traps, etc., which had no number designating a running back, it was understood that the fullback carried on these plays. The second part of the play name (Power, Isolation, etc.) usually denoted certain blocking assignments that were required:

- ♣ "Power" meant the fullback blocked the middle linebacker.
- ♣ "Isolation" or "Iso" meant the fullback blocked the defensive end or outside linebacker.
- ♣ "Special" meant fullback blocked a down lineman—usually a defensive tackle.
- ♣ A "trap block" meant that an offensive lineman ran parallel behind the line of scrimmage and struck a defensive lineman from the side. Trap plays were favorites among offensive linemen in that they presented opportunities to obliterate defensive lineman if they did not see the block coming, hence the name "trap."

Basic Plays

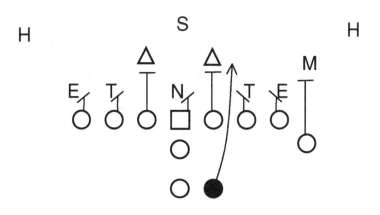

14 Dive

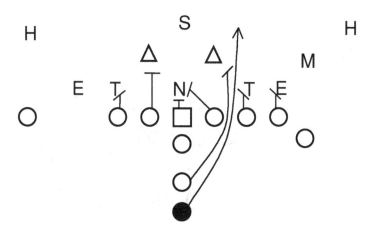

24 Power

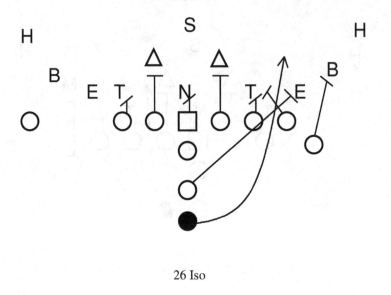

26 Iso

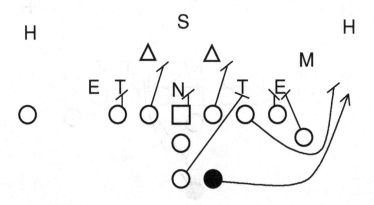

18 Quick Pitch

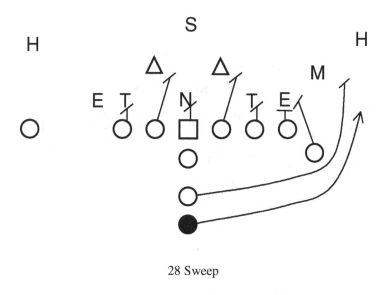

28 Sweep

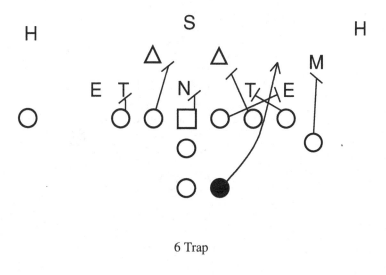

6 Trap

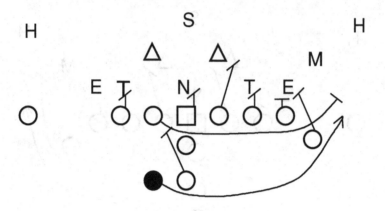

28 Counter Sweep

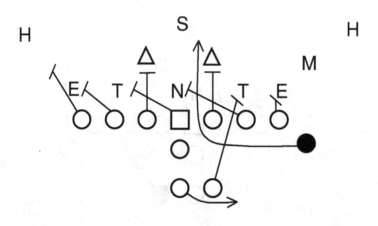

Flanker Trap Zero

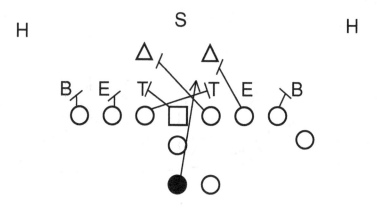

Zero Trap
(against 6-2 Defense)

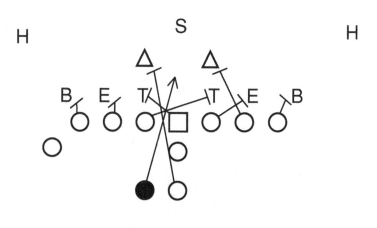

30 Trap
(against 6-2 Defense)

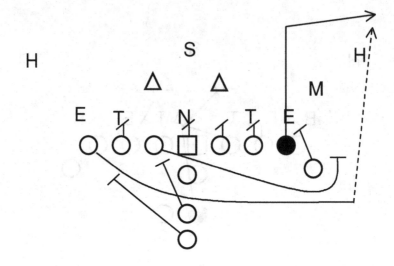

48 Counter Pass

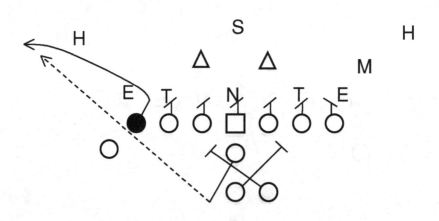

Tight End Delay

Explanation of Symbols

S = Safety
H = Halfback
B = Outside Linebacker
E = Defensive End
T = Defensive Tackle
N = Nose Tackle
Triangles are Middle Linebackers

Note: The intention of these play diagrams is not to teach football. Rather, they are to illustrate some of the more common plays mentioned throughout this manuscript and thus provide an understanding of the technical jargon. There are a multitude of formations from which to run plays and a multitude of blocking schemes depending on the defense, most of which are not shown for the sake of space and simplicity.

6-2 Defense

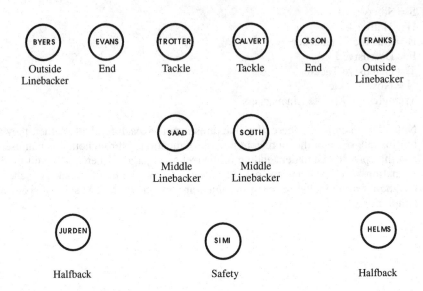

A 40-Defense consisted of Byers and Franks dropping back for pass-defense, leaving four men on the line of scrimmage.

Appendix B

1985 Newark Catholic Football Statistics*

Game Results:

NC – 14 Tuscarawas Central Catholic – 3
NC – 51 at Northridge – 0
NC – 16 Watkins Memorial – 13
NC – 28 at Johnstown – 21 (OT)
NC – 17 at Coshocton – 3
NC – 35 Heath – 0
NC – 7 at Licking Valley – 6
NC – 28 at Granville – 0
NC – 29 Utica – 0
NC – 42 Lakewood – 0
NC – 48 Richmond Dale Southeastern – 18
NC – 27 Bainbridge Paint Valley – 0
NC – 42 Mogadore – 28
NC – 19 Delphos Jefferson – 0

Record:

Licking County League: 8-0
Regular Season: 10-0
Overall Season: 14-0

Championships:

Licking County League
United Press International Class A
Computer Region 19, Division V
Ohio Division V State Playoff

Team Statistics

	NC	Opp
First Downs	247	93
By Rushing	126	48
By Passing	105	38
By Penalty	16	7
Yards Rushing	2,239	956
Avg. Per Game	159.9	68.3
Total Attempts	554	409
Avg. Per Rush	4.1	2.3
Yards Passing	2,615	795
Avg. Per Game	186.8	56.8
Completions	153	72
Attempts	279	199
Percentage	55%	36%
Had Intercepted	8	14
Total Net Yardage	4,854	1,751
Avg. Per Game	346.7	125.1
No. of Offensive Plays	833	608
Avg. Per Play	5.8	2.9
Punts	39	81
Avg. Per Punt	29.2	34.2
Had Blocked	1	0
Punt Returns	32	16

Avg. Per Return	8.9	5.2
Kickoff Returns	26	69
Avg. Per Return	23.7	14.5
Penalties	81	78
Yards Lost	638	653
Fumbles / Lost	26-16	33-16
Touchdowns	57	12
By Rushing	28	4
By Passing	28	8
By Fumble Recovery	1	0
Points Scored	403	92
Avg. Per Game	28.8	6.6

1985 Individual Statistics

Rushing

Player	Att	Yds	Avg	Lg	TD
Joe Bell	208	1,108	5.3	66	14
Jeff Ronan	87	365	4.2	17	4
Scott Saad	63	280	4.4	43	2
Tom Parker	33	174	5.3	65	3
Darby Riley	48	166	3.5	22	0
John Jurden	35	151	4.3	18	1
Tim McKenna	18	52	2.9	17	0
Bill Franks	5	25	5.0	15	0
Jeff Poulton	2	10	5.0	10	0
Monte Byers	1	2	2.0	2	0
Scott Rogers	1	-4	-4.0	-4	0
Andy Kubik	45	-25	-0.6	17	4
Dale Backlund	1	-31	-31.0	-31	0
Jeremy Montgomery	7	-34	-4.9	-6	0

Passing

Player	Att	Comp	Yds	PCT	Avg. Comp	TD	Int	LG
Andy Kubik	255	138	2,379	54%	17.2	23	8	69
J. Montgomery	19	11	164	58%	14.9	2	0	28
Joe Simi	5	4	72	80%	18.0	3	0	31

Receiving

Player	Rec	Yds	Avg	Lg	TD
Monte Byers	56	1,050	18.8	55	9
Joe Simi	44	762	17.3	69	11
John Jurden	20	363	18.2	52	3
Jeff Ronan	9	61	6.8	19	2
Joe Bell	8	124	15.5	24	0
Bill Franks	6	116	19.3	52	1
Scott Saad	4	66	16.5	29	1
Tom Parker	3	49	16.3	28	0
Albert Ghiloni	2	13	6.5	9	0
Tom Helms	1	11	11.0	11	1

Scoring

Player	TD	P-1	P-2	FG	Sfty	Total
Joe Bell	14	0	2	0	0	88
Joe Simi	11	0	0	0	0	66
Monte Byers	9	0	0	0	0	54
Dale Backlund	0	40	0	3	0	49
Jeff Ronan	6	0	0	0	0	36
John Jurden	4	0	0	0	0	24
Andy Kubik	4	0	0	0	0	24
Tom Parker	3	0	0	0	0	18
Scott Saad	3	0	0	0	0	18
Bill Franks	1	0	0	0	0	6
Tom Helms	1	0	0	0	0	6
Todd South	1	0	0	0	0	6
Boo Cook	0	4	0	0	0	4
Matt Dase	0	2	0	0	0	2
Team Score	0	0	0	0	1	2

Punting

Player	No.	Yds	Avg	Lg	Blocked
Dale Backlund	26	806	31.0	45	0
Joe Bell	11	379	34.5	43	1
Jim Winters	2	54	27.0	31	0

Punt Returns

Player	No.	Yds	Avg	Lg
John Jurden	9	91	10.1	26
Joe Bell	7	75	10.7	20
Joe Simi	7	70	10.0	41
Darby Riley	3	21	7.0	19
Joe Wiley	3	3	1.0	2
Monte Byers	2	10	5.0	6
Damon Schumaker	1	14	14.0	14

Kickoff Returns

Player	No.	Yds	Avg	Lg
Joe Bell	11	286	26.0	57
John Jurden	9	210	23.3	33
Monte Byers	2	37	18.5	26
Jeff Ronan	2	21	10.5	14
Damon Schumaker	1	58	58.0	58
Scott Saad	1	5	5.0	5

All-Purpose Yardage

Player	Rush	Pass	Rec	PR	KOR	Total
Andy Kubik	-25	2,379	0	0	0	2,354
Joe Bell	1,108	0	124	75	286	1,593
Monte Byers	2	0	1,050	10	37	1,099
Joe Simi	0	72	762	70	0	904
John Jurden	151	0	363	91	210	815
Jeff Ronan	365	0	61	0	21	447
Scott Saad	280	0	66	0	5	351
Tom Parker	174	0	49	0	0	223
Darby Riley	166	0	0	21	0	187
J. Montgomery	-34	164	0	0	0	130
Bill Franks	25	0	116	0	0	141
Damon Schumaker	0	0	0	14	58	72
Tim McKenna	52	0	0	0	0	52
Albert Ghiloni	0	0	13	0	0	13
Tom Helms	0	0	11	0	0	11
Jeff Poulton	10	0	0	0	0	10
Joe Wiley	0	0	0	3	0	3
Scott Rogers	-4	0	0	0	0	-4
Dale Backlund	-31	0	0	0	0	-31

Pass Interceptions

Player	No.	Yds	Avg.	Long
Joe Simi	4	17	4.3	13
Tom Helms	3	35	11.7	14
John Jurden	2	5	2.5	5
Todd South	2	5	2.5	5
Darby Riley	1	17	17.0	17
Monte Byers	1	6	6.0	6
Joe Bell	1	0	0.0	0

Opponent Fumble Recoveries

By: Scott Saad had three; Tom Helms and Monte Byers each had two; Bill Evans, Mike Trotter, Bill Franks, Joe Wiley, Matt Gilmore, Jim Calvert, Todd South (for TD), Bill Keaser and Jim Olson each had one.

Score By Quarters

	1st	2nd	3rd	4th	OT	Total
Newark Catholic	69	166	89	72	7	403
14 Opponents	16	23	16	37	0	92

New School Records

Team- Single Game:
Passing Yardage- 334 vs. Utica

Team- Single Season:
Most Wins- 14
Passes Attempted- 279
Passes Completed- 153
Passing Yardage- 2,615

Individual- Single Game:
Passing Yardage- 308 by Andy Kubik vs. Utica
Receiving Yardage- 212 by Monte Byers vs. Utica
TD Receptions- 3 by Joe Simi vs. Richmond Dale Southeastern (ties mark)

Individual- Single Season
Passes Attempted- 255 by Andy Kubik
Passes Completed- 138 by Andy Kubik

Passing Yardage- 2,379 by Andy Kubik
Pass Receptions- 56 by Monte Byers
Receiving Yardage- 1,050 by Monte Byers
TD Receptions- 11 by Joe Simi (ties mark)

More Accomplishments

1985 was the first year Newark Catholic had three receivers catch 20 or more passes-
Monte Byers (56); Joe Simi (42); John Jurden (20).

In 1985, the fourth-highest individual rushing total for a single game was compiled by
Joe Bell: 215 yards vs. Mogadore.

In 1985, for the first time in Newark Catholic history, Green Wave players were
honored by the Associated Press with Central District Player of the Year (Andy
Kubik) and Lineman of the Year (Kevin Donnelly) awards in the same season.

In 1985, Newark Catholic became the first Division V school to compile more than
100 computer points in the Ohio High School's five-divisional computerized
rankings.

In 1985, Newark Catholic's defensive unit pitched seven shutouts, gave up
touchdowns in just four games, held seven opponents under 100 yards in total
offense, and held nine opponents to five first downs or less. Winning streaks for
Newark Catholic now stand:

27 for all games
25 for regular season play
21 in Licking County League play (ties mark)

*Note: Statistics shown here were taken from the "1985 Newark Catholic Football
Statistics" sheets supplied by John Cannizzaro. Records were as they stood at the end of the
1985 season only. Many have been broken since.

Additional data: Career record of the seniors of the 1985 Green Wave.

	As a starting class	As team members
Grade 8	7-0	7-0
Grade 9	6-1	6-1
Grade 10	8-0 (Reserve)	11-2 (+Reserve)
Grade 11	----	13-0
Grade 12	14-0	14-0
Total	**35-1**	**59-3**

Appendix C

Where Are They Now?

In addition to their present-day information, some individuals were asked to reflect upon what playing football for Newark Catholic has meant to them.

Dale Backlund served four years in the U.S. Navy and earned a Bachelor's degree in History from the Ohio State University. Dale is currently pursuing his teacher's license and a Master's degree in Education. Dale is a faculty member of Newark Catholic High School and is an assistant lineman coach for the football team—a position he has had since 1997.

> I think of four things when I think of my Newark Catholic football days: 1) Tremendous discipline, which helped me in the military and in college and I know it will help me in my teaching career. 2) Hard work. Coach Graham was right. Nothing has ever been harder. It taught me to persevere, to never quit and to face adversity and beat it. 3) Teamwork. There were no individuals on the team. Life is the same way. You need to surround yourself with people you can work with who all desire a common goal. 4) Team Masses, which were a very important part of the tradition. Coming together as a team and thanking God that we had the ability to do what we did was very special.[1]

Joe Bell obtained a degree in Accounting from Kent State University. A few years later, he became a certified public accountant and now oversees internal auditing for the Ohio Attorney General's Office in Columbus. Joe currently resides in New Albany with his wife Peggy and children Robert and Samantha.

> Playing football for J.D. Graham and Newark Catholic was a valuable lesson about discipline, building character and learning that continued hard work and persistence will overcome adversity—be it in football or life in general. Many times, it would have been easy to pack up the bags and quit when the going got tough. However, by staying the course and pursuing our vision, we achieved our team goals. J.D. was an expert on motivating players and teaching the concept of teamwork. He made each player strive to achieve more than they thought they were capable of, thus turning average athletes into good players and good athletes into great players. By making each person realize the chain is "only as strong as its weakest link," we felt compelled to give our best efforts so as to not let down our teammates.
>
> Teenage years were filled with many distractions, yet these years were also the most impressionable as we began our transition into adulthood. I will always remember J.D. emphasizing the values and priorities that hold true today: 1) God; 2) Family; 3) School; and 4) Football. Although football seemed like my life at that time and it still holds many special memories, I later realized that teamwork and a hard work ethic were

fundamental traits that were to be carried over into all aspects of life. It was a difficult and demanding journey, but the rewards reaped will last a lifetime.[2]

Monte Byers received a football scholarship to Michigan State University. After a year-and-a-half stay, he transferred to University of Akron and Western New Mexico University over the next two years. The frequency of his moves stemmed from a digestive problem that caused rapid weight loss. Monte enlisted into the U.S. Navy's nuclear program, scoring 20 points higher than the national average on the entrance examination. Naval doctors correctly diagnosed Monte's problem and prescribed proper medication, but the ordeal resulted in a medical discharge. In 1995, Monte joined the family business, the BT Pro Golf Shop in Heath, Ohio. He has enjoyed huge success with his Kids of America Junior Golf Equipment, which Monte created and was the primary engineer. Monte lives in Heath with wife Cindy and children Alexis and Logan.

Jim Calvert spent a few years in Atlanta, Georgia where he was a warehouse manager for a heavy equipment company. Since then, Jim entered the truck-driving profession and currently drives for Layton Excavating in Newark, Ohio. Jim lives in Newark with wife Kim and children Matt and Haley.

> Coach Graham was a good coach. He put it into our heads that we could play better than we thought we were capable of playing. He built us all into one machine and there were no individuals. He told us to never let anyone intimidate us and I still live by that to this day. I learned more than just football from him. I learned about life. I learned how to deal with problems.[3]

Coach Jim Campolo stayed with the Newark Catholic football program until after the 1987 season. He then went on to serve as offensive coordinator for the Newark Wildcats until 1996. Today he is an assistant football coach for Watkins Memorial High School and is the head softball coach for Gahanna Lincoln High School.

Pat Cooperrider remained in Newark and entered the plumbing profession. He and his wife Beth have two children: Lindsey and Tanner.

> Playing for Newark Catholic made for good work habits later in life. It was definitely a positive experience. How many people can say that they played on the state championship level—and won? It was a lot of hard work, but it paid off in the end.[4]

Coach Paul Cost has been an assistant lineman coach for NC on and off for approximately 13 years. Paul lives in Cincinnati, Ohio, where he is employed by State Farm.

Kevin Donnelly took up skydiving following high school. This hobby led to an interest in flying. Kevin subsequently obtained his pilot's license and is now flying on a nightly cargo route from Columbus, Ohio to Chicago, Illinois. Kevin lives in Columbus.

> I did not fully realize it at the time, but Coach Graham gave us a great gift. That gift—the desire to work hard and to stay focused—has stayed with me ever since. In my time in the real world, I have not met another person like J.D. Graham. In addition, when I think of Newark Catholic football, I am proud of how I played and acted and I am proud of my teammates and classmates. [5]

Coach Dave Erhard remained an assistant coach for Newark Catholic until the end of the 1996 season. He left his teaching position at Blessed Sacrament in 1997 and is now an independent financial adviser in Newark.

Bill Evans- After graduation, I knew I was obligated to the U.S. Navy given the fact that I enlisted before the 1985/86 school year began. This was not a problem. Even though I did receive letters from West Virginian Wesleyan College and Ohio Northern University about playing football, I had no desire to play any longer for two reasons: One, I had played the sport for eight years and felt blessed that I made it through with no serious injuries. Two, I knew that no collegiate football experience would compare to what I had been privileged to be a part of at Newark Catholic. My career ended on an up-note.

I served four years in the U.S. Navy as an aircraft mechanic, specializing in oxygen systems, air-conditioning systems and ejection seats. (They actually permitted me to handle high explosives!) I enrolled in The Ohio State University in the fall of 1990. I earned a B.S. in Agriculture and a minor in Natural Resources Management. This field of study led to my current job with the Licking County Soil and Water Conservation District. I live in Newark with my wife Jo-Ella. I learned to play the guitar while in the Navy. This skill has lead to the rewarding experience of writing and recording jazz/rock/fusion music in a trio comprised of bassist Brent Crowley, drummer Mike Evans (brother) and me on guitars and keyboards.

Billy Franks and his teammates returned to Ohio Stadium in their senior year to play Defiance Ayersville (yet another team from northwest Ohio) in the 1986 Division V State Finals. Trailing 27-21 with 2:24 left in the game, the Greenies marched down the field and Franks made the winning touchdown reception with 47 seconds left in the game. NC took home its third straight title by a score of 28-27! (A terrific footnote to this story that I just love has often been told by Doug Heffley, a scout for Newark Catholic. Doug says that he and other Green Wave fans entered the Varsity Club on Lane Avenue after the game. They had been noticed by some celebratory Defiance fans and one of them said, "Hey, great game. I'm sorry you guys had to lose." Mr. Heffley had the pleasure of informing these folks that they had exited the stadium prematurely!)

Franks went on to play football at the University of Dayton where he won a national championship and was an All-American in 1989. After earning a B.S. degree in Physical and Health Education and a Master's in Educational Administration, Bill became an assistant football coach for the Newark Wildcats and eventually held the head-coaching position from 1996-2001. And in February of 2002, Bill became the athletic director and head football coach of the Newark Catholic Green Wave.

> I would like to publicly thank Coach Graham for giving us—the Newark Catholic community—his "all" for nearly one quarter of a century. He influenced us in ways that are impossible to describe with words. Coach Graham had a saying about his football program: "If you can get through this, nothing again will ever be a challenge to you." Coach, You were right![6]

Coach Dave Gebhart left Newark Catholic after the 1985 season to become the defensive secondary coach at Denison University, a position that he held for six years. Coach Gebhart received additional collegiate coaching experience in the spring of 1992 when he was a volunteer graduate assistant coach at The Ohio State University. In the fall of 1992, Coach Gebhart returned to elementary education while also serving as defensive coordinator, secondary coach and passing-game coach for Columbus Bishop Ready High School. In Coach Gebhart's four years at Ready, they qualified for the playoffs two times and Dave was named Central District Assistant Coach of the Year in 1994. In 1996, Coach Gebhart became the defensive coordinator for Fairbanks High School—a Division V school south of Marysville, Ohio. In the three seasons prior to Coach Gebhart's arrival, Fairbanks had a record of 3-27. With Coach Gebhart on board, however, Fairbanks would go 26-4 in the next three seasons, including 10-0 records in 1996 and '98. For these successes, Coach Gebhart was again named Central District Assistant Coach of the Year in 1996 and '98. Coach Gebhart moved into the head coach's job at Fairbanks in 1999 and led the team to a 10-0 season, qualifying Fairbanks for their first-ever playoff appearance. They lost in the first round to Sidney Lehman Catholic. In 2000, Coach Gebhart led Fairbanks back to the playoffs, which resulted in their first-ever playoff victory. The team they defeated was Columbus Ready—Coach Gebhart's previous assignment. Dave pointed out that he not only coached a team to their first playoff victory, but he has also played on a team that was the first to win a playoff game for its school—Newark Catholic's 1975 squad. Coach Gebhart was named the West Central Ohio Conference Coach of the Year in 1999 and 2000. In 2001, Coach Gebhart returned to Newark and served as head coach of the junior high team at Wilson Middle School. As of 2002, Coach Gebhart has returned to his alma mater—Newark Catholic—to serve as an assistant coach once again. I'm sure others will agree that Dave is a valuable addition to the coaching staff!

Albert Ghiloni joined Label Graphix in Heath, Ohio in the spring of 1987 where he worked on the production floor. Today he is the general manager of this location and lives in Newark.

> When I stop and look back at playing football at Newark Catholic for Coach Graham, I remember all of the seat rolls, sprints, push-ups, sit-ups, hours of watching films and those famous scouting reports. Then I think of everything we accomplished in our four years and what we learned from that experience. There is nothing I would change about any of it.[7]

Matt Gilmore attended Capital University after high school. He majored in History and is now employed with Farmers Insurance in Westerville, Ohio.

Coach J.D. Graham continued as head coach of Newark Catholic through the 1991 season. In his final game as coach of Newark Catholic, Coach Graham led the Green Wave to a 34-13 victory over the Bluffton Pirates (another team from northwest Ohio) in the Division V State Championship. In 21 seasons at Newark Catholic, Coach Graham tallied 220 wins, 30 losses and one tie. His teams made 16 appearances in the state football playoffs with a record of 35-9 including 16 regional computer championships; 11 title-game appearances (8 consecutively); seven state championship teams: 1978, '82, '84, '85, '86, '87, '91; and four state runner-up teams: 1975, '80, '81, '83. Coach Graham also recorded 7 Associated Press poll titles, 7 United Press International poll titles and 15 league titles.

After Newark Catholic, Coach Graham took a position as recruiting coordinator for the Ohio State Buckeye football program, where he stayed for one season. Coach Graham currently lives in Medina, Ohio with his wife Kelly and is employed by State Farm.[8]

Tom Helms graduated magna cum laude from the University of Notre Dame and works in the accounting profession. He has not become president of the United States—yet.

Tony Johns received an Associate degree in Computer Programming from Central Ohio Technical College and an Associate degree in Human Resources from the Community College of the Air Force. He also received a B.A. degree in Computer Science from Otterbein College and his Master's certificate in Project Management from George Washington University. He currently works for Nationwide Financial as a Project Manager. Anthony is also a Master Sergeant for the U. S. Air Force Reserves. He served stateside during Operation Desert Storm and is supporting our current military operations.

Coach Jeff Jones continues to serve at Newark Catholic not only as an assistant football coach but also as a Social Studies and Science teacher.

John Jurden went to Rio Grande College for one year and played baseball. After returning home in the summer of 1987, John began working in the family business—Heritage Sportswear Inc.—where he has been for 15 years. John lives in Newark with his wife Mary and three sons and tinkers with draft horses in his spare time.

> I feel that playing for Newark Catholic made me more dedicated at my job today. Coach Graham instilled that hard work ethic in us day in and day out. It pays off in the long run and the ones that don't work the hardest don't come out on top. I think he instilled confidence in me by enabling us to compete at the championship level of high school football making us successful. His language never bothered me. It's football, not golf, and nothing was taken to heart. The way I saw it, if he cared enough to get that upset about a game he couldn't play in, then I should care as much as him or more.[9]

Andy Kubik received a full scholarship to the University of Akron in Akron, Ohio. Under the tutelage of ex-Cincinnati Moeller and University of Notre Dame coach Gerry Faust, Andy lettered four years in football as quarterback for the Zips. Andy earned his Business degree from the University of Akron and now works in Newark as the marketing manger for W/S Packaging of Cincinnati. Andy says that during his time at Akron, he met up with Mr. Jamie Popa, the outstanding running back/linebacker from the 1985 Mogadore team. "Popa was a friendly person," Andy said. "We talked about our semifinal game, of course, and Popa said that he never did watch the film of that game."

> Playing football for Newark Catholic and J.D. Graham was definitely a positive experience. I remember J.D. saying that three-a-days would be the toughest thing we would ever have to do. If we could do three-a-days, we could do anything. That has always stuck with me. Personally, I don't feel I would have had the opportunity to play in college if it were not for J.D. and the tradition of the Newark Catholic program. I feel I had an edge over other guys in college because of that mental toughness we developed. Aside from those aspects, I had the most fun in my life playing football at Newark Catholic, culminated by winning a state championship. Nothing I have done since—any college games or experiences—has compared to that fall of 1985. It wasn't just about the winning, but it was being around the best friends I ever had, sharing the good times and the bad times and knowing we would make it through. It is something of which we all can be very proud. [10]

Tim McKenna attended college at Eastern Kentucky University and majored in Criminal Justice. He is currently employed at the Licking-Muskingum Community Correction Center and lives in Newark his wife Brooke and newborn daughter Caroline.

> Playing football for Newark Catholic was a long-time goal of mine and I believe it helped shape who I am today. J.D. was a god to me and I was his foot soldier. He had his creative way of getting me to play above and beyond my abilities. If he were to say,

"Timmy, I want you to run through that brick wall for Newark Catholic and for everything that green helmet represents," I would have done it. I often joke with myself, saying that I would trade my soul to the devil for the chance to play one more game. It was a privilege to have been a part of something so special.[11]

Jeremy Montgomery attended Ashland College and earned his Bachelor's degree in Finance and Marketing. Jeremy has spent the last seven years as Finance Manger for a BMW dealership in Columbus, Ohio.

Tom Ogilbee did not return to Newark Catholic for his senior year. Today, he is a policeman and lives in Loveland, Ohio with his wife Rowena and children Megan and Nicole.

Jim Olson attended the University of Dayton and majored in Education. While a student at Dayton, Jim began working for Marriott. This led to full-time employment after college, which has taken Jim to Atlanta, Georgia, Charleston, West Virginia and back to Dayton, Ohio as of August 2002.

Coach Wes Poth has remained the offensive and defensive lineman coach for Newark Catholic. The year 2002 will mark his thirty-second year in this assignment. In 1999, he stepped down from his position as Social Studies and Physical Education teacher at Blessed Sacrament School and is now a guidance counselor at Newark Catholic High School.

Darby Riley returned to Newark Catholic in the late 90's to serve as defensive coordinator for the varsity football program through the 2000 season. After one year out of football, Darby accepted the head coaching position at Portsmouth Notre Dame High School in 2002. Newark Catholic and Portsmouth Notre Dame have engaged in some great battles in the past. Perhaps these two schools will meet again someday.

Jeff Ronan enlisted into the Unites States Air Force after high school. While in basic training, his problem with concussions resurfaced and he was released on a medical discharge. After a few years with Heritage Sportswear and Arwebb Office Supply, Jeff began working at Holophane in Newark, Ohio where he has been for 10 years. Jeff is also studying Criminal Justice at the Central Ohio Technical College and plans to start a career in law enforcement. Jeff lives in Newark with his wife Julie and sons Tyler, Drew and Nathan.

> Playing for J.D. Graham required great discipline. We were under his thumb and I apply this discipline to my own kids and the kids I coach in baseball. He was right when he said, "This will be the hardest thing you'll ever go through." Physically, there has been nothing harder in my life. I remember him saying, "No matter how hard you think it is for you, the guy next to you may be suffering more."[12]

Scott Saad was a key player on two additional state-championship teams in his final two years at Newark Catholic. In 1987, Scott's senior year, Newark Catholic and Mogadore met again—this time in the title game. Newark Catholic won the duel 16-13 and the game remains the most-cherished victory of Saad's Green Wave career. After high school, Saad continued his football career as a middle linebacker for the University of Dayton (1988-1992). The Flyers won the NCAA Division III National Championship in 1989 and were runner-up in 1991. After his senior year in college, Saad was awarded the Sheriff Bernard L. Keiter Award, which honors the senior with the outstanding four-year contribution to the program. Graduating in 1992 with a B.S. in Business Administration, Saad started his professional career at Merrill Lynch in Dayton, Ohio where he is now Vice President and Senior Financial Advisor. Scott resides in Kettering, Ohio with his wife, Beth and children Ali, Penn, Kennon.

> I took many positive influences away from NC that have had a lasting impact on me professionally, academically and athletically. I still remember to this day a quote that Graham used all the time: "Look sharp, play sharp." He even insisted on us polishing our shoes before each game or we wouldn't be playing. He demanded that we look like a first-class operation at all times. He believed that if you looked your best, you had a much better chance of playing your best. I apply this thought professionally to this day. I try to look my best each day because in my profession, I cannot afford to be perceived as sloppy. That would cost me business. Another thing I took away from Graham was the habit of setting your goals and expectations high. Our goals were always to win the state championship. In order to attain that goal, we had to outwork and outthink our competitors on a daily basis. Graham showed us that through desire, discipline and hard work, anything was possible. Back in the mid to late '80s, every player knew that Graham was a disciplinarian and expected excellence. We knew that football was tough at Newark Catholic, but the players were willing to accept that in hopes that we would be successful in winning the state title. To this day, I set my goals high professionally and in my home life. In order to achieve my goals, I have to outwork and outthink my competition. This sounds a lot like what we did playing NC football. Graham also taught us that in order to be successful, we had to play as a team. We could not be worried about only ourselves. The team came first. This taught me that in life, sometimes you have to make sacrifices for the greater good of your family or co-workers. In summary, Graham taught us how to be winners on and off the field. [13]

Joe Simi attended Bowling Green State University on a baseball scholarship. After working at RRD Direct in Heath, Ohio for 11 years, Joe relocated to Minneapolis, Minnesota in February of 2003 where he is an account manager for Japs Olson. Joe married Newark Catholic cheerleader and classmate Denise Diebert. They have three children: Ryan, Kyle and Andrea.

> Playing football at Newark Catholic for J. D. Graham was the most difficult but most rewarding thing I have experienced. It was without a doubt the toughest thing to go through both physically and mentally. I look back and appreciate it more so now

than when I went through it. Obviously, I learned a great deal about football, but more importantly, I learned a great deal about life. Coach Graham always talked to us about discipline, hard work and dealing with adversity and how these things would affect us later in life. I remember these things more than I remember the things I was taught about football. [14]

Todd South remained in central Ohio after high school. He currently lives in the Buckeye Lake area and is employed with Eco Lab in Hebron, Ohio. Todd is an avid hunter.

Mike Trotter went to Urbana University in Urbana, Ohio on a half-scholarship for football. Mike was a starting defensive tackle until a massive ankle injury ended his football career in his first quarter at Urbana. After spending one quarter at OSU-Newark, Mike then enrolled into Central Ohio Technical College where he earned his associate degree in Criminal Justice. Mike served two years as a police officer in Alexandria, Ohio before joining the Newark Police Department in 1996. Mike lives in Newark with his wife Jennifer and son Dillon.

Joe Wiley attended the Ohio State University in Newark for 6 months before joining the U.S. Navy. His first duty station was Washington, DC in 1987, where he was accepted onto the All-Navy Softball team in Norfolk, Virginia. Joe played on this team until 1989 when he met his future wife Jennifer and married in March. Taking college courses off and on while stationed in Washington, DC and Louisiana, Joe graduated from Liberty University in June 2000 with a B.A. in Business Administration. Joe played shortstop for the Louisiana Armed Forces State Championship team, where he was named the All-State Most Valuable Player. The team advanced to the Word Championships in August of 2001 and took 2nd place. Joe was named the All-World Shortstop for the Armed Forces team. Joe is currently a Chief Petty Officer in the Navy and a junior at St. Leo University, where he is pursuing a B.S. in Management Information Systems. Joe recently purchased seven acres of land in Fallsburg (northeast Licking County) where he plans to build his "retirement home" after completing his naval career. Joe and Jennifer have two children—Heather (14) and Alicia (12).

Notes

1. Dale Backlund, Conversation with author, Aug. 23, 2002.

2. Joe Bell, electronic mail to author, Aug. 13, 2002.

3. Jim Calvert, Telephone conversation with author, Aug. 18, 2002.

4. Pat Cooperrider, Telephone conversation with author, Aug. 19, 2002.

5. Kevin Donnelly, electronic mail to author, Jan. 19. 2002.

6. Bill Franks, electronic mail to author, Aug. 23, 2002.

7. Albert Ghiloni, electronic mail to author, Aug. 15, 2002.

8. Jim Wharton, "Roast and Toast for retiring Newark Catholic Coach J.D. Graham" program, Jun. 27, 1992.

9. John Jurden, electronic mail to author, Aug. 15, 2002.

10. Andy Kubik, electronic mail to author, Aug. 23, 2002.

11. Tim McKenna, Telephone conversation with author, Aug. 12, 2002.

12. Jeff Ronan, Telephone conversation with author, Aug. 18, 2002.

13. Scott Saad, electronic mail to author, Aug. 20, 2002.

14. Joe Simi, electronic mail to author, Aug. 14, 2002.

Bibliography

Advocate, The: *Football '85*, (Aug. 28, 1985), p. 8, 10; (Aug. 31, 1985), p. 8; (Sep. 7, 1985), p. 7; (Sep. 14, 1985), p. 7; "Newark Catholic at Johnstown," (Sep. 19, 1985), p. 16; (Sep. 21, 1985), p. 12; "NC dodges loss to keep No. 1 spot," (Sep. 24. 1985), p. 11; "Newark Catholic at Coshocton," (Sep. 26, 1985), p. 13; (Sep. 26, 1985), p. 14; (Sep. 28, 1985), p. 6; (Oct. 1, 1985), p. 11; (Oct. 3, 1985), p. 16; (Oct. 5, 1985), p. 6; (Oct. 10, 1985), p. 14; (Oct. 12, 1985), p. 7; "Mogadore edges NC for top 'A' billing," (Oct. 15, 1985), p. 11; (Oct. 17, 1985), p. 16; (Oct. 22, 1985), p. 12; (Oct. 24, 1985), p. 26; (Oct 26, 1985), p. 8; (Oct. 29, 1985), p. 11; (Oct. 31, 1985), p. 15; (Nov. 4, 1985), p. 14; "NC, Sheridan in playoffs; unbeatens left out," (Nov. 4, 1985), p. 13; (Nov. 5, 1985), p. 12; "NC, area gridders grab top honors on all-district team," (Nov. 6, 1985), p. 15; (Nov. 7, 1985), p. 14; (Nov. 24, 1985), p. 2C.

Backlund, Dale. Conversation with author, Newark, Ohio, Apr. 4, 2002; Aug. 23, 2002.

Bell, Joseph. Electronic mail to author, 26 Nov 2001; Jan. 7, 2002; Feb. 28, 2002; Aug. 13, 2002. Conversation with author, Newark, Ohio, Dec. 28, 2002; Jan. 25, 2002.

Byers, Monte. Telephone conversation with author, Jan. 1, 2002.

Calvert, Jim. Conversation with author, Newark Ohio, Apr. 4, 2002. Telephone conversation with author, Jan. 13, 2002; Aug. 18. 2002.

Cannizzaro, John. 1985 Newark Catholic Football Statistics Report; 1985 Division V State Semifinals Statistics Report; 1985 Division V State Finals Statistics Report.

Cannizzaro, Rick. "Irish win over Heath sets up Friday title game," *Newark (O) Advocate*, (Nov.5, 1973), p. 18; "Heath stuns Newark Catholic," *The Advocate*, (Oct. 2, 1983), p. 1C; "Catholic makes title game with playoff win," *The Advocate*, (Nov. 20, 1983), p. 1C. "Redskins' chief looks to ground attack," *The Advocate*, *Football '85*, (Aug. 28, 1985), p. 11; "Revamped machine powers Green Wave," *The Advocate*, (Sep. 1, 1985), p. 1C; "NC throttles Watkins for key victory," *The Advocate*, (Sep. 15, 1985), p. 1C; "Undefeated Green Wave frustrates Coshocton," *The Advocate*, (Sep. 28, 1985), p. 5; "Kubik passes Wave to victory," *The Advocate*, (Oct. 20, 1985), p. 1C; "NC breaks record, Redskins," *The Advocate*, (Oct. 27, 1985), p. 1C; "Newark Catholic crushes Lancers; playoffs await," *The Advocate*, (Nov. 3, 1985), p. 1C; "Poll champs named; real titles undecided," (Nov. 5, 1985), p. 11; "Catholic defense gives PV dose of own medicine," *The Advocate*, (Nov. 17, 1985), p. 1C.

Cooperrider, Pat. Telephone conversation with author, Dec. 11, 2001; Jan. 13, 2002; Aug. 19, 2002.

Crowley, John. Conversation with author, Newark, Ohio, Jun. 2, 2002.

Daubenmire, Dave. Electronic mail to author, Feb. 26, 2003.

Donnelly, Kevin. Electronic mail to author, Jan. 19, 2001.

Erhard, Dave. Telephone conversation with author, Mar. 3, 2002.

Evans, Cara. Telephone conversation with author, Mar. 10, 2002.

Evans, Joseph. Electronic mail to author, Dec. 28, 2001.

Evans, M. Joan. Conversation with author, Newark, Ohio, Mar. 10, 2002.

Franks, Bill. Telephone conversation with author, Feb. 14, 2002; Conversation with author, Newark, Ohio, Apr. 4, 2002; Electronic mail to author, Aug. 23, 2002.

Gebhart, Dave. Telephone conversation with author, Jul. 2, 2002.

Ghiloni, Albert. Electronic mail to author, Mar. 26, 2002; Aug. 15, 2002. Conversation with author, Newark, Ohio, June 13, 2002.

Gilmore, Joseph. Conversation with author, Newark, Ohio, Apr. 4, 2002; Aug. 3, 2002.

Graham, J.D. Telephone conversation with author, Mar. 3, 2002; Jul. 1, 2002; Conversation with author, Newark, Ohio, Aug. 3, 2002.

Johns, Anthony. Electronic mail to author, Jan. 7, 2002; Jan. 21, 2002.

Jurden, John. Electronic mail to author, Aug. 15, 2002.

Krizay, Kane M. Cheers and Tears: 25 Years of the Ohio High School Football Championships. Medina, Ohio: KMK Publishing Company, 1997.

Kubik, Andy. Electronic mail to author, Nov. 29, 2001; Aug. 23, 2002.

Marquis, Ted. Conversation with author, Newark, Ohio, Jan. 25, 2002.

McClelland, Sean. "NC shows no mercy in rout of Vikings," The Advocate, (Sep. 8, 1985), p. 1C; "Wave quarterback completes mission despite handicap," The Advocate, (Sep. 15, 1985), p. 1C; "Baldwin leads Johnnies' attack," The Advocate, (Sep. 7, 1985), p. 5; "Green Wave blanks Heath; Valley awaits," The Advocate, (Oct. 6, 1985), p.1C; "Black, defense lead Panthers to shutout win over Lexington," The Advocate, (Oct. 5, 1985), p. 5; "Green Wave trips LV; Kubik TD aerial stops Panthers," The Advocate, (Oct. 12, 1985), p. 12; "Simi stars with three TD receptions," The Advocate, (Nov. 10, 1985), p. 1C; "Newark Catholic tailback has message for Jefferson," The Advocate, (Nov. 27, 1985), p. 9; "Catholic claims second straight title," The Advocate, (Nov. 30, 1985), p. 9; "Catholic's unlikely hero emerges from shadow," The Advocate, (Nov. 30, 1985), p. 10.

McKenna, Tim. Telephone conversation with author, Jan. 29. 2002; Aug. 12. 2002.

McNabb, Mark. Conversation with author, Newark, Ohio, Apr. 4, 2002.

Monroe, Derek. "Wave's crowns piling up," The Columbus Dispatch, (Nov. 30, 1985), p. 3B.

Naegele, Mark. "New Lancer boss begins to search for game players," The Advocate, Football '85, (Aug. 28, 1985), p. 12; "Vets help Johnnies to improve," The Advocate, Football '85, (Aug. 28, 1985), p. 13; "Warriors hoping for 'typical' year," The Advocate, Football '85, (Aug. 28, 1985), p. 18; "Valley shows power when all are healthy," The Advocate, Football '85, (Aug. 28, 1985), p. 19; "NC, Watkins to battle for local bragging rights," The Advocate, (Sep. 13, 1985), p. 7; "Valley hopes to gain respect with win over NC," The Advocate, (Oct. 10, 1985), p. 13; "Polls show worth again," The Advocate, (Oct. 18, 1985), p. 7; "Wave offsets rush shortage with defense," The Advocate, (Nov. 8, 1985), p. 11; "NC prepares to tackle 'unseen' Southeastern," The Advocate, (Nov. 7, 1985), p. 13; "Weak offense, strong defense propel Bearcats" The Advocate, (Nov. 15, 1985), p. 7; "Newark Catholic to renew battle with Mogadore," The

Advocate, (Nov. 18, 1985), p. 13; "Mogadore, NC show similar styles," *The Advocate*, (Nov. 21, 1985), p. 13; "Newark Catholic faces season's toughest test," *The Advocate*, (Nov. 20, 1985), p. 7; "Mogadore game stirs emotions in Catholic camp," *The Advocate*, (Nov. 22, 1985), p. 7; "Berth in championship tilt 'special' for NC squad," *The Advocate*, (Nov. 25, 1985), p. 11; "Delphos gridders take advantage of initial chance," *The Advocate*, (Nov. 26, 1985), p. 11; "Jefferson rushes into title contest with big numbers," *The Advocate*, (Nov. 28, 1985), p. 1C; "'Biggest win' for NC coach," *The Advocate*, (Nov. 30, 1985), p. 10; "Long Wildcat run spurs defense," *The Advocate*, (Nov. 30, 1985), p. 9.

Neumeyer, James. Telephone conversation with author, Mar. 14, 2002.

Newark Catholic vs. Johnstown Football Program, (Sep. 18, 1982), p. 26.

Newark Catholic vs. Tuscarawas Central Catholic Football Program, (Aug. 31, 1985), p. 16-19.

Newark Catholic vs. Granville Football Program, (Oct. 31, 1986), p. 20-21.

Newark Catholic vs. Tuscarawas Catholic game broadcast, Adelphia Cable of Newark, Ohio, (Sep. 1, 1985).

Poth, Wes. Telephone conversation with author, Jan 14, 2002; Conversation with author, Newark, Ohio, Jan. 30, 2002; Jun. 27, 2002.

Ronan, Jeff. Telephone conversation with author, Nov. 30, 2001; Jan 9, 2002; Feb. 11, 2002; Aug. 18, 2002.

Saad, Scott. Electronic mail to author, Feb. 16, 2002; Aug. 20, 2002.

Shaw, Mark. "Heath boss expresses confidence in QB," *The Advocate, Football '85,* (Aug. 28, 1985), p. 9; "Northridge mentor guns for first in last," *The Advocate, Football '85,* (Aug. 28, 1985), p. 20; "Football takes huge strides at Southeastern," *The Advocate*, (Nov. 6, 1985), p. 15; "Wave thrashes Southeastern in round one," *The Advocate*, (Nov. 10, 1985), p. 1C; "High-tech NC puts byte on Jefferson," *The Advocate*, (Nov. 30. 1985), p. 9.

Simi, Joseph. Conversation with author, Newark, Ohio, Dec. 1, 2001; Dec. 18, 2001. Electronic mail to author, Jan. 7, 2002; Aug. 14, 2002.

Trotter, Michael. Telephone conversation with author, Jan 3, 2002; Mar. 14, 2002. Conversation with author, Granville, Ohio, Jun. 7, 2002.

Waitkus, Dave. "Young Johnnies fight inexperience," *The Advocate, Football '83,* (Aug. 31, 1983), p. 25; "Johnstown 'traps' winless Northridge," *The Advocate*, (Sep. 14, 1985), p. 5; "'Attitude adjustment' pays dividends for NC," *The Advocate*, (Nov. 24, 1985), p. 1C.

Wharton, Jim. "Lettermen key Johnstown secret," *The Advocate, Football '84,* (Aug. 31, 1984), p. 25; "Roast and Toast for retiring Newark Catholic Coach J.D. Graham" program, Jun. 27, 1992.

Wilder, Rod. Conversation with author, Newark, Ohio, Dec. 19, 2001.

Wiley, Joe. Electronic mail to author, Nov. 25, 2001.

World-wide web. http://www3.uakron.edu/src/Demographics/Mogadore-Demographics-CPS.htm
    (January, 2002); http://memoryInsports.com/usahkremarkable.html (Jan. 2002);
    http://www.noacsc.org/allen/dl/high/highschool.htm (Jan. 2002).

Wright, Joe. "Newark Catholic clips Coshocton," *The Times-Reporter*, (Sep. 28, 1985), p. B-5.

Van Hove, Gary. Electronic mail to author, Feb. 4, 2002.

1985 Regional Football Tournament Program, Division I, II, III, IV, V, (Nov. 1985), p. 1.

1985 OHSAA Football Championship Game Program, Division I, II, III, IV, V, (Nov. 1985), p. 17.

Printed in the United States
By Bookmasters